'This is an important and timely book for school: technology can help hard-pressed teachers in the schools to know who to believe as new products : time. This academic analysis answers

Lord Jim Knight, Chief Education and External Officer for TES, and former Schools Minister

'This is a box of delights: it draws together an exceptional range of contributions to focus what we currently know – and highlight what we don't – about enhancing learning with technology. For all the variety, the focus is strongly, as it should be, on learning. It's accessible and well-structured – a great reference source for busy practitioners.'

Professor Chris Husbands, Vice-Chancellor, Sheffield Hallam University, and TEF Chair

'A wide-ranging and fascinating exploration of what we know about effective learning and how the many uses and applications of technology can enhance impact. This is a must-read for teachers keen both to understand "what works", and to gain awareness of areas that show promise in pedagogy that seeks to embrace technology.'

Professor Dame Alison Peacock, DBE, DLitt, Chief Executive, Chartered College of Teaching

'Keeping a pace with research on teaching is exhausting. Step forward Rose Luckin and her cast of experts who guide us effortlessly through all the latest thinking on sifting through the wheat from the chaff.'

Sir Anthony Seldon, Vice-Chancellor, University of Buckingham

Enhancing Learning and Teaching with Technology

Enhancing Learning and Teaching with Technology

What the research says

Edited by Rosemary Luckin

IOE Press

First published in 2018 by the UCL Institute of Education Press, University College London, 20 Bedford Way, London WC1H 0AL

www.ucl-ioe-press.com

British Library Cataloguing in Publication Data:
A catalogue record for this publication is available from the British Library

ISBNs
978-1-78277-226-2 (paperback)
978-1-78277-227-9 (PDF eBook)
978-1-78277-228-6 (ePub eBook)
978-1-78277-229-3 (Kindle eBook)

Typeset by Quadrant Infotech (India) Pvt Ltd
Printed by CPI Group (UK) Ltd, Croydon, CR0 4YY
Cover image ©iStock.com/liuzishan. Cover design by Liron Gilenberg.

Contents

PART 6 How technology can support teaching

Notes on contributors

Shaaron Ainsworth is Professor of Learning Sciences at the University of Nottingham. She combines her background in psychology and artificial intelligence to research representational learning technologies such as games, simulations and good old-fashioned pen and paper.

Allison Allen is a Director of Outstream Consulting and a governor for STEP Academy Trust. She has a proven reputation at senior level within education and specializes in the use of technology to enhance the life chances of all learners.

Richard Allen is a Director of Outstream Consulting. He is a specialist in education transformation and an experienced educator to Master's Level. He has a background of business management in international high-tech industries.

David Barlex is an acknowledged leader in design and technology education, curriculum design and curriculum materials development. He directed Nuffield Design and Technology and was educational manager of Young Foresight.

David Baume is an international higher education consultant, academic developer, evaluator, researcher and writer. He was founding Chair of the Staff and Educational Development Association (SEDA), co-founder of the International Consortium for Educational Development and founding editor of the International Journal for Academic Development.

Miroslava Černochová is Vice Dean of the Faculty of Education at Charles University in Prague, and teaches in the Department of Information Technology and Technical Education.

Koula Charitonos is a lecturer in the Institute of Educational Technology, The Open University. Her research focuses on learning in schools and museums, and she is interested in how technology impacts and transforms learning across formal and informal settings.

Tim Coughlan is a lecturer in the Institute of Educational Technology at The Open University. His research works towards more open, accessible, creative and inclusive forms of learning.

Charles Crook is a developmental psychologist and Professor of Education based in the School of Education and the Learning Sciences Research Institute at the University of Nottingham.

Mutlu Cukurova is Lecturer in Digital Technologies in Education at the UCL Institute of Education. His research interests are broad and eclectic, revolving around investigating the potential of educational technologies to continuously support and evaluate students' skill development.

Patricia Davies is Senior Lecturer in Computer Science at the University of Wolverhampton. She is Co-convenor of the BERA Educational Technology SIG. Her research interests include educational technology leadership and policymaking, and educational data mining.

Benedict du Boulay is Emeritus Professor in the Department of Informatics at the University of Sussex. He is president of the International Society for Artificial Intelligence in Education, has been a school teacher, and is interested in motivation.

Stuart Edwards is an Honorary Research Associate at the UCL Knowledge Lab. Previously, a senior civil servant, he advised ministers on technology to enhance learning.

Rebecca Ferguson is a Senior Lecturer in the Institute of Educational Technology at The Open University and a leading member of the FutureLearn Academic Network (FLAN). Her research interests include learning at scale, learning analytics and the future of learning.

Terry Freedman is an independent education technology consultant, speaker, trainer and freelance writer, based on 40 years' experience. He is a member of the committee of the Association for Information Technology in Teacher Education, and a Mirandanet Fellow. He publishes the 'ICT & Computing in Education' website at www.ictineducation.org and the Digital Education newsletter at www.ictineducation.org/newsletters.

Tony Gardner-Medwin is Emeritus Professor of Physiology, University College London. He is a research neuroscientist interested also in improving techniques for learning, studying, teaching and assessment. His personal website is http://tmedwin.net.

Mark Gaved is a lecturer in the Institute of Educational Technology at The Open University. His research explores mobile, informal, community-based and location-triggered learning.

Christothea Herodotou is a lecturer in the Institute of Educational Technology at The Open University. She is interested in the evaluation of technologies for learning through crowdsourcing and learning analytics.

Wayne Holmes is a lecturer in the Institute of Educational Technology, The Open University. His research interests are in the learning sciences and the use of AI to enhance teaching and learning, and to help us learn more about learning.

Kim Issroff was a Senior Lecturer at UCL and The Open University before deciding that she is better suited to a freelance career.

Ann Jones is a Reader in Educational Technology in the Institute of Educational Technology at The Open University. Her research interests include social and affective uses of technologies, and also how informal learning can be supported by technology.

Agnes Kukulska-Hulme is Professor of Learning Technology and Communication in the Institute of Educational Technology at The Open University, United Kingdom. Her expertise includes mobile learning and language learning.

Charlotte Lærke Weitze is an Assistant Professor at LearnT, Center of Digital Learning Technology, DTU Compute, Technical University of Denmark. She works on the development of innovative, motivating and effective ways of learning for both students and teachers.

Rosemary Luckin is Professor of Learner Centred Design at the UCL Knowledge Lab and Director of EDUCATE. Her research involves the design and evaluation of educational technology using theories from the learning sciences and techniques from artificial intelligence (AI).

Rafael Marques de Albuquerque is a lecturer at the University of Vale do Itajaí (Univali), Brazil. He researches serious games, learning and the influences of playing digital games

Manolis Mavrikis is a Reader in Learning Technologies at the UCL Knowledge Lab. He is particularly interested in educational data mining and learning analytics.

Norbert Pachler is Professor of Teaching and Learning and Pro-director: Teaching, Quality and Learning Innovation at the UCL Institute of Education and Pro-Vice-Provost: Education at UCL.

Alice Peasgood is an educational technology consultant and researcher. She is currently a visiting fellow in the Institute of Educational Technology at The Open University.

Kaśka Porayska-Pomsta is a Reader in Adaptive Technologies for Learning at the UCL Knowledge Lab. Her background is in artificial intelligence and her research focuses on computational modelling of non-cognitive aspects of learning, including learners' emotional and motivational self-monitoring and self-regulation.

Alexandra Poulovassilis is Professor of Computer Science and Director of the Birkbeck Knowledge Lab, Birkbeck, University of London. Her research focuses on computational techniques to support knowledge discovery, organization and sharing in learning communities.

Christina Preston is Professor at the Institute for Education Futures at De Montfort University and founder of the MirandaNet Fellowship, and specializes in practice-based research with teachers often funded by companies like BrainPOP, BBC, Gaia Technologies, IRIS Connect, Oracle and Promethean.

Michael J Reiss is Professor of Science Education at the UCL Institute of Education, University College London, and a Fellow of the Academy of Social Sciences.

Eileen Scanlon is Regius Professor of open education and associate director of research and innovation in the Institute of Educational Technology at The Open University. She is also honorary professor at Moray House School of Education, University of Edinburgh and a Trustee of Bletchley Park.

Mike Sharples is Emeritus Professor of Educational Technology at The Open University.

Torben Steeg is a teacher and teacher educator involved in writing, curriculum development, CPD, ITE, evaluation and research in D&T, electronics, science, computing and maker education.

Phil Thornton is a freelance economics and business writer and consultant, formerly of *The Independent*, who now runs www. clarityeconomics.com. He has written two books: *Economics Demystified* and *The Great Economists*.

Keith Turvey is Principal Lecturer in the Education Research Centre at the University of Brighton. His research focuses on teacher education, pedagogy and digital technologies.

Kristen Weatherby is a researcher at the UCL Knowledge Lab. Previously she worked at the OECD, Microsoft and in the classroom

Lawrence Williams is an experienced classroom practitioner who currently teaches Literacy, ICT and Computing on ITE courses at several universities in London and abroad.

Sarah Younie is Professor at The Institute for Education Futures at De Montfort University, and director of the MirandaNet Fellowship. She has published research on educational technologies funded by UNESCO, EU, TDA, DfE, Becta, BBC, HEA and JISC.

Nageela Yusuf is a Director at Cerebriam Technology, an engineering company with expertise in video, image processing and user interface design.

Glossary

accommodation	when learners either modify an existing schema or idea or form an entirely new schema to deal with a new object or event
affective state	the state of a student's emotion or mood
artificial intelligence	the capability in computers to perceive, understand, reason and react to the world in an intelligent way
artificial intelligence in education	the study of the use of techniques from artificial intelligence in understanding or supporting teaching or learning
assimilation	when learners respond to a new event in a way that is consistent with an existing schema (a model of ideas) of them
Bloom's Taxonomy	a set of three hierarchical models (cognitive, affective and sensory) used to classify educational learning objectives into levels of complexity and specificity
cognitive load theory	a learning theory (introduced by John Sweller) that holds that extraneous material in instructional design can distract learners and hamper learning (because working memory becomes overloaded)
cognitive psychology	the branch of psychology concerned with mental processes (such as perception, thinking, learning and memory)
collaboration	two or more people working together with a common purpose to generate shared understanding
constructionism	a learning theory (introduced by Seymour Papert) that holds that learning is most effective when students learn through project-based learning, when they are active in making (constructing) tangible objects in the real world, and where the teacher acts as a facilitator

constructivism	a learning theory (mostly associated with Jean Piaget) that holds that humans learn (make meaning or construct an understanding) through the interaction of experience and ideas
constructivist	a theory that people construct their own understanding and knowledge of the world through experiencing things and reflecting on those experiences
CPD	continuing professional development
Creative Commons licence	a licence issued by the creator of an Intellectual Property (IP, e.g. a design or video) that allows, within some predefined constraints, others to use, reuse or amend that IP
determinism	the doctrine that all events, including human action, are ultimately determined by causes external to the will
digital literacy	ability to confidently, critically, skilfully and appropriately select and use digital technologies to achieve goals
digital natives	a highly-contested term (introduced by Marc Prensky) that claims that younger people are 'native speakers' of the digital language of computers, video games, social media and other sites on the Internet (in contrast to older people who are 'digital immigrants')
domain model, domain knowledge	in a teaching system, the understanding of the topic being taught
econometrics	the application of statistical analysis to economic data
exploratory learning environment	a computer-based system for learning where the learner can explore and largely has the agency about what to do
FabLabs	Practical workshops stocked with state-of-the-art but low-cost digital designing and making tools, with a focus on community use

feedback	when simply defined it means any kind of usable response
gamer	a person who plays video games or participates in role-playing games
gamification or gamifying	applying elements of game design to non-game contexts (for example, applying points, badges and leaderboards to learning or fitness activities)
genetic inheritance	the process by which information encoded in DNA is passed on from parents to their offspring
hackers	usually we think of 'hackers' as people who use coding skills to sneak into and manipulate computer programs, often for disreputable reasons; however, in maker culture, 'hacker' is used to describe programmers who are adept at taking apart code and altering it for new purposes
hackspace	a community-operated workspace where people with common interests, often in computers, technology, science or digital art, socialize and collaborate. Also see 'makerspace'
instructional design	the practice of creating experiences designed to support learning
intelligent tutoring system	a system for learning in which the learner solves problems or explores a domain where the system largely has the agency about what the learner should do
interface	that part of a computer-based system through which the user and the system communicate
inverted pyramid	the name given to the 'shape' of a news story, in which the main questions of who, what, when, where, etc., are given in the very first paragraph of the article
just in time learning	an expression sometimes used in maker spaces to indicate that there is no shame in asking for help from those who know more or are more skilled than you are

long term memory	the part of memory that holds information for long periods of time, from where it can be retrieved as and when required (although naturally things are a bit more complicated than that)
longitudinal studies	studies that repeatedly examine or observe the same set of subjects over an extended period of time (usually months or years) in order to collect data
maker movement	see 'makers'
makers	people who like to make stuff, often using high technology tools
makerspace	a community-operated workspace where people with common interests (often in computers, technology, science or digital art) socialize and collaborate; see also 'hackspace'
meta-analyses	a statistical analysis that combines the results of multiple scientific studies
meta-analysis	a study that synthesizes a number of randomized controlled trials (RCTs) to gain an overarching view of a field; it's important to note that meta reviews or analyses can only summarize or average results – so details can be lost sometimes giving misleading impressions
meta-review	see 'meta-analysis'
metacognition	being self-aware of your own cognition (of your own learning)
microworld	a computer program simulating a fragment of the world, e.g. a pond eco-system or a jet engine, that can be manipulated and explored by learners
mobile learning	Using mobile devices to learn, but also that the learner himself or herself is mobile
MOOC	massive open online course (a model for delivering learning content online to any person who wants to take a course, with no limit on attendance)

Open Source Initiative	organization dedicated to promoting open source software (software with source code that has been made freely available for anyone to change and distribute for any purpose)
pedagogical model	in a teaching system, the understanding by the system of its way to teach
qualitative research	empirical investigation prioritizing understanding the phenomena that it studies – an interpretivist approach; see also 'quantitative research'
quantitative research	empirical investigation prioritizing measuring the phenomena that it studies (using numbers) and using statistical, mathematical or computational techniques – a positivist approach; see also 'quantitative research'
randomized	set up or distributed in a deliberately random way
randomized control trials (RCT)	a quantitative research approach often used to evaluate 'what works'. An RCT involves two groups, the experimental and the control group, the first of which are given the intervention being evaluated and the second an alternative intervention or 'business as usual'. The numerical outcomes of the two groups are then compared using various statistical techniques. Some argue that RCTs are the gold-standard of empirical research; other researchers disagree, arguing that RCTs only provide averages and hide the details and can be misleading
retention	keeping something in one's memory
rote learning	a memorization technique based on repetition – the idea is that one will be able to quickly recall the meaning of the material the more one repeats it
scaffolding	a process in which teachers model or demonstrate how to solve a problem, and then step back, offering support as and when needed.
self-regulated learning	learning that is self-motivated and that involves taking control of and evaluating one's own learning; see also 'metacognition'

Glossary

sociocultural	a learning theory (associated with Lev Vygotsky) that sees social interaction as having a fundamental role in the development of cognition (learning)
steampunk	a science fiction inspired approach to design that combines historical elements (e.g. steam engines) with anachronistic technologies (e.g. computers)
STEM	science, technology, engineering and mathematics
student model	in a teaching system, the understanding by the system of the student(s) being taught
tangential learning	the process by which people self-educate if a topic is exposed to them in a context that they enjoy
textspeak	shorthand text sometimes used on mobile devices (for example, 'CuL8R' to mean 'see you later')
tinkering	exploring through fiddling, toying, messing, pottering, dabbling and fooling about with a wide range of things that happen to be available – in a creative and productive pursuit to make, mend or improve
transmedia	commonly defined as a narrative or project that combines multiple media forms
unproblematized	not problematized; especially not subjected to analysis or questioning
virtual learning environment	a computer program to deliver educational material and tests to students and collect data about their progress, as well as providing other facilities such as links to related material and a forum for communication between students and with teachers
virtual space	a platform or environment where people can interact, facilitated by networked computers
working memory	a 'store' where small amounts of information are retained for a short period of time, such as the duration of solving a problem (although naturally things are a bit more complicated than that)

What the research says

Rosemary Luckin and Phil Thornton

When I was first prompted by a publisher to form the idea of a *What the research says* book I knew that I could not write such a book alone. A *What the research says* book about learning and teaching with technology would require input from a range of experts who would need to be willing to review the research in the areas of their expertise and produce a succinct account of the consensus from this research, brought to life through carefully selected case studies. I floated the book idea to the community of researchers, technologists and educators who had been attending a series of seminars at the London Knowledge Lab, now the UCL Knowledge Lab, with the same title: *What the research says*. This series of seminars had been designed for non-academic and academic audiences as a channel for communicating research findings for significant issues of interest to those who were using technology to support their learning and/or teaching. I knew that this community would be key to the success of a *What the research says* book and I was delightfully overwhelmed by the enthusiasm of the response I received when I suggested the book to them. This is an enthusiasm that has been maintained throughout the process of producing this book and it is an enthusiasm without which this book would not exist. The job of editing this volume has been an immense pleasure and I look forward to this book being the first in a series of *What the research says* books; there is so much to be said about this topic and it is important that we work together to ensure that everyone interested in this subject has access to quality research syntheses to improve the quality and enjoyment of their learning and/or teaching with technology.

This first *What the research says* book is designed to progress the work of the *What the research says* seminars through which we established a diverse core community of more than 1,000 people. The community is a knowledge exchange society for all sectors of education. Membership includes educational technology corporates, small and medium enterprises, independent consultants, students, teachers, lecturers, researchers, entrepreneurs and policymakers. All the seminars have been over-subscribed with attendees drawn from a wide range of backgrounds. The *What the research says* book aims to capture some of the enthusiasm of the events and is an opportunity for us to extend the reach of the seminars and provide good quality, accessible research summaries to everyone interested in how technology can be designed and used for learning and teaching to best effect.

There is an increasing appetite for evidence about learning and education. There are organizations such as The Education Endowment Foundation (https://educationendowmentfoundation.org.uk), CEBE (www.cebenetwork.org) and Evidence for the Frontline (www.evidenceforthefrontline.com), that contribute to the growing body of educational evidence made available outside academia. There are also bodies explicitly aimed at teachers, such as: ResearchEd (www.workingoutwhatworks.com). In terms of partnership with industry, the MirandaNet Fellowship (http://mirandanet.ac.uk/), a professional organization of edtech innovators from schools and universities, has been working with associate companies in practice-based research and development projects in classrooms since 1992. However, there is no existing organization or publication that specifically targets the evidence relating to learning and teaching with technology. The *What the research says* books and events hope to start to address this gap.

This *What the research says* volume is divided into six parts. The first two parts provide a set of learning principles and an account of some of the factors that influence how and when learning takes place, and a flavour of the range of technologies that can be used to support learning. The remaining four parts of the book offer more detailed accounts of four important educational challenges that technology may help us to address: how we use technology to engage learners to learn; how we support learners to get the best from their technologies; how we can use technology to support adult learners, and how technology can be used to support teachers.

Part 1 sets out seven principles of learning that are needed – but that are not necessarily sufficient alone – to ensure learning is as effective as possible. Based on analysis by David Baume and Eileen Scanlon of a vast literature, and in particular two key meta-reviews that identify the most consistent and reliable research papers, they provide a foundation for the principles of good practice that will be relevant throughout this book. Chapter 1.1 by Michael J. Reiss highlights how a better understanding of genetic inheritance may help schools work with children with ADHD, dyspraxia and other conditions. Chapter 1.2, by Tony Gardner-Medwin, looks at the benefits of encouraging students to challenge themselves, privately in self-tests and by using mark schemes that reward them for weighing up their reservations and reasons for being confident about answers. The last chapter in this part: Chapter 1.3, is by Rosemary Luckin and presents a range of evidence about the nature of a learner's context and the influence this has upon their learning. The chapter presents the Ecology of Resources, which provides a mechanism for talking about context and a checklist that can be used to help teachers and learners to design effective ways of using technology to support learning that take into account learners' important contextual factors and influences.

Part 2 looks at some of the many new ways in which technology is used to support teaching and/or learning. This part includes six chapters that provide some evidence of the potential of specific technologies. Two chapters look to change the way children learn in school, two more chapters explore the potential for learning when on the move, while the remaining two chapters look at videos and games. The strong message is that *regardless of the design purpose of the technologies, it is always essential to provide evidence for using technologies as part of teaching and learning.*

The remaining four parts of the book each focus on a particular educational challenge. Part 3 explores the role of technology to engage and motivate learners and teachers: Rafael Marques De Albuquerque and Shaaron Ainsworth look at the positive and negative aspects of computer games and conclude that if games are to be used in the classroom to positive effect, educators must work to overcome the negative views that many parents have about their role in the home. Charles Crook opens up another tricky issue in Chapter 3.2: the potential of online source material and teaching aids to foster both collaboration and collusion. He says teachers need to equip themselves with a better sense of how students use new media to help students search, select, abstract, integrate, critique and finally reassemble that information in a distinctive voice. The final chapter in Part 3, by Richard Allen and Allison Allen shows how lessons on architecture from first century BCE Rome offer guidance for designing virtual learning spaces. They also provide some useful tips that won't break the bank, but will help teachers who want to change their environment to promote better learning.

Part 4 starts off with a brief discussion about contemporary digital capabilities and the need for learners to develop these if they are to be effective learners. In Chapter 4.2 Keith Turvey and Norbert Pachler examine the divisive issue of the use of tablets in both education and home game-playing. Their research indicates that tablets and smartphones can help children become critical and creative learners, but there should be regular opportunities for children, teachers and parents to critically review the ways they use technology. Chapter 4.3 takes us into the realms of the Maker World with Torben Steeg and David Barlex. It is something of a roller coaster trip through a landscape of hackspaces, FabLabs, tinkering and the Greatest Show (and Tell) on Earth. However, there are serious points to be made about the constructivist and constructionist foundations of maker activity and its learning potential for schools. Ann Jones, Eileen Scanlon and Koula Charitonos complete the chapters in Part 4 with their look at how learning can be supported across different settings, for example between schools and after-school clubs or between museums and schools.

Adult learners are the focus for Part 5, which looks at ways in which technology can improve the way educators impart knowledge to adults. Stuart Edwards warns that the increase in the number of adults taking courses masks concerns that digital courses may be replacing traditional options hit by fiscal austerity. He also flags up concerns about the way the data suggests that digital technologies are not reaching the most needy, nor are they attracting new learners. Rather, they are providing more ways for existing learners to learn. In Chapter 5.2 the focus is on how massive open online courses, or MOOCs, now engage millions of learners. Rebecca Ferguson, Christothea Herodotou, Tim Coughlan, Eileen Scanlon and Mike Sharples highlight eight issues universities must tackle to ensure MOOCs exploit their potential to open up education around the world. In Chapter 5.3 the importance of both adult education and widening participation are cast in yet sharper relief when considered in light of the fact that across the globe, populations are living longer and the workplace is evolving swiftly as a result of increasing automation. It is clear that lifelong learning will be essential for all adults. And yet it is also clear that while technology has significant potential to extend education for the adult population, as Stuart Edwards points out in Chapter 5.3, we return to the lack of evidence that technology is having a significant impact on adult access to education. There is some positive evidence and increasing signs of significant investment by industry in training with technology and a growing e-learning industry. However, there is no rigorous evidence base to call upon.

The sixth and final part of the book highlights the important role that educators play and the need for them to be the focus of attention when it comes to technology in education. Chapter 6.1 looks at the continual growth of Learning Analytics and Educational Data Mining. Research suggests the possibilities for personalization of learning and improving teaching are greater than the inherent risks, especially when Artificial Intelligence is introduced to enhance the Learning Analytics software. However, there is a pressing need to develop analytics that take into account the learners' context when engaging in learning activities. Chapter 6.2 considers the potential for fast-moving technological information to help improve education. Benedict du Boulay, Alexandra Poulovassilis, Wayne Holmes and Manolis Mavrikis look at artificial intelligence (AI) and 'big data'. While AI is still a young technology within education, initial studies point to some positive conclusions in terms of helping to close the attainment gap by lifting up poorer-performing students. The immense volumes of data generated within education systems can be used to design visualization and notification tools for teachers. The final chapter in the part and the book: Chapter 6.3, looks at three ways in which teachers can build metacognitive skills – thinking about thinking what to do – to help them adapt to different situations. One is collaborative thinking established to support teachers using a video conferencing tool. Another is video and audio technology that includes a camera used to observe and capture classroom activity, and an in-ear receiver so the teachers may hear feedback and suggestions from a coach in real time. Finally, a chat interface enabled tutors to talk aloud about their feedback to students and the resulting data from that enabled them to see how they could improve.

The communication of research

Before progressing to the heart of book, let's pause for a moment and consider the way research is often reported beyond the standard academic journals and conferences. To this end Terry Freedman has lent his voice to the enterprise and provided an extremely readable introduction to how research is often communicated. Terry looks at how education research tends to be reported, how the nature and economics of newspaper reporting account for how it tends to be reported, and how even an article's headline can influence the information a reader gleans from the article. Even if the research is accurately reported, can its findings be divorced from the views held by the teachers who participated in it?

How research is reported in the news

Terry Freedman

Let's start by considering how research is reported in the news. This section will focus on newspapers, but similar considerations about the reporting, though not the economics, apply to other types of media too.

As a preamble, it is worth stating that misleading reporting is not confined to research items. A good example of this may be seen by something that occurred in 2007. In July of that year, several newspapers in England ran articles with headlines declaring that the QCA – the Qualifications and Curriculum Authority – advocated five-minute mathematics lessons.

Clearly this had to be a mistake. How could a school have five-minute lessons? Even apart from the time it would take for pupils to get to the lesson, by the time they'd settled down it would be time to ask them to get ready to leave! A search on the web to find out where this had come from proved fruitless. An email to the QCA enquiring about the origin of the story elicited the reply 'We don't know.'

After some frantic searching within the QCA someone finally worked out where it had come from. Apparently, somebody from the organization had said in a press conference that quick five-minute sessions in languages or mental arithmetic could be quite useful – as part of normal lessons. Yet some newspapers at the time reported that the government had told schools to scrap the timetable and replace it with five-minute lessons. In other words it turned out be a non-story. Good teachers have always spent five minutes or so doing things like quick-fire questions about their subject, spelling or mental arithmetic, especially at the beginning or end of lessons.

This is an extreme example of some of the things that are wrong about journalism in the United Kingdom, and therefore why research in education technology is often poorly reported. It has several key characteristics. First, although the story wasn't exactly made up, it was based on flimsy evidence. There was a kernel of truth, and it's important to remember this. That kernel of truth was written about imaginatively. Secondly, in some papers, the nature of the evidence wasn't given, so the reader did not have an opportunity to see the wider picture and realize that what was said was probably more nuanced than it would appear. Thirdly, the press reported this uncritically. There was no questioning of how five-minute lessons might work in practice. One does not have to be a professor of education to realize that timetabling five-minute lessons could present difficulties. But if they **had** been unsure they could have interviewed a few deputy headteachers who are responsible for the timetabling in their schools, or even 'ordinary' classroom teachers to ask how they would cope with 300 five-minute lessons a day. But it also illustrates the importance of not taking things at face value, and that with some persistence it is usually possible to find out what the truth of the matter is, if one has the time.

Let's consider a few more misleading headlines, because headlines have particular importance, and because the five-minute lesson story was not an isolated case.

First, the reporting of the decision by Michael Gove, the then secretary of state for education in England and Wales, to suspend the ICT Programme of Study. Many newspaper headlines stated that ICT had been 'scrapped'. This is what Michael Gove **really** said: 'ICT will remain compulsory at all key stages, and will still be taught at every stage of the curriculum' (Gove, 2012).

A more recent example is the OECD (2015) study entitled 'Students, Computers and Learning: Making the connection'. Many headlines cried that, according to the OECD research, by spending on computers, schools were wasting money. However, the research itself was far more nuanced than that, making the point that many schools have not taken full advantage of the potential of education technology. The research also found that using computers had not led to noticeable improvements in specific areas of the curriculum: reading, mathematics and science. That is to say, not across the board, as the headlines suggested.

Unfortunately this is not an isolated example. In a paper entitled 'Ill communication: Technology, distraction and student performance', Beland and Murphy (2015: 1–46) reported that banning mobile phones in the classroom can improve outcomes for low-achieving students but has no significant impact on high-achieving students. Perhaps predictably, newspaper headlines declared that mobile phones should be banned in schools as they adversely affect student performance.

One could cite many similar examples of this phenomenon, which may be summarized thus:

1. An organization issues a summary of the results of a research project in the form of a press release.

2. Newspapers report the results, often leaving out any caveats that may have been provided.
3. Article headlines present the results in a single sentence that gives a misleading impression of what the research actually says.

Why does this happen?

The process of making a newspaper, and economics, both play an important part.

Economic considerations

Where do journalists get their news from? Sometimes from investigations, although really big ones are now very rare because they are so expensive. For example, *The Times*'s exposure of child abuse in Rotherham involved Andrew Norfolk, a journalist, sitting in court for day after day listening and taking notes, which is very expensive. Because of redundancies made necessary by falling circulation, more is demanded of all reporters and that can cause problems in having the time to research a story as fully as might have been possible in the past.

In a report entitled *Journalists in the UK*, Thurman, Cornia and Kunert (2016) found that some journalists worked on 50, 60 or 75 stories a week; when editors were included, the figure rose to the hundreds, even to as high as 500. The authors of the study commented that this raises concerns about standards of verification. The same report also shows that in terms of specialist 'beats', no journalist in their survey of 699 respondents self-identified as an education reporter. A category designated as 'social affairs', which may be presumed to include education, was cited by only 2 per cent of the survey sample. These two findings from the report may help to explain why educational research is often reported on so uncritically. To summarize: fewer journalists, even fewer education specialists, plus having to fill the same number of pages, means less time and other resources to evaluate and report on research in any depth, and a greater reliance on press releases.

We must also consider the process of moving from a research report to a news article as summarized above. It is, in effect, a continuous process of leaving out detail, and therefore nuance. Before we look at how the very 'shape' of a news story affects how research is reported, we need to consider the press releases on which the articles are based.

The primary function of a press release is to get itself published. Obviously, the reason that an organization wants the press release to be published is because it wants to make people aware of the information referred to in the release, but that will only happen if the press release is published.

Here we meet our first obstacle. Anecdotal evidence suggests that a national newspaper will receive hundreds, if not thousands, of press releases every day. In order to increase the chances of a press release being published, the information the issuing organization includes in it, and the headline, have to be chosen carefully. If the press release were to say, for example: 'Sometimes computers help pupils, and sometimes they don't', that may be an accurate summary of the research but a journalist reading that headline would almost certainly think it's a non-story and then rapidly move on to the next one in the pile. Unfortunately, a headline or first paragraph that read: 'Computers help kids achieve. Schools are spending their money wisely' would probably only have a small chance of being published, because from a media point of view good news is no news.

An organization's best chance of having a press release read and then published is if there's a hint of taxpayers' money being wasted or some other kind of debacle. The press release may include some caveats in a section headlined 'Notes to editors', but whether or not these notes find their way into the final article is another matter.

The shape of a news story

Another aspect that we need to consider is the shape of a news story, which is sometimes referred to as an inverted pyramid. As shown in the illustration below, the conclusion comes at the top.

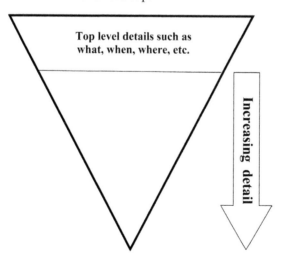

Figure 1: The inverted pyramid. This illustrates the 'shape' of a typical news story. The essential details are packed into the first paragraph. Finer details are revealed as the article progresses.

The first paragraph contains the meat: who, where, how, etc. Further paragraphs contain more and more detail. If any nuance or caveats are included at all they will be in subsequent paragraphs. The reason for writing news stories in this way is simple: it is so that busy commuters can obtain the gist of the news articles without having to read further than the first paragraph in each case.

Headlines are written by sub-editors rather than the journalists who write the articles. They are the people who come up with clever, distinctive headlines, often a play on words. For example, a headline might read: 'Schools' spending on technology does not compute'. Headline writing is quite a skill, so much so that some newspapers employ editors who only write headlines. But the important thing from our point of view is that the headline is written by someone who may be unfamiliar with the detail of the story. (In fact in some cases the headline may have nothing to do with the article, or even convey the opposite of what the article says.)

How we interpret research reporting in newspaper articles

At this point the reader may be thinking, what difference does it make? People will read the article, and then they will see the 'truth'. Unfortunately, even if the article contains all the correct information, that is not necessarily going to be the case, for the following reasons.

First, the way people read newspapers is an issue. According to Wastler (2013) more people are skimming newspaper articles. This observation pertains to the United States, but it almost certainly applies in the United Kingdom as well. Secondly, according to Konnikova (2014), the headline of an article determines the frame of mind in which you approach the article. In other words, first impressions count. Reading the article does not correct that. Not only does the headline frame the way one reads the article, but it even prevents one remembering details that contradict the impression given by the headline.

Unfortunately, if the headteacher or chair of governors or bursar (if the school has one) or academy trustee in your trust has just been reading that the money spent on education technology may as well have been flushed down the drain, the head of computing or e-learning co-ordinator may be placed in a difficult position. What practical steps can he or she take to ensure that requests for more funding will not be dismissed out of hand?

Defence mechanisms

An important first step is to become familiar with the research. Here are some suggestions:

- If the article is based on a press release, find and read the press release. One can usually tell if it's a press release because the same information, often using the same wording, will be seen in several newspapers.
- One can find the press release on the organization's website, usually under a menu item called News, or PR, or Blog.
- The press release will usually provide information about the report and where one can find it.
- Next, read the original report, if it's available.
- If it is not available, read the executive summary.
- If that's not available, read the press release as a last resort.

The experimenter effect

As stated earlier, the headline can influence the way we read and remember an article, and this is an example or a variation of something called the experimenter effect. This describes the situation in which people perform a task well or badly according to whether they have been informed that the task is easy to do or almost impossible to do, even when the instructions are identical in each case.

The reason seems to be that the experimenters give subtle cues that they are not even aware of, and that the subjects pick up on without realizing it. Might a similar thing be happening even in a written report, through the choice of words used? This seems feasible, and is something implied on the Media Bias website at https://mediabiasfactcheck.com/. This site enables one to enter the name of a news source in order to find out if it is biased and, if so, in which direction. The answer returned is sometimes justified by a statement to the effect that, while factual information is given, the reporting uses value-laden words.

The experimenter effect may be said to have been demonstrated by some research in the field of educational ICT that shows that teachers' beliefs affect how they use computers and pupils' attainment. For example, Higgins and Moseley (2001: 191–210) found that pupil outcomes in literacy and numeracy are strongly linked with their teachers' views about ICT and how they used it. They also discovered that teachers tend to use computers in ways that reflect their views on teaching and learning. Similarly, Gobbo and Giradi (2001: 63–85) found that how teachers implement ICT in their classrooms largely depends both on their level of competence in using the technology and on their personal theories of teaching.

To summarize, teachers' faith in ICT and their views of how children learn, as well as their competence in using computers, affects pupil outcomes. While these findings may not be surprising, it calls into question the validity of a lot of the research we read about, even if we believe that the way the research has been reported in the media is scrupulously accurate. Put simply: would the outcomes have been different if they'd looked at a different set of teachers? And how does this affect our view of research that appears to show that a new innovation or a particular type of technology has resulted in excellent pupil outcomes? Might such outcomes have come about because the person implementing the new technology expected them to?

Conclusions

When educational research is reported on in the media it goes through several 'filtering' processes. The report itself tends to be condensed into an 'executive summary'. This often forms the basis of a press release that, more often than not, will emphasize the negative aspects of education technology rather than the positive ones. The essence of the press release will be further condensed into a single paragraph at the start of the article. Once the article has been written, the headline will typically be penned by someone who specializes in writing headlines, and who has not read the evidence on which the article is based. Finally, even if the research has been reported accurately, it may contain implicit bias according to the theories of teaching and learning held by those who took part.

Possible triggers for future research

- A comparative review of the way in which articles about the same research differ from one news source to the next. This was undertaken as research for this chapter, but a more formal and larger scale piece of work could be enlightening.
- The 'experimenter effect' could be tested for by giving similar groups of teachers education technology to try with their pupils, but with different information about the likely efficacy of the technology given to the people chosen to give the instructions. For this to be effective, they themselves would have to be ignorant of the truth of such claims.

Acknowledgements

Special thanks must go to Mutlu Cukurova, Wayne Holmes, Kim Issroff and Allison Allen for their invaluable assistance with editing this volume.

References (Preface and Introduction)

Beland, L.-P. and Murphy, R. (2015) 'Ill Communication: Technology, distraction and student performance' (CEP Discussion Paper 1350). London: Centre for Economic Performance. Online. http://cep.lse.ac.uk/pubs/download/dp1350.pdf (accessed 29 March 2017).

Gobbo, C. and Girardi, M. (2001) 'Teachers' beliefs and integration of information and communications technology in Italian schools'. *Journal of Information Technology for Teacher Education*, 10 (1–2), 63–85.

Gove, M. (2012) 'Michael Gove speech at the BETT Show 2012'. Online. www.gov.uk/government/speeches/michael-gove-speech-at-the-bett-show-2012 (accessed 29 March 2017).

Higgins, S. and Moseley, D. (2001) 'Teachers' thinking about information and communications technology and learning: Beliefs and outcomes'. *Teacher Development*, 5 (2), 191–210.

Konnikova, M. (2014) 'How headlines change the way we think'. *New Yorker*, 17 December. Online. www.newyorker.com/science/maria-konnikova/headlines-change-way-think (accessed 29 March 2017).

OECD (Organisation for Economic Co-operation and Development) (2015) *Students, Computing and Learning: Making the connection*. Paris: OECD Publishing. Online. www.oecd.org/education/students-computers-and-learning-9789264239555-en.htm (accessed 29 March 2017).

Thurman, N., Cornia, A. and Kunert, J. (2016) *Journalists in the UK*. Oxford: Reuters Institute for the Study of Journalism. Online. http://reutersinstitute.politics.ox.ac.uk/publication/journalists-uk (accessed 29 March 2017).

Wastler, A. (2013) 'Newspaper bane: Nobody reads the stories'. *CNBC*, 10 August. Online. www.cnbc.com/id/100952247 (accessed 29 March 2017).

Part One

Learning

1

What the research says about how and why learning happens

David Baume and Eileen Scanlon

In this first Part of the book we provide a brief synthesis of the research on learning as relevant to the use of technology. This synthesis is followed by three case studies, each of which provides a very different example of evidence that can help us to better understand why, how and when learning happens.

Learning: A brief synthesis of the research

From the mid nineteenth century the nature and process of learning has been researched extensively and from different perspectives and disciplines including, for example, psychology, anthropology and education. The main findings from much of this research have been summarized into meta-analyses, and in some cases these meta-analyses have been synthesized. This process enables the most robust of results and findings from the research and the review articles to be extracted. In this chapter we have selected four syntheses of meta-analyses and extracted from these some key points about learning that can be stated with a good degree of certainty. Most of the results we use in this chapter come from two meta-studies that focus on learning by Chickering and Gamson (1987) and by James and Pollard (2011). Additional confirmation comes from the two additional meta-studies, which are more concerned with teaching: Hattie (2015) and Pascarella and Terenzini (2005).

To start this first chapter, we identify seven principles for learning that help us to understand the conditions in which learning is most effective. Specifically, effective learning has been shown to happen when the following conditions are met:

1. A clear structure, framework, scaffolding surrounds, supports and informs learning.
2. High standards are expected of learners, and are made explicit.

3. Learners acknowledge and use their prior learning and their particular approaches to learning.
4. Learning is an active process.
5. Learners spend lots of time on task, that is, doing relevant activities and practice.
6. Learning is undertaken at least in part as a collaborative activity, both among students and between students and staff.
7. Learners receive and use feedback on their work.

We are not saying that these are the only seven conditions in which learning will be effective. We are, however, saying that we can be confident about these seven principles being evidence based. However, this does not mean that just observing these seven principles will mean that all will be well. Principles have to be applied in particular situations, combinations and ways. This is where the skill and the craft of the teacher, and of the learner, come into play. Simple principles can lead to complex practices.

You may feel that most, or possibly all, of these principles are obvious, intuitive, perhaps even common sense. This shouldn't be a surprise. Look at this in another way. It would surely be surprising if any of these seven key learning principles, that have been extracted from decades of research and analysis, were counterintuitive. We are all learners and have a huge amount of experience of learning. We all probably also have some experience of teaching, or at least of supporting learning. We all therefore know something about what works when it comes to our own learning and when supporting the learning of others.

We all have models or theories about our own learning, whether or not we make these explicit. Likewise, teachers, managers and politicians also have models of learning and all of us can hold both true and false beliefs about learning. For example, the prevalence of the practice of lecturing on a topic for 50 minutes suggests that many people believe that being lectured to for 50 minutes is a good way to learn. Unfortunately, in this case there is considerable evidence that in many situations the 50-minute lecture strategy is rather poor (Bligh, 1998). A lecture may inspire, motivate and inform, but rarely fulfils the seven principles for effective learning; it is certainly inadequate for developing high-level skills.

On a more positive note, Bain (2004) has shown that one of the qualities of a truly outstanding teacher is that their own internal models of learning and teaching are broadly similar to what is known from research evidence about learning and teaching. This is true whether or not these outstanding teachers have undertaken formal study in learning and teaching, and whether or not they make their models and theories explicit.

We now go into more detail about the seven key principles for successful learning outlined earlier.

Learning is most effective when:

1. A clear structure, framework, scaffolding surrounds, supports and informs learning.
2. High standards are expected of learners, and are made explicit.

As we learners blunder about on the lower slopes, we need to see the mountain top – our ultimate destination. The sight of the mountain top, the thought of arriving there, should inspire us. If it doesn't, then perhaps we have chosen the wrong quest. Or perhaps nobody has successfully shown us a perspective on the destination that could inspire us. Here we see a vital role for the teacher – that of motivating learners.

But the mountain top may look remote, scary, or even perhaps unattainable. So we also need to see waypoints, intermediate goals, cabins where we can consolidate achievements and recuperate as we plan the next stage of the climb. Better still if we also have a route map, showing the path, or ideally a range of paths, to allow ourselves to choose the path best suited to our current capabilities and enthusiasms. We also need to learn about ourselves: to judge the security of our progress and how confident we are in tackling different kinds of challenges. We need to know when we are getting out of our depth, and we need to have available a framework of routes by which we can achieve a secure footing again. We need tools and resources, information and feedback about our progress, and we need companionship and competition, to ensure that our achievements are real and worthwhile. One of the most important activities we can do as learners or teachers is to try and make our beliefs explicit and map them back to the evidence.

We have compared learning to the process of climbing a mountain. Perhaps the most vivid aspect of this analogy arises when we reach the mountain top. Then we can see the full horizon, typically with higher peaks presenting new inspiring challenges that now seem, with effort, achievable. Education has no Everest, no highest peak: rather, there is always something more challenging to achieve.

Moving away from mountain climbing metaphors, structures for learning can take the form of clear intended learning outcomes, course schedules and an appropriate set of learning activities. High standards can include, once again, clear learning outcomes, together with examples of work that achieves these outcomes. Achieving high standards also needs the opportunity to articulate and then use criteria to identify good work.

3. Learners acknowledge and use their prior learning and their approaches to learning.

Learning can usefully be seen as a process whereby learners get from where they are to where they want to be. So it makes sense for learners to acknowledge whatever it is they currently know and can currently do. Learners need to build on, which of course will sometimes include tearing down, their current knowledge, and maybe also some of their current ways of working. Learning is aided through collaboration, but learning is also in part an individual process. Unfortunately, the need for large-scale mass education can tug against this individuality.

It is hard to learn if we do not know ourselves. It is hard to teach if our learners do not know themselves. It is hard to teach if we do not know our learners. Good learners are often those who have learned to manage their own learning, based on knowledge of themselves as learners. One important job of a teacher therefore is to facilitate learners' self-knowledge.

4. Learning is an active process.

We are doing (at least) two distinct things when we are learning.

Firstly, we are trying to fit what we are reading or hearing into our current model or picture of the world. For example, when we read or hear about a new country, we can fit or assimilate what we are hearing into our current concepts of 'country'. We have a, perhaps implicit, concept of 'country-ness', if you like. This concept may include ideas including borders, culture, government, policy, language, currency. Seeking to assimilate new information, new ideas, into our existing world-view, is often a valid and productive approach to learning.

But sometimes this assimilation process does not work. We therefore need other approaches. Any example involving countries is likely to be contentious, but, if we consider the island of Guernsey, we may struggle to accommodate Guernsey into our current account of a country. We may discover that we need to re-conceptualize what we mean by 'country' to accommodate Guernsey. The ideas of assimilation and accommodation, originated by Jean Piaget, are well explained in Boden (Boden, 1980).

Learning is an active process, but activity alone is no guarantee of learning. A skilled pro-active learner will learn to ask internally the kind of questions that make for productive thinking, and hence learning. It is in this context that peer interaction, explored later under principle 7, can be incredibly valuable. Any conversation about a shared experience – a visit, a piece of music, a show – will immediately demonstrate how new ideas, even untidy nonsensical ones, can stimulate understanding and make sense of experiences.

5. Learners spend lots of time on the task, that is, doing relevant activities and practising.

Time on task is essential for any kind of learning. Tasks need to be sequenced appropriately, undertaken with constructive collaboration and feedback, and with reference to clear, high expectations and standards. Structures are needed in which to think about the issues, and to make relationships between what we are learning and what we know already. You will recognize all this from the list of seven principles.

Learning should be relevant for the learner. An implicit theory of learning in much formal education is that we need, first, to learn the core concepts and ideas. Only then can we learn to apply them. Consideration of time on task suggests a different approach. Often it may be more productive to start with the intended outcomes of learning: with what we want to achieve and why it is worthwhile. Then, as we initially tackle simple, then progressively more sophisticated versions of the tasks described in the outcomes, we become motivated and more able to use and test principles that underlie what we are doing.

John Holt (1977) asked whether he was engaged in learning the cello or playing the cello. Of course, he was doing both. He was playing, for his current pleasure, and with the intention of playing even better, for even greater future pleasure.

Is this how you or your current learners describe their learning?

6. Learning is undertaken at least in part as a collaborative activity, both among students and between students and staff.

In good, open, honest, critical and constructive conversations, sharing, testing and developing ideas and practices are how we learn and how we progress our knowledge and understanding.

The teacher may have two distinct roles in educational conversations. Of course the teacher is an expert in the subject being taught and learned, and students value the subject expertise that the teacher brings. But the teacher must also facilitate learning, judging when to ask and answer a question, when to steer students towards possible answers or sources for answers, and when to help students develop their own approaches to answering questions. Conversation is an essential skill, for teaching and for learning.

Collaboration is also an excellent example of how the seven principles we identify are ideally integrated. It is important to consider the various principles together, rather than in isolation. That we learn through collaboration should not be a surprise, given the other principles. Principle 1, the need for a clear structure or framework, describes a prerequisite for effective collaboration rather than an automatic consequence of collaboration. We have probably all worked in poorly structured collaborations, which were less than effective. A constructive, well-motivated group is constantly striving to do better (principle 2). In an effective collaboration, participants value and build on what everyone brings, as well as challenging and questioning as appropriate (principle 3). Effective collaboration involves actually doing things together (principles 4 and 5). Collaboration and conversation include receiving and using feedback on our thoughts (principle 7).

7. Learners receive and use feedback on their work.

Action and reaction, thesis and antithesis and synthesis, call and response, question and answer. The idea of interaction, of conversation, of a statement and critical and/or constructive response, is fundamental to much human interaction. It also turns out to be fundamental to how we learn.

Feedback can come from the teacher, from a fellow learner, from a computer program. At a basic level, usable feedback can talk about:

- what was good in the work, and why, and therefore what the person producing the work should continue to do and build on in future pieces of work;
- what was less good, and again why it was less good, and what the person producing the work might do differently in future pieces of work.

Usable feedback goes well beyond saying 'good' or 'poor', 'like' or 'don't like'. Usable feedback is specific and constructive. Crucial to usable feedback is the word 'because', as in this example:

> *'This answer was good because it clearly and directly answered the question; sourced and then marshalled evidence for both sides of the argument; reached a reasoned conclusion, while acknowledging the weight of countervailing arguments; and identified future lines of enquiry.'*

> *'In future work, you might additionally look at sources including these ... and adopt a more critical stance, perhaps using approaches including ... '*

The person who produced the original work could use feedback like this to guide their future work, as well as feeling appropriate pride in what they have produced this time.

Feedback can also come from the learner themselves (Falchikov, 2004). Learners can answer basic questions including 'What is good about this work, and why?' and 'In what ways could it be better, and again why?' That, after all, is what we do when we consider the first draft of something we have produced, and set about improving it. Learners can also become good at giving accurate and useful feeback to peers (Boud, 1995).

Feedback goes well beyond a single act of production and a single response. The kinds of collaborative learning explored in principle 6 above involve a rapid cycle of production and response; a conversation leading to learning. This is, after all, how much of the real world conducts itself. Self- and peer-feedback could usefully play a much larger and more constructive role in education than they currently do.

Talking about learning

Beyond these seven evidenced principles, we can make a further important point about learning. In formal education, whether in school, college or higher education, we rarely talk much with our learners about learning. It would be good to talk about it more. It would be good to talk about: what we mean by learning, about the conditions for learning, about our individual preferences for learning, and about what we know about how we learn and like to learn. These should be conversations, not lectures. The more we all know about learning in general, and about our own learning, our peers' learning and our learning preferences, the better our chances to become and remain effective and enthusiastic lifelong learners.

The three chapters in Part 1 of this book consider three very different perspectives on learning and why and how it takes place. In Chapter 1.1 Michael J. Reiss considers the impact of inheritance on a learner's progress. The second chapter 1.2 by Tony Gardner-Medwin considers the value of self-testing. The third and final chapter is by Rose Luckin and it provides an overview of the importance of a learner's context to their progress, and a checklist for use when designing learning activities so that context is taken into account.

The role of genetic inheritance in how well children do in schools

Michael J. Reiss

It is widely accepted that the cultural and material benefits children obtain from their parents play an important role in how well they do at school. However, there is a surprising disconnect between what most academics in education and what many academics in biology think about the role of genetic inheritance in many areas of human life, including how well children do in schools. What we want to do here is first look at why there is this disconnect and then to examine the core issue of the role of genetic inheritance in school performance. As a result, I hope to show three things:

1. Education needs to stop putting its head in the sand about the possible role of genetic inheritance in school performance.
2. Genetic inheritance can play a significant role in how well children do in schools.
3. This does not mean that children's school performance is predetermined, i.e. fixed in advance.

Education needs to stop ignoring the possible role of genetics in school performance

Ever since the publication of Darwin's momentous *On the Origin of Species* in 1859, biologists have accepted that inherited variation plays a central role in the evolution of the enormous number of traits (distinguishing qualities or characteristics) exhibited by organisms. The early twentieth century advances in genetics, followed by the mid-twentieth century advances of neo-Darwinism and the subsequent developments in molecular biology, have underlined this conclusion.

In the case of humans, this means that just about everything of interest about us has an inherited component. It doesn't matter whether one is looking at height, or weight, or reaction time, or longevity, or the likelihood of developing heart disease, or anything else; inheritance generally plays a

9

role. And this is true too of such educationally significant factors as general intelligence, reading ability and examination success.

Many people – including parents and teachers – are happy to accept that children differ greatly in their abilities or potential (e.g. at music, mathematics or ball sports). However, educators have been reluctant to accept the mounting weight of evidence for the importance of genetic inheritance in school performance. There are a number of reasons for this reluctance – mostly understandable and indeed well-intentioned.

For one thing there is a terrible legacy of genetics and human history. Various historians of science (e.g. Gould, 1981; Lewontin, 1991) have shown how genetics has been used, both consciously and unconsciously, in attempts to argue for the inferiority of women, of black people and of those not in the ruling classes. Faced with this legacy of sexism, racism and cultural imperialism, it is hardly surprising that educators, who by and large have liberal leanings and are in favour of social justice, have rejected genetics as a way of understanding what is important about humans. What has happened is that genetics, rather than the misuse of genetics, has been rejected. It is as if books, in general, were rejected because some books are harmful. The reality, though, is that a better understanding of genetics, not the abandonment of genetics, is what is needed.

Figure 1.1.1: Cyril Burt, who probably falsified some of the data that helped lead to an acceptance of the role of inheritance in intelligence. *Source:* https://en.wikipedia. org/wiki/Cyril_Burt

A second major reason for the widespread scepticism among educators concerning the importance of inheritance in educational attainment is because of the legacy of Cyril Burt (Figure 1.1.1). Cyril Burt (1883–1971) was an educational psychologist. Although there have been revisionist accounts, it is generally accepted that he systematically engaged in scientific fraud, falsely claiming to have collected data in his studies on the heritability of intelligence. However, what is beyond doubt is that the findings he produced on the extent to which intelligence is inherited were and are consistently in line with other studies. In other words, even if we ignore all of Burt's work, there would be no effect on the conclusions to be reached from the evidence in the research literature.

A third major reason why educators have tended to ignore the ever-increasing growth in what is known about inheritance is, I believe, because of a widespread, often implicit, presumption that inheritance is to be equated with determinism. I shall deal with this misunderstanding below, but first I turn in a bit more detail to the role that inheritance plays in school performance.

Inheritance does play a role in how well children do in schools

Let me explain a bit about how scientists decide whether or not inheritance plays a role in a trait. It doesn't matter whether we are talking about the height of plants, the milk yield of cows or the reading ability of children.

First, for the sake of clarification, by 'inheritance' we mean 'genetic inheritance'. Everyone realizes, for example, that family background is important. If one is brought up in a home with lots of books and where reading is valued, it is hardly surprising that one is likely to do better at reading as a child than another child of the same age who has not enjoyed such benefits. Indeed, much of the skill in arriving at measures of 'heritability' – that is the extent to which genetics plays a role – is precisely to do with disentangling the effects of shared environments.

Without going into a full-scale statistical treatment of how biologists and statisticians determine the importance of genes for the expression of any trait, it should be clear that what one needs to do is:

- Get reasonably objective measures of the trait in question. This is fairly easy for milk yields in cows; it's harder – but not impossible – for most things of educational interest such as reading ability or musicality.
- Collect such data from a large number (ideally many thousands) of individuals.
- Get some measure of the extent to which these individuals have similar genetic backgrounds.

- Get some measure of the extent to which these individuals have similar environmental backgrounds.

It's the last two of these that are the most difficult to do and for this reason a number of studies have relied on twin studies. Twin studies are of value because there are two sorts of twins – identical twins and non-identical twins. Non-identical twins are no more genetically similar than are any two non-twin siblings but, by virtue of having been born from the same pregnancy, they have shared an early environment that is more similar than that shared by non-twin siblings. Identical twins have an early environment that is as similar or even more similar as that shared by non-identical twins but in addition, they are virtually genetically identical. What this means is that by looking at the extent to which monozygotic (identical) twins are more similar in certain traits than are dizygotic (non-identical) twins, one can obtain a measure of the heritability of the trait.

To give an extreme example: identical twins typically have a very similar eye and hair colour – more similar than is the case for non-identical twins. We, therefore, conclude that eye and hair colour have high heritabilities. However, the language that identical twins speak best is no more similar than is the case for non-identical twins. (In most cases, of course, siblings, whether or not twins, have the same mother tongue but if they are separated at some point in their childhood – for example because they are adopted by families in different countries – they may end up speaking different languages best.) We therefore conclude that the language one speaks best has a very low heritability.

There are various ways nowadays of calculating heritabilities and they give very similar values – which is encouraging from a scientific point of view. What is important is that virtually all human behaviours tend to have heritabilities of about 0.3 to 0.6 (Bouchard, 2004). Heritabilities lie between 0 (e.g., the language one speaks best) and 1 (e.g. eye colour). This means that human behaviours are moderately heritable – not as heritable as height (with a heritability in the West of about 0.9) but more so than religiosity (which has a heritability of about 0.1 to 0.2). Examples of human behaviours are such things as personality, intelligence, artistic interests and the chances of developing a psychiatric illness.

Children's school performance is not predetermined

Despite the fact that intelligence, along with most other human behaviours, is moderately inheritable, this does *not* mean that intelligence itself or school performance more generally are predetermined. The way that heritabilities are calculated depends on the range of environmental variation that exists in the sample. This is why earlier I wrote that height has 'a heritability in *the West* of about 0.9'. In the West, relatively few children are malnourished. Obviously, if you are malnourished you don't end up growing as tall, other things being equal, as you would otherwise. So, in the West, the extent of relevant environmental variation for the determination of human height is quite small. Sadly, there are plenty of countries where this is not the case – where many children grow up malnourished. In such countries calculations of the heritability of height result in values that are smaller than they are in the West.

This simple but vital point about heritability calculations is all too often not understood. To repeat: values of the heritabilities of traits can vary greatly depending on the environment. And herein lies one of the crucial tasks of education, I would argue, from a social justice perspective. Just as we hold that no child, whatever their family circumstances, should be malnourished or fail to receive treatment for medical conditions (including those like short-sightedness that can damage their educational performance), so we need to develop our ways of teaching, including those that draw on new technologies, to minimize the deleterious effects of each child's circumstances.

Let me end with some crystal ball gazing. We are only just beginning to get to grips with how teachers should tackle such conditions as dyslexia, ADHD (Attention Deficit Hyperactivity Disorder) and dyspraxia. All such conditions will have both heritable and environmental components. It is possible that as we learn more about how schools can better teach children who manifest with such conditions, calculations of their heritabilities will reduce, as will educational inequalities. This will be good for the children concerned – and for society more generally.

The value of self-tests and the acknowledgement of uncertainty

Tony Gardner-Medwin

Introduction

Student testing can be controversial. Why should students, especially children, repeatedly be given stressful exercises designed to rate them relative to their peers, often on measures that have limited relevance to the real world or limited value for stimulating their individual strengths and interests? It is important therefore to make it clear that the issue I examine here is not this use of formal assessment in education. Testing is not just assessment. I'm looking at the value to students of challenging themselves by doing self-tests for their own benefit, in private or with friends: learning from mistakes, discovering how arguments interrelate, gaining immediate feedback about misconceptions and interconnections, and above all learning to think positively without the fear of humiliation that can arise from teacher interactions or exams.

Learning and knowing what we know

How do we learn things? As a teacher and neuroscientist, I, of course, know that there are many answers to this question, to take account for example of different contexts and different levels. But the question is always worth bearing in mind. I learned that 7×8=56 at the age of around 8. Maybe I learned it much as a parrot could learn it – as an English phrase that just tripped off the tongue: '*rote learning*'. Now, more than 60 years later, it doesn't seem to trip quite so reliably: 48? 54? 56? However, with good teaching, I learned the importance of getting such things right and how to get them right even when memory recall of the fact is unreliable. I learned that there were ways to check against things I had learned differently: my understanding of what the question means and how it relates to other memory traces: 7×7=49, so with an extra 7, this is 56. This strategy is something beyond even the smartest parrot. Confucius is credited as having said: 'Learning without thought is labour lost'. I'm not sure I go so far as this because simple associative or rote learning can be very useful. But in education, we need to stimulate thinking to promote deeper learning and understanding.

Challenge, self-testing and mock combat

What do we learn from examples outside the classroom? Ask any musician or sportsperson how they learn and they will say the key is practice. Watch a young leopard learning to stalk prey by pouncing on its mother and you will see the same thing. These examples combine challenge, enjoyment and sometimes supreme achievement. Practice is a context where you make mistakes with impunity and without humiliation, where you can think about what you get right and wrong, and choose new situations and tactics that challenge you near your limits. That is how you expand your areas of competence and confidence. Challenge, self-testing and mock combat constitute the evolutionary origin of games, to which we owe so much in childhood and from which we can learn much in adulthood. In all our skills we each have areas of competence and inadequacy. We need good judgement about where these limits are, to work to improve them. Caution is needed when we are unsure of success, and boldness when confidence is warranted. Teachers can guide the learning process through inspiration and example or explanation, but much of the constructive work in learning is done away from public view or high-stakes competition. It involves thinking and perhaps dreaming about new challenges and things that went right and wrong. Somehow we – or at least the lucky among us – have been programmed and brought up to enjoy such self-testing wherever it can help.

Maths and 'maths anxiety'

I once had to run maths and physics classes for first year medical and physiology students at University College London. Though highly selected, these students have a huge range of ability in those subjects. They were not treated as priority subjects on the medical timetable: I had just two lectures, despite the fact that lack of numeracy and physical insight can have dire consequences in medicine and can be a huge handicap in science. So how can one try to deal with the all too prevalent syndrome '*I'll never be any good at maths*'? The fact is, everyone can do some maths reliably and everyone can get out of their depth at some point. My approach was to use self-tests combined with what I called 'Certainty-Based Marking' (CBM) to help students establish their own boundaries. Trainee doctors must know what jobs they can do reliably and when they need help or extra time. Students were required to repeat self-tests (with randomized question selections and randomized data) as often as they wanted, indicating with each answer how sure they were that it was correct. They received instant feedback with penalties if they expressed confidence in a wrong answer. Submission of results was optional, except that at some point they had to submit at least an 80 per cent grade on each test. This scheme was popular with students: good students passed quickly in a single trial, while weak students made as many as six attempts and even continued after gaining 80 per cent because they saw that the issues being tested were issues they really needed to understand. Even good students learned from the process since with over-confidence they often made snap decisions without thinking – eliciting a clear wake-up penalty. My approach to those who felt maths was not their thing was to encourage them to find the areas where they were genuinely competent and to extend these by identifying and working at the boundaries.

How sure are you?	C=1 (unsure)	C=2 (middling)	C=3 (pretty sure)	No Reply			
Mark if correct:	1	2	3	(0)		C=3	100% / 80%
						C=2	67%
Mark if wrong :	0	-2	-6	(0)		C=1	
Chance of error?	More than 1 in 3 (>33%)	Around 1 in 4 (25%)	Less than 1 in 5 (<20%)	-			0%

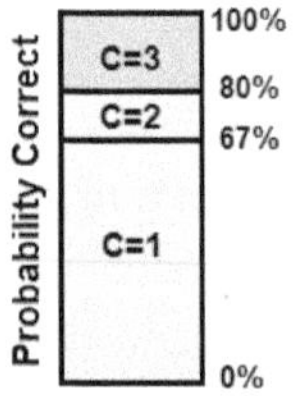

Probability Correct

Figure 1.2.1: A. The mark scheme used for Certainty-Based Marking. B. The rational basis for choosing a certainty level in (A), given one's judgement of the probability that an answer is correct, in order to expect (on average, with similar judgements) the highest marks

Certainty-Based Marking

Certainty-Based Marking (CBM) in one form or another has a long history, back as far as the 1930s (Ahlgren, 1969; Hassmén and Hunt, 1994). It is only with computers that it has become really easy to implement. But surprisingly it is still not widely used. Post-instruction tests where students rate confidence in individual answers have been shown to enhance long-term retention. Unaware of this literature, but certain of the importance to a student of knowing where their knowledge is and is not reliable, I set up my own CBM scheme (Gardner-Medwin, 1995; www.ucl.ac.uk/lapt; www.tmedwin.net/cbm) (Figure. 1.2.1). It is simpler and more intuitive than earlier schemes, and properly motivates students always to be honest. It asks for a rating of certainty for each answer on one of three levels: C=1, C=2 and C=3. If the answer is correct they will receive 1, 2, or 3 marks (or in the United States 'points'). If the answer is wrong there is no penalty as long as uncertainty (C=1) was acknowledged, whereas with C=2 and C=3 there are penalties of -2 and -6 marks for wrong answers. With this scheme, it is obviously best to click C=3 if sure and C=1 if very unsure, with no option to 'game' the system differently to improve one's score. A rational threshold (where the blue and orange lines cross in Figure 1.2.2) is around 75 per cent chance of being correct, and if students are unsure whether to judge above or below this, they choose the middle option C=2. This requires thinking about reservations and justifications for an answer.

In a survey following extensive use of CBM in self-tests including core medical topics (Issroff and Gardner-Medwin, 1998) students supported its use strongly, with a majority saying they thought about confidence for most answers and sometimes revised their answers as a result. A later survey (2005, unpublished) supported continuing use of CBM in year 1 and 2 medical exams and agreed that negative marks were appropriate if answers were confident and wrong, as well as reduced marks for correct answers that were unconfident. Both at UCL and in many previous studies, CBM has been shown to improve reliability in exam grades (Ahlgren, 1969, Gardner-Medwin and Gahan, 2003, Salehi *et al.*, 2015). CBM is not widely used in exams at present, perhaps due to its somewhat increased complexity and the need – in the interests of fairness – to ensure that students have had prior experience with CBM. Within self-tests, CBM is more unequivocally beneficial – incentivizing careful thinking and enhancing feedback. The sting of a penalty for confidence in a supposedly wrong answer helps teachers too: comments and discussion flow freely when students feel the issue unclear or contentious, so there is opportunity to clarify misconceptions and improve questions and explanations.

CBM provides a new quality of feedback to students through self-testing. Figure 1.2.2 shows data from subjects previously unfamiliar with CBM, practising online for a prospective application to medical school. Feedback with just conventional grades on such tests can lead to crude and often dispiriting student responses (orange). Adding the information from CBM (the vertical axis) allows much clearer categorization of a student's status and issues (blue). These are difficult self-tests, and about 10 per cent of the subjects obtained negative overall CBM marks. Since it is obvious that they would have done better by acknowledging uncertainty (C=1) all the time, the feedback provides a wake-up call that, even with quite good conventional grades over 60 per cent, they may need to address issues where they don't realize they are weak. Such negative overall CBM scores are of course much rarer in final exams, since misconceptions (when defined as confident wrong ideas) have, for most students, largely been dispelled. CBM tests at the end of a course may show a lack of knowledge, but typically indicate good discrimination between what is and is not known. Gender biases sometimes observed with conventional (especially negative) marking – perhaps due to females being more inclined to disadvantage themselves by omitting uncertain answers – seem to be absent or much reduced with CBM (Gardner-Medwin, 1995; Hassmén and Hunt, 1994; Salehi *et al.*, 2015).

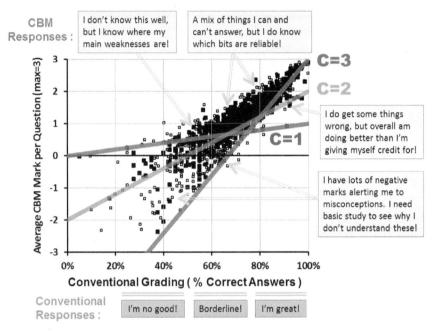

Figure 1.2.2: Data from 1500 CBM self-test sessions taken voluntarily online (www. ucl.ac.uk/lapt/?bmat) as practice for the Biomedical Admissions Test (http://bmat. org.uk) used by several UK medical schools. Large symbols: students completed all questions (40–69 per test). Typical responses are shown for just conventional grades (orange) and for CBM grades (blue). Coloured lines show CBM marks that would have been awarded if students always used the same certainty level. About 60 per cent of grades are above these lines, indicating successful discrimination. This is reflected as a bonus in feedback to the students, added to their conventional grade

Voluntary self-tests in a medical course

At Imperial College Medical School, with Prof. Nancy Curtin and colleagues, we have kept track since 2008 of the relationship between voluntary use of CBM self-tests in the first-year course (October–June) and pass/fail rates in formative (January) and summative (June) exams (Curtin and Gardner-Medwin, 2013). The self-tests were mostly drafted by students in previous years, with vetting by staff. The statistics over seven years (averaged in Figure

1.2.3) are striking. Failure rates for students who used relevant self-tests before the exams were, in both contexts, consistently and markedly lower than for students who had not used self-tests. After the first year, students were each year (at the end of Term 1 and before the first exam) shown such data from previous years in lectures; but the discrepancy nevertheless persisted.

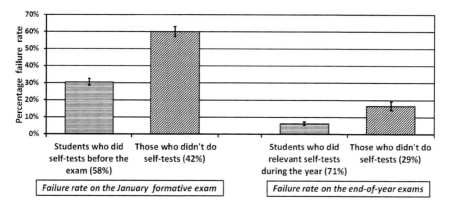

Figure 1.2.3: Failure rates in exams for students who did and did not choose to attempt CBM self-tests in year 1 of a London medical course. The exams did not employ CBM. Averages (± 1 s.e.m.) over seven years 2008–2015. Student numbers 270–330 per annum

We do not suggest that the students who tried self-tests necessarily did better in exams because of the self-tests. We certainly hope these may have contributed, but good students are doubtless more likely both to use available learning tools and to pass exams. Around 30 per cent of the students who failed the formative exam without trying self-tests did start using them later in the year. But it is worrying that many students who were destined to fail these exams did not have the insight to foresee the problem, and at least try something that the data suggested might help. This lack of insight is exactly where self-tests, especially with CBM, should help: identification of weak areas through practice, challenge and mistakes. Medical students are smart and have all done well at school. Perhaps this is part of the problem: some of them need to learn that in a wider world there are always limits to what you understand, and without self-testing, it is difficult to realize how uncomfortably close these limits may be.

Conclusion

To quote Confucius again, 'Real knowledge is to know the extent of one's ignorance'. The most valuable element of self-tests and CBM is perhaps to reward acknowledgement of uncertainty as something more valuable than self-confidence. Teachers often have trouble getting students to acknowledge uncertainty. In the privacy of a self-test and with the unconventional structure of certainty-based marking it is possible to reap some of the benefits of Confucius's insight.

Context and learning

Rosemary Luckin

Introduction

The context of learning has an important impact on the learning process and the gains made by learners. This impact has been noted by many researchers (see, for example, Cole 1996). We know that context matters to the learning and teaching process, we do not, however, know exactly how the relationship between context and learning works. Some people consider context to be something like a container in which learners interact as they learn, others believe context is a complex set of interlinked experiences and interactions that are weaved together to form a person's context (Luckin, 2010). This book has a particular focus on learning and teaching with technology and here, too, context is important. Technology cannot, in itself, improve learning. The context within which educational technology is used is crucial to its success or otherwise. Evidence clearly suggests that technology in education offers potential opportunities that will only be realized when technology design and use takes into account the context in which the technology is used to support learning.

In this chapter, we present a particular definition and way of talking about context that can be used to help us decide upon the ways in which technology can best be designed and used to support learning and teaching. The definition, its supporting theory and the associated design framework, are combined into an approach that is called the *Ecology of Resources* and it is discussed in detail in Luckin (2010).

The theoretical background for the Ecology of Resources

Context is a complex concept that is discussed across many disciplines and from a variety of perspectives. However, previous research into the manner in which context impacts upon learning has been largely limited to specific environmental locations, such as school classrooms. Environmental location is only one of the contextual factors that impact upon learning and teaching. There are others of importance, such as people and technologies, plus of course the individual learner's past experiences and their character traits, experience, knowledge and expertise. The proliferation of ubiquitous technologies has added to the complexity of discussions about context. These technologies also provide an increasing impetus for the integration of research into the blended physical and digital environment: through for example, the *Internet of Things*.

Context is 'perhaps the most prevalent term used to index the circumstances of behaviour' (Cole, 1996: 132). It requires that we interpret mind 'as distributed in the artefacts which are woven together and which weave together individual human actions in concert with and as part of the permeable, changing, events of life' (Cole, 1996, 136). This is a perspective that is also echoed in the work of Lev Vygotsky ([1978]; 1986).

The Ecology of Resources draws upon previous research and provides a learner-centred definition of context:

> Context is dynamic and associated with connections between people, things, locations and events in a narrative that is driven by people's intentionality and motivations. Technology can help to make these connections in an operational sense. People can help to make these connections have meaning for a learner. A learner is not exposed to multiple contexts, but rather has a single context that is their lived experience of the world; a 'phenomenological gestalt' (Manovich, 2006) that reflects their interactions with multiple people, artefacts and environments. The partial descriptions of the world that are offered to a learner through these resources act as the hooks for interactions in which action and meaning are built. In this sense, meaning is distributed amongst these resources. However, it is the manner in which the learner at the centre of their context internalizes their interactions that is the core activity of importance. These interactions are not predictable but are created by the people who interact, each of whom will have intentions about how these interactions should be. (Luckin, 2010: 18)

This definition of context is informed by a particular interpretation of Vygotsky's Zone of Proximal Development or ZPD (Vygotsky, 1986), called the Zone of Collaboration. The Zone of Collaboration emphasizes the important role played by the society within which the learner interacts, and in particular the role of more knowledgeable, or more able, members of that society: lecturers, teachers, trainers and parents, for example. The Zone of Collaboration involves two sub-concepts, namely: the Zone of Available Assistance (ZAA); and the Zone of Proximal Adjustment (ZPA). The ZAA describes the variety of resources within a learner's world that could provide different qualities and quantities of assistance to the learner at any particular point in time. The ZPA represents a sub-set of the ZAA; a sub-set that is deemed appropriate for a learner's needs. The concept of the Zone of Collaboration is integrated with the definition of context outlined earlier to form the Ecology of Resources model of context.

The Ecology of Resources model of context

The Ecology of Resources model (EoR) is illustrated in Figure 1.3.1. The EoR develops the ZAA and ZPA concepts into a characterization of a learner along with the potential interactions that form that learner's context. Its full detail can be found in Luckin (2010). Here we describe it briefly to help readers to understand the practical implications for the use of technology to support learning and teaching that we outline later in this chapter.

The resources that make up a learner's ZAA are wide ranging. They include, for example: the knowledge and actions of the subject or skill to be learned ('Knowledge and Skills' in Figure 1.3.1); the books, pens and paper, and the technology that can be used by the learner ('Tools' in Figure 1.3.1); the other people who know more about the knowledge or skill to be learnt than the learner does with whom the learner can learn ('People' in Figure 1.3.1); and the location and surrounding environment with which the learner interacts as they learn: for example, a school classroom, a park, a virtual world, or a place of work ('Environment' label in Figure 1.3.1). In order to support learning, the relationships between the different types of resource with which the learner interacts need to be identified and understood.

In addition to the resources with which learners can interact as they learn, there are factors that constrain the way learners can use and interact with the resources in their context. These factors are identified by the 'Filter' labels in Figure 1.3.1. For example, the teacher as a resource for learners is *filtered*. For example, he or she is probably only available during a class, or perhaps at some other times via email. A learner's access to their environment is also filtered by the environment's organization and any rules and conventions that apply to it. For example, in a lecture hall it is expected that students will sit and listen to their lecture, complete activities as required and ask questions when appropriate. It is not expected that students will jump up and down or stand at the front and talk about their weekend. These are well-understood conventions that *filter* the way that learners behave when in the lecture environment. Filters can be positive or negative and they are often also interrelated. For example, the way in which a chemistry lab is constrained or filtered for learners is related to the nature of the chemistry curriculum. In turn, this curriculum filters the way learners interact with the subject of chemistry by structuring it in a certain way.

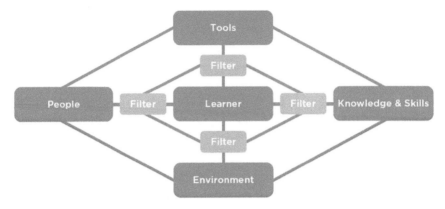

Figure 1.3.1: The Ecology of Resources Model of Context (Luckin *et al.*, 2012)

In addition, it is also important to understand that the learner at the centre of their Ecology of Resources has their own history of experience that impacts upon their interactions with each of the resources in their Ecology.

The Ecology of Resources design framework

The EoR offers a way of characterizing a learner in terms of the interactions that form that learner's context. It is based upon identifying the resources that can provide assistance to a learner as they interact. The EoR could be viewed statically as merely a snapshot of the set of resources that describe a learner's ZAA. However, the EoR can also be seen as the basis for a dynamic process of designing, initiating and maintaining learning interactions, in particular learning interactions that use technology. The key aim of this design process is to create a ZPA for a learner by helping them to identify and interact with the resources in their ZAA that are most suitable for their needs.

The aim of the EoR design framework is to structure the process of designing and monitoring teaching and learning interactions with technology so that they take into account learners' (and teachers') contexts. This does not mean that the entire complexity of a learner's context can be indexed into the design of learning activities, merely that this complexity can be effectively simplified in a manner that can be usefully applied to the development of teaching and learning interactions.

The EoR Design Framework offers a structured process that is iterative and has three phases, each of which has several steps:

1. Phase 1: Create an Ecology of Resources Model to identify and organize the potential forms of assistance that can act as resources for learning.

    Step 1 – Brainstorming potential resources to identify learners' ZAA

    Step 2 – Specifying the focus of attention

    Step 3 – Categorizing resource elements

    Step 4 – Identify potential resource filters

    Step 5 – Identify the learner's resources

    Step 6 – Identify potential more able partners.

2. Phase 2: Identify the relationships within and between the resources produced in Phase 1. Identify the extent to which these relationships meet a learner's needs and how they might be optimized with respect to that learner.
3. Phase 3: Develop the scaffolds and adjustments to support learning and enable the negotiation of a ZPA for a learner. Phase 3 of the framework is about identifying the possible ways in which the relationships identified in Phase 2 might best be supported or scaffolded. This support might for example be offered through the manner in which technology is introduced, used or designed.

Each phase and step is intended to be completed through collaboration with learners and/or teachers as part of a participatory design process. A full account of the framework can be found in Luckin (2010).

The practical application of the Ecology of Resources design framework

The Ecology of Resources approach has been used in a variety of projects to design both technology, a mobile phone application for example; and to design learning activities that use technology. For example the EoR was used with a teenage EFL class to support students in designing their own activities for learning. This work produced engaging, effective activity designs that were subsequently used successfully with other groups of learners with some evidence that the process changed learners' attitudes to learning. One learner remarked for example, 'before I thought the best way to learn was to study now I know more ways to learn' (Underwood *et al.*, 2011: 20).

The approach was also used to index a literature review written for Nesta and published as the Decoding Learning report in 2012 (www.nesta. org.uk/publications/decoding-learning). When we were writing this report we noted how little of the research evidence about technology in learning and teaching we reviewed provided sufficient evidence about the context in which the research was conducted. Without this information it is very hard to know how generally applicable the research being reported can be. For example, a technology that has been used in a particular way with a group of students in a grammar school in Kent may not be amenable to the same style of use in a coastal school in the same county of the United Kingdom, where deprivation and poverty result in a dramatically different learning context.

To make it easier for teachers and learners to use the EoR approach when planning how to use technology to support learning, we developed a simple set of steps that can be followed when planning the use of technology to support learning. These steps take the form of a set of questions that provide a checklist for planning and recording how technology is used to support learning:

1. What type of learning do you want to support? For example, is it a collaborative activity or an activity for a learner to complete alone?
2. How will you set up the activity? Will it be tightly structured or more free flowing?
3. How will learners be managed and organized?
4. How will you know that the activity has worked? What evidence will you collect to help you know this?
5. In what environment will the activity take place? For example, how will the physical resources in the environment be organized?
6. What are the constraints in the environment? For example, are there any rules and practices that impact on the way people behave in this environment?
7. Who else will be involved in the learning activity? For example, if the environment is in a school there may be a teaching assistant involved? What knowledge and skills do these people bring to the environment? Note: people not directly involved in the learning can nevertheless impact upon it; managers and technicians for example.
8. What are the rules, regulations and conventions that influence how other people interact in the environment? How will these constraints impact upon the learning and the way the technology can be used?

9. What technology are you planning on using? How much will it cost? Why is it appropriate for this learning activity? How much time will you need to invest to make sure that you can use this technology confidently?

Conclusion

No one promised that learning would be easy. But it will always be essential. It will take us to new places, to important and rewarding new achievements. The principles described and explored here can guide our own learning and the ways in which we help others to learn, although we shall always have to apply these principles to particular settings and learning needs. They are not the last words about learning, but they provide useful starting points.

The EoR offers a way to talk about learners holistically to sensitize us to the range of interactions that constitute their contexts. The EoR is based upon a definition of context that recognizes the interconnectedness of all the elements with which learners interact and that shape their understanding of the world. A learner's context is made up of the billions of interactions that they have with other people, with artefacts, and with their environment. These interactions provide 'partial descriptions of the world' that help learners to build understandings that are personally crystallized through a process of internalization. The EoR checklist offers a simple tool that enables teachers and learners to take some of the contextual complexity of learning into account when they plan, particularly when planning the use of technology to support learning.

Conclusion

Rosemary Luckin and Mutlu Cukurova

In this chapter we have explored the nature of learning and have presented seven learning principles that have been extracted from the wealth of research carried out into how we learn. These principles are evidence based and should be useful to anyone involved in learning for themselves or to support others. We then discussed three very different factors that impact upon learning: what we inherit from our parents, how we can better know what we know, and the context of our learning: how it impacts on learning and how it can be taken into account when we decide how best to support learning, particularly with technology.

The discussion of the three factors in Chapters 1.1, 1.2 and 1.3 illustrate some important findings. For example, the vital point about heritability calculations is that the values of the heritabilities of traits can vary greatly depending on the environment. This point links into the discussion of context in Chapter 1.3 and highlights the difficult and yet crucial task that education must fulfil: no learners' context should be detrimental to their education, because we know that each learner's context, including their environment, has a significant impact upon their learning achievements. Chapter 1.2 shows how self-testing can help identify areas of confidence and uncertainty. Research has shown that this can promote deeper understanding and retention. Everyone's reliable knowledge can grade at some point into guesswork or even misconception, and self-testing can help students to identify these limits. This is particularly important in a world where abundance of information can lead people to think that they know more than they understand. The processes of justifying certainty or doubt about a particular issue, both rewarded in certainty-based self-tests, are prime stimuli to better learning.

What the research says about learning

- Research has established some key principles of learning. Learning is most effective when:

  i. A clear framework surrounds, supports and informs the learner.
  ii. High standards are expected of learners, and are made explicit.
  iii. Learners acknowledge and use their prior learning and preferences.
  iv. Learning is an active process.
  v. Learners spend lots of time on task and practising.
  vi. Learning is undertaken at least in part as a collaborative activity.
  vii. Learners receive and use feedback on their work.

- Genetic inheritance can influence how well children do in schools.
- Genetic as well as environmental diversity provides a challenge to teachers, but should not be seen as a deterministic constraint.
- Doing private self-tests alone or with peers, without fear of making mistakes, can stimulate insight into knowledge and weaknesses through challenge, and can help focus effective study.
- Certainty-based marking (CBM) is a strategy that rewards students for identifying uncertainties and justifications relating to their answers, developing links to other knowledge in a way that improves long-term retention.
- CBM technology can help teachers and students through better feedback and more reliable grading, promoting understanding above rote-learning in both self-tests and formal assessments.
- Context is important to learning and we need to understand it and use this understanding effectively when learning and teaching.
- The Ecology of Resources (EoR) is a way of talking about context and has associated design framework that has been used effectively, both to design technologies themselves and to design activities that use technology to support learning.

> • The EoR checklist provided in Chapter 1.3 offers a way to talk about learners and their contexts holistically to sensitize us to the range of interactions that constitute learners' contexts and to plan the use of technology to support learning more appropriately to meet individual learner's needs.

Acknowledgements

Thanks to Professor Bob Farmer for conversations about the work of James Hattie, and to Professor Alan Tait and the late Dr Roger Mills for collaboration on an earlier synthesis of the research on learning.

References (Part 1)

Ahlgren, A. (1969) 'Reliability, predictive validity, and personality bias of confidence-weighted scores'. Remarks delivered at the "Confidence on Achievement Tests – Theory, Applications" symposium at the 1969 meeting of the AERA and NCME. Online. http://assessmentpriorart.org/wp-content/uploads/2012/08/ahlgren.pdf (accessed 15 September 2017).

Bain, K. (2004) *What the Best College Teachers Do*. Cambridge, MA: Harvard University Press.

Bligh, D.A. (1998) *What's the Use of Lectures?* 5th edn. Exeter: Intellect Books.

Boden, M.A. (1980) *Jean Piaget*. New York: Viking Press.

Bouchard, T.J. (2004) 'Genetic influence on human psychological traits: A survey'. *Current Directions in Psychological Science*, 13 (4), 148–51.

Boud, D. (1995) *Enhancing Learning Through Self Assessment*. Abingdon: RoutledgeFalmer.

Brown, J.S. (1990) 'Toward a new epistemology for learning'. In Frasson, C. and Gauthier, G. (eds) *Intelligent Tutoring Systems: At the crossroads of artificial intelligence and education*. Norwood, NJ: Ablex Publishing, 266–82.

Brown, J.S., Collins, A. and Duguid, P. (1989) 'Situated cognition and the culture of learning'. *Educational Researcher*, 18 (1), 32–42.

Chickering, A.W. and Gamson, Z.F. (1987) 'Seven principles for good practice in undergraduate education'. *AAHE Bulletin*, 39 (7), 3–7.

Clark, A. (2008) *Supersizing the Mind: Embodiment, action, and cognitive extension*. New York: Oxford University Press.

Cole, M. (1996) *Cultural Psychology: A once and future discipline*. Cambridge, MA: Harvard University Press.

Cummins, S., Curtis, S., Diez-Roux, A.V. and Macintyre, S. (2007) 'Understanding and representing "place" in health research: A relational approach'. *Social Science and Medicine*, 65 (9), 1825–38.

Curtin, N. and Gardner-Medwin, A.R. (2013) 'Self-tests with certainty-based-marking in early years of medical course'. Poster presented at the 37th International Union of Physiological Sciences Congress, Birmingham, 21–26 July, 2013. Online. www.tmedwin.net/~ucgbarg/tea/IUPS_2013_Curtin.pdf (accessed 15 September 2017).

Darwin, C. (1859) *On the Origin of Species by Means of Natural Selection, or the Preservation of Favoured Races in the Struggle for Life*. London: John Murray.

de Kerckhove, D. and Tursi, A. (2009) 'The life of space'. *Architectural Design*, 79 (1), 48–53.

Falchikov, N. (2004) *Improving Assessment through Student Involvement: Practical solutions for aiding learning in higher and further education*. London: Taylor and Francis e-Library.

Gardner-Medwin, A.R. (1995) 'Confidence assessment in the teaching of basic science'. *Research in Learning Technology*, 3 (1), 80–5.

Gardner-Medwin, A.R. and Gahan, M. (2003) 'Formative and summative confidence-based assessment'. In *Proceedings of the 7th International Computer-Aided Assessment Conference*. Loughborough: Loughborough University, 147–55. Online. https://dspace.lboro.ac.uk/dspace-jspui/bitstream/2134/1910/1/gardner-medwin03.pdf (accessed 15 September 2017).

Gould, S.J. (1981) *The Mismeasure of Man*. New York: W.W. Norton and Company.

Hassmén, P. and Hunt, D.P. (1994) 'Human self-assessment in multiple-choice testing'. *Journal of Educational Measurement*, 31 (2), 149–60.

Hattie, J. (2015) 'The applicability of visible learning to higher education'. *Scholarship of Teaching and Learning in Psychology*, 1 (1), 79–91.

Holt, J. (1977) *Instead of Education: Ways to help people do things better*. Harmondsworth: Penguin Books.

Issroff, K. and Gardner-Medwin, A.R. (1998) 'Evaluation of confidence assessment within optional computer coursework'. In Oliver, M. (ed.) *Innovation in the Evaluation of Learning Technology*. London: University of North London, 168–78.

James, M. and Pollard, A. (2011) 'TLRP's ten principles for effective pedagogy: Rationale, development, evidence, argument and impact'. *Research Papers in Education*, 26 (3), 275–328.

Lave, J. (1988) *Cognition in Practice: Mind, mathematics and culture in everyday life*. Cambridge: Cambridge University Press.

Lave, J. and Wenger, E. (1991) *Situated Learning: Legitimate peripheral participation*. Cambridge: Cambridge University Press.

Lewontin, R.C. (1991) *Biology as Ideology: The doctrine of DNA*. New York: HarperCollins.

Luckin, R. (2010) *Re-designing Learning Contexts: Technology-rich, learner-centered ecologies*. London: Routledge.

Luckin, R., Bligh, B., Manches, A., Ainsworth, S., Crook, C. and Noss, R. (2012) *Decoding Learning: The proof, promise and potential of digital education*. London: Nesta.

Manovich, L. (2006) 'The poetics of augmented space'. *Visual Communication*, 5 (2), 219–40.

NPR (National Public Radio) (1999) 'The science in science fiction'. *Talk of the Nation*, 30 November. Washington, DC: NPR. Online. www.npr.org/templates/story/story.php?storyId=1067220 (accessed 15 September 2017).

Pascarella, E.T. and Terenzini, P.T. (2005) *How College Affects Students: A third decade of research*. 2nd ed. San Francisco: Jossey-Bass.

References (Part 1)

Salehi, M., Sadighi, F. and Bagheri, M.S. (2015) 'Comparing confidence-based and conventional scoring methods: The case of an English grammar class'. *Journal of Teaching Language Skills*, 6 (4), 123–52.

Underwood, J., Luckin, R. and Winters, N. (2011) 'Harnessing resources for personal and collaborative language inquiry'. Heidelberg: Springer, 87–98.

Vygotsky, L. (1986) *Thought and Language*. Ed. Kozulin, A. Rev ed. Cambridge, MA: MIT Press.

Wertsch, J.V. (1984) 'The zone of proximal development: Some conceptual issues'. *New Directions for Child and Adolescent Development*, 23, 7–18.

Wood, D., Bruner, J.S. and Ross, G. (1976) 'The role of tutoring in problem solving'. *Journal of Child Psychology and Psychiatry*, 17 (2), 89–100.

Wood, D., Underwood, J. and Avis, P. (1999) 'Integrated learning systems in the classroom'. *Computers and Education*, 33 (2–3), 91–108.

Part Two

The use of different
technologies to
enhance learning

What the research says about the use of different technologies to enhance learning

Mutlu Cukurova and Rosemary Luckin

Discussions surrounding technology and education often take for granted that technologies can enhance learning and teaching. However, the research evidence behind such assumptions is rarely included in the discussions themselves, and the assumptions are rarely clarified with respect to key issues and questions (Kirkwood and Price, 2014). For example, the specification of what will be enhanced when technologies are used for teaching and learning, how enhancements can be achieved, and how enhancements can be evaluated. In fact, the question: 'do the technologies enhance learning?' is not even the right one to ask, because it implies that any technology regardless of the purpose of its design or the manner of its use can enhance learning and teaching. As Richard Noss argued (2013), the right question is 'how can we design technologies that enhance learning, and how can we measure that enhancement?'

In the previous chapters, Baume and Scanlon discussed how people learn. Here, we frame the chapters in this section of the book with a description of the learning activities that have been identified as occurring when people learn with technology. We then provide a series of case study chapters about how specific technologies and technology related activities have been evidenced as being used to support learning and teaching. We hope that these examples will provide sufficient support to reflect the potential of specific technologies to enhance learning and teaching when used appropriately. The nature of the evidence in this chapter varies broadly, yet focuses mainly on the improvement of student learning outcomes (quantitatively and/or qualitatively). Initially Lawrence Williams and Miroslava Černochová explore the research behind the new Computing curriculum, and the models that can help develop students' computer programming and literacy skills, in a creative way. Then Charlotte

Lærke Weitze shows that learning through game development may be an appropriate approach to support and evaluate students' learning processes and can lead to increased collaboration among students. The games-based learning discussion is followed by the use of technology in citizen science, in which Christothea Herodotou argues that citizen science projects have the potential to improve the public's knowledge of scientific content, their understanding of the scientific process and their attitudes towards science and scientists. In Chapter 2.4 Nageela Yusuf shows that video in learning may lead to an increased ability in learners to transfer knowledge, and in Chapter 2.5 Mark Gaved and Alice Peasgood present the results of two recent research projects to argue that learning at a relevant location, or in a context associated with a specified learning goal, is more likely to make the learning activity effective. Finally, Patricia Davies presents a chapter on the use of iPads in classrooms in which she shows that the investigation of student diaries about the use of their iPads revealed that students often use iPads in classrooms for tests and revision, and that the 'ownership' of an iPad is a key issue in their effective use for teaching and learning.

The acts of learning

Not all learning activities are the same. This is fairly obvious, for example watching a video about an earthquake is not the same activity as building a working simulation of an earthquake, even though both these activities may cover the same area of the curriculum. Table 2.1 illustrates the 19 Learning Acts that have been observed to occur when learning happens with digital media. These are grouped into four meta-categories (Manches *et al.*, 2010). A standard video would promote and support *Exposition* as a Learning Act. This Act is characterized as a private interaction with an author or speaker who is presenting a narrative account of knowledge to a learner. Knowledge is thereby 'exposed'.

This practice is well suited to situations where expertise can be transmitted in structured narrative form. The success of this form of learning depends on the depth of the private interaction elicited from the (otherwise passive) learner. Thus technology may support such depth of interaction by making material vivid or representationally rich. Interactive video is likely to also promote Learning Acts such as *Browsing, Ludic, Simulation and Problem Focused*. The effectiveness with which the range of different Learning Acts is supported through the interactive medium will impact upon its learning effectiveness.

Table 2.1: The Acts of Learning with technology

	Learning Act	Learner's mediated interaction
Personal	*Browsing*	Improvise an exploration of subject materials
	Annotation	Record elaborating commentary on subject materials
	Rehearsal	Recall and exercise relevant domain elements and processes
	Representing	Design and manipulate symbolic formats of subject matter
	Ludic	Un-directedly explore materials to generate positive affect
	Construction	Build artefacts, knowledge or representations relevant to some subject domain
	Reflection	Consciously systematize one's own evolving learning
Dialogic	*Exposition*	Implicit dialogue with authorial voice
	Tutorial	Engage in dialogue with more knowledgeable other
	Assessing	React to feedback from an authoritative other
Social	*Performative*	Publically present a domain-relevant construction
	Networked	Distributed and intermittent exchange of subject-related understandings
	Participative	Integrate with a community of learners who share knowledge-building ambitions
	Collaborative	Exchange to deliberately create shared knowledge
Scenarioed	*Cross-contextual*	Integrate and manage activities over multiple contexts
	Case-based	Engage with the components of a subject-relevant case
	Simulation	Manipulate a functional reproduction of subject-relevant system
	Problem-focused	Solve a specific problem defined as subject relevant
	Scripted inquiry	Execute a scaffold of investigation or articulation

Manches *et al.* (2010) describe each of these Learning Acts as follows:

BROWSING

An interaction with knowledge structures whereby the learner searches for relevant items. This search may be improvised and opportunistic (more traditional sense of 'browsing') or may be guided by principled rules ('strategic' search). Education should furnish an interest in exploration through unguided browsing but also the skills necessary to be more strategic.

ICT in the form of the Internet access furnishes a rich context in which to exercise browsing, however, it also demands skills – while offering tools.

Examples
- search term technologies
- CiteULike and other data mining and collecting tools

ANNOTATION

An interaction with existing knowledge material (particularly text) such that tools allow the learner to construct a personal elaboration of that material. This might take the form of elaborative commentary closely attached to the original ('marginal notes') or it might be a form of personal précis or reflection ('summarizing', etc.). Knowledge is thereby elaborated or personalized.

This practice suits situations where a body of well-formed material is available for study. Its cognitive benefit arises from the effort of actively recasting material and selectively linking it with existing knowledge. Clearly annotation is something that can be done more or less skilfully and demands practice and support.

ICT offers tools that can structure (such as notetaking) as well as an infrastructure of composition and storage tools for writing and filing the products of 'active study' pursued in this manner.

Examples
- web page annotation tools
- word processing functions adapted to structured note taking
- review features of word processors
- practices of organizing personal notes in personal computer filing systems

REHEARSAL

An interaction in which the learner is able to exercise key skills and knowledge relevant to the domain. For instance carry out arithmetical operations or practise language vocabulary.

Such activity supports the learner in building a robust database of knowledge relevant to some domain that can be recalled for processing in required contexts (e.g. solving arithmetic-based problems or conversations in a foreign language).

ICT can be a presentational tool for such problems that allow exercise of core skills and recovering of core facts.

Examples
- drill and practice software
- language pronunciation demonstrations

REPRESENTING

An interaction whereby some experience in the world (an artefact, event or process) is reproduced by invoking and manipulating some system of representation. Such activity allows the learner to make their understanding overt and explicit – as well as creating a space within which that understanding can be manipulated.

ICT provides representational tools that can be readily manipulated, stored and shared.

Example
- the concept map and other screen-based systems for constructing representations

LUDIC

An interaction allowing playful, relatively undirected engagement with domain-relevant material such that exploratory manipulation of that material is rewarded with positive affect.

Such activity allows the learning to *experiment* with knowledge and thereby explore properties and affordances of the domain.

ICT can provide microworlds in which such exploration is readily offered along with the possibility of playful creations.

Example
- Logo

CONSTRUCTION

An interaction with material that supports the building of artefacts, knowledge or representations.

Such activity allows the learner to exercise principles of some knowledge domain through the demands of constructing some end product calling upon that knowledge.

ICT may provide tools that allow creative development such as the construction of video, montage, narrative representations and so forth.

Examples
- Animoto
- Movie Maker
- PowerPoint

REFLECTIVE

An elaborating interaction with a record of one's own learning activities. This might take the form of some sort of diary with evaluative personal commentary. Personal knowledge building is thereby subjected to critical scrutiny and adjustment.

This practice cultivates the metacognitive skills necessary to refine and structure personal knowledge building activities.

ICT offers tools that assemble the achievements of learning and allow some form of (shareable) reflective commentary to be superimposed upon them ('annotation' where the object of annotation is a personal record).

Examples
- the e-portfolio

EXPOSITION

A private interaction with an author or speaker who is using some tool to present a narrative account of knowledge to a learner. This might take the form of a lecture, or a textbook or a multimedia presentation. Knowledge is thereby 'exposed'.

This practice is well suited to situations where expertise can be transmitted in structured narrative form. The cognitive benefit arises according to the depth of private interrogation and meaning-making encouraged in the listener/reader/viewer.

ICT offers tools that package and make accessible such structured accounts. However, the success of this form of learning practice depends on the depth of the private interaction elicited from the (otherwise passive) learner. Thus technology may support such depth of interaction by making material vivid or representationally rich.

Examples
- podcasts of lectures
- YouTube explanatory videos
- eBooks
- Wikipedia and other reference materials online

TUTORIAL

An interaction in which the learner takes part in a dialogue with a more informed other. The quality of the interaction depends upon the manner in which the dialogue is orchestrated towards building and interrogating knowledge.

This practice externalizes process of scrutiny and questioning as well as furnishing a context for more explicitly interrogated exposition (see above, under 'exposition').

ICT can support dialogues in text or voice, particularly where partners are not co-present. Technology may also blend that conversation with forms of visual representation on associated whiteboards etc. It may simulate the human partner in such dialogues.

Examples
- intelligent tutoring systems
- chat-based discussion forums
- Skype exchanges

ASSESSING

An interaction that optimizes opportunities for one person to feed back on the knowledge-building product of a learner. This practice equips the learner to recognize and respond to a critical voice applied to their own efforts.

<u>ICT</u> provides tools to traffic in assessment interactions – potentially making them more prompt, representationally rich and interactive.

Examples
- VLE structures that support online submission and commentary on student work
- tools for embedding voice or images as feedback to submitted files

PERFORMATIVE

An interaction with an (implicit or explicit) audience. Personal knowledge is shaped in such a way that it is actively disseminated – made the object of attention (and critique perhaps) by others.

This practice encourages an awareness of personal knowledge in terms of how it may be seen by, and how it influences others. This requires engaging with those alternative perspectives and considering how knowledge allows itself to be shaped to come into relationship with them.

<u>ICT</u> offers tools for dissemination and audience reaction.

Examples
- blogs
- expository videos on YouTube
- wikis

NETWORKED

An interaction in which learners make intermittent contact with others for data co-ordination of interrogation, although usually separated in time and space. Knowledge patterns are thereby established for navigation and querying.

This practice cultivates a model of knowledge as distributed and facilitates patterns of engagement that support creative questioning of such structures.

<u>ICT</u> provides an infrastructure for assembling and managing networked knowledge and for navigating to nodes where informants may be interrogated.

Examples
- topic-centred mailing lists, discussion forums or ning.com sites
- personal databases of contacts for one-to-one or one-to-many querying
- Delicious and other shared bookmarking tools

PARTICIPATIVE

A structure of interaction that creates circumstances for fostering integration among a group of individuals who have an evolving history of shared understanding and practice, and a motive to work towards elaborating this. The cognitive gain of this concerns the confidence and identity of the individual as a 'member' of some learning community/ discipline. It also creates a knowledge structure within which the individual learner can seek other learner relations.

<u>ICT</u> can provide infrastructures that establish and shape the felt sense of communication and community and which create tools for individuals to become participants rather than mere communicants.

Example
- The Knowledge Forum and other networked designs for shaping and making visible corporate identity and products

COLLABORATIVE

An interaction in which two or more individuals deliberately strive to create shared knowledge.

This practice allows an individual to acquire interest, skills and confidence in knowledge construction activities that take advantage of the expertise of others and which gives an affective motive for that knowledge building.

ICT can provide a context at which collaborators may assemble and share representations.

Examples

- classroom arrangements within which small groups may work together at a shared site of representation and recording
- Internet communications may support collaborative knowledge building at a distance and synchronously

CROSS-CONTEXTUAL

An interaction in which learners integrate meaning across different contexts of representation or activity. The cognitive benefits arise from positioning the same ideas in more than one setting or by simply extending the range of knowledge searching and integration.

ICT equips the learner with tools to capture, store, compare and integrate material from multiple contexts.

Example

- mobile recording and communication tools such as PDAs, cameras, phones and GPS enabled devices

CASE-BASED

An interaction in which the structure and working of a disciplinary 'case' is pursued. This allows the learner to understand knowledge in the context of an authentic example, providing an integrated and meaningful context for disciplinary content.

ICT can provide a structuring and exploratory context for the presentation of case material. It offers a condensed form of representation with interactive possibilities – allowing the case to be viewed and explored in an economical manner.

Examples
- semantic technologies that support investigation of cases
- self-contained case realizations in virtual format

SIMULATION

An interaction allowing control over some model system representing domain-relevant processes. The learner is allowed to manipulate qualitative or quantitative parameters in order to investigate functioning or construct desired outcomes.

The activity benefits learners by allowing the functional properties of some system to be experienced directly such as to support experiment.

ICT can provide self-contained environments in which such systems are modelled and which allow active manipulation.

Examples
- Civilization
- Astroversity
- Racing academy
- Savannah

PROBLEM-FOCUSED

An interaction in which the learner is challenged and resourced to solve domain-relevant problems. The learner thereby encounters domain knowledge in the context of authentic problems and is motivated to exercise that knowledge.

ICT can be a presentation resource for encountering problems designed by others. That presentation may include tools for the exploration of the problems made available.

Example
- presentational contexts for defining a problem and offering solution and dissemination tools

SCRIPTED INQUIRY

An interaction in which the route through an inquiry space is defined and guided by a script of steps. The learner thereby is scaffolded in the relevant problem solving strategy.

__ICT__ can offer tools that guide the learner though some process of enquiry by specifying a succession of moves relevant to approaching some agreed goal. These scripts may scaffold a conversation in collaborative contexts or drive a pathway for individuals.

Example
- LMS and other learning design scaffolds

It can be very useful to bear these 19 different Learning Acts in mind when thinking about and designing activities that use technology to support learning. It is worth bearing these in mind as you read through the next six chapters in Part 2.

The new Computing curriculum in England

Lawrence Williams and
Miroslava Černochová

Introduction

In this chapter we explore the research behind the new Computing curriculum in the United Kingdom and the reasons for developing this new subject in our schools, and for seeing computational thinking as an intrinsically worthwhile activity.

The first reason for developing the new Computing curriculum can be seen in the fact that the curriculum covers a wide range of teaching and learning activities. We are happy for our pupils to develop mathematical, scientific and problem-solving skills. Some primary schools in England even teach introductory philosophical thinking. What needs to be added to this important list, however, are computational thinking skills: concepts that underpin a huge range of human activity. Practical human activities are based on a wide range of computational thinking skills, though there is obvious overlap with other skills and concepts.

The second reason is that much in the new Computing curriculum is not, in fact, new at all (Noss, 2010). Both Piaget and Papert are well-known names to teachers for their constructionist approaches to teaching and learning, and significant parts of the new Computing curriculum flow from their work.

It is also appropriate here that we acknowledge the outstanding contribution of the late Jerome Bruner; his legacy is an important one. Bruner showed us that learning is an active process in which learners construct new ideas or concepts, based on their current or past knowledge. The pupil selects and transforms information, constructs hypotheses, and makes decisions, relying on a developing cognitive structure to do so (Bruner, 1960). Bruner's original development of the framework for reasoning processes is described in Bruner, Goodnow and Austin (1956). In this model, the teacher tries to encourage students to discover fundamental principles for themselves. This is achieved by the student and teacher engaging in an active dialogue. So we could actually argue that some elements of constructionism go back as far as Socrates.

The principle of creating a 'spiral' curriculum derives from this. The student learns at a basic level, but then returns to the same concepts at a slightly older and mature stage, and builds on the information learned. This is particularly true when learning a language, as Vygotsky shows us (Vygotsky, 1934). He argues that the semantic horizons of words expand as the child develops a wider understanding of the world. For example, the word 'drink' begins life in the child's mind simply as mother's milk, and water, but as the child grows, the word's meaning expands with his or her life experience to include fruit juices and squash, and so on. The word's meaning, or the rule for its use, expands with experience. As Wittgenstein (1953: 109) puts it, 'The problems are solved, not by giving new information, but by arranging what we have known since long.'

Logo and Computing in the classroom

The Logo computer program is the practical result of some of these ideas from psychology, and it has been widely and successfully used in schools for many years. These teaching and learning ideas are further developed through the work of Mitch Resnick (the creator of Scratch) and others (Resnick and Brennan, 2010).

What, then, are the issues? First, there needs to be clarity about the definitions of what the various terms mean: Computing, with a capital C, is now the new curriculum topic in England that includes the former requirements for developing skills in using ICT tools. Computer Science (CS) is a wider term that includes the development of computer software and hardware. Computational thinking, on the other hand, is also a very wide term covering general thinking processes themselves. It is sometimes called Computation and can include 'unplugged' activities, i.e. activities undertaken off a computer (Charlton and Luckin, 2012).

It is important to appreciate that the ideas that led to the Computing curriculum in England have not been to help or require schools to produce an army of computer programmers for industry, but rather to develop computational thinking, through constructivist and constructionist models of learning. Constructionist models derive, as we have indicated, from the work of Piaget, who looked at how children actually think, and construct their own view of the world. The focus of learning is on working through various stages to help construct meaning. Papert (1980) then emphasized the need for children to make things, in order to help them understand how things work. The children could 'talk' to the computer, and, using Logo, work with words, sentences and symbols to control the outcomes as part of an active process. This helps to explain why a whole community of like-minded teachers has developed steadily across the world.

The success of the Logo program later spawned the creation of Scratch, the block coding (or visual coding) language, developed at MIT by Mitch Resnick and others. This is a child-friendly, creative programming language that has huge potential for developing a wide range of skills in the classroom. One approach in using it, which has had some success, is the classroom project called 'Literacy from Scratch'. This started at Brunel University, London, but was quickly adopted by Charles University, Prague, and in attached primary schools.

'Literacy from Scratch': A creative classroom solution to developing coding skills

This section describes an ongoing and internationally successful curriculum model for the teaching and learning of computer programming skills that is based on the MIT visual block coding language, Scratch. 'Literacy from Scratch' is also based, pedagogically, on Piaget's and Papert's constructionist models, with pupils planning, problem-solving, constructing, developing and then coding their original animated narratives, with their own Sprites and Backgrounds, with music and bilingual voice-over sound files (see Figure 2.1.1). Pupils involved in this cross-curricular project range in age from 5 to 14 years, with stories made by students in further age and ability ranges (16 to 24 years) currently under development. The 'Literacy from Scratch' project is supported by a dedicated, cost-free support website for teachers, with information in several languages (www.literacyfromscratch. org.uk), and has an accompanying textbook, *Introducing Computing: A guide for teachers*. The project is currently running in schools in the United Kingdom, the Czech Republic, Italy and Pakistan, and has been presented at conferences in Poland (WCCE), Germany (IFIP), Italy (Torino University), Lithuania (IFIP), Thailand (Eel) and South Korea (Computational Thinking). The success of the project lies in its constructionist approach to the teaching and learning of coding, while it also encourages the development of creativity in language, art and music.

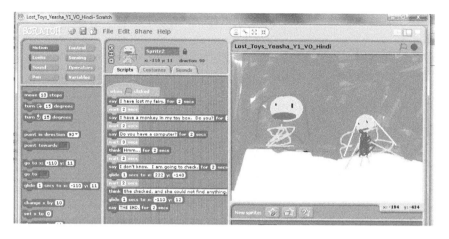

Figure 2.1.1: Bilingual story, with a 'voice-over' in Hindi, created entirely by a pupil aged 5 years

The origins of the project

'Literacy from Scratch' is a constructionist curriculum project that has been developed from a series of earlier projects using ICT tools to support the teaching of English, as well as developing cross-curricular teaching and learning activities. These projects were created at a south London comprehensive school, and are published on MirandaNet (www. mirandanet.org.uk/publications/williams.htm).

One of the earlier narrative models, for example, began with London pupils, aged 11 years, working by email and video-conferencing with NASA scientists in Cleveland, Ohio, United States, to develop science fiction stories (as part of their English work and ICT skills) but also with an emphasis on having an accurate scientific basis, by researching and using NASA space science data. It was called 'Science Through Arts', or 'STAR' (www. literacyfromscratch.org.uk/star/).

This cross-curricular project later developed into the writing of stories in more than one language, created at this earlier time in PowerPoint. Stories were developed by, and shared with, pupils in other countries, by email and by video-conferencing. The work simultaneously developed creativity and literacy skills, alongside ICT skill development. For a delightful example of one of these animated, bilingual stories, see 'Hot Dog and Kit Kat' (www. worldecitizens.net/projects/curriculum-development/stories-for-children/).

Figure 2.1.2: From 'Hot Dog and Kit Kat', an animated, bilingual story by a pupil aged 11 years

The whole process brought about such outstandingly high levels of engagement and pupil achievement that their creative work was presented variously at ICT, English and Science conferences across the world, and led to several UK (BBC and Channel 4), Japanese (NHK) and Korean (EBS) television programmes about the project.

When, in 2012, the curriculum in England changed to include the addition of computer programming, along with ICT, under the new all-embracing title of Computing, we therefore set about developing these earlier ICT projects in creative writing, and cross-curricular teaching and learning, into a new curriculum project called 'Literacy from Scratch', reasoning that the MIT program was a far more powerful tool for developing animated narratives than PowerPoint and Moviemaker had ever been. The above Kit Kat presentation, for example, uses some 150 separate PowerPoint slides. This does also clearly show the dedication and commitment of the pupil in creating her bilingual story.

As a response to the new curriculum needs of teachers and pupils in Computing, we started also to develop a free website (www. literacyfromscratch.org.uk), and an accompanying textbook for teachers: *Introducing Computing: A guide for teachers*, based on these earlier teaching and learning models. Material for the project was also created by MA and PGCE students both in London and in Prague.

The paradox of creativity

We have learned, during many years of teaching in the classroom, that 'creativity' is developed by pupils who have been given a very clear, even strict, set of guidelines and structures within which to work. It seems paradoxical to argue this, but the more restricted the pupils' parameters, the wider the range of creative responses that is developed. For example, for the bilingual story project, pupils were asked to develop ideas within a very limited framework of about ten slides, to create only two or three characters, to develop their story with a beginning, middle and end, to have some sort of climax to the story, and in the case of the space science project (Science Through Arts) to add a scientific fact on each PowerPoint page, or within each paragraph of Word, depending on the ICT format.

Having set all of these parameters in place, the pupils were then instructed to do whatever they liked, *without being given concrete examples of what was expected*. On one classroom wall a poster was placed saying, 'The answer is: Yes. What is your question?' Pupils were then encouraged to *negotiate* any alterations they felt would be of benefit to their self-designated task. Our experience with classroom practitioners is that whenever specific examples are given, pupils invariably offer up nearly identical responses ('It's what Sir/Miss wanted … '), and the resulting range of outcomes is severely restricted. Vagueness, within the rigid structures set, allows pupils to widen their own creative responses. This, incidentally, is particularly evident if the outcome is a collaborative venture. So, too, it has been with 'Literacy from Scratch'.

The development of the constructionist Computing project: Key Stage 3 (pupils aged 11 to 14)

Work on the project began at the Bishop Ramsey CE School, Ruislip Manor, west London, an all-ability, mixed secondary school. The headteacher, Andrew Wilcock, kindly allowed me to work with his entire ICT Department (as they were then called), and the whole of the Year 8 cohort (186 pupils, aged 12 / 13 years). Over a period of eight weeks, pupils created narratives along the lines of 'Stories for Children', and every pupil, regardless of ability, successfully completely the project without 'teacher pressure', and a small group of pupils proudly presented their finished stories to teachers and other delegates at the BETT 2013 exhibition in London.

The full process of the project development is detailed on the website: www.literacyfromscratch.org.uk.

Development at Key Stages 2 and 3 (pupils aged 5 to 11 years)

Encouraged by the success at Bishop Ramsey, Brunel PGCE students, within their 'Curriculum Enhancement' option for Computing, tried out the project in schools during their school placements. This, too, proved highly successful and one of the teacher trainee students, Ashlie Cox, completed very valuable work with her Key Stage 2 pupils.

Finally, the project was further developed at the Swaminarayan School in Neasden, west London, with the support of the headteacher, Mr Raja, and, together with the classroom teachers, we taught the 'Literacy from Scratch' course to pupils at Key Stage 2 (Year 1 pupils aged 5 years, and Year 2 pupils aged 6 years). The results showed clearly that all of these students were capable of understanding elementary computer programming concepts through this constructionist learning model.

PGCE students (teacher trainees)

As part of the PGCE course at Brunel, students created projects in Scratch, to present as support materials to their primary school pupils. Once again, the freedom to work within a set of clearly prescribed limits resulted in a wide range of outcomes. These are listed on the 'Literacy from Scratch' website (www.literacyfromscratch.org.uk/teaching/).

Conclusion

'Literacy from Scratch' succeeds as a curriculum project at all levels from age 5 pupils to postgraduate levels because it is based on a constructionist approach. It becomes pupil-driven in the classroom because pupils want to watch their own clown turn somersaults or to see their witch flying across the screen. Accordingly, they *demand from their teacher* access to the skills that allow them to construct and develop their narratives.

The project develops both computational thinking skills (even at age five) as well as encouraging creativity at all ages, including those at postgraduate level. The next step is to widen participation in the project to include students with learning difficulties, and at higher age ranges, such as from 16 to 24 years. This work has just been completed at Lambeth College, a Career College in south London.

The new Computing curriculum should, we feel, be welcomed as a means of developing constructionist as well as cross-curricular approaches to teaching and learning both at primary and secondary school level. There is, as we have seen, considerable research supporting this. For a good summary of the way that teaching programming languages in school education develops computational thinking and algorithmic skills this article by Ivan Kalaš and colleagues (Kalaš *et al.*, 2011) is well worth reading.

Using game design for learning

Charlotte Lærke Weitze

Introduction

Educators and educational theorists have long advocated learning games as an active way of learning through experience. If carefully designed, learning games can allow learners to interact with learning situations that cannot be replicated in a traditional classroom setting (Barab and Dede, 2007; Gee, 2003; Squire, 2011). However, not all games are equal when it comes to learning and there is, for example, an active debate emanating from the serious game movement as to whether the educational potential of games is realized best through commercial games or skill-and-drill exercise games. Kafai and Burke (2015) argue that there may be a valid alternative to this binary debate and suggest that the real question is about whether the practice of *playing* games or the practice of *making* games is more learning effective. There is a growing body of research that evidences the potential value of extending game-based learning – be it the use of simulations, virtual worlds or games developed with the purpose of learning – to the creation of games as a means of learning (Earp, 2015; Weitze, 2015). Instead of giving the student a less active role as a game player, creating games as a means of learning positions the student in a more active role as game designer (Oygardslia, 2015; Weitze, 2015).

Learning-game creation as a means of learning originates in a constructionist pedagogical approach. As we have seen in Chapter 2.1 constructionism is also central to the Computing curriculum in the United Kingdom. It builds upon the thesis that there is a strong connection between designing and learning. When students design learning games, the activities involve making, building and programming, all of which provide a rich context for learning (Harel and Papert, 1991; Kafai and Resnick, 1996; Weitze, 2016b, forthcoming). The learning-game designer needs to think about the meta-structures of the game. This involves interactions and game mechanics (what you can do in the game) as well as how the game's learning design is set into play. The term *learning design* describes (1) how a teacher shapes social processes and creates conditions for learning; and (2) the phenomenon of the individual student constantly re-creating or redesigning information in his or her own meaning-creating processes (Selander and Kress, 2012: 2). When using game design as a means of learning, the focus is often on learning to program and develop computational thinking skills (Brennan and Resnick, 2012); teachers seldom have an expressed expectation that students must attain specific learning goals.

In contrast, the purpose of the experiment discussed in this chapter was for students to incorporate specific learning goals in the process of creating their own learning games. *The aim was to create an overall gamified learning design that would facilitate the students' learning processes since both teachers and students were novices to game design.* In designing their own digital learning games to achieve specific learning goals in cross-disciplinary subject areas, students would themselves attain specific learning goals in those subjects. But how can students be supported to create a learning design for specific learning goals in analogue and digital games as a means of learning? And what learning trajectories emerge in those digital games that succeed in creating learning events for the characters in the games – and thereby for the players (learners) of the games?

Adult students building learning games

Our experiment was part of a series of four iterations that took place at VUC Storstrøm, an adult learning centre in Denmark. The students attended an upper-secondary general education programme, a full-time education programme lasting two years. Two teachers and 19 students participated in an experiment in which the overall learning design was made into a big Game while students designed learning goals for specific subject matter – history and English as a second language – into small digital games. The learning goals were focused on the American Civil War, human rights, and the liberation of the slaves. Teachers initially participated in a workshop, were introduced to the overall learning design, and tried some of the learning game design methods. Before the student workshops started the teachers briefly introduced students to the subject matter, showed a film about the subject area and introduced a few texts.

The teachers and students then participated in a five-hour workshop once a week for three weeks that involved creating learning game concepts, making paper prototypes and transforming them into digital learning games (with the game design tools Scratch and RGB-Maker) in a gamified learning environment (Figure 2.2.1).

Figure 2.2.1: Students designing analogue learning game concepts and digital learning games

The Smiley Model

The project used the Smiley Model (Figure 2.2.2; Weitze, 2016a) a learning game design model for building engaging learning games that combine learning design and game design (Weitze, forthcoming). The Smiley Model uses a framework for learning design that encompasses designing for the students' learning prerequisites, the setting or learning situation, the learning goals, the content and the creation of relevant learning processes and evaluation processes (Hiim and Hippe, 1997).

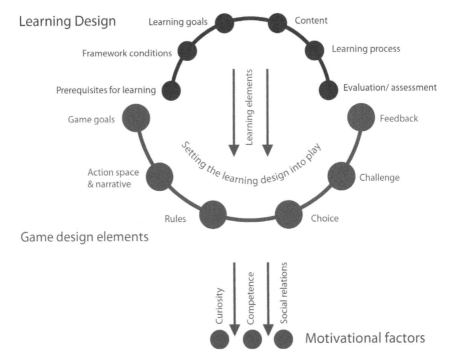

Figure 2.2.2: The Smiley Model (reprinted with permission from Weitze, 2016a)

The framework is accompanied by six game elements that are used to set the learning design into play: game goals, action space or narrative, rules, choices, challenges and feedback. Each of these game elements is intertwined. While 'setting the learning into play' the Smiley Model advises to keep the three primary driving forces for our intrinsic motivation to learn in mind and design for: (1) curiosity; (2) the feeling of achieving competence; and (3) reciprocity/relatedness (Bruner, 1966). The Smiley Model thus addresses the need to design the learning process, to set the learning elements into play through traditional game-elements and the need to design for motivational factors.

The big Game and the small games

The goal of this particular experiment was to facilitate a motivating learning experience by making the whole learning design into a big Game (Gee, 2011). Inside this overall big Game, the students worked in teams and created digital learning games, while they embedded learning goals from the curriculum into each game (Figure 2.2.3).

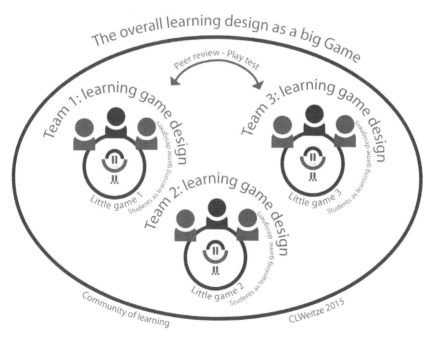

Figure 2.2.3: The gamified learning design (Weitze, 2014a, 2014b)

The big Game for this project was designed in 25 levels, encompassing tasks for building learning games; the framework was presented in a Google document for each of the teams. The Smiley Model (Weitze, 2016a) inspired the learning design of both the big and the small games, with guidelines for how to make engaging learning experiences. In addition to the motivational purpose of gamifying the learning game design process, another goal was structuring and scaffolding the learning process to help students and teachers, novice to game design, create the small games (Weitze, 2014a, 2014b). Therefore, the aim of this learning project was that the students would discuss, negotiate and finally master the intended learning goals while building and implementing these learning goals into their small digital games. In other words, the student-game-designers were learning inside the big Game while designing the small games. Another ambitious sub-goal was that students from other teams would be able to learn by playing the different small games and discussing game concepts, thus gaining knowledge, skills and competence within the relevant subject matters during this process.

Learning game example – the American Civil War and emancipation

The following is an example to illustrate how the students constructed digital learning games. Three of the four games the student teams created used Scratch as the game design tool. But the fourth student game design team chose another game design tool: RGBMaker. The affordances of this game design tool, as well as the hard work the students put into the design process, led to the creation of a quite advanced digital learning game. The learning trajectories in this game were complex and made it possible to learn in various ways while playing the game (Figure 2.2.4). This game succeeded in using both learning and game elements from the Smiley Model in an engaging way (please note the **emphasized** words).

In this game, a character in the game represented the player and the **learning process** took place through the characters' experiences. Representing events that took place during the American Civil War the character in the game was being suppressed and, at the end of the story in the game, was finally helped to flee, experiencing various historical events on his way through the story (**action space**). The player of the game had several opportunities to become emotionally engaged in the scenes in the game. Afforded by the game tools' possibilities (RGBMaker), the player was initially introduced to the story by listening to the character. The character/player could explore the game and choose (**choice**) to enter various areas in the game. He could approach other game-characters choosing between (1) doing or asking something learning related (historical); or (2) doing or asking something game-related (game-play; Figure 2.2.4b). When choosing between these possibilities (**choice**) the consequences (**rules**) were equivalent to the historical consequences. This allowed the player to learn as he played (**learning by doing**). The game character met other characters on the way. They gave hints on where he should go and what to do. If following these (authentic historical) suggestions the character could move on in the game, and these opportunities worked as examples of stealth assessment (Shute, 2011) – that is, being assessed during game play while not disrupting the fun (**evaluation**).

The student game designers used the affordances of the game tool. For example, they interpreted/used a build-in game mechanic in the game-tool (escaping enemies) as part of the original story, where the enslaved character tried to avoid being caught while fleeing (**challenges**). If the character made the wrong choices, or if he was caught, he would be set back (**feedback**). The **game-goal** thus was to be free, and when the character succeeded in becoming free, he would meet another character in the game that read the declaration of independence aloud.

The main focus of the process was on creating innovative and engaging learning designs for students. As expected, the students learned the most while designing learning games as they created learning situations and built learning content into these games. According to the teachers' formative assessments, the students reached their learning goals: they could explain, discuss and critically think about the concepts from the curriculum, confirming that they had reached a complex level of understanding (Weitze, 2015, forthcoming). The quality and characteristics of the learning situations built into the games were found to be important for the depth of the students' learning processes.

The purpose of the study was to generate knowledge about how to create motivating learning designs for the students. Therefore, the aim of these experiments was to develop a reusable learning design for teachers and students who were game design novices. The following are empirically based models illustrating how the students learned in these game design processes.

Figure 2.2.4a: Analogue prototype and digital interface of game four. See Figure 2.2.4b for a map of the possible learning trajectory in the game example.

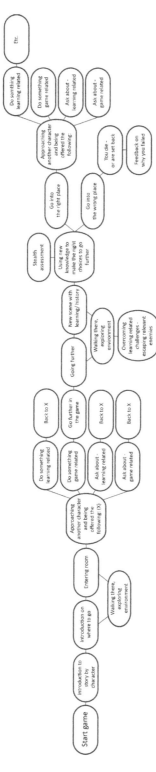

Figure 2.2.4b Map of the possible learning trajectory in the game example (Weitze, 2016c)

Iterative learning game design processes

When analysing the students' learning trajectories within this method of learning, we found that during the learning-game design process, students went through an iterative process consisting of seven areas, including conceptualizing and building the games as illustrated in Figure 2.2.5.

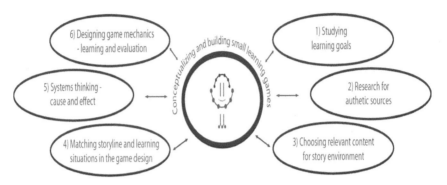

Figure 2.2.5: Seven areas of building small digital learning games (Weitze, 2015)

A hierarchy of learning designers

In this experiment the learning design was constructed as a hierarchy supported by various learning-designer roles contained within one another (Figure 2.2.6). The teacher was the primary learning designer guiding the students. The students became their own learning designers, leading their own innovative learning processes with educational technology. They discussed the subject matter, found content and conscientiously negotiated how to implement learning into the small digital games they were creating for future players/learners to learn – becoming learning designers for their fellow students as well (Weitze, 2015). Finally, the small games were learning designers for the students that played them – facilitating their learning processes.

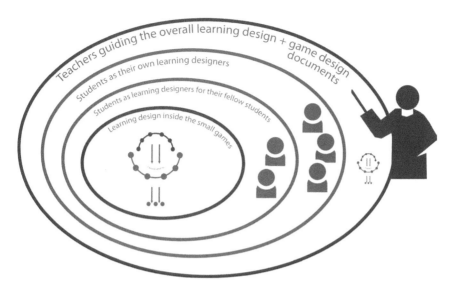

Figure 2.2.6: Learning designers in the game development process (Weitze, 2015)

Learning and design processes in the gamified learning design

The gamified learning design supported the innovative learning processes for the students. The teacher participated as an inspirational guide and contributed to the students' cognitively complex learning processes as they designed curriculum-based learning games (Anderson and Krathwohl, 2001; Illeris, 2007). Four parallel types of processes for designing and learning supported the gamified learning design:

(1) the structured game-design process – 25 levels of assignments presented in a document
(2) concept-building processes in which prototypes served as materials for learning
(3) teaching processes in which the teacher's learning- and game-inspired metaphors were used to support the learning processes in the big and small gamified learning designs
(4) the students' individual, collaborative and motivational learning processes (Figure 2.2.7)

Learning and design processes in the learning-game design environment

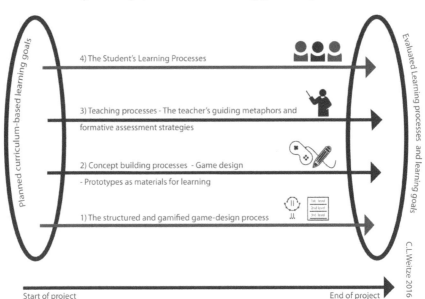

Figure 2.2.7: Four parallel types of processes for designing and learning supported the gamified learning design (Weitze, forthcoming)

Evaluating the use of game design as a means of learning

The teachers found it easy to support and evaluate the students' learning processes, with the help of concepts and metaphors guiding the students in their learning game development process. The teachers observed an increase in socially engaged interactions among the students, which contributed to deeper learning processes with more collaborative activity. The study found that the students experienced deep and motivating learning; and that the teachers found this problem-based and activating learning design inspiring and easy to use as a variation on more traditional teaching approaches. The students benefited from this way of learning as a valid variation on more conventional teaching approaches, and teachers found that the students learned at least the same amount or more compared with traditional teaching processes. The findings were that activities that involved making, building or programming provided a rich context for learning, as the construction of artefacts, in this case, learning games, enabled reflection and new ways of thinking. The students learned from reflection and interaction with the tools, both individually and in collaboration with peers. Consequently, the maker-culture (Hatch, 2013) and its potential constructionist pedagogical approach – learning by creating – can also be used in formal learning situations with adult students, enabling motivating and cognitively complex learning processes.

Conclusion

The above models may be of inspiration for teachers that have the courage to enter the endeavour of using learning game design as a means of learning. The Smiley Model (Figure 2.2.2) provides a learning game design model for building engaging learning games that combine learning design and game design. The next step in our research will be to extract the students' successful learning trajectories in their games and to create game examples in the game design tool Scratch to support students' future learning games processes while at the same time enabling deep learning processes for the students. This teaching method has also been tried out with success together with students from the primary school.

Citizen science and informal learning

A brief commentary

Christothea Herodotou

Introduction

Citizen science and crowdsourcing are often used interchangeably to denote the participation of the general public in social activities or projects. The 'crowd' becomes a source of information when it contributes ideas, content or services to solve a problem, generate content, raise funds and vote best solutions. Wikipedia is a crowdsourcing example where a large number of people add or curate information online resulting in the collective creation of a considerably large encyclopaedia. Kickstarter (www.kickstarter.com) is an online crowdsourcing website where people share their project ideas and request funds from the general public to implement these ideas. The term citizen science is more specific; it is used to denote the participation of the public in scientific or research projects. Members of the public volunteer to support the work of scientists by contributing data to projects initiated by professionals and research institutions. The *Oxford English Dictionary* defines citizen scientists as amateurs who engage in scientific work in collaboration or under the supervision of professional scientists with the aim to serve the community.

There is a diversity of citizen science projects available ranging from exclusively online initiatives to offline field-based research activities. One example of online citizen science is the iSpot platform (www.ispotnature. org) developed and run by The Open University, United Kingdom. Members of the public identify species such as birds, reptiles and insects, by taking and posting pictures of them on iSpot, recognizing species others have posted and commenting about their contributions in forums. To recognize people's contributions and demonstrate their level of expertise, iSpot activities are rewarded with points through a system of reputation. This system can help people distinguish expert users from novices. One example of offline field-based citizen science is BioBlitz. Instead of recognizing species individually and uploading pictures of them online in platforms such as iSpot, groups of people (e.g. schools or families) gather together in a specific area (such as a park) and work together to get an overall account of the species identified in an area, often in a limited time. One example of this are the National Geography Society Bioblitz events (http://nationalgeographic.org/projects/bioblitz/). As argued by Edwards (2015), environmental and ecological issues and the engagement of the public in field work have been the main focus of most citizen science projects. The power of citizen science has yet to be harnessed in fields such as medicine and humanities. The crowdsourcing game *Fold-it* is an example that shows the potential of citizen science for medicine. Through engaging with protein-folding puzzles, members of the public managed to identify the structure of an enzyme involved in the reproduction of HIV, helping scientists to devise drugs to fight it (Cooper *et al.*, 2010).

Benefits for scientists and learners

For scientists who initiate citizen science projects, the contributions of the public to research entail certain benefits including the accomplishment of time-consuming and expensive projects that could not be easily implemented, or even implemented at all, without the support of the public. For the general public taking part in citizen science, benefits are often connected to learning about science and the scientific method, appreciating nature and supporting conservation initiatives including ensuring that species are secured and recovered (Freitag and Pfeffer, 2013). To understand how participation in citizen science projects might be a source of informal learning for the general public, we first need to detail the forms this participation may take. The classification of citizen science projects by Shirk and colleagues (Shirk *et al.*, 2012) sheds light in this respect. Five types of projects are proposed indicating the type of people's involvement in scientific activities: (a) contractual projects: projects are initiated by scientists due to requests by communities to conduct scientific research and report outcomes; (b) contributory projects: projects are designed by scientists and the role of the public is to collect data; (c) collaborative projects: apart from contributing data, the public contributes to refining the design of the project, analyses and disseminates findings; (d) co-created projects: projects are designed in collaboration with the public – members of the public are engaged in all the aspects of the research project from defining the research questions to collecting, analysing and reporting data; and (e) collegial contributions: non-professional members of the public conduct research independently.

With the exception of contractual projects, the last four types of projects indicate how the public may engage with citizen science. The criterion that differentiates types of participation is the level of involvement in scientific research. Participation in all the stages of scientific research has been coined as 'extreme science' (Haklay, 2012) and 'citizen inquiry' (Sharples, *et al.*, 2015). The latter raises the need for citizen science projects that will provide opportunities to the public to initiate and conduct their own personally meaningful research and will explicitly target informal science learning. According to Edwards's (2015) concluding remarks in a recent review of the field, it is questionable whether learning is a structured part of the design of citizen science projects. There is still the need to investigate the educational impact of citizen science projects on the public and provide opportunities for participation in all the range of scientific activities. In this direction, online platforms such as nQuire-it (www.nquire-it.org) have been designed to provide to the public the technology to initiate and implement citizen science projects and tools to scaffold the process of data collection and analysis including the use of mobile sensing apps (Herodotou, *et al.*, 2014). Yet having the public devise their own research agendas is not without challenges such as the creation of scientifically robust investigations, the validity of the collected data, the need for moderation and advice from experts and long-term engagement in citizen science projects to develop skills to conduct reliable research.

The type of participation a citizen science project allows affects the learning outcomes emerging from it. Bonney *et al.* (2016) reviewed the learning outcomes of four different citizen science projects as defined by the way participants are engaged with the scientific activities, and commented on the learning potential of citizen science. In particular:

(a) Data collection projects: evidence suggests improvements in the knowledge of the general public about scientific content such as knowledge about bird biology and invasive species, and awareness of the effects of invasive species on the environment. Improvements in their understanding of the scientific process were also identified yet these were limited. No changes in attitudes about science were recorded, an outcome that might be explained by people already possessing positive attitudes when volunteering to participate in citizen science projects.

(b) Data processing projects have the potential to contribute to the understanding of science, as they engage people in activities such as transcription and interpretation of the collected data. Evaluation of these projects is limited yet promising. Bonney *et al.* (2016) make reference to the evaluation of the 'Citizen Sky' project and the reporting of improvement in participants' attitudes about science and their epistemological beliefs about the nature of science after taking part in the project.

(c) Curriculum-based projects yielded very promising outcomes in terms of youth engagement and learning from citizen science, especially when facilitated by teachers. In particular, improvements were measured in students' content knowledge, communication, knowledge of the scientific method (including sampling, measurement, data interpretation) and science-based inferences about the natural world. Yet, as authors note, the fact that these projects take place in school restricts their impact on community development and personal empowerment can lead to social change.

(d) Community science projects: these projects may hold the greatest potential for learning improvements as they involve the public in all stages of the scientific research from the shaping of research questions to the development of protocols for data collection, data analysis and interpretation. Evidence suggests that community science projects gave a voice to people to document environmental problems they could not have done otherwise and gained insights about the scientific method when working along with scientists.

How can people gain the most from citizen science?

This review reveals that our understanding of what the public gains from its participation in citizen science projects is still in its infancy. More and systematic work is needed to detail the learning impact of those projects on participants. Citizen science is a new approach to teaching and learning yet to be well understood and utilized for the public's benefit (Herodotou *et al.*, 2018). Such knowledge could inform the design of citizen science projects by documenting the design elements and mechanisms that better support learning and engagement. Quoting Bonney *et al.* (2016: 11), 'practitioners who design and implement citizen science projects without specific learning objectives or lesson plans must realize that learning does not just "happen" via project participation. Citizen science participants are unlikely to change their perspectives about science unless their participation includes reflection about their role and how it relates to the processes of science.'

Conclusion

Participation in citizen science projects might be an effective way to engage young people with Science, Technology, Engineering and Maths (STEM) areas where youth is found to be disinterested, with rather negative attitudes and aspirations for future careers (Tapscott, 2012). Evidence suggests there is a connection between participation in informal (out-of-school) science activities (e.g. in the form of family initiatives) and positive attitudes towards science (OECD, 2012). Participation in existing citizen science projects or initiation of personally meaningful projects might raise youth interest in STEM domains and bridge this gap. For the general public, citizen science might be a teaching experience that can educate on how to think critically through awareness of the scientific method and general reflection on the learning processes involved in citizen science projects.

In a society abundant with information, it becomes *sine qua non* to educate citizens in how to access and evaluate information in order to make informed decisions that consider and balance both the pros and cons of a given situation. To put this into practice, a scientifically educated public could engage critically in debates such as the provision of certain vaccinations to young children (see debates around MMR). An educated public would have the skills to access original sources of information around the arguments made by mass media, compare and contrast resources in terms of their reliability and validity, weigh the pros and cons of each approach and make informed decisions considering their impact on generations to come.

Video for learning

Nageela Yusuf

Introduction

Multimedia, including educational video content, has been used by higher education providers such as The Open University since at least 1971 when broadcasting on the BBC began. However, this decade has seen a momentous increase in the creation and use of video for educational purposes. Advances in the Internet, computing, video and imaging technology on the one hand and student expectations on the other have spurred on its rise in popularity. In addition, educators want to enhance the learning experience for their students and are increasingly willing to experiment with what can be achieved using new technologies. In tandem with this increased appetite for the use of video in teaching and learning, several scientific studies have been published looking at the impact of video on engagement and learning. In this chapter, we look at some of the evidence behind how using video in teaching supports the learning process.

We initially explore some of the research evidence from neuroscience and learning and report the findings from several recent experimental studies. We follow this with evidence from the social sciences: a case study of video being used to teach physics at a large campus university. We then present the EVE model as a tool to assist us frame the discussion around video in education in order to develop more effective use of video in education. But first a quick word about memory and learning that is relevant to our discussions about video in education.

Memory appears at the bottom of Bloom's Taxonomy of learning (Bloom, 1956). This may account for its lack of prioritization in the learning design of some educators working in further and higher education. However, it is important to remember that Bloom's classification is a method of building up to a desired level of cognition and that one must have some level of mastery of the foundation blocks before moving to the step immediately above. Furthermore, memory and learning, though a very broad field, is an integral part of our existence. It is memory that gives us the ability to retain and utilize information or knowledge, and from psychology to neuroscience, it is considered significant to learning (Blakemore and Frith, 2005; de Jong *et al.*, 2009; Colvin, 2016). For example, Finke

(1996) investigated the extent to which memory enhances visual creativity, and suggests that people can mentally synthesize and remember novel combinations of objects and their component parts, which can often result in creative insights and discoveries.

Neuroscience and learning with video

The debate about the passive consumptive nature of viewing certain educational video continues to evolve. Educational video content of a real-life lecture, for example, can be seen as a passive mode of learning with video, because there is little operational interaction required on the part of the learner. If we reflect on the presentation of the Learning Acts at the start of this part, you will recall that learning with such a video would be described as an act of *exposition* and as such in order for the learner to interact cognitively with the concepts being presented in the lecture, the video will need to be highly engaging to prompt the viewer to participate mentally and interact with the subject matter.

The publication of recent research from neuroscientists is interesting in the context of this discussion. For example, Kemp and Manahan-Vaughan (2012) have demonstrated in rats that passive perception of two-dimensional images of an environment displayed on a computer screen, similarly to a video, facilitate the brain chemical process by which specific synapses are selectively weakened in order to make way for new synaptic strengthening and the simplified representation of new information. Synaptic plasticity is the means through which we learn and the researchers suggest not only that passive learning influences synaptic plasticity but also that '2D' spatial imagery has a significant impact on synaptic plasticity in rats. Such experiments carried out in a highly controlled environment by neuroscience experts help us to understand the mental processes underlying learning and memory, and the temporal and spatial changes that underlie successful, or unsuccessful, educational attainment in a more detailed way than that achievable by behavioural testing alone. However, ultimately, as Colvin (2016) argues, studies such as this would be most insightful if they consider what other brain activities take place at the time of passive viewing of the video, as well as looking at the longitudinal impact of passive perception.

Blakemore and Frith (2005) have also made a useful contribution to the literature seeking to connect educational practices in evidence derived from neuroscience involving humans. They note that visual imagery, or visualization, is a powerful technique that an individual can use to imagine, or recall, things in their mind. Patients with damage to the occipital lobes of the brain, where the visual cortex lies, often have visual memory problems and do not benefit from visual imagery when trying to memorize words. Being able to view visual material at a comfortable pace helps to internalize it, and thereby recall and imagine it at a later stage.

Social science and video and education

Eric Dey, Helen Burn and David Gerdes (Dey *et al.*, 2009) have published an informative case study looking at the link between learning outcomes and the use of audio-visual multimedia in the context of an undergraduate physics course at a large selective university. A total of 195 students participated in the study, and each individual was assigned to one of three groups: personalized video, neutral video or a control group.

Students in the personalized video group viewed an online presentation consisting of a video image of a lecturer along with his voice and slide presentation. The neutral video group viewed an online presentation, which included the audio of the same lecturer synchronized with the slides. Students in the control group attended the live lecture delivered by the lecturer. Preliminary analyses of the quantitative data showed that the three groups were similar in terms of demographics, academic achievement, aspirations and technical proficiency. Evaluation included a post test of what learners had been able to retain and apply from their experiences.

The study concluded that there were no statistical differences detected between the groups in their performance on the questions that tested their memory retention. There were, however, significant differences in the results of the groups in their competence in answering questions that probed their ability to transfer or apply their learning from the lecture. The neutral and personalized video group outperformed the live group (Figure 2.4.1). However, there were no significant differences between the neutral video and the personalized video groups.

Treatment group	Mean	SD
Transfer question		
Neutral video (*n* = 69)	1.30	0.79
Video (*n* = 76)	1.37	0.83
Live (*n* = 50)	0.92	0.80
Two-tailed sig. $p < .01$		
Retention question		
Neutral video (*n* = 69)	3.51	1.59
Video (*n* = 76)	3.45	1.61
Live (*n* = 50)	3.70	1.31
Two-tailed sig. $p > .05$		

Figure 2.4.1: Analysis of Variance (ANOVA) results on retention and transfer questions (Dey *et al.*, 2009: 387)

The live group (M = .92) scored significantly lower than the neutral video (M = 1.30) and personalized video group (M = 1.37) in the transfer question. This significant difference in the performance between the live group and the two multimedia groups may be explained by the slower pace of the latter, and the fact that students had the controls to pause and resume the multimedia content.

The authors of the study suggest that the video of the lecturer had no significant effect on student learning. However, using video appropriately presents affordances that do not exist in live classrooms, or with slide presentations, and not exploiting these affordances could result in sub-optimal use of video. Drawing on the largest known collection of computer logs associated with educational video content, Guo *et al.* (2014) have been able to identify emerging best practice in video production techniques for educational content. Having categorized and analysed data from 6.9 million video watching sessions across four edX computer science courses, the authors have made the following observation-based recommendations:

1. Shorter videos, six minutes or under, are much more engaging.
2. Videos that intersperse an instructor's talking head with presentation slides are more engaging than showing only slides.
3. Videos produced with a more personal feel could be more engaging than highly polished studio recordings. Try filming in an informal setting such as an office to emulate a one-on-one 'office hours' experience.
4. Khan-style tablet drawing tutorials are more engaging than presentation slides or code screencasts. Introduce motion and continuous visual flow into tutorials, along with audio guidance, so that students can follow the instructor's thought process.
5. High-quality pre-recorded classroom lectures are not as engaging when chopped up into short segments for a MOOC. See recommendation 1.
6. Videos where instructors speak fairly fast and with high enthusiasm have been shown to be engaging.
7. Students engage differently with lecture and tutorial videos. For lectures, focus more on the first-time watching experience. For tutorials, add more support for re-watching and skimming, such as inserting sub-goal labels in large fonts throughout the video.

Four main types of video production techniques are typically used on the edX platform. These production types could also be used in other scenarios utilizing video in education and they are presented in Figure 2.4.2.

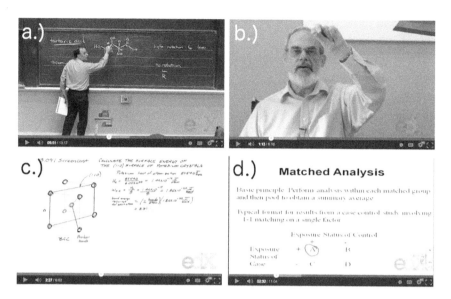

Figure 2.4.2: MOOC video production styles

The above image from Guo *et al.* (2014: 1) depicts:

  a) a recorded classroom lecture
  b) an instructor's talking head
  c) a Khan-style digital tablet drawing (popularized by Khan Academy http://khanacademy.org)
  d) a slide presentation.

The EVE model for framing video in learning

The debate about video in education is often not well evidenced and under-investigated. Consequently, learners are ultimately underserved. Good video in learning design will optimize the student learning experience. Improvements to course content require a good understanding of: the technologies in question; the pedagogy underpinning learning design (a multidisciplinary approach involving cognitive psychology, neuroscience, and so on); the key stakeholders concerned (learners and educators) and the affordances created by the intersection of these three factors. The Enhanced Video in Education Model (EVE Model) takes these factors into account and provides a framework through which to understand video in learning design that is based upon an adaptation of Koole's (n.d.) Mobile Learning FRAME model.

In this framework, we intersect the Learner (L), Pedagogy (P) and Video aspects (V) in a Venn diagram. These are the major stakeholders, frameworks and technologies that will affect the quality of learning. The Venn diagram is illustrated in Figure 2.4.3. Looking at the intersections of Learner (L), Pedagogy (P) and Video Technology (V) you will see that three further parameters are created: Video-Learner (VL), Learner-Pedagogy (LP), and Pedagogy-Video (PV). Learning via video is therefore a combination of the interactions between learners, video content and pedagogical frameworks (including educator and peer support).

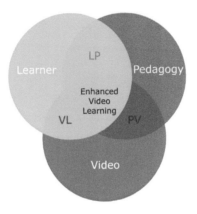

Figure 2.4.3: Enhanced Video in Education Model (EVE Model)

(L) Involves Learners' prior knowledge, self-motivation, history, memory, emotions, learning preferences, metacognition, the ability to transfer skills and knowledge, etc.

(P) The Pedagogical framework being used by the educator to support learners' efforts such as flipped learning, reinforced learning, group collaboration or constructivist methods, for example.

(V) Video content and quality can vary. For example, is it custom video for a particular purpose, standard video recording of a lecture, high/low video quality, good/bad audio quality, multimodal (audio and video; audio and slides; audio, video and slides), and is it accessible?

The Video–Learner intersection (VL) can vary according to the learning environment, human-computer interaction, psychological comfort, and personalized content, for example.

The Learner–Pedagogical intersection (LP) can vary according to the amount of user generated content, the learning environment, and how the learners' personal experiences and history interact with the educational framework, for example. This leads to questions such as: If the learner exhibits a lot of self-directed learning, what impact would this have in a learning environment where peer learning is encouraged?

At the Pedagogy–Video intersection (PV) variance can include how learning concepts are supported by: collaboration tools, peer learning, social presence, for example.

It is interesting to note that rarely did the research literature reviewed for this chapter include all the aspects of the EVE model. This means that these studies may not be identifying all the factors that impact upon the benefits learners can derive from video in learning, nor all the factors that can impede these benefits being realized.

Conclusions

In the past seven to ten years numerous published case studies show the extent to which the implementation of video has enhanced learning experiences. However, the research methodology used in these studies often makes it difficult to see clearly the cause and effect of learning. We have also highlighted a significant piece of research carried out with a large campus-based class, which provides some indication that transfer of knowledge can be evidenced more among students who viewed multimedia content than those who took part in a live lecture. We also note that growing evidence from neuroscience research looks at imagery, memory and learning and is written in a manner accessible to those involved in educational design. We expect to see greater application of the research published in such studies in the years to come, because it gives us a finer grained understanding of how a learner's mind evolves from novice to expert (Thomas, 2013).

We have highlighted the complexity involved in understanding how and when video can best be used to support learning and have presented the EVE Model as an approach that can optimize the design and use of video for learning.

Learning when out and about

*Mark Gaved, Alice Peasgood and
Agnes Kukulska-Hulme*

Introduction

Mobile digital devices such as tablet computers and smartphones (mobile phones that can run apps and access the Internet), enable learners to access learning materials while out and about during their daily lives. This enables networked digital learning to move from beyond the classroom and to become part of everyday routines. Smartphones and tablets are increasingly likely to be the first devices a wide range of people will turn to for technology enhanced learning, incorporated into their everyday activities and carried with them. Learning becomes ubiquitous, making use of 'domesticated' technologies that serve a variety of purposes in daily life.

In this chapter, we consider how smartphones can trigger location-specific learning resources to support adults learning languages when out and about, and consider two projects, MASELTOV and SALSA.

There has been increased interest in exploring the potential of 'smart cities' – urban environments with high-tech infrastructures – to support learning. We look at an example, the SALSA project, where a combination of smartphones, location-based technologies and learning resources has been used to prompt language learners, and to understand whether this motivates them to extend their learning.

Location and context triggered learning

Educators recognize the power of specific locations or contexts to make learning activities relevant; travel and cultural guidebooks have been popular learning tools for hundreds of years. Until recently similar results were difficult to achieve with information technologies that could react to the users' location/context and personalize resources based on their preferences or history of activities.

Language learning educators identify that location-based and context-sensitive resources and activities can be a powerful resource (Edge *et al.*, 2011): learning at a relevant location or in a context associated with the learning goal is more likely to make the activity effective. Smartphones, with their ability to connect to networks, provide text, audio, and video through apps and web browsers, and take advantage of a wide range of onboard sensors, are becoming a powerful, practical platform for mobile learning and have enabled exploration of digital learning beyond the classroom.

There is a range of different ways of identifying where a smartphone is and hence providing resources relevant to the user's location or context. Global Information System receivers (e.g. GPS) can identify location if the user is outside, or position can be estimated with less accuracy from nearby WiFi points or cellphone towers. Alternatively, markers such as QR codes can be placed on objects or locations and scanned by the phone to identify location or trigger resources. More recently, Bluetooth beacons have been used, sending radio signals to nearby smartphones. These have the advantage of working indoors as well as outdoors and enable a more discreet interaction than mechanisms such as QR that require the phone user to actively engage with a visible object. However, like QR codes, they require prior installation in target locations.

In two of our recent projects (MASELTOV and SALSA), we have explored how location- and context-triggered learning might be supported by smartphones: in both cases to support recent migrants with language learning and social inclusion.

The SALSA and MASELTOV projects

The MASELTOV project explored a range of services to support immigrants' learning through their daily activities in urban environments, while the SALSA project has investigated how learners engage with location-triggered language activities around a town.

MASELTOV (www.maseltov.eu) was a European Union funded project exploring how smartphones might be used by recent immigrants to Europe to support their language learning and social inclusion. A central element was the development of a smartphone suite of tools ('MApp') containing a range of integrated services that the target audience can use in their daily lives.

The MApp application includes navigation tools, language learning activities, a social forum, a translation tool and a help radar that enables the user to find local volunteers and other community members who might be nearby and willing to solve a problem. Underpinning the system is a recommendation engine that gathers data from the user's interactions, contexts and preferences.

We drew on the concept of incidental learning, 'unintentional or unplanned learning that results from other activities' (Kerka, 2000: 1), using situations occurring in daily lives as the basis for learning, recognizing the power of authentic situations and personally relevant contexts to motivate learners.

Several of the tools in the MApp drew on locational data gathered by the phone to support services. In some cases this was explicit, for example guiding the user around the city using a pedestrian sat-nav, or identifying potential nearby volunteers who could help (both using the phone's GPS receiver). In other cases the locational aspect of the services was not visible but improved the functionality of the tools. For example, by allowing the MApp to identify the user's location (in the settings tool), better contextual recommendations for learning resources could be made. Users were given the ability to switch this geolocational tracking on and off.

The SALSA project (Sensors and Apps for Languages in Smart Areas), funded by The Open University, investigated location-triggered language learning activities via smartphones for learners out and about in an urban environment (www.open.ac.uk/blogs/salsa/). The project was started in 2014 in response to a call from the Milton Keynes smart city project, 'MK:Smart'.

SALSA is designed to improve the spoken English skills of adults who are living in Britain and already have a basic level of English, and drawing on the same principles as MASELTOV, explored learners' responses to receiving learning prompts when out and about in the city. We wanted a system that worked indoors and outdoors, and discreetly: we were aware that language learners might not wish to be identified as such, so explicit interaction with a trigger (e.g. walking up to a QR code and taking a photo of it) might not be appropriate.

We therefore chose to experiment with Bluetooth beacons that would send prompts to a custom-built Android based smartphone app, and trigger relevant content when a learner's smartphone was within range (up to approximately 30 metres). For example, while waiting at a bus stop, a learner who has downloaded the SALSA app might be in the vicinity of a SALSA beacon. This would trigger a phone notification (like an SMS prompt) and indicate that there is a relevant language activity for the location, including content such as how to purchase a bus ticket and ask the driver or ticket office about ticket options (e.g. 'single', 'concession', 'off-peak', 'season ticket').

Working with tutors and English language learners from a local adult education centre, we identified locations and contexts around Milton Keynes where communications challenges might occur, and that were commonly visited during learners' daily routines. We devised 12 different scenarios and worked with an educational publisher to produce contextually relevant educational resources including text, images and audio delivered through a dialogue, vocabulary, grammar and idiomatic phrases.

The app containing all the learning resources was designed to be downloaded at the learners' convenience in a location where there is free WiFi (e.g. library or community centre) and it works without a network connection: MASELTOV participants had previously identified that concern about data download costs acted as a barrier against engaging with mobile learning apps.

Both MASELTOV and SALSA apps were trialled in the United Kingdom with volunteer language learners.

Findings from SALSA and MASELTOV

SALSA field trial participants found the technology easy to use and helpful in supporting their language learning. Although they only used the app for two weeks during the field trial, many reported learning something useful from the app. In particular, they found the idiomatic phrases and audio recording of a dialogue useful, especially as the written transcript of the dialogue was available on the phone, so they could listen and read at the same time. The relevance of the learning content to each location was helpful, particularly phrases and ways of starting a conversation that enabled them to 'speak like a native'. The SALSA participants already had conversational English, so for many of them their priority was to 'fit in' and enhance their social skills in English. They did not tend to use the app content at the location or in the situations for which it was designed. For example, rather than approach the bus ticket sales desk with the app open on the page about purchasing a ticket, one participant preferred to study that content discreetly nearby, then enter the ticket office to practise the phrases she had just learned. Learners adapted the use of the app to meet their personal goals, taking into account the social and cultural context.

It is worth noting that feedback from MASELTOV participants has indicated that requiring the active and obvious use of a smartphone to trigger learning resources (such as taking a photo of a sign in a public place) can deter users from taking advantage of potential learning opportunities.

Conclusion: The opportunities and issues for learning with smart mobile technology

There are many opportunities for further work in this area. For example, one possibility for future development is extending a context-based learning experience into a more prolonged or reflective learning experience over time. This may be achieved through application designs by prompting learners to continue learning or revisit past learning. Another possibility would be to design some speaking practice so that it mimics natural phone conversations. This may be a way to overcome various barriers to learners practising just-in-time oral language skills on the phone in public.

There are, however, some issues that must be overcome if these opportunities are to be fulfilled. For example, tracking users' activities and locations raises ethical, privacy and data-security issues. Users may be concerned about how their contextual information is stored or who has access to it, and how it may be used. Contextually aware language learning systems must inform users clearly how their data will be used and stored, and offer the opportunity to opt out of some or all data gathering (though users will need to understand that this may reduce the quality of recommendations that can be made to them). GPS and WiFi-based location systems store data about the user's location. Bluetooth beacons do not store any user information.

Learning with iPads

'Makes learning fun'

Patricia Davies

Introduction

Tablets are small touchscreen computers that are slim, lightweight and can easily be connected to a wireless network. They have evolved rapidly over the past decade. Inclusive of these are iPads; there have been more than a dozen models since Apple launched the original version in 2010. iPads run on iOS – the operating system used by Apple mobile devices – and are available in one of three screen sizes: 7.9, 9.7, or 12.9 inches. More than 300 million iPads have been sold worldwide since their debut. Many of these are now being used in schools and colleges, to enhance student engagement and learning in the classroom.

The capability of one-to-one mobile devices to increase learning remains highly contentious. Over the past four years, the need for schools to provide pupils with mobile digital tools has increased, however, the potential of these technologies to advance student learning is yet to be determined. The cost involved in deploying iPads to learners is huge, and those who make this investment often want to be sure that they are getting value for money. More recently, guidelines have been produced for helping schools adopt these mobile learning technologies more seamlessly (Clark and Luckin, 2013). Also, many schools now employ instructional technology experts to work with them to ensure teachers' uses of iPads is grounded in pedagogical knowledge – knowing how to generate understanding through the uses of iPads.

The present chapter draws on recent work done at a preparatory school in south-east England, to help integrate iPads into the curriculum. The school was piloting the use of iPads for learning and teaching, and had recently distributed these mobile devices to learners in Years 4 and 7. The project explored learners' perspective on their uses and experiences of the iPads distributed by the school for academic purposes (hitherto referred to as School iPads). It also examines some related issues raised by these learners.

The project

The project utilized qualitative case study methodology, using a variety of data sources. This was one way of ensuring that the issue of learning with iPads is not explored through a single lens, but rather through varied views, allowing for multiple facets of the phenomenon to be revealed and understood. Data were collected from 100 learners (60 in Year 4 and 40 in Year 7), in three rounds, to examine the following research question: *How do learners perceive the uses of School iPads?*

In the first round of data collection learners reported on their experiences with School iPads through reflective writing in a personal diary kept over one week. The diaries were anonymized and confidential; they did not include participants' names and learners were asked not to include names of teachers. Over five days each pupil recorded in his/her diary where the iPad was used, and how, and then rated each activity using one of the following descriptors:

☺ – **Great:** I enjoyed using the device and feel it helped me learn.

☺ – **Good:** I enjoyed using the device and don't feel I learn much by using it.

☹ – **Disappointing:** I did not enjoy using the device.

Students were encouraged to report on up to three sessions per day, for each of the five days; Figure 2.6.1 shows one reporting row of the student diary. They could use any combination of text and diagrams to describe how the iPad was used in a lesson.

Where?	How?	It was ... (tick one)
		☐ ☺
		☐ ☺
		☐ ☹

Figure 2.6.1: A row of the student diary

In addition, learners in Year 7 were asked to comment in their diaries on whether and, if so, how they used School iPads at home. Learners in Year 4 did not take the iPads home so they were asked instead to report on other kinds of digital technologies used at home, and whether or not they would have preferred to use their School iPad instead.

The second round of data collection provided a deeper understanding of some of the issues raised in the learners' diaries. All learners in both year groups were asked to discuss and answer several questions, including what was special about using iPads in lessons, in 'buddy groups' of threes or fours. The questions focused on the following themes, which had evolved from the diary entries: classroom use, choice, home use, ownership.

Learners were also asked to what extent they thought certain activities using their iPads, including taking notes, watching videos and creating products, helped them learn. These conversations were recorded.

The third round of data collection involved learners making recommendations on the changes they would like to see relating to the uses of School iPads, and concerning other issues raised in their diaries. They did this in the form of 'concentric circles' – working in the group of fours or fives, and switching groups until each one had a chance to be in a group with every other person in the room – which could be envisioned as a kind of intellectual 'speed dating', in groups. It was agreed in advance that each group could make up to three recommendations, which made it necessary for each proposer to persuade others in the group to select his or her recommendation(s). Each group then voted to determine the three statements to put forward as their suggested recommendations. Naturally there was some overlap in the group suggestions. Those that occurred more frequently were deemed most favourable.

Findings

Data from the diaries collected in round 1 were analysed by reading through the entries, and then coding them. The audio files were also analysed, and this data was used to verify data in learners' diaries. The findings are discussed below under the key themes identified in the learners' logs, plus another that came out of the audio data.

CLASSROOM USES

The two main ways in which participants reported using School iPads in the classroom were for revising and testing. When asked if they preferred revisions led by the teacher, on their own or with their classmates, the overwhelming response was that they preferred revising with their peers. They stated that far too many lessons were teacher-led, and added that they would cherish the opportunity to do more presentations during lessons using School iPads. Regarding testing on the iPads, learners felt it made the experience more fun, and that tests on the iPad were, in fact, easier since these mainly involved multiple-choice or true/false questions. Learners also seemed to relish the fact that such tests involved little writing.

The participants were provided with a list of classroom iPad activities to rate using a Likert scale, according to how much each one helped them learn. Those activities that involved alternate forms of content representation – watching videos, creating products, seeing pictures, working on projects – ranked highest. Other activities, such as taking notes and reading a text, were moderately rated, but learners argued, 'it makes a difference if you can actually see something', and 'you don't really need technology to [read or write]'.

Choice

The majority of the participants stated that they enjoyed being given a choice of when and how to use their iPads during lessons. Several activities during which teachers offered them a choice of whether or not to use School iPads, or how to use them, were documented. These included lessons in which they were asked to create products such as posters, or comment on a video. The learners were able to give practical reasons why they should be allowed a choice, including that their iPad may have run out of battery life. Other reasons they gave demonstrated an understanding of the need for differentiation in the use of digital technologies; one group argued that 'some pupils learn differently and may find it easier to use paper and pencil instead'. Another group thought that 'dyslexic pupils should be allowed apps [that] help them learn [better]'.

Differentiated classroom instruction provides teaching strategies that give today's learners, having a variety of learning preferences, the opportunity to assimilate and process knowledge content by making sense of ideas, and expressing their understanding, in a variety of ways. Digital technologies have been shown to support differentiation by personalizing the environments in which learners interact with software and hardware, communicate, create products, and conduct research in the twenty-first century.

Home uses

The majority of Year 7 participants reported that they never use School iPads at home. The main reason given was that the level of permission set for them on the devices did not allow them to use social apps, such as Messenger and YouTube, to communicate with their friends. In addition, they said that the homework or preparations set by teachers never require the use of School iPads.

OWNERSHIP

Participants in the project had a good sense of what ownership means: their answers included, 'you take care of it, like you do when you have a dog' and that 'you can do what you want with it'. These sentiments make it easy to understand why the majority of them, including Year 7 pupils, who were allowed to take the iPads home, did not feel they owned the iPads given to them by the School. One group commented, 'We feel like we half own the iPads', and went on to argue that they were unable to use School iPads for a majority of the things they enjoy doing outside the school, including taking pictures and communicating with friends and family in online chatrooms. As a result, they rather tended to use their own (or their parents') personal devices at home. Ownership of School iPads is an issue worth exploring further to understand how, and to what extent, pupils learn better when they feel the device (or any other learning aid) is indeed theirs. It is not difficult to imagine how an activity as simple as making a call on a mobile phone could become quite an arduous task if one had to borrow someone else's phone, particularly if it is a different make or model.

'MAKES LEARNING FUN'

The consensus of the participants in the project was that using School iPads during lessons 'makes learning fun' – as put succinctly by students in one 'buddy group'. They also reported that it was easy for them to become disengaged and disinterested in classes that did not involve iPad use because 'the lessons are boring and [we] find it hard to concentrate'. It might be that the finger-driven iPad provides active and collaborative learning, and increases student-teacher interaction. The participants also reported enjoying the experience of 'being in charge' of their own learning. It was clear that the increased sense of responsibility attached to the more investigative approaches of classroom iPad use could be exciting for learners.

Pupil recommendations

At the end of the project, the participants drew up the following list of recommendations to make to the teachers and administrators at the school. A plan was put in place for a focus group, made up of teachers and pupils at the school, to discuss and finalize these to determine what should be adopted as practice and policy regarding iPad use.

- Year 4 pupils should be allowed to take School iPads home from next year (i.e. in Year 5 and upwards).
- Pupils should be allowed to keep School iPads once they leave the School.

- Year 3 pupils should be provided with School iPads.
- Pupils should be assigned preps that require use of the School iPads (with some suggestion that they are used in every lesson).
- Pupils should be allowed access to social apps: camera, Twitter, music, etc., at least at home, also allow headphones so the iPads could be used to reward pupils for completing their work early during lessons.
- Allow special apps for pupils with special needs, for example dyslexia.
- Consider a 'bring your own device' (BYOD) approach perhaps this would work better.
- Allow pupils to choose or buy their own cover for School iPads.
- Introduce an app that could allow pupils to order lunch in advance.
- Introduce an iPad reward system: for example, if you get special recognition in a lesson then you are allowed to use your iPad during break (only).
- Allow pupils to use iPads on coaches.
- Provide more educational apps, especially fun ones, including ones that could be used for Prep and Homework.
- Increase privacy for pupils; stop spying on us (this came exclusively from Year 7 students).

Conclusion

The findings suggest that the excitement of these new digital technologies has the potential to prompt novel ways of teaching and learning, and that there is a need to understand better what works for learners, and how they could be tailored to address their individual needs better. Educators who work to document and understand what is educational about technology have noted that the uses of educational technology should be anchored in the requirements for learning provided by both learners and teachers.

Recent discourses around the uses of digital technologies in education have been replete with ideas to do with personalization, individualization and pupil engagement. However, as we grapple with the expanding influence of technology in education, rulemaking, regulation and resistance remain central to the place that iPads could have in learning. In contrast to the era of 'fixed' desktop computers (prior to 2010), the contemporary growing presence of digital technology in our lives means that schools now play a much more reduced part in facilitating pupil access to digital technology; mobile technologies are more commonplace with young people outside school than in school. As a result, the fine line between formal and informal learning with technology has become blurred. While lauded for their educational potential, iPads can unsettle a school's capacity to control pupils' actions and behaviours. They also introduce a new set of practices that potentially require regulation. The initial step of examining learners' viewpoints is important in determining a way forward for those who teach with iPads, and for those meant to be beneficiaries of learning with iPads.

Conclusion

Mutlu Cukurova and Rosemary Luckin

At the start of this section we highlighted the absence of evidence in many discussions about technology and education. We also suggested that asking how we can design and use technologies so that they enhance learning is much more fruitful than asking if technologies *per se* enhance learning. Initially, we presented the 19 *Learning Acts* that have been identified as happening when learners learn with or through technology and then discussed a range of technologies along with suggestions from the research evidence about how each technology can be used to support learning.

Lawrence Williams and Miroslava Černochová discussed the new Computing curriculum in the United Kingdom and the success of the work done through the 'Literacy from Scratch' curriculum project based on a constructionist approach. The project has been shown to develop both computational thinking skills as well as creativity at all ages: from 5 to young adults. The chapter authors suggest that we should value the approach taken in the new computing curriculum, because its design is supported by good research evidence. They highlight the fascinating 'creativity paradox' seen by the fact that students need very clear, potentially strict guidelines and structures within which to work creatively: the more restricted and structured the parameters the more diverse the creative responses developed by learners.

In Chapter 2, Charlotte Lærke Weitze discusses the value of engaging learners in making their own computer games and provides some useful examples of teachers working with students in game making activities. Charlotte introduces the Smiley Model (Figure 2.2.2) for learning game design to help teachers build engaging learning games that combine learning design and game design. Christothea Herodotou explores the potential of citizen science in Chapter 2.3, particularly to engage learners in STEM subject learning. She identified evidence from work completed by the OECD that suggests that there is a connection between participation in informal (out-of-school) science activities and positive attitudes towards science. There are potential gains for the general public too: helping people to think critically through awareness of the scientific method and learning processes. This last point is particularly important as more and more information becomes available to us. It is essential that we can evaluate this information effectively to support informed decision making.

How to make the best use of video to support learning was the subject of Chapter 2.4. Nageela Yusuf presented evidence from neuroscience experiments and social science evaluations about the potential value of video for learning and provided the EVE framework to guide those who want to integrate video into their teaching or learning. Mark Gaved and Alice Peasgood discussed the value of context-based learning experience in Chapter 2.5. This work highlighted both the opportunities for using mobile devices to extend learning beyond a single location, such as the classroom. They also identified the significant ethical, privacy and data-security issues involved when tracking people's activity across tasks and locations. The final chapter in this section by Patricia Davies tackled a topic frequently discussed in schools and colleges: the use of iPads or other tablet devices and how to get the best results when using these devices. Patricia stresses the central role played by rulemaking, regulation and resistance when it comes to iPads and learning. The growing presence of digital technology, particularly smart, mobile devices, such as the iPad, reduces the role of schools in facilitating pupil access to digital technology and can lead to the fine line between formal and informal learning with technology becoming blurred and the potential need for regulation.

What the research says about the use of different technologies to enhance learning

- The ideas behind the new Computing curriculum in England can easily be linked back to constructivist and constructionist approaches to teaching and learning.
- As exemplified with the 'Literacy from Scratch' project, successful Computing curriculum models can help students develop computer programming skills, as well as literacy skills, in a creative way. Computing can also support cross-curricular approaches to teaching and learning, including literacy, Computing, ICT, art, music and bilingual work.
- There is evidence to support the value of developing computational thinking and coding skills through teaching programming languages.
- Learning through game development, as opposed to game playing, can be an appropriate approach to support and evaluate students' learning processes, and it can lead to increased collaboration among students. The evidence reported in Chapter 2.2 shows that students can learn from making games as much as they can from conventional teaching.
- Citizen science projects have the potential to improve the public's knowledge of scientific content, their understanding of the scientific process and their attitudes towards science and scientists. To achieve this potential, public participation must be appropriately guided, and must include reflection about the public's role and how it relates to the processes of science.
- Evidence about the impact of various citizen science approaches is just emerging and it has multiple challenges such as the creation of scientifically robust investigations, the validity of the collected data, the need for moderation and advice from experts and long-term

engagement in citizen science projects to develop skills to conduct reliable research.

- Research about the use of video in learning is rarely conclusive due to the methodological challenges of controlling potential variables, which can impact on student performance. However, there is some evidence that video in learning may lead to an increased ability to transfer knowledge, as it provides opportunities to view visual material at a comfortable pace for learners. This has the potential to help learners to internalize knowledge, and thereby recall it at a later time.

- Learning at a relevant location, or in a context associated with the learning goal, is more likely to make the learning activity effective.

- Initial evaluations of the potential of urban environments with high-tech infrastructures to support learning with location and context associated learning activities are promising. However, research mostly relies on self-declarations of participants, and further investigations are required to interpret the potential of these approaches.

- The requirement for learners to make obvious use of smart tools to trigger learning resources (such as taking a photo of a sign in a public place or scanning QR codes) may deter potential users from taking advantage of potential learning opportunities in location-based learning approaches.

- iPads are nowadays commonly used in educational settings with the purpose of enhancing student engagement and learning. Students' feedback on the use of iPads in schools evidences that these new digital technologies have the potential to contribute to teaching and learning. However, the value of these educational technologies is to be found in the way they are implemented rather than the technologies themselves.

- Evidence from student diaries about the use of iPads illustrated that the two main ways in which students used School iPads in the classroom were for revising and testing. Students stated that tests on the iPad were easier because they mainly involved multiple-choice type questions and little writing. The majority of the participants enjoyed being given a choice about when and how to use their iPads during lessons. The consensus of the participants in the project was that using School iPads during lessons 'makes learning fun'. They also reported enjoying the experience of 'being in charge' of their own learning.

References (Part 2)

Ackermann, E.K. (2010) 'Constructivism(s): Shared roots, crossed paths, multiple legacies'. In Clayson, J.E. and Kalaš, I. (eds) *Constructionist Approaches to Creative Learning, Thinking and Education: Lessons for the 21st century: Proceedings of the 12th EuroLogo Conference (Constructionism 2010), 16–20 August 2010, Paris, France.* Paris: AUP.

Agalianos, A., Whitty, G. and Noss, R. (2006) 'The social shaping of Logo'. *Social Studies of Science*, 36 (2), 241–67.

Anderson, L.W. and Krathwohl, D.R. (eds) (2001) *A Taxonomy for Learning, Teaching, and Assessing: A revision of Bloom's Taxonomy of Educational Objectives (Complete Edition).* New York: Longman.

Barab, S. and Dede, C. (2007) 'Games and immersive participatory simulations for science education: An emerging type of curricula'. *Journal of Science Education and Technology*, 16 (1), 1–3.

Blakemore, S.-J. and Frith, U. (2005) *The Learning Brain: Lessons for education.* Oxford: Blackwell.

Bloom, B.S. (ed.) (1956) *Taxonomy of Educational Objectives: Handbook 1: Cognitive domain.* New York: Longman.

Bonney, R., Phillips, T.B., Ballard, H.L. and Enck, J.W. (2016) 'Can citizen science enhance public understanding of science?'. *Public Understanding of Science*, 25 (1), 2–16.

Brennan, K. and Resnick, M. (2012) 'New frameworks for studying and assessing the development of computational thinking'. Paper presented at the Annual Meeting of the American Educational Research Association, Vancouver, British Columbia, Canada, 13–17 April 2012.

Bruner, J. (1960) *The Process of Education.* Cambridge, MA: Harvard University Press.

Bruner, J. (1966) *Toward a Theory of Instruction.* Cambridge, MA: Harvard University Press.

Bruner, J.S., Goodnow, J.J. and Austin, G.A. (1956) *A Study of Thinking.* New York: John Wiley and Sons.

Černochová, M., Dorling, M. and Williams, L. (2015) 'Developing computational thinking skills through the Literacy from Scratch project: An international collaboration'. Paper presented at the IFIP TC3 Working Conference, Vilnius, Lithuania, 1–3 July 2015.

Charlton, P. and Luckin, R. (2012) *Time to Re-Load? Computational thinking and computer science in schools* ('What the Research Says' Briefing 2). London: London Knowledge Lab. Online. https://knowledgeillusion.files.wordpress.com/2012/03/time-to-re-loadwhattheresearchsaysbriefing27april2012.pdf (accessed 15 September 2017).

Chen, G., Davis, D., Hauff, C. and Houben, G.-J. (2016) 'Learning transfer: Does it take place in MOOCs? An investigation into the uptake of functional programming in practice'. In *L@S 2016: Proceedings of the 3rd ACM Conference on Learning at Scale, April 25–26, 2016, University of Edinburgh, Edinburgh, United Kingdom.* New York: Association for Computing Machinery, 409–18.

Clark, W. and Luckin, R. (2013) *What the Research Says: iPads in the classroom.* London: London Knowledge Lab.

Colvin, R. (2016) 'Optimising, generalising and integrating educational practice using neuroscience'. *Science of Learning*, 1, Article 16012, 1–4.

Cooper, S., Khatib, F., Treuille, A., Barbero, J., Lee, J., Beenen, M., Leaver-Fay, A., Baker, D., Popović, Z. and *Fold-it* players (2010) 'Predicting protein structures with a multiplayer online game'. *Nature*, 466 (7307), 756–60.

de Jong, T., van Gog, T., Jenks, K., Manlove, S., van Hell, J., Jolles, J., van Merriënboer, J., van Leeuwen, T. and Boschloo, A. (2009) *Explorations in Learning and the Brain: On the potential of cognitive neuroscience for educational science*. New York: Springer.

Demouy, V., Jones, A., Kan, Q., Kukulska-Hulme, A. and Eardley, A. (2016) 'Why and how do distance learners use mobile devices for language learning?'. *EuroCALL Review*, 24 (1), 10–24.

Dey, E.L., Burn, H.E. and Gerdes, D. (2009) 'Bringing the classroom to the web: Effects of using new technologies to capture and deliver lectures'. *Research in Higher Education*, 50 (4), 377–93.

Earp, J. (2015) 'Game making for learning: A systematic review of the research literature'. In Gómez Chova, L., López Martínez, A. and Candel Torres, I. (eds) *ICERI2015: Proceedings of the 8th International Conference of Education, Research and Innovation, Seville, Spain, 16–18 November 2015*. Valencia: IATED Academy, 6426–35.

Edge, D., Searle, E., Chiu, K., Zhao, J. and Landay, J.A. (2011) 'MicroMandarin: Mobile language learning in context'. In *CHI'11: Proceedings of the SIGCHI Conference on Human Factors in Computing Systems, May 7–12, 2011, Vancouver, British Columbia, Canada*. New York: Association for Computing Machinery, 3169–78.

Edwards, R. (2015) *Enhancing Informal Learning through Citizen Science: Background literature*. Stirling: University of Stirling. Online. www.informalscience.org/sites/default/files/Enhancing_Informal_Learning_Through_Citizen_Science_Review__PDF.pdf (accessed 15 September 2017).

Enterbrain (2016) RPG Maker. Tokyo: Enterbrain. Software retrieved from www.rpgmakerweb.com

Finke, R.A. (1996) 'Imagery, creativity, and emergent structure'. *Consciousness and Cognition 5* (3), 381–93.

Freitag, A. and Pfeffer, M.J. (2013) 'Process, not product: Investigating recommendations for improving citizen science "success"'. *PloS One*, 8 (5), Article e64079, 1–5.

Gaved, M., Greenwood, R. and Peasgood, A. (2015) 'Using and appropriating the smart city for community and capacity building amongst migrant language learners'. In Avram, G., de Cindio, F. and Pipek, V. (eds) *Proceedings of the Work-in-Progress Track of the 7th International Conference on Communities and Technologies* (International Reports on Socio-Informatics). Bonn: International Institute for Socio-Informatics, 63–72.

Gaved, M., Luley, P., Efremidis, S., Georgiou, I., Kukulska-Hulme, A., Jones, A. and Scanlon, E. (2014) 'Challenges in context-aware mobile language learning: The MASELTOV approach'. Paper presented at the 13th World Conference on Mobile and Contextual Learning (mLearn 2014), Istanbul, Turkey, 3–5 November 2014.

Gee, J.P. (2003) *What Video Games Have To Teach Us About Learning and Literacy*. New York: Palgrave Macmillan.

Gee, J.P. (2011) 'Reflections on empirical evidence on games and learning'. In Tobias, S. and Fletcher, J.D. (eds) *Computer Games and Instruction*. Charlotte, NC: Information Age Publishing, 223–32.

Guo, P.J., Kim, J. and Rubin, R. (2014) 'How video production affects student engagement: An empirical study of MOOC videos'. In *L@S 2014: Proceedings of the 1st ACM Conference on Learning at Scale, March 4–5, 2014, Atlanta, Georgia, USA*. New York: Association for Computing Machinery, 41–50.

Haklay, M. (2012) 'Citizen science and volunteered geographic information: Overview and typology of participation'. In Sui, D., Elwood, S. and Goodchild, M. (eds) *Crowdsourcing Geographic Knowledge: Volunteered geographic information (VGI) in theory and practice*. Dordrecht: Springer, 105–22.

Harel, I. and Papert, S. (eds) (1991) *Constructionism: Research reports and essays, 1985–1990*. Norwood, NJ: Ablex Publishing.

Hatch, M. (2013) *The Maker Movement Manifesto: Rules for innovation in the new world of crafters, hackers, and tinkerers*. New York: McGraw-Hill.

Herodotou, C., Sharples, M. and Scanlon, E. (eds) (2018) *Citizen Inquiry: Synthesizing science and inquiry learning*. Abingdon: Routledge.

Herodotou, C., Villasclaras-Fernández, E. and Sharples, M. (2014) 'The design and evaluation of a sensor-based mobile application for citizen inquiry science investigations'. In Rensing, C., de Freitas, S., Ley, T. and Muñoz-Merino, P.J. (eds) *Open Learning and Teaching in Educational Communities: 9th European Conference on Technology Enhanced Learning, EC-TEL 2014, Graz, Austria, September 16–19, 2014, Proceedings* (Lecture Notes in Computer Science 8719). Cham: Springer, 434–9.

Hiim, H. and Hippe, E. (1997) *Læring gennem oplevelse, forståelse og handling*. København: Gyldendal.

Ho, A.D., Reich, J., Nesterko, S.O., Seaton, D.T., Mullaney, T., Waldo, J. and Chuang, I. (2014) *HarvardX and MITx: The first year of open online courses, fall 2012–summer 2013* (HarvardX and MITx Working Paper 1). Cambridge, MA: Harvard University.

Honey, M. and Kanter, D.E. (eds) (2013) *Design, Make, Play: Growing the next generation of STEM innovators*. New York: Routledge.

Illeris, K. (2007) *How We Learn: Learning and non-learning in school and beyond*. London: Routledge.

Kafai, Y.B. and Burke, Q. (2015) 'Constructionist gaming: Understanding the benefits of making games for learning'. *Educational Psychologist*, 50 (4), 313–34.

Kafai, Y.B. and Resnick, M. (1996) *Constructionism in Practice: Designing, thinking, and learning in a digital world*. New York: Routledge.

Kalaš, I., Kabátová, K., Mikolajová, K. and Tomcsányi, P. (2011) 'Konštrukcionizmus: Od Piageta po školu v digitálnom veku'. Keynote speech at DidInfo 2011, Banská Bystrica, Slovakia, 7–8 April 2011.

Kemp, A. and Manahan-Vaughan, D. (2012) 'Passive spatial perception facilitates the expression of persistent hippocampal long-term depression'. *Cerebral Cortex*, 22 (7), 1614–21.

Kerka, S. (2000) *Incidental Learning* (Trends and Issues Alert No. 18). Columbus, OH: ERIC Clearinghouse on Adult, Career, and Vocational Education. Online. http://files.eric.ed.gov/fulltext/ED446234.pdf (accessed 15 September 2017).

Kirkwood, A. and Price, L. (2014) 'Technology-enhanced learning and teaching in higher education: What is "enhanced" and how do we know? A critical literature review'. *Learning, Media and Technology*, 39 (1), 6–36.

Kluzer, S., Ferrari, A. and Centeno, C. (2011) *Language Learning by Adult Migrants: Policy challenges and ICT responses* (JRC–IPTS Policy Report). Luxembourg: Publications Office of the European Union.

Koole, M. (n.d.) 'The FRAME Model of Mobile Learning'. Online. http://kooleady.ca/thoughts/?page_id=1068 (accessed 15 September 2017).

Learning Games (ECGBL 2014) Proceedings of the 8th European Conference on Games Based Learning. Berlin, Germany, 9–10 October 2014. (2) 594–603. Academic Conferences and Publishing International Limited.

Lifelong Kindergarten Group (2016) Scratch. Cambridge, MA: MIT Media Lab. Software retrieved from http://scratch.mit.edu.

Manches, A., Phillips, B., Crook, C., Chowcat, I. and Sharples, M. (2010) CAPITAL-Curriculum and Pedagogy in Technology Assisted Learning. Online. https://halshs.archives-ouvertes.fr/hal-00593082/document (accessed 2 November 2017).

Noss, R. (2010) 'Reconstructing constructionism'. In Clayson, J.E. and Kalaš, I. (eds) *Constructionist Approaches to Creative Learning, Thinking and Education: Lessons for the 21st century: Proceedings of the 12th EuroLogo Conference (Constructionism 2010), 16–20 August 2010, Paris, France*. Paris: AUP.

Noss, R. (2013) 'Does technology enhance learning? Some findings from the UK's Technology Enhanced Learning (TEL) research programme. Online. http://www.tlrp.org/docs/enhance.pdf (accessed 25 September 2017).

OECD (Organisation for Economic Co-operation and Development) (2012) *Equity and Quality in Education: Supporting disadvantaged students and schools*. Paris: OECD Publishing.

OED (*Oxford English Dictionary*) (2014) 'New words list June 2014'. Online. http://public.oed.com/the-oed-today/recent-updates-to-the-oed/previous updates/june-2014-update/new-words-list-june-2014/ (accessed 15 September 2017).

Oygardslia, K. (2015) 'Students as game designers: Learning by creating game narratives in the classroom'. In Schoenau-Fog, H., Bruni, L.E., Louchart, S. and Baceviciute, S. (eds) *Interactive Storytelling: 8th International Conference on Interactive Digital Storytelling, ICIDS 2015, Copenhagen, Denmark, November 30–December 4, 2015, Proceedings* (Lecture Notes in Computer Science 9445). Cham: Springer, 341–4.

Papert, S. (1980) *Mindstorms: Children, computers, and powerful ideas*. New York: Basic Books.

Resnick, M. (2013) 'Mother's Day, warrior cats, and digital fluency: Stories from the Scratch community'. In Reynolds, N., Webb, M., Sysło, M.M. and Dagienė, V. (eds) *Learning while We Are Connected: Proceedings of the 10th IFIP World Conference on Computers in Education (WCCE 2013), Toruń, Poland, July 1–7, 2013 (Vol. 3)*. Toruń: Nicolaus Copernicus University, 2–8.

Resnick, M. and Brennan, K. (2010) 'Getting to know Scratch'. In Clayson, J.E. and Kalaš, I. (eds) *Constructionist Approaches to Creative Learning, Thinking and Education: Lessons for the 21st century: Proceedings of the 12th EuroLogo Conference (Constructionism 2010), 16–20 August 2010, Paris, France*. Paris: AUP.

Selander, S. and Kress, G. (2012) *Læringsdesign i et multimodalt perspektiv*. København: Frydenlund.

Sharples, M., Aristeidou, M., Villasclaras-Fernández, E., Herodotou, C. and Scanlon, E. (2015) 'Sense-it: A smartphone toolkit for citizen inquiry learning'. In Brown, T.H. and van der Merwe, H.J. (eds) *The Mobile Learning Voyage: From small ripples to massive open waters: 14th World Conference on Mobile and Contextual Learning, mLearn 2015, Venice, Italy, October 17–24, 2015, Proceedings* (Communications in Computer and Information Science 560). Cham: Springer, 366–77.

Shirk, J.L., Ballard, H.L., Wilderman, C.C., Phillips, T., Wiggins, A., Jordan, R., McCallie, E., Minarchek, M., Lewenstein, B.V., Krasny, M.E. and Bonney, R. (2012) 'Public participation in scientific research: A framework for deliberate design'. *Ecology and Society*, 17 (2), Article 29, 1–20.

Shute, V.J. (2011) 'Stealth assessment in computer-based games to support learning'. In Tobias, S. and Fletcher, J.D. (eds) *Computer Games and Instruction*. Charlotte, NC: Information Age Publishing, 503–24.

Squire, K. (2011) *Video Games and Learning: Teaching and participatory culture in the digital age*. New York: Teachers College Press.

Tapscott, D. (2012) 'Introduction: Creating digital capability in Europe'. In Bergaud, C., Kurop, N., Joyce, A. and Wood, C. (eds) *The e-Skills Manifesto*. Brussels: European Schoolnet, 4–11.

Thomas, M.S.C. (2013) 'Educational neuroscience in the near and far future: Predictions from the analogy with the history of medicine'. *Trends in Neuroscience and Education*, 2 (1), 23–6.

Vygotsky, L. (1934) *Thought and Language*. Cambridge, MA: MIT Press.

Weitze, C.L. (2014a) 'An experiment on how adult students can learn by designing engaging learning games'. In *Proceedings of the 4th International Academic Conference on Meaningful Play, October 16–18, 2014 (I-35), East Lansing, Michigan*. East Lansing: Michigan State University.

Weitze, C.L. (2014b) 'Experimenting on how to create a sustainable gamified learning design that supports adult students when learning through designing learning games'. In Busch, C. (ed.) *Proceedings of the 8th European Conference on Games Based Learning (ECGBL 2014), Berlin, Germany, 9–10 October 2014 (Vol. 2)*. Reading: Academic Conferences and Publishing International, 594–603.

Weitze, C.L. (2015) 'Learning and motivational processes when students design curriculum-based digital learning games'. In Munkvold, R. and Kolås, L. (eds) *Proceedings of the 9th European Conference on Games Based Learning (ECGBL 2015), Nord-Trondelag University College, Steinkjer, Norway, 8–9 October 2015*. Reading: Academic Conferences and Publishing International, 579–88.

Weitze, C.L. (2016a) 'Designing for learning and play: The Smiley Model as a framework'. *Interaction Design and Architecture(s)*, 29, 52–75.

Weitze, C.L. (2016b) *Innovative Pedagogical Processes Involving Educational Technology: Creating motivating learning through game design and teacher competence development in a hybrid synchronous video-mediated learning environment*. PhD thesis, Aalborg University.

Weitze, C.L. (2016c) 'Student learning-game designs: Emerging learning trajectories'. In Connolly, I.T. and Boyle, L. (eds), *Proceedings of the 10th European Conference on Games Based Learning: ECGBL 2016* (1 vol. no. 1, 756–64). The University of the West of Scotland: Academic Conferences and Publishing International.

Weitze, C.L. (forthcoming) *Learning and Design Processes in a Gamified Learning Design in which Students Create Curriculum-Based Digital Learning Games.* London: Sense Publishers.

Williams, L. (2013) 'Introducing computing in the UK: A creative response to government policy'. Paper presented at the Computational Thinking International Seminar, Seoul, South Korea, 6 December 2013.

Williams, L., Černochová, M., Demo, G.B. and Younie, S. (2014) 'A working model for teacher training in computing through the Literacy from Scratch project'. In Passey, D. and Tatnall, A. (eds) *Key Competencies in ICT and Informatics: Implications and issues for educational professionals and management: IFIP WG 3.4/3.7 International Conferences, KCICTP and ITEM 2014, Potsdam, Germany, July 1–4, 2014, Revised Selected Papers* (IFIP Advances in Information and Communication Technology 444). Heidelberg: Springer, 25–33.

Wing, J.M. (2006) 'Computational thinking'. *Communications of the ACM,* 49 (3), 33–5.

Wittgenstein, L. (1953) *Philosophical Investigations.* Oxford: Blackwell.

Part Three

Engaging learners
through technology

Engaging learners through technology

Kim Issroff

A recent advertisement talked about the values that underlie the provision of education at a new school near Cambridge. The school was described as an 'innovative, forward-facing school' and the advert recognized 'the critical interdependency of pedagogy, technology and the spatial environment for successful active learning'. The wording discussed active, student-centred learning and the design of the learning environment. The advert was for school furniture. The clear message was that having the right furniture can foster engagement and improve learning.

While there are significant differences between educators, researchers, policymakers and parents, one thing is clear and concerns all of them: they want to see active and engaged learners. And they all believe this can be achieved by the way in which the learning is structured. To actively engage students in learning is a challenge for all of us.

What do we mean when we discuss active and engaged learners? What should we expect to see when we walk into a learning environment? Do we want children sitting individually, deeply engaged in drawing a diagram on a worksheet? Or chatting vigorously to each other about the subject they are learning about? Or manipulating tools and materials to create something? And how do we know which of these are important?

Understanding the ways in which the learning context impacts on what is learnt is crucial to our understanding of the learning. The context is not just the environment and its physical and virtual equipment, but also the curriculum, the expectations, the tasks and the other people involved in the learning. You will remember that we considered this earlier in our discussions about context and its impact on learning in Chapter 1.3.

The three examples of research reported in the chapters in this section of the book each focus in very specific detail on one facet of a learning context: games, integrity and space. The first two chapters discuss issues when engagement may be problematic and there is a real risk of inappropriate behaviours and the development of undesirable human characteristics. The last chapter is focused on how to make learning contexts more engaging through the design of spaces and the curriculum.

Together these three chapters show how researchers have attempted to understand and evaluate different facets of the learning context. All the research discussed has a range of metrics for measuring the aspects of the learning context with which they are concerned.

In the first chapter, Rafael Marques de Albuquerque and Shaaron Ainsworth discuss the use of games. They directly address parents' and educators' concerns about engagement in games and the risks involved. They focus on concerns about aggression and the use of gender and racial stereotypes.

In the second chapter, Charles Crook discusses academic integrity, focusing on when engagement with digital media results in cheating. He discusses both expository and collaborative engagements and how the presence of technology impacts on cheating.

In the third chapter, Allison Allen and Richard Allen discuss the design of both physical and virtual learning spaces, with particular focus on flipped classrooms. They discuss research about spaces in relation to engagement and use a range of metrics to measure the learning.

Unintentional learning

Are digital games friends or foes?

Rafael Marques de Albuquerque and Shaaron Ainsworth

Introduction

Let's start with a scene from a typical family's life. It's a sunny Sunday afternoon and Anne hopes her 13-year-old son, Andy, will come with the rest of the family to the park. But he refuses, preferring to play *Warcraft III: Reign of chaos* (Blizzard Entertainment, 2002) instead. Anne is not a 'gamer' herself, but she has seen her son playing games like this frequently, and they seem to her both violent and rather pointless. She also heard someone on TV worrying about the addictive power of games and a friend told her video games are damaging children's minds. She is also afraid that her son will spend all day alone in his bedroom not doing his homework or socializing with his friends. But Andy could not disagree more. He tells her playing games helps you to be smarter and think faster as they provide complicated and engaging challenges to solve. He meets his friends online and they play together – how is that different from meeting up in the street? Isn't he allowed to have fun? It did not help Anne when she talked with Andy's teachers later that week as they also seem divided. While some advised her to severely restrict Andy's play, another planned to start an after-school club for creating videogames. Anne struggles with what to do for the best.

A concerned mum like Anne would probably enjoy watching a *Horizon* documentary such as 'Are video games really that bad?' (BBC, 2015a), where researchers explored in detail claims concerning the positive and negative influences of playing games. However, it is fair to say that documentaries such as these are an exception in the media, which not only is dominated by negative views of gaming (Whitton and Maclure, 2017), but seldom presents either positive or negative findings in a critical manner. For instance, in the article entitled 'Boy saves sister from moose attack using "World of Warcraft" knowledge' (Key, 2013), the journalist describes a Norwegian 12-year-old boy who apparently used combat strategies (such as taunting and playing dead) learnt in *World of Warcraft* (Blizzard Entertainment, 2004) to rescue his sister. Although such stories are intriguing and at least offer a more positive vision, they illustrate a somewhat naive understanding of how gaming can be good for players, which arguably makes the discussion even more problematic.

At this point in the twenty-first century the issue of whether videogames are good or bad for players interests a wide section of the community. Many parents seem to struggle with responsibilities around children's gaming (Steinkuehler, 2015). It is also reasonable to expect that the influences of gaming are important to players themselves, both adults and underage players. Finally, this question is of interest to teachers and other educators. Games are seen in schools in many ways, in class, for homework, or as the central purpose of after-school clubs, but they are also commonly a reason to ban mobile devices from entering the classroom.

Consequently, this chapter aims to provide a concise summary of what the research says about the matter, with the aim of helping all of the parties described above with an opportunity to enrich their discussions with insights from research. We restrict our analysis to commercial entertainment games, leaving the field of educational games for another day. Consequently, the next section presents some of the most frequently considered issues in academia. Then we problematize some of the conclusions we can take based on this research, in order to present a critical perspective of how we can translate research findings into concrete decisions and actions.

What would we rather NOT learn by playing games?
Violent behaviours
It is sometimes argued that digital gaming provides a crucible for intense learning. Many games are very complex, and in order to play them well players have much to learn about the game itself, and so games (and gaming communities) employ a variety of strategies to instruct players about how to play. However, there is also much that players can learn from games that is not intentional (i.e. was not designed for by the game designer), and some of this unintentional learning is, in general, considered very undesirable. Here we will address three of these possible consequences: violence and aggression, gender stereotyping and racial stereotyping.

The topic of violence in games is probably one of the most frequently addressed. Many digital games have narratives based on violence in which players are requested to use violence to solve the challenges, and in some games the resulting depictions can be particularly graphic. The main concern, both now and over the last decades, is that by interacting with violent games players will become more aggressive, perhaps to the point of committing serious crimes. When shooting tragedies happen, this topic tends to reappear in the popular media. For example, consider the response to the tragic Columbine massacre in 1999, which left two students killed and many more injured in their school. But does the research evidence support this concern?

On the one hand, researchers have conducted experiments and longitudinal studies concerning violent video games and found that their players expressed more aggressive emotions, behaviours and thoughts, leading Anderson *et al.* (2010) to conclude on the basis of their meta-analysis that this connection is undeniable. Other researchers criticize the methods typically employed in such studies, arguing that laboratory tests used to measure aggression are too flawed and artificial to support such generalized conclusions (Ritter and Eslea, 2005). Yet others suggest a more nuanced response; for example, finding that although some players get more aggressive, some become less aggressive, and others are unaffected, depending both upon players' psychological traits and how they were feeling when they began to play (Unsworth *et al.*, 2007). Moreover, it is not clear what in games might influence aggressive responses. Some argue it is the competition in games rather than the depictions of violence (Adachi and Willoughby, 2011). Furthermore, the size of the effect is unclear with some researchers suggesting that even if violent gaming is a determining factor in youth violence, the real world impact is minor and that youth violence has decreased in recent years as violent game sales have increased (Ferguson, 2015). What is clear is that digital games, whether they are inclined to increase aggression in players or not, should not be the sole focus of a media preoccupied by finding a single simple cause for a horrific event. Moreover, they should certainly not become a strategy to distract the wider public from other relevant problems, such as the relationship between gun availability and violent crime. At this point research is still mixed but there seems little to be gained from ignoring age ratings for games, to ensure that younger children are not exposed to computer violence. We hope that discussion can become more about what is a reasonable degree of worry, and what steps can be taken to ensure that young people are not exposed to an unproblematized series of graphically depicted aggressive actions that results in players experiencing positive consequences within the gaming world. Age ratings might not be perfect, but advancing this discussion will hopefully help these ratings to become increasingly realistic and helpful to parents and guardians.

Unwelcome stereotypes

Another unintended lesson that players may be learning from games, which we wish they were not, is unwelcome stereotypes. For example, the question of whether negative representations of race and gender can affect how players see women and non-white people (Dill *et al.*, 2008). Unfortunately, gaming culture is infamous for being misogynistic, and it is argued that this is true both by what is represented within games and among player communities. The game industry as a whole is accused of not representing leading female characters enough, and for using many stereotypical, sexualized and/or misogynistic representations. One of the most notorious games in this respect is *Grand Theft Auto V* – Rockstar, 2013 – with its explicit scenes of the protagonist killing of female prostitutes. However, sexualization and objectification of women is pervasive and presented in games with a much more innocent marketing tone and intended audience; for example, when female characters are disempowered and depend on male heroes to save them such as Princess Peach needing Mario in *Super Mario Galaxy* – Nintendo, 2007. When the media critic Anita Sarkeesian produced an online series pointing this out called *Tropes vs. Women in Video Games*, she became one of the most hated personalities within part of the game community, frequently abused online and receiving many death threats (Feminist Frequency, 2009, YouTube channel, available at https://www.youtube.com/user/feministfrequency; accessed May 2016). It is not surprising therefore that in some online gaming environments female players – who are a minority among the fans of many game titles – prefer to hide their gender, fearing such harassment.

Similarly, games are also accused of conveying racist representations. For example, black people are frequently portrayed as criminals, thugs or athletes. It is symptomatic that one of the few widely popular games that portrays a black protagonist is *Grand Theft Auto: San Andreas* – Rockstar, 2004 – from a game series the theme of which is centred on crime. Games became more even more infamous in this regard after other titles raised racial controversy, such as *Resident Evil 5* – Capcom, 2009 – which was criticized for portraying white protagonists slaying black zombies in an African village.

Clearly, problematic representations of race and gender are not unique to digital games. In a 'census' of game characters, researchers found that compared to television, ethnic minorities are not particularly underrepresented, but are stereotyped. However, in the case of female characters, they are both largely underrepresented when compared to television, as well as being stereotyped (Williams *et al.*, 2009). It could be argued that digital games have had less time to develop as an artistic and cultural phenomenon than television and cinema, and that changes are slowly occurring in the game industry that will make it more inclusive. However, this must be tempered by the fact that games have come to the fore at a time when racial and sexual discrimination is no longer legal or officially tolerated. In 2014, the debate heightened between conservative players (who became known as #*GamerGate* supporters) and progressive voices (who supported female designers and journalists who suffered sexist attacks). An optimistic view on the episode would suggest that the game community is beginning to take issues of representation more seriously, but sadly this is not without resistance. Finally, it should be remembered that not all games depict stereotypes and/or violence, and careful players can find more inclusive representations if they so wish.

What do we HOPE we are learning by playing games?

Less pessimistic scholars have suggested that by gaming, players are also learning useful skills, abilities and attitudes, even when they play commercial games that were not explicitly designed to teach.

In experimental research, players' specific skills are measured before they play a game, then they play in a controlled environment for a specific time, and finally the same skill is measured again at the end to assess whether the skill has improved. Typical skills that have been addressed and claimed to improve are: spatial resolution and visual performance (Spence and Feng, 2010), cognitive speed of processing with no decrease in accuracy (Dye *et al.*, 2009a), attention skills (Dye *et al.*, 2009b), evidence-based decision making (Green *et al.*, 2010) and working memory (Kühn *et al.*, 2014). Additionally, outside these more cognitive skills and in contrast to the research on games and violence, scholars have found that certain social games can encourage pro-social behaviour (Gentile *et al.*, 2009). Other scholars have considered naturally occurring game play through observation, interview and analysis of the games played and the online community interaction – and pointed out a variety of skills that are used in games. For instance, scholars have suggested that some games require players to practise collaborative skills (MacCallum-Stewart, 2011), leadership (Jang and Ryu, 2011), literacy (Marsh, 2011), scientific habits of mind (Steinkuehler and Duncan, 2008), and ethical decision making (Simkins and Steinkuehler, 2008). A fundamental assumption of the benefits of gaming is that a skill developed and refined in the game environment can be transferred to another environment outside the game. At this time, the extent to which this assumption can be met is unclear, as skills employed in games are often very specific to those games. However, this research reminds us that although gaming can sometimes be seen as isolated from other activities, in fact players are being challenged by games and responding to them by employing a variety of skills that are, perhaps, being transferred to other spheres of their lives.

Another aspect of learning associated with commercial games is tangential learning whereby players become curious about a theme found in a game resulting in searching for and learning from external sources that discuss it. For example, a player becomes intrigued by a game set in Ancient Egypt and so later searches for and reads an article about Cleopatra and then the wars of the Roman Republic. Although research in this area is only just beginning and so we don't know how common or successful a practice this is, studies have found that players describe it as one of the ways they learn from gaming (Iacovides *et al.*, 2014).

What does this mean for us?

Among the myriad claims and counterclaims, sometimes it can be difficult to make sense of what are the desired and undesired aspects of learning enabled by gaming. In the following section of this chapter we outline two principles that provide a way to navigate these turbulent waters.

Games are very diverse and so are their influences upon players

It is important to keep in mind, when talking about the influence of playing games, that when the term 'digital game' is used as a singular concept, it actually encompasses a large variety of games and modes of play. At least in part, a game's influence on a player will depend on what game the player chooses to play. To illustrate this, we can compare two games. *Diablo III* – Blizzard Entertainment, 2012 – is a game that allows the player to kill hundreds of monsters in the role of a hero or heroine, collect items, engage in a complex narrative and play online, either co-operatively or competitively. It allows players to create clans online and play with friends or strangers. It requires players to explore scenarios, judge the quality of magic items and be very skilled with the mouse and keyboard (or console). In order to finish the game players are required to play for many hours, probably in long sessions. Contrastingly, *Farmville* – Zynga, 2009 – allows the player to manage a virtual farm by purchasing crops, animals and other props, and interacting (normally co-operatively) with friends from the players' social network. There is an aesthetic element in designing your farm according to personal taste, and the pace of the game can be very slow. Although the game has no formal end (therefore can be played for a very long time), players are rewarded for accessing the game frequently (allowing intervals for the crops to grow), rather than spending a long time in one session.

When the two games are analysed, it is clear that the potential consequences of playing them differ greatly from one another. The cognitive processes involved are very different, the kind of socialization opportunities vary, the problems posed by each game have to be solved by completely different strategies, and even the schedule of play will probably be very different. Their themes, narratives and game mechanics contrast in almost every way. And analysing the game itself is only one aspect of players' gaming. For example, we could consider for how long people play: playing *Diablo III* for three hours every week is likely to have a different influence on a player compared to playing for 50 hours a week. Furthermore, although there is not as yet much research into this, styles of play can change a game's influence. For instance, one player of *Farmville* might focus on calmly creating a beautiful farm, while another might play to make a successful and rich farm, and compare it to the farms of others.

In summary, there are just too many possibilities encompassed in the term digital game to allow for simple unproblematized generalizations. A debate that hopes to be resolved by stating that playing games is either 'bad for you' or 'good for you' can never succeed. In most cases, the studies presented in this chapter were conducted focusing on one particular game played in a particular manner. Therefore, it might be better to try to be specific when discussing games, rather than trying to be too conclusive about the whole games category.

There are no simple answers, but there can be inquisitive minds

Although it is difficult for a player to be confident about the outcomes of playing a specific game in a specific manner, it is possible to use research findings to help inform choice. For instance, if a player is familiar with ideas – such as 'action games can decrease reaction time without loss of accuracy' – he or she could take this into account when playing games. So, if a game requires players to give accurate responses increasingly quickly, one might suspect playing the game would be more likely to result in such an outcome in the longer term than games without such pacing. However, in order to undertake this kind of judgement ideally one would need to be familiarized with the game to be analysed – by playing it, understanding the game culture that surrounds that game as well as being familiar with the debate around transfer of learning – so it is not an easy or superficial judgement to make.

One option to support a judgement might be to spend time learning and playing the game. Secondly, one could analyse the game critically, especially with regard to the consequences of playing; just by playing a game we may not always be conscious of the full consequences of playing it, for example games may not make us act aggressively but could influence our implicit aggression (Bluemke *et al.*, 2010).

Thirdly, enjoy the experience. As Andy asks in our introduction 'aren't I allowed to have fun?'. Digital games are designed mostly for entertainment, although normally gamers describe some periods of frustration too. However, many players may associate gaming with a waste of time, and so feel guilt. Furthermore, it's possible they may limit the potential positive consequences of gaming by not engaging with 'such a waste of time'. Perhaps it's a good idea to accept the challenge the game is posing for you, and allow yourself to make an effort and appreciate the rewards that can come from it, albeit in a way that does not take over all of your life.

If we, as learners, teachers or parents, are able to acknowledge that the media misinformation regarding digital games and the consequences of playing them is out of proportion to the actual concern, then we may engage more with gaming. Consequently, communication between players and non-players (or should it be less frequent players?) will be more fruitful, because both sides have experiential knowledge of what digital gaming can be about.

A balanced view

Research suggests that playing games has consequences for players, but then so does everything we do as a hobby: the magazines we read, the sports we watch, the guitar solo we play. We shape ourselves continuously by the activities in which we engage. This may seem an obvious point, but it is hard to avoid the impression that gaming has an especially strong influence on players. It can be portrayed as an addictive 'drug' that will ruin lives, or a magic medicine that will immediately and immeasurably boost our intelligence, rather than simply another activity with which we can engage, in more or less healthy ways. Should we judge all gardening as evil if you put your back out while weeding or participate a little too enthusiastically in competitions to grow the biggest marrow? Similarly, despite our argument concerning the importance of thinking about the consequences of gaming, we would still argue that the most important reason to play a game is that it allows the player and their friends to have fun.

Games – as with other activities such as drawing, watching movies or visiting museums – can be effective pedagogical methods. But the case of games seems to generate stronger (negative) reactions in teachers and parents than these others. Would it be better to acknowledge that playing games in schools for educational purposes is very different from playing games at home, for entertainment only? Whatever view one has of what digital games mean to the society as a whole – either as a danger, a blessing, or something in between – how much should this view influence how we see games in education? So even if one believes games are harmful in general, they can be fruitful in the classroom if well-chosen and supported. And even if one believes games are a great medium for people in general, focused educational games have to be designed and supported in an effective way so they are not merely a superficial – and perhaps even ineffective – method (Habgood and Ainsworth, 2011).

We have the power to analyse games critically, and take action in order to transform game practices into positive, healthy ones. For instance, as an example of a model parents or educators might emulate, Marques de Albuquerque (2016) created a short course to encourage young people to reflect critically about gaming and its positive and negative consequences. For the time being though, let's suggest that our fictional character Anne should pay attention to suggested age ratings of games and ensure Andy is also engaging in other activities, but that Andy can be allowed this afternoon in his bedroom playing with his friends online. And if he chooses the right games and plays them in a reflective manner then maybe he is not only just having fun.

Engagement with games clearly causes concerns, which all stakeholders need to consider when thinking about the value of gaming. Cheating is also a common concern around the use of digital media, and in the next chapter in this part, Charles Crook explores cheating in more detail.

Issues of academic integrity and cheating in digital learning and assessment

Charles Crook

Introduction

In many areas of cultural practice, reference to 'integrity' can arouse feelings of anxiety. Practitioners may wonder: 'Is my own practice at a high standard?' or even 'Do I actually recognize those areas in which high standards are expected?' Education is one domain within which matters of integrity are scrutinized and debated – while students are often those with the greatest feelings of anxiety about doing the proper thing.

'Academic integrity' is a topic that now boasts its own Handbooks (Bretag, 2016; Velliaris, 2017) and to which whole journals are devoted, such as the *Journal of Academic Ethics* and the *International Journal for Educational Integrity*. There is even a MOOC on the topic (www. futurelearn.com/courses/academic-integrity). For anxious educators, browsing these sources reveals the issues of academic integrity that are judged by the community to be most urgent. These turn out to be: research ethics, journal review processes, institutional marketing, external influences on curricula, community partnerships, staff–student relationships and teaching evaluation procedures. However, by far the greatest volume of research-led scrutiny and debate is directed towards a set of issues that together might, in the vernacular, be termed 'student cheating'. And within that category plagiarism is the biggest single topic.

This chapter, in the 'engaging learners' section of the book, considers how the growth of digital media relates to practices of cheating by students. Managing this theme of academic integrity attracts several slippery concepts: notably, 'ownership', 'honesty' and 'authenticity'. Matters of *ownership* arise in relation to the products of student learning – the things that get assessed. Here the reader or examiner will ask if submitted work is the unique voice of its author and, therefore, whether any grade awarded to the student who submitted it offers a useful indication of what that student knows. Matters of *honesty* then concern the transparency of an author in relation to how such work is presented. Finally, *'authenticity'* becomes an evaluative adjective applicable to work that is being judged in these ownership terms. Yet authenticity is a troublesome descriptor. The student must reconcile institutional beliefs that all scholars are 'standing on the shoulders of giants' with institutional imperatives that students should strive for authorial ownership. Moreover, some teachers of these students may have their own postmodern doubts about the validity of the concept of an autonomous 'author' (Howard, 1999). Still others may add confusion by encouraging assignment composition that involves the *intentional* blending of already-existing voices – as in the cases of transmedia (Jenkins, 2010) and remix (Lessig, 2008) initiatives.

To review this dimension of academic integrity – and relate it to ubiquitous digital media – the discussion here will consider the learning practices of students under two headings: two varieties of student engagement that involve digital media. First, students may engage with *expository* material. Traditionally, this would be either disciplinary texts (books, videos, etc.) or teachers' classroom 'performance' of their discipline (lectures, etc.). Second, students may engage in *collaborations*. That is, they learn from conversation with others (peers, tutors, family, etc.). There is, of course, a third mode of engaging with a discipline. That is, through actively exploring that discipline's material resources (using tools, observing places of work, etc.). However, those study practices do not raise such clear integrity issues for students.

Tensions of academic integrity that do arise in both expository and collaborative contexts will be noted below in the next two sections of this chapter. Then, in the final part of the chapter, consideration will be given to important conceptual themes. These emerge from within contemporary thinking about teaching and learning and exert an overarching influence on the integrity tensions under discussion here.

Integrity issues around students' engagement with expository material

A great deal of student learning involves this form of engagement. The study material involved may be traditional educational texts but it may be expository material that was not explicitly designed to be 'teaching' in format (journal articles, datasets, for example) and it may be material that is in a variety of presentational formats (infographics, videos, for example). Increasingly, this implies that expository practices will be encountered in digital media.

A central characteristic of expository learning is that the student engages autonomously with such sources. They make choices among them and selections within them – all to guide their building of new knowledge. That knowledge may often be motivated by an assignment or the need to create a shareable product. Naturally, the resulting assignment will be based upon the sources that a student has sought and studied. The tension here arises over how (or whether) that dependency is acknowledged and articulated. Plagiarism can take many forms and, accordingly, can be judged to manifest varying degrees of seriousness. Software that strives to detect it – to support the judgement of seriousness – has been welcomed by educational institutions. Both the market leader for these tools (Turnitin, 2012) and, independently, Alzahrani *et al.* (2012), have published taxonomies of plagiarism. Both identify ten varieties – a continuum of apparent severity. In short, plagiarism is not, therefore, an easy violation of integrity to judge.

Students finding dishonest solutions to the demands of their study is a practice much older than digital technologies. Many researchers have stressed that cheating has a long history at all educational levels. McCabe and colleagues have documented this over a considerable period for American students (McCabe *et al.*, 2012). Yeo (2007) notes in her review that the extent of cheating is likely to be greater than that detected. It has been found to be commonplace in secondary education (Jensen *et al.*, 2002). Even MOOCs have attracted cheating (Northcutt *et al.*, 2016) – as, presumably, achievements on these self-regulated learning initiatives start to acquire recognized status through certification.

Does digital media encourage dishonest study?

Has technology therefore simply aggravated an established problem? A most digitally distinctive form of academic dishonesty is cut-and-paste plagiarism. The practice is linked to the widespread availability of digital texts, yet it is hard to judge whether they have *increased* rates of plagiarism. After all, the same technology has furnished detection services and these may have simply exposed a level of cheating previously concealed. On the other hand, detection may also have *deterred* plagiarizing. Or perhaps it has pushed it further underground as 'patchwriting' (cosmetically adjusted plagiarized text). The situation is difficult to diagnose and it is clearly in flux – as detection algorithms become ever more sensitive (Alzahrani *et al.*, 2012).

However, it is not just enhanced detection complicating any consideration of digital impact. Many other factors in the environment of studying (as well as the constituency of students) have changed in recent years: all making the impact of technology on plagiarism hard to judge. Selwyn (2008) and Szabo and Underwood (2004) both present data indicating that digital plagiarizers had previously also plagiarized from *written* sources. However, as Kauffman and Young (2015) argue (and to some extent demonstrate) working with digital sources may create a potent opportunity: '(c)heating is not the implementation of a premeditated cheat-plan, but instead results through interactions on-the-fly as the writer proceeds on a trajectory toward their goal, guided by their perceptions' (46). In other words, the context of digital study space seems to 'invite' it.

Estimates of the extent to which students engage in this digital copy/ paste practice vary considerably. Moreover, as with many empirical studies of plagiarism, conclusions depend on self-reporting methods with students, who may be anonymous, but who may still be unsure as to what defines the offence (Risquez *et al.*, 2013). At one extreme, Chang *et al.* (2015) find that only 2.8 per cent (of school students in Taiwan) report cheating as something done 'frequently'. While Selwyn (2008) reports that 62 per cent of UK undergraduates admit some form of online plagiarism during the previous 12 months. Such a wide range of estimates must surely reflect variations in research procedure: the different forms of interrogation, the respondents' confidence in their anonymity, the local institutional culture, and many other such contextual factors. However, when browsing a range of studies on self-reported copy/paste plagiarism, one commonly finds that the number of students who admit to having done this lies at around 40–50 per cent (e.g., Ellery, 2008; Ma *et al.*, 2007; Sisti, 2007; Stogner, Miller and Marcum, 2013; Szabo and Underwood, 2004). Selwyn (2008: 476) summarizes his survey of UK undergraduates by noting: 'Our data have found a majority of students reporting instances of copying non-attributed sentences and lines of material into their own assignments, with around one-quarter of students doing so at the more sustained level of copying paragraphs or pages of material.'

In summary, breeches of integrity seem deeply rooted in the domain of studying – as they are in other areas of cultural life. Copy/ paste plagiarism has not, therefore, invented this problem. Neither is it the only way in which digital media invite academic dishonesty. While the authoring of assignment and project work may be particularly vulnerable to its influence, Dawson (2016) highlights other contexts of concern. In particular, the various ways in which personal digital devices can bypass the constraints associated with traditional examinations – an important caution given suggestions that such examinations are plagiarism-resistant alternatives to assignment-based assessment (http://theconversation.com/more-exams-the-way-to-beat-cheats-buying-contract-essays-32399).

Some researchers have attempted to link this family of practices to demographic and individual differences variables, gender being the most often discussed. Where such differences are reported (and they are not always found), then they reliably indicate that male students are more prone to plagiarism. Cultural factors are also invoked – particularly when individuals are studying outside of their native culture. This is often linked to coping with unfamiliar practices of study. However, unfamiliar language alone may be a factor, because recent research shows how moral decisions can be made differently when issues are presented in a second language (Corey *et al.*, 2017).

With its emphasis on quantifying the self-reported occurrences of copy/paste plagiarism, research may be just scratching a surface. Mechanically lifting text from some source to your own page is merely one extreme on a continuum of engaging with sources – albeit the least useful extreme. This continuum needs to be better understood. Research should explore how students' access to extensive, ubiquitous and plastic text shapes the depth and patterning of their cognitive engagement with its ideas. Research might aim to capture such a dynamic as it is in progress. We need a closer understanding of how the student's ongoing processes of translation and transcription are exercised in the new and rich spaces of digital media.

How is digital plagiarism rationalized?

The temptation to plagiarize may be independent of whether the media is digital or print, yet judgement of its appropriateness may not be. Some researchers (e.g. Poole, 2007) have suggested that young people are more accepting of a whole range of unethical conduct when it involves digital technologies – compared to when the same offences occur in the 'offline world'. Accordingly, several researchers have reported students as more tolerant of plagiarism that is based on digital rather than print material. Ellery (2008), in questioning self-reported frequent plagiarizers, finds that many of them provide in-text citations for print sources but not for electronic sources. These students argue that the Internet is different: it is 'open', public domain and therefore it is 'for everyone'. Other researchers describe undergraduate students as saying Internet plagiarism is 'less dishonest' (Baruchson-Arbib and Yaari, 2004). High school students may declare a sense of excitement around finding short-cutting material on the Internet (Ma *et al.*, 2007). This echoes findings that such dishonesty need not necessarily generate such negative emotions as guilt – often the opposite response is reported, as a kind of 'cheaters' high' (Ruedy *et al.*, 2013).

However, student judgement in this area can be more nuanced. In close conversation with 25 high school students, Kolikant (2010) reports a different perception of digital resources: 'Almost half of the students interviewed (48 per cent), judged their partnership with the Internet as dis-empowering. The Internet was thought to make schooling too easy, exempting students from the need to "really" study' (1388). Ma *et al.* (2007) reinforce this concern in reporting that nearly one-third of their 36 high school students admitted that they had gone online to get solutions for homework without actually digesting the information. Ellery (2008) makes the same point differently: while 79 per cent of their sampled undergraduate students always wrote personal notes when working from print books, only 40 per cent said they wrote such notes when working from digital sources. Yet the taking of notes makes possible a deeper processing of the core information. Therefore, such depth of processing may be inhibited when working from digital sources. This is a possibility empirically demonstrated by Mueller and Oppenheimer (2014) when comparing the quality of paper note taking with laptop note taking.

In sum, the opportunities for knowledge building created by ubiquitous and extensive digital sources are indeed great. Yet this final observation above – relating source transcription to depth of study – identifies a wider range of researchable issues than just those associated with this context of lapses in academic integrity.

How should education respond?

If the inherently plastic and mobile nature of digital sources is affording too easy cut-and-paste plagiarism – what is to be done about it? Any consideration of repair must start from recognizing the loose grasp that students often have on the nature of the problem. When they are asked to talk about plagiarism they often reveal difficulty in recognizing what counts as a misdemeanour, or agreeing on its seriousness (Ellery, 2008; Gullifer and Tyson, 2010; Löfström; 2011; Park, 2003) – although this may vary across disciplines and cultures (Hayes and Introna, 2005). For example, Chang *et al.* (2015: 363) report that: 'Some students … admitted that they would copy and paste online texts because they were afraid of misusing the data or misinterpreting the original content.' Of course, such *interpretation* is exactly what assignment tasks are demanding.

These student uncertainties may lead to anxiety over plagiarism occurring by accident (Ashworth *et al.* 1997). Where it is clearly understood to have occurred, there remains a variety of views among students as to the seriousness of what they have done (Sutton *et al.*, 2014). As might be expected in this confusion, staff and students do not necessarily have a *common* view of the offence or its standing (Flint *et al.*, 2006). Consequently, any discourses of cheating employed by students do not always match well those employed by their institutions (Adam *et al.*, 2017).

The university sector, in particular, struggles to respond to the challenges involved in academic dishonesty. Coren (2011) reports findings in which almost half of academics polled admit to ignoring cases of plagiarism, while McGrail and McGrail (2015) find considerable variation across institutions in how cheating is defined and Gullifer and Tyson (2010), in a survey of 3,000 students, find that only half of them had ever read such policies. In tackling this issue, institutions increasingly wrap their assignment tasks up with various forms of warnings, or requirements to endorse honour codes. Yet it is not clear that these make very much impact. Corrigan-Gibbs *et al.* (2015) explored this with students taking online courses. These were assessed with an examination involving a mix of multiple choice questions and free text answer questions. Typical of online course assessment, the timed examination was taken online with no invigilation. However, a 'honey-pot' website had been created on the open Internet and it contained the questions and answers. Elaborate tracking revealed that a quarter of the 400 candidates cheated through Internet text search (despite its prohibition), either directly to the honey-pot or by conventional copy/paste plagiarism of text for their free format answers. Moreover, group contrasts showed that neither honour codes nor vigorous warnings made a great impact on the probability of such cheating.

However, it may be more constructive not to view cut-and-paste plagiarism as a self-contained and circumscribed problem. Such practices are the extreme point on a continuum of cognitive engagement with sources. What assignments must achieve is more than an avoidance of that lazy extreme, they need to inspire engagement that rests at the more probing and reflective points of the study continuum.

Integrity issues around students' engagement in collaboration

As with matters discussed in the previous section of this chapter, it is uncomfortable to be dwelling here on negative aspects of new technology for education, when that technology offers so many *positive* opportunities. In particular, such opportunities are most keenly apparent for the forms of communication that are connected with Web 2.0 – participatory practices online that stimulate the creation of learning communities, creative collaborations, and audiences for student work (Greenhow *et al.*, 2009; Stewart, 2015). Moreover, there is a further resonance here with discussion in the previous section of this chapter: namely that the threats to academic integrity to be considered below are not new, they have not been created by digital media. All the concerns to be discussed here have troubled previous generations of educators. In short, both opportunities and threats have always existed: digital tools have merely reconfigured their presence and reach.

Collaboration or collusion?

The communication that digital media allows can have a collaborative quality. That is, it can support the construction of shared knowledge through students' joint activity. Such collaborations are mediated by technology in three basic ways: learners interacting *at* technology, *around* technology or *through* technology (Crook, 1996). The first is the most familiar. Students can work synchronously at a shared digital device – such as is common in classrooms. On the other hand, interacting around technology is a looser form of this arrangement – such as is illustrated in the new library designs called 'learning commons' that create a collaborative 'social ambience' (Crook and Mitchell, 2012). It is interactions *through* technology that are potentially the most troublesome in terms of challenging academic integrity.

The Internet has created a rich environment for always-on communication. For students, digital media such as email or Skype allow exchanges typical of traditional communications. However, exchanges in new media may also mirror more *communal* structures: for example, through social media services such as Facebook or through a wide range of text discussion boards. Given the increasingly central place of social media in young people's informal communication, it would be surprising if students did not allow their 'classroom' experiences to find expression in these media. It might also be surprising if educators did not appropriate these social media into their teaching repertoire. Increasingly they do (Stewart, 2015). Moreover, young people regard the potential of these media for learning very positively (Mao, 2014). How far they pursue that potential as informal learning conversations with peers is less certain. Interviews with students suggest that it *can* function this way – at least through brief back-and-forth exchanges, if not through fully orchestrated but informal collaborative projects (Hrastinski and Aghaee, 2012). Generally, such exchanges might be regarded positively by teachers. On the other hand, Stöckelová and Virtová (2015) describe a website set up by disgruntled Czech students for more organized mutual support (including the exchange of scripts): this was an initiative that left their institution very uncomfortable about its potential to disturb the certainties of traditional assessment.

There is little research that reveals how far out-of-class assignments are tackled within these online social relationships. Although, at least for undergraduates, this way of working may not be so appealing. When students are questioned about the kind of collaboration and publishing that Web 2 practices make possible, they are most worried that their (social media published) ideas might be stolen by peers (Schroeder *et al.*, 2010; Sutton and Taylor, 2011). Their lecturers confirm this concern but also express a tension of their own – around the challenge of promoting collaboration among students while having to assess them as individuals (Waycott *et al.*, 2010).

Such uncertainties of ownership need not only arise from exchanges among peers and friends. They may be cultivated in less intimate forms of social contact, such as those made possible by 'social referencing' sites (Shachaf, 2010). Here, questions and answers are exchanged within an informal digital community. It is not unusual for homework questions to be submitted to such sites (Gazan, 2007) although research has not determined reliable estimates of how widely such resources are used in this manner. With such services as social referencing sites, it is clear that the ties between 'collaborating' partners have become very distant. There may still be a dialogue and it may even be warm but it is typically between the student and person or persons that exist within a diffuse community of relative strangers. In the next section of this chapter, we consider how this very loose coupling can mutate into an authoring relationship that seems no longer to justify the positive associations of the phrase 'collaborative understanding' but which represents its very dark side.

Can collaboration be commercialized?

Student plagiarism becomes commercialized when ideas dishonestly represented as a student's own have been uniquely provided for that student by another party. Although, to be more precise, they have been 'traded' rather than simply 'provided'. Because the distinctive feature of issues to be discussed here is that the appropriation of another's ideas are part of a business transaction. In short, the student is *outsourcing* the construction of their assignment to another author.

Again, the offence exists in a space of exchange with very blurred boundaries. There has always been a legitimate profession of individuals who offer support for the copy-editing or proofreading of text. The blurring arises from the *purpose* of a document being edited in this way. When its purpose is primarily to demonstrate a student's control of linguistic expression, then such outsourcing violates the trust of an assessor who is judging the student's confidence with language. However, it should be noted that the same outcome is achieved by the foreign language student who uses online and software-based translators for their assignments – turning their teacher into what Correa (2014) sorrowfully terms a 'forensic linguist'.

A second kind of boundary-blurring arises in relation to the *depth* to which such commercial consultation goes. For example, commissioning surface proofreading may be an innocent enough practice for a dissertation, but 'substantive editing' is not. Lines (2016a) reflects on these practices as she witnessed them while running a professional editing service: she was keenly aware of the extent to which postgraduate students seek such support and the extent to which many businesses seem willing to respond to it.

The final blurred boundary occurs in relation to the degree of *joint* involvement the partners in a co-authoring relationship agree to. At one extreme, the student may be merely seeking conversational exchanges with a confident disciplinary voice – a kind of private tutoring. At the other extreme, the confidence of that voice may be recruited to independently author an entire assignment. Individuals available for relationships at both extremes advertise this – and can readily recruit digital media to do so. In fact, the Internet has created structures whereby such freelancing individuals can make their availability more visible and their assignment trading more efficient (for instance, Amazon's Mechanical Turk at mturk.com, which is a marketplace service where people can buy and sell human skills). The range of services available have been tabulated and defined by Newton and Lang (2016).

To investigate this, Harris and Srinivasan (2012) acted as go-betweens for a fictional website ('homework assist') and recruited such crowdsourced workers with an invitation to author student assignments. Seventy-nine per cent of these workers were indifferent to the intended destination of their work and were thereby willing to be complicit in producing text to be submitted as homework or for an examination. Sivasubramaniam *et al.* (2016) have interviewed a number of such ghost writers to explore their motives. Often, they are qualified postgraduates who have failed to gain an academic post. They rationalize their work in terms of the helping students who they see as being under pressure from high fees, or poor language skills, or a lack of adequate support from their tutors.

Perhaps unsurprisingly the Internet has created an infrastructure to co-ordinate these freelance authors, with increasingly sophisticated processes for managing their work. Clarke and Lancaster (2007) coined the term 'contract cheating' to describe the practices associated with what are sometimes termed 'essay mills'. Lancaster and Clarke (2014) have monitored activity on sites that are easily tracked and focused on traffic from students taking online courses. They identified 17 different institutions whose students were using this service. The concern is not simply with the scale of their operation in the higher (and, increasingly, the secondary) education system (Lancaster and Clarke, 2014), but also with the fact that the quality of their 'products' are often good (Lines, 2016b). Moreover, turnaround on delivery can be so quick that the educators who shorten the time available for doing an assignment as a response is unlikely to be a deterrent (Wallace and Newton, 2014)

Such observations invite a cost-benefit perspective on student motives. Economic researchers who report on such decision making (in cheating simulations) were shocked by the willingness of students to outsource coursework (Rigby *et al.*, 2015). These authors comment: 'At a time when the university student is increasingly treated as a consumer demanding value for money it would appear that subcontracting some of the work required to achieve their degree is seen as a rational choice for many consumers on campus' (36). We see this literature as making the case for a firmer understanding of student practices and motives.

Theorizing a digital influence

The preceding two sections of this chapter presented a research review focused on issues of student academic integrity as they relate to new digital media. Such reviews may risk creating more fog than focus – at least if they represent the state of research only as a collection of isolated studies. Hopefully, within such a corpus, readers may still find useful points of clarity or inspiration but, ideally, there should be a legacy of the assembly as a whole that offers some organizing and overarching themes: frameworks for viewing the landscape discussed.

In what follows I shall sketch just three frameworks that are suggested by the research corpus assembled here and which may provide useful windows for finding a perspective on our central topic.

Contrasting student inquiry in and out of school

Inquiry and discovery activities outside of school have always been possible for young people. But the scale and accessibility of traditional media (libraries, museums, personal correspondence, for example) have been greatly surpassed by digital technologies. Yet new media present their own challenges to young researchers. Much has been made of students' limited strategies for Internet *searching* (e.g. Kuiper *et al.*, 2005). However, commentators have also drawn attention to a wider problem: this arises from the different norms and practices that characterize informal Internet research versus formal (schooled) Internet research (Zhang, 2009). While it is encouraging that so many young people use digital media to pose and pursue topics of interest to them, the fabric of such 'recreational' research activity may be very different from that typical of schooled research. Indeed, some authors have constructed tables that contrast formal and informal research practices in relation to a range of criteria – goals, collaborations, dissemination, etc. (Crook, 2012; Kimmerle *et al.*, 2015).

One way of characterizing the contrast between personal research out of school (Internet mediated) may be in terms of goals. Unlike schooled projects, more recreational research is likely to be driven by finding a singular and satisfactory answer – rather than pursuing a particular research method or feeling any responsibility to be accountable for that method. As digital media increasingly become the inquiry context for research both in school and out, then it might be expected that the more casual attitude to method natural for out of school research could (unhelpfully perhaps) be appropriated into classroom tasks.

Another possible contrast of the inquiry context relates to the format in which goals or discoveries are often presented out of school. Digital tools have encouraged inquiry practices that are sometimes termed 'curation' (http://mashable.com/2010/05/03/content-curation-creation/). That is, fragments of media relevant to the topic under research are assembled and configured into a personal perspective. Evidently, such assembling practices imported into classroom inquiry could sometimes be understood as a version of plagiarism. The fact that digital curation is so familiar in out-of-school creative activity (for example mashups) again generates tensions when the same media is recruited for school inquiry. Such tensions are heightened for teachers because there are compelling arguments that celebrate this curating format as legitimate for schooled inquiry (Lessig, 2008; Potter, 2012).

The socialization of knowledge and knowing

Theories addressing human learning and cognition have taken a 'social turn'. To which some might argue: '... of course learning is *social* – isn't *knowledge* constructed in social life and doesn't *learning* take place within our communication with other people?' However, a 'social turn' involves a radical re-calibration of theory, such as to make social forces central to an understanding of knowledge, knowing and learning. This trend may be clarified by asking: 'What is the "turn" of theory turning *away* from?' To which the answer might be: 'Turning away from understanding the human mind in narrowly computational terms'. That is, questioning the principle that cognition and learning are processes entirely contained 'in the head' – and to be understood by probing only there. In short, this recalibration entails research questions shifting from 'what's inside the head?' towards 'what's the head inside of?'

This is conveniently consistent with messages from the world of work that urge educators to prepare learners for effective *team work*. Accordingly, tensions of academic integrity discussed above arise because of the blurred boundaries between productive collaboration and unwelcome collusion. So, the contemporary stress on the social construction of knowledge can be a source of confusion for students and their teachers.

The mediated nature of academic dishonesty

A popular metaphor for explaining the impact of new media on cognitive processes is 'amplification' (Bruner, 1965). Applying this metaphor, a digital tool might 'amplify' our mental capabilities. This seems an innocent enough way of talking. At least if it means that a tool allows some desired outcome to be more quickly or more frequently or more economically realized. However, the quantitative tone of 'amplification' distracts attention from a *qualitative* impact: one that is more about 'reconfiguring' what is done than 'strengthening' it. When a new technology is adopted into an existing practice (such as studying) it does not simply amplify what is done, it alters the structure of what is done. Theorists now tend to discuss this perspective by invoking a language of 'mediation'.

Accordingly, it would be argued that the core study practices of learners have not altered in kind over time. The influence of digital media is to shift the balance and tools whereby they are conducted. One way in which this may be experienced is in how the student relates to research sources. That so much of such material is in the same digital medium and, moreover, that it exists in such an accessible and plastic form must create a distinctive dynamic between 'reader' and research source. One consequence may be a degree of confusion in the student's mind as to whether and how to use the voice of other authors.

Concluding comments

This short review has discussed the relation of pervasive digital media to challenges of academic integrity that confront learners. Attention has been focused on the topic of dishonesty arising from traditional plagiarism and from unwarranted collusion. Important points to arise from this review are the following:

- Dishonesty around study practices remains widespread among students.
- A prominent form of dishonesty is centred on misrepresenting the ownership of submitted text.
- Yet student understanding of digital plagiarism offences is often limited.
- Digital media do not create these practices but do offer distinctive opportunities for them.
- Software detection tools are increasingly the way in which these problems are confronted.
- Honour codes and vigorous warnings may have only limited impact.
- Digital sources may be less often acknowledged by student authors than print sources.
- Internet communication offers students a wide range of services for informal sharing, exchange and support in relation to assignments.
- These services include freelance authors who are often casual about the destination of their commissions.
- Such authors are increasingly co-ordinated by overarching websites using a sophisticated business model and its tools.
- The degree of engagement with these services is poorly monitored but appears to be extensive.
- How do deal with 'contract cheating' is rarely discussed in any sector of education.
- Practices typical of recreational Internet inquiry may be innocently but unhelpfully imported by students as methods for schooled research.

Prevention may partly rest on research that equips individual teachers with a better sense of how students study with new media. In particular, to understand the micro-structure of engagement with digital sources: searching, selecting, abstracting, integrating, critiquing, extending and, finally, communicating them in a distinctive voice. Lapses of integrity may arise less from students' intention to avoid these challenges and more from a poor understanding of how to master them. Teachers see and judge the *products* of study but the *processes* are hidden from them. Micro-structural research that reveals more of such processes may help teachers understand the cognitive and affective challenges of student inquiry in digital media and, thereby, offer richer and more realistic support. Such understanding should become a research priority.

Improving learning through engaging spaces

Allison Allen and Richard Allen

> *Environments that provide experience, stimulate the senses, encourage the exchange of information, and offer opportunities for rehearsal, feedback, application, and transfer are most likely to support learning.*
>
> (Chism, 2006)

Introduction: Why consider learning spaces?

When asked, most people feel that the design of the spaces in which we live and work makes a difference to how we feel and may affect how well we perform activities. This perception has not been supported until now by a strong or actionable evidence base, leading the Education Endowment Foundation (Higgins *et al.*, 2014) to note in its influential review of factors affecting pupils' learning how limited the research was in this area and to conclude that: 'changes to the physical environment of schools are unlikely to have a direct effect on learning beyond the extremes'.

Recent research (Tanner, 2009; Mazuch, 2013; Barrett *et al.*, 2015; Heppell, 2016a; 2016b) suggests that learning spaces have surprisingly powerful effects on learning and yet teachers are rarely given the chance, much less the funding, to design them. Vicki Phillips, of the Bill and Melinda Gates Foundation, commented in 2015 that technology can bring teachers and students closer together, but that teachers often have little or no input into the design process of learning spaces, the functionality of which should support teachers and learners using emerging technologies and evolving pedagogical strategies.

The term 'learning space' suggests place and environment – a school, a classroom, a library – and much Third Millennium learning (Naace, n.d. b) takes place in such physical locations. But in our connected and technology-rich world, a learning space can also be virtual, online and remote. Schools are beginning to think of Third Millennium learning spaces that support the conditions that optimize learning systems including personal needs, and support positive, collaborative learning.

Planning learning spaces is complex – where this process used to involve providing places for quiet, individual concentration, today it means creating more places that accommodate a wide range of activities, technologies, and participants – both physically and virtually. In these spaces, learners need to be able to create, retrieve, combine, display, share and collaborate on information, repeating the process over again as needed, in a space that they can easily remodel and that is well supported by staff who meet and anticipate their needs.

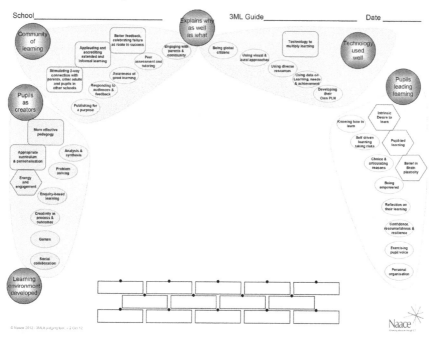

Figure 3.3.1: Naace: Third Millennium Award Judging Tool. Copyright Naace 2012. Reprinted with permission.

Physical learning spaces

> *Architectural embodiments of educational philosophies.*
> (Monahan, 2002)

We are in an era when the school curriculum is changing. High stakes assessment is the focus of teachers, and pedagogy is under close scrutiny, with the government funding activities to encourage a return to whole-class teaching (DfE, 2016). There is apparent dissatisfaction among ministers at the attainment of learners in the United Kingdom (BBC, 2015b) and yet, aside from teaching and learning, other potential factors are ignored; for example, research undertaken by Royal Institute of British Architects (RIBA) in 2014, found that 80 per cent of schools are operating beyond their life cycle – suggesting that the majority of our schools are unable to provide effective learning environments as they are past their best, or at worst not fit for purpose. The same research found that schools built now are 15 per cent smaller than those built under the Building Schools for the Future programme that was abandoned in 2010 (BBC, 2011).

With heavy demands for education a century ago, schools were built to deliberately mimic the industrial designs that had transformed the workplace. According to the historians Tyack and Cuban (1995), this factory approach to schooling has been remarkably long-lasting; children enter school at the same age, are sorted into age-based grades, exposed to standardized curricula, textbooks and resources, assessed at fixed points, and expected to progress at the same rate as their peers. Even now, many school buildings and classrooms with their rows of seats resemble the factories they were built to emulate.

Torin Monahan (2002) describes educational architecture literature as grounded in a conviction that the design of built spaces influences the behaviours and actions of individuals within those spaces. He calls such architectural embodiments of educational philosophies '*built pedagogy*'. To a certain extent, these spaces embody the pedagogical philosophies of their designers:

> Designs for classrooms not only tell us much about the didactic means that were used in them; they also reveal the essence of the pedagogy that directed the educative efforts of past times. (McClintock and McClintock, 1970: 2)

This passage, in Monahan's view, implies that a trained eye can read these spaces for the pedagogies they facilitate: a classroom with neat rows of desks embodies pedagogies of discipline and conformity, whereas spaces personifying flexible properties can be said to embody pedagogies of freedom and self-discovery.

Teachers in a large survey (Association of Teachers and Lecturers, 2010) were almost unanimous in believing that the school's learning environment had an effect on pupil behaviour and more than a quarter felt the environment was not effective. Professor Stephen Heppell's research (2014; 2016a; 2016b) confirms that – poor light levels, the wrong temperatures, inappropriate sound volumes and rhythms, humidity, air pollution, CO_2 and air pressure can all impair learning; he argues that his results show how these conditions can unfairly skew the outcome of children's work because the environment they are in is damaging to their performance. Yet there remains a gap between research on internal environment quality (IEQ) that focuses on such measurable aspects of heat, light, sound and air quality; and more quantitative aspects such as Ulrich's (1984) evidence of the positive healing effects of views of nature in the hospital environment, and understanding the holistic effects of environments on people.

These ideas are not new; the Roman architect Marcus Vitruvius Pollio in his treatise on architecture, De Architectura (Vitruvius, 2006), asserted that there were three principles of good architecture:

- Firmatis (durability) – it should stand up robustly and remain in good condition.
- Utilitas (utility) – it should be useful and function well for the people using it.
- Venustas (beauty) – it should delight people and raise their spirits.

Few of us would challenge the Vitruvian principles; school buildings should be fit for purpose and should work (utility); they should be well built and sustainable (durability); and they should have an impact on the human sensory experience (delight). The value of design in this context is often misunderstood, and people see only the aesthetic, without considering function. In point of fact, the three criteria are entwined within the design process and disregard of all three in balance leads to poor results – frequently (but understandably) school design is often focused on 'function' with consequent loss of learner experience and feeling of wellbeing.

Rooted in the child-centred philosophy of John Dewey (1902), current educational research and broader thinking about learner achievement add urgency. In America, the Whole Child initiative (ASCD, 2017) has been established, encouraging schools and communities to work together to create learning environments that enable children to be healthy, safe, engaged, supported and challenged.

Without the scale of investment such as Building Schools for the Future (BBC, 2011), it is still possible for schools to have inspiring learning environments enhancing learning, teaching and wellbeing. Research by Professor Peter Barrett at the University of Salford (Barrett *et al.*, 2015) found that if an average learner moved from the least effective to the most effective learning environment, their attainment could increase by 1.3 sub-levels (National Curriculum levels converted to NC points) which is surprising when teachers expect children to progress by two sub-levels a year overall.

> The single most important finding reported here, is that there is clear evidence that the physical characteristics of primary schools do impact on pupils' learning progress in reading, writing and

mathematics. This impact is quite large, scaling at explaining 16 per cent of the variation in the overall progress over a year of the 3,766 pupils included in the study. By fixing all factors to their mean scores, except the physical environment factors, the impact of moving an 'average' child from the least effective to the most effective classroom has been modelled at around 1.3 sub-levels, a big impact when pupils typically make two sub-levels progress a year. As far as we are aware, this is the first time that clear evidence of the effect on users of the overall design of the physical learning space has been isolated in real life situations. (Barrett *et al.*, 2015)

Barrett's research found that whole-school factors such as size, navigation routes, specialist facilities and play facilities do not seem to be as important as the design of the individual classrooms. This point is reinforced by evidence that schools often have a mix of more and less effective classrooms in the same school. The significant point is that each classroom must be well designed. Subsequently, a positive finding is that users (teachers) can affect many of the factors, and suggestions show that small changes, costing very little or nothing, can make a real difference – examples include changing the layout of the room, the choices of display, or colour of the walls.

Three types of physical characteristic of the classrooms were assessed: Stimulation, Individualization and Naturalness – the 'SIN' design principles. The factors Barrett found to be particularly influential are:

- Naturalness: light, temperature and air quality – accounting for half the learning impact.
- Individualization: ownership and flexibility – accounting for about a quarter.
- (Appropriate) Stimulation: complexity and colour – again about a quarter.

Barrett quotes Tanner (2009) whose survey of 71 US elementary schools examined the impact of natural light and sources of artificial light in classrooms. The results provided evidence that good lighting significantly influences reading vocabulary and science test scores.

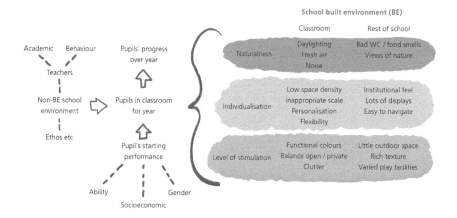

Figure 3.3.2: Organising Conceptual Model (SIN) adapted with permission from Barrett *et al.*, 2015

This approach places the individual at the centre of the analysis between non-built environment factors to the left, such as the effect of teachers, and, to the right, the built/physical features of the school environment. Structured into axes then, there is a vertical flow from the pupil's starting position academically, individual characteristics; time in the classroom; to their achievements, measured in terms of their academic improvement.

The University of Salford research builds on the concept of 'Sense Sensitive Design' (IBI Group, 2012), developed by Nightingale Associates in response to 12 years of extensive research that has shown that a range of built environmental characteristics can have powerful healing and therapeutic benefits. Explained by Richard Mazuch (2013), the design ideas are based on the way the body perceives and responds to sensory stimuli.

According to Mazuch, using the basics of light levels, colour, vista, sound, touch, temperature and atmosphere, we can impact on learning through physiological, psychological, emotional and physical means. For example, dimming light leads to quieter movement in school while good levels of natural lighting in classrooms can increase productivity by 18–20 per cent; whereas poor ventilation leading to CO_2 build-up negatively impacts learning and attentiveness. There are cost-effective ways to address ideas of improving classroom ambience through sense-sensitive design: low natural light can be enhanced through the use of inexpensive natural light bulbs; colour can affect mood, for example through paint, and projection could be used to subtly change the environment throughout the day; olfactory planning is often forgotten, but smell can affect attitude – for example citrus oil enlivens the environment and increases productivity;

sound is used extensively in retail but not in schools – can learners benefit from music, birdsong or gentle wind through trees?

These values of 'durability, utility and beauty', informed by current thinking on salutogenic (supporting human health and wellbeing) and sense-sensitive design in the context of people, time and place, are a force for design of our buildings now and in future.

20th Century Classroom	21st Century Learning Spaces
Time-based	Outcome-based
Focus: memorization of discrete facts	Focus: what students 'know', 'can do' and 'are like' after all the details are forgotten
Lessons focus on the lower level of Bloom's Taxonomy – knowledge, comprehension and application	Learning is designed on the upper levels of Bloom's – synthesis, analysis and evaluation (includes lower levels as curriculum is designed top-down)
Textbook-driven	Research-driven
Passive learning	Active learning
Learners work in isolation – classroom within four walls	Learners work collaboratively with classmates and others around the world – Global Classroom
Teacher-centred: teacher is centre of attention and provider of information	Student-centred: teacher is facilitator/coach
Little to no student freedom	Great deal of learner freedom
'Discipline problems' – educators do not trust students and vice versa; no student motivation	No 'discipline problems' – students and teachers have mutually respectful relationship as co-learners; students are highly motivated
Fragmented curriculum	Integrated and interdisciplinary curriculum
Grades averaged	Grades based on what was learned
Low expectations	High expectations – 'if it isn't good it isn't done'. We expect, and ensure, that all students succeed in learning at high levels. Some may go higher – we get out of their way to let them do that
Teacher is judge. No one else sees student work	Self, peer and other assessments. Public audience, authentic assessments
Curriculum/school is irrelevant and meaningless to the students	Curriculum is connected to students' interests, experiences, talents and the real world
Print is the primary vehicle of learning and assessment	Performances, projects and multiple forms of media are used for learning and assessment
Diversity in students is ignored	Curriculum and instruction address student diversity
Literacy is the 3 'R's – reading, writing and maths	Multiple literacies of the 21st century – aligned to living and working in a globalized new millennium
Factory model, based upon the needs of employers for the Industrial Age of the 19th century. Scientific management	Global model, based upon the needs of a globalized, high-tech society
Driven by standardized, high-stakes testing	Driven by exploration, creativity and 21st-century skills

Figure 3.3.3: Twenty-first century skills; adapted with permission from NfER

If we are to use technology effectively in our learning spaces we need to consider what that might be and how it might fit into our physical spaces. In a new build, technology should be part of the fabric and thus considered at the start of planning. Vitruvian principles can also be the basis for good virtual space design and can be used to help analyse why we prefer certain websites to others. In addition, using the principles of 'sense-sensitive design', austerity-driven schools can also cheaply and effectively enhance the learning environment. Layout and visuals are already important in a virtual space, but perhaps as augmented reality improves, more of the principles can be employed for effective learning in cyberspace.

Virtual learning spaces

Our concept of the use of learning technology has changed considerably this century. In 2005 Ruth Kelly, then secretary of state for education and skills for England, outlined a leap in technology to include online spaces:

> In the future it will be more than simply a storage place – a digital space that is personalised, that remembers what the learner is interested in and suggests relevant web sites, or alerts them to courses and learning opportunities that fit their needs.

Learning spaces are the structures, tools and communities that inspire students and educators to attain the knowledge and skills to live successfully in the twenty-first century. It is a profound change requiring the courage to modify practice from teachers, and new kinds of pedagogy that enable learners to take control, and where teachers are another resource to be called upon when needed. Indeed the role of teacher and learner becomes fluid.

However, this fluidity will not be realized if online tools and spaces are poorly designed with resources that are only reached via complex passwords and multiple clicks, making it difficult to use the tools or complete an activity – frustration stops us trying again. If we are seeking to empower our learners through technology, we need well-designed technologies and it appears that the Vitruvian principles apply equally well to technology:

- Firmatis (durability) – it won't break, is sustainable and it can scale.
- Utilitas (utility) – it should do what the teacher and learner need and function well.
- Venustas (beauty) – learners should enjoy the experience and want to revisit it.

Embedded in the principles is the concept of keeping learners safe – the ability to engage in a learning space 'anytime, anywhere' implies a planned online safety education programme and concern for potential risk to information.

Virtual learning spaces allow for the development of learning communities and communities of practice – concepts introduced by Lave and Wenger (1991). In *Digital Habitats: Stewarding technology for communities*, Wenger (2009) states that what makes interactions on the

Internet attractive and productive is the ability to experience 'learning friendships' that occur when there is a common interest and a space to learn together.

Learning spaces with community affordances can reflect a constructivist approach to knowledge (Cross, 1998), whereby knowledge is not simply 'discovered' but is socially constructed. Rather than the teacher transmitting information, learners actively construct and assimilate knowledge through a reciprocal process (Bruffee, 1995; Schön, 1995; Whipple, 1987). These approaches are linked with positive behaviours, like increased academic effort and outcomes such as social tolerance and interpersonal development (Johnson and Johnson, 1994).

Flipped learning

> *If you can design the physical space, the social space, and the information space all together to enhance collaborative learning, then that whole milieu turns into a learning technology and people just love working there and they start learning with and from each other.*

John Seely Brown (2000)

According to Keene (2013) the term 'flipped classroom' was coined in 2007 when teachers Bergman and Sams recorded their live lessons and posted these online for students who missed their class. The online lectures began to spread student to student and school to school and the term 'flipped learning' was born.

In many schools in reality, the practices of 'flipped classroom' and 'flipped learning' were never introduced by design, but rather evolved when certain resources and technologies were available. The importance is that knowledge materials are available to students online and recorded lectures are only one possible source. Exploiting such materials outside the classroom allows for the best possible rich learning experience for each of a widely mixed cohort of students. Students can absorb knowledge at their own pace and repeat or use alternative sources as suits their personal learning. Supporting the materials with online safe and secure chat facilities to promote peer to peer learning activities can deepen the learning experience.

'Flipped learning' now allows the best use of classroom time and involves the teacher as guide and mentor rather than as the didactic imparter of knowledge at the low end of Bloom's taxonomy. The teacher has class time to focus on the relevant higher level thinking skills applicable to the topic or subject and ensures that each student achieves their best outcomes and the required mastery before progressing (Sams and Bergmann, 2013).

Some schools have introduced courses that focus on 'learning to learn' specifically to cover the processes and skills to support 'anytime/anywhere/any subject' learning.

One example case study (Allen, 2013) showed the following impacts:

- Saves class time to allow children to apply what they have learned.
- Makes children more confident, independent and highly engaged.
- Teachers are also more positive and engaged.
- Real impact on the quality and quantity of work produced.
- Each child has an 'assessment buddy' and both staff and students are collegiate.
- Using MLE forums and email has a massive impact on improved communication.
- Flipped learning often shows a big impact on parental communication and engagement.
- The pedagogy is changing from the didactic model of 'Starter, Introduction, Main and Plenary' to lessons and structures based on 'What do students need to learn?', 'What skills are missing?', 'Where are the gaps?' and 'How are we going to fill them?'
- There was massive evidence of engagement from log-in statistics (highest in the borough).
- Steady upward trend in progress and results.

Employing such learning structures that rely heavily on access to technology and resources outside of the classroom does mean that such access is regularly audited. Although this is normally not a problem for the vast majority of students or staff, where there is such a problem measures must be set in place to compensate. Most organizations have ways to support equality of access. It is important that such learning practices do not disadvantage any student or teacher.

From a number of ICT Mark assessment reports (Naace, n.d. a) such use of learning spaces and the technology changes the way pupils and teachers interact. The children trust more and are not scared to ask questions, are more confident and less scared of making mistakes. They use their forums and support each other, relying less on needing answers only from their teacher.

Pupils are requesting and practising independent learning and have, in some year groups, prepared and delivered short lessons to their classmates on their special interest topic. This is an extension of the group research and delivery to classmates that is a regular part of Discovery Time learning and the Flipped Classroom in-classroom activities.

Conclusion

As articulated by Sams and Bergmann, education is for everyone, but the way we deliver education – and the way learners receive it – is not the same for everyone. Well-designed learning spaces give teachers the flexibility to meet the learning needs of all their students and they give students the flexibility to have their needs met in multiple ways, creating the opportunity for deep and enjoyable personalized learning and the best achievable outcomes.

Conclusion
Rosemary Luckin

The three chapters in Part 3 of this book have offered three different perspectives on learner engagement and all highlight the complexities involved. What can we take away from the research our Part 3 authors report?

Albuquerque and Ainsworth tackle a difficult and controversial subject in their discussion of the values and problems involved with digital games in Chapter 3.1. They make clear that there are unintentional learning consequences involved in game playing. However, the three unintentional learning consequences they focus on in this chapter: violence, gender bias and racism, are not simply characteristics or beliefs that result from game playing activity in general. Albuquerque and Ainsworth urge us to take a broader view when citing games as the cause of problems involving these three unintentional and undesirable learning consequences and stress that when violence occurs and games are blamed there are other more powerful influences at play too, such as gun availability, for example. Problematic representations of race and gender are evidenced as not being equally problematic in comparison to TV: ethnic minorities are not particularly underrepresented for example, but they are stereotyped; female characters, by contrast, are both underrepresented and stereotyped.

Useful practical advice about how we can prevent these unintentional learning consequences is provided: observe age ratings for games to ensure that younger children are not exposed to computer violence; and remember that not all games depict stereotypes and/or violence in the same way or to the same extent, therefore careful selection of games can result in more inclusive representations.

The potential for intentional learning consequences is also discussed with positive evidence about skills such as collaboration, scientific habits of mind and ethical decision making in the research reported. However, there is another clear warning about the need to avoid assuming that skills developed and refined in the game environment can be transferred to another environment outside the game. The evidence to support such an assumption is unclear, but Albuquerque and Ainsworth outline two guiding principles: firstly, games are very diverse and so are their influences upon players, and secondly, there are no simple answers, but there can be inquisitive minds. Research suggests that as with everything we do, playing games has consequences for players, and they can be fruitful in the classroom if well-chosen and supported, and their use in formal education must be supported in an effective way so they are not merely a superficial learning approach.

In Chapter 3.2 Charles Crook provides a fascinating review of the research concerned with academic integrity and student cheating. Charles distinguishes between students' engagement with *expository* material, such as books, videos and lectures, and secondly, students' engagement in *collaborations*. He highlights that research suggests that the level of cheating is likely to be greater than that detected, but that while detection has increased through digital media, this does not necessarily mean that digital media have produced an increase in cheating. Other factors in the study environment and the constituency of students have also changed in recent years and these too will have an impact on the amount of cheating among students. Evidence indicates that digital plagiarizers had also been analogue plagiarizers, but that the context of digital study does seem to 'invite' cheating. Digital tools have merely reconfigured the presence and reach of opportunities and threats that have always existed.

Research reports a wide range of estimates in the number of students who take part in plagiarism, but the most commonly reported number of students who admit to having plagiarized is around 40–50 per cent. This is a significant number and to make the problem more demanding of attention, the prevalence of cheating is not restricted to course work. Various ways have been reported that enable personal digital devices to bypass the constraints associated with traditional examinations, often thought to be more cheat resistant. What can we do about this serious problem? Neither honour codes nor vigorous warnings appear to have much impact on the probability of cheating and Charles suggests that we need to view cheating of this sort as being on a continuum of cognitive engagement with information sources. Educators therefore need to design assignments that achieve more than an avoidance of these lazy copy-and-paste behaviours and inspire engagement in curious exploration and reflection on the part of the student instead.

It is interesting to note that interactions *through* technology are suggested to be potentially the most troublesome. For example, out-of-class assignments that are completed through online social relationships, or via paid for marketplace services that allow students to outsource their work. This is sometimes referred to as 'contract cheating'. Charles provides a useful summary of the important points to arise from his review and urges us to more actively engage in the discussion of 'contract cheating'. He suggests that prevention may require us to support teachers with a better sense of the micro-structure of student engagement with digital sources: searching, selecting, abstracting, integrating, critiquing, extending and, finally, communicating them in a distinctive voice. Teachers need to focus on the processes of student engagement rather than the products, through micro-structural research that reveals more of such processes and enables the provision of richer and more realistic support.

The final chapter in this part saw Allison and Richard Allen reviewing the research evidence about learning spaces and their impact on learner engagement. They lament the fact that educators are rarely involved in the design of the spaces where they work and provide some practical ways in which teachers can manipulate their environments to support better student engagement. For example, by changing the layout of the room, changing the display, or the colour of the walls. Allison and Richard report research evidence that indicates that basics of light levels, colour, vista, sound, touch, temperature and atmosphere can impact on learning through physiological, psychological, emotional and physical means. Dimming light, for example, can lead to quieter movement in school; whereas good levels of natural lighting in classrooms can increase productivity by 18–20 per cent. They suggest that low natural light levels can be enhanced through the use of inexpensive natural light bulbs; and projection can be used to subtly change the display and colour of the environment throughout the day.

Technology should be integrated effectively into physical spaces and keeping learners safe should be an embedded principle. In particular, we are encouraged to consider digital learning spaces that stimulate community building activity and social interactions through which learners actively construct and assimilate knowledge through a reciprocal collaborative process. When technology changes the way pupils and teachers interact in this way, learners are more confident, trusting, are not scared to ask questions and are less scared of making mistakes.

What the research says about engaging learners through technology

- Observe age ratings for games to ensure that younger children are not exposed to computer violence.
- Not all games depict stereotypes and/or violence in the same way or to the same extent, therefore careful selection can result in more inclusive representations.
- Skills developed and refined in the game environment are not necessarily transferred to other environments outside the game.
- Games are very diverse and so are their influences upon players.
- Playing games can be fruitful in education if the games are well-chosen and supported in an effective way so they are not merely a superficial learning approach.
- Digital media is not the only change in education that might account for cheating behaviour. Study environments and the constituency of students will also have an impact on cheating among students.
- Digital tools have merely reconfigured the presence and reach of cheating opportunities and threats that have always existed.
- Digital plagiarizers are also likely to be analogue plagiarizers.
- The most commonly reported number of students who admit to having plagiarized is around 40–50 per cent.
- Neither honour codes nor vigorous warnings appear to have much impact on the probability of cheating.
- Educators need to design assignments that achieve more than an avoidance of lazy copy-and-paste behaviours, and inspire engagement in curious exploration and reflection on the part of the student instead.
- Prevention of contract cheating may require us to support teachers with better tools to enable them to focus on the *processes* of student engagement rather than its *products* through micro-structural research that reveals more about such processes.

- Educators are rarely involved in the design of the spaces where they work, but they can manipulate their environments to support better student engagement.
- Dimming light can lead to quieter movement in school, whereas good levels of natural lighting in classrooms can increase productivity by 18–20 per cent.
- Moving an 'average' child from the least effective to the most effective classroom has been modelled at around 1.3 sub-levels – a big impact when pupils typically make two sub-levels' progress per year.
- Keeping learners safe should be an embedded principle for technology used in education spaces.
- Digital learning spaces that stimulate community building activity and social interactions change the way pupils and teachers interact: learners are more confident, trusting, are not scared to ask questions and are less scared of making mistakes.

References (Part 3)

Adachi, P.J.C. and Willoughby, T. (2011) 'The effect of video game competition and violence on aggressive behavior: Which characteristic has the greatest influence?'. *Psychology of Violence*, 1 (4), 259–74.

Adam, L., Anderson, V. and Spronken-Smith, R. (2017) '"It's not fair": Policy discourses and students' understandings of plagiarism in a New Zealand university'. *Higher Education*, 74 (1), 17–32.

Allen, R. (2013) 'The flipped classroom: Gonville Academy'. Online. http://edfutures.net/The_Flipped_Classroom_-_Gonville_Academy (accessed 15 September 2017).

Alzahrani, S.M., Salim, N. and Abraham, A. (2012) 'Understanding plagiarism linguistic patterns, textual features, and detection methods'. *IEEE Transactions on Systems, Man, and Cybernetics, Part C (Applications and Reviews)*, 42 (2), 133–49.

Anderson, C.A., Shibuya, A., Ihori, N., Swing, E.L., Bushman, B.J., Sakamoto, A., Rothstein, H.R. and Saleem, M. (2010) 'Violent video game effects on aggression, empathy, and prosocial behavior in Eastern and Western countries: A meta-analytic review'. *Psychological Bulletin*, 136 (2), 151–73.

ASCD (Association for Supervision and Curriculum Development) (2017) 'Whole Child'. Online. www.ascd.org/whole-child.aspx (accessed 15 September 2017).

Ashworth, P., Bannister, P. and Thorne, P. (1997) 'Guilty in whose eyes? University students' perceptions of cheating and plagiarism in academic work and assessment'. *Studies in Higher Education*, 22 (2), 187–203.

Association of Teachers and Lecturers (2010) 'School buildings not fit for learning'. London: ATL.

Barrett, P., Zhang, Y., Davies, F. and Barrett, L. (2015) *Clever Classrooms: Summary report of the HEAD Project (Holistic Evidence and Design)*. Manchester: University of Salford.

Baruchson-Arbib, S. and Yaari, E. (2004) 'Printed versus internet plagiarism: A study of students' perception'. *International Review of Information Ethics*, 1, 29–35.

BBC (2011) 'Q&A: Building schools for the future'. *BBC News*, 14 June. Online. www.bbc.co.uk/news/education-10682980 (accessed 15 September 2017).

BBC (2015a) 'Are video games really that bad?'. *Horizon*, 16 September. Online. www.bbc.co.uk/programmes/b06cjypk (accessed 15 September 2017).

BBC (2015b) 'Pisa tests: Top 40 for maths and reading'. *BBC News*, 14 October. Online. www.bbc.co.uk/news/business-26249042 (accessed 15 September 2017).

Beagle, D., Fox, W., Parkinson, J. and Plotka, E. (2014) *Building a Better Britain: A vision for the next government*. London: Royal Institute of British Architects.

Bluemke, M., Friedrich, M. and Zumbach, J. (2010) 'The influence of violent and nonviolent computer games on implicit measures of aggressiveness'. *Aggressive Behavior*, 36 (1), 1–13.

Bretag, T. (2016) 'Defining academic integrity: International perspectives – introduction'. In Bretag, T. (ed.) *Handbook of Academic Integrity*. Singapore: Springer, 3–5.

Bruffee, K.A. (1995) 'Sharing our toys: Cooperative learning versus collaborative learning'. *Change*, 27 (1), 12–18.

Bruner, J.S. (1965) 'The growth of mind'. *American Psychologist*, 20 (12), 1007–17.

Chang, C.-M., Chen, Y.-L., Huang, Y. and Chou, C. (2015) 'Why do they become potential cyber-plagiarizers? Exploring the alternative thinking of copy-and-paste youth in Taiwan'. *Computers and Education*, 87, 357–67.

Chism, N.V.N. (2006) 'Challenging traditional assumptions and rethinking learning spaces'. In Oblinger, D.G. (ed.) *Learning Spaces*. Washington, DC: Educause, 2.1–2.12. Online. http://digitalcommons.brockport.edu/cgi/viewcontent.cgi?article=1077&context=bookshelf (accessed 15 September 2017).

Clarke, R. and Lancaster, T. (2007) 'Establishing a systematic six-stage process for detecting contract cheating'. In *Proceedings of the 2nd International Conference on Pervasive Computing and Applications (ICPCA 2007), 26–27 July 2007, Birmingham, United Kingdom*. Piscataway, NJ: Institute of Electrical and Electronics Engineers, 342–7.

Coren, A. (2011) 'Turning a blind eye: Faculty who ignore student cheating'. *Journal of Academic Ethics*, 9, 291–305.

Corey, J.D., Hayakawa, S., Foucart, A., Aparici, M., Botella, J., Costa, A. and Keysar, B. (2017) 'Our moral choices are foreign to us'. *Journal of Experimental Psychology: Learning, Memory, and Cognition*, 43 (7), 1109–28.

Correa, M. (2014) 'Leaving the "peer" out of peer-editing: Online translators as a pedagogical tool in the Spanish as a second language classroom'. *Latin American Journal of Content and Language Integrated Learning*, 7 (1), 1–20.

Corrigan-Gibbs, H., Gupta, N., Northcutt, C., Cutrell, E. and Thies, W. (2015) 'Deterring cheating in online environments'. *ACM Transactions on Computer–Human Interaction*, 22 (6), Article 28, 1–23.

Crook, C. (1996) *Computers and the Collaborative Experience of Learning*. London: Routledge.

Crook, C. (2012) 'The "digital native" in context: Tensions associated with importing web 2.0 practices into the school setting'. *Oxford Review of Education*, 38 (1), 63–80.

Crook, C. and Mitchell, G. (2012) 'Ambience in social learning: Student engagement with new designs for learning spaces'. *Cambridge Journal of Education*, 42 (2), 121–39.

Cross, K.P. (1998) 'Why learning communities? Why now?'. *About Campus*, 3 (3), 4–11. Online. www.nhcuc.org/pdfs/CrossLC.pdf (accessed 15 September 2017).

Dawson, P. (2016) 'Five ways to hack and cheat with bring-your-own-device electronic examinations'. *British Journal of Educational Technology*, 47 (4), 592–600.

Dewey, J. (1902) *The Child and the Curriculum*. Chicago: University of Chicago Press.

DfE (Department for Education) (2016) 'South Asian method of teaching maths to be rolled out in schools'. Press Release, 12 July. Online. www.gov.uk/government/news/south-asian-method-of-teaching-maths-to-be-rolled-out-in-schools (accessed 15 September 2017).

Dill, K.E., Brown, B.P. and Collins, M.A. (2008) 'Effects of exposure to sex-stereotyped video game characters on tolerance of sexual harassment'. *Journal of Experimental Social Psychology*, 44 (5), 1402–8.

Dye, M.W.G., Green, C.S. and Bavelier, D. (2009a) 'Increasing speed of processing with action video games'. *Current Directions in Psychological Science*, 18 (6), 321–6.

Dye, M.W.G., Green, C.S. and Bavelier, D. (2009b) 'The development of attention skills in action video game players'. *Neuropsychologia*, 47 (8–9), 1780–9.

Ellery, K. (2008) 'An investigation into electronic-source plagiarism in a first-year essay assignment'. *Assessment and Evaluation in Higher Education*, 33 (6), 607–17.

Ferguson, C.J. (2015) 'Does media violence predict societal violence? It depends on what you look at and when'. *Journal of Communication*, 65 (1), E1–E22.

Flint, A., Clegg, S. and Macdonald, R. (2006) 'Exploring staff perceptions of student plagiarism'. *Journal of Further and Higher Education*, 30 (2), 145–56.

Gazan, R. (2007) 'Seekers, sloths and social reference: Homework questions submitted to a question-answering community'. *New Review of Hypermedia and Multimedia*, 13 (2), 239–48.

Gentile, D.A., Anderson, C.A., Yukawa, S., Ihori, N., Saleem, M., Ming, L.K., Shibuya, A., Liau, A.K., Khoo, A., Bushman, B.J., Huesmann, L.R. and Sakamoto, A. (2009) 'The effects of prosocial video games on prosocial behaviors: International evidence from correlational, longitudinal, and experimental studies'. *Personality and Social Psychology Bulletin*, 35 (6), 752–63.

Green, C.S., Pouget, A. and Bavelier, D. (2010) 'Improved probabilistic inference as a general learning mechanism with action video games'. *Current Biology*, 20 (17), 1573–9.

Greenhow, C., Robelia, B. and Hughes, J.E. (2009) 'Learning, teaching, and scholarship in a digital age: Web 2.0 and classroom research: What path should we take now?'. *Educational Researcher*, 38 (4), 246–59.

Gullifer, J. and Tyson, G.A. (2010) 'Exploring university students' perceptions of plagiarism: A focus group study'. *Studies in Higher Education*, 35 (4), 463–81.

Habgood, M.P.J. and Ainsworth, S.E. (2011) 'Motivating children to learn effectively: Exploring the value of intrinsic integration in educational games'. *Journal of the Learning Sciences*, 20 (2), 169–206.

Harris, C.G. and Srinivasan, P. (2012) 'With a little help from the crowd: Receiving unauthorized academic assistance through online labor markets'. In *Proceedings of the 2012 ASE/IEEE International Conference on Privacy, Security, Risk and Trust and 2012 ASE/IEEE International Conference on Social Computing (SocialCom/PASSAT 2012), 3–5 September 2012, Amsterdam, Netherlands*. Piscataway, NJ: Institute of Electrical and Electronics Engineers, 904–9.

Hayes, N. and Introna, L.D. (2005) 'Cultural values, plagiarism, and fairness: When plagiarism gets in the way of learning. *Ethics & Behavior*, 15 (3), 213–31.

Heppell, S. (2014) 'Learnometer Project: Research data'. Online. http://rubble. heppell.net/learnometer/old/research_data (accessed 15 September 2017).

Heppell, S. (2016a) 'Learner led learning research'. Online. www.heppell.net/ learner_led/default.html (accessed 15 September 2017).

Heppell, S. (2016b) 'Learnometer'. Online. http://rubble.heppell.net/learnometer/ (accessed 15 September 2017).

Higgins, S., Katsipataki, M., Kokotsaki, D., Coleman, R., Major, L. and Coe, R. (2014) *The Sutton Trust–Education Endowment Foundation Teaching and Learning Toolkit*. Online. https://educationendowmentfoundation.org.uk/ evidence-summaries/teaching-learning-toolkit (accessed 15 September 2017).

Howard, R.M. (1999) *Standing in the Shadow of Giants: Plagiarists, authors, collaborators*. Stamford, CT: Ablex Publishing.

Howard, R.M. (2007) 'Understanding "internet plagiarism"'. *Computers and Composition*, 24 (1), 3–15.

Hrastinski, S. and Aghaee, N.M. (2012) 'How are campus students using social media to support their studies? An explorative interview study'. *Education and Information Technologies*, 17 (4), 451–64.

Iacovides, I., McAndrew, P., Scanlon, E. and Aczel, J. (2014) 'The gaming involvement and informal learning framework'. *Simulation and Gaming*, 45 (4–5), 611–26.

IBI Group (2012) *Sense Sensitive Design*. London: IBI Group. Online. www. ibigroup.com/wp-content/uploads/2013/03/IBI-Group-Brochure-Sense-Sensitive-Design.pdf (accessed 15 September 2017).

Jang, Y. and Ryu, S. (2011) 'Exploring game experiences and game leadership in massively multiplayer online role-playing games'. *British Journal of Educational Technology*, 42 (4), 616–23.

Jenkins, H. (2010) 'Transmedia storytelling and entertainment: An annotated syllabus'. *Continuum: Journal of Media and Cultural Studies*, 24 (6), 943–58.

Jensen, L.A., Arnett, J.J., Feldman, S.S. and Cauffman, E. (2002) 'It's wrong, but everybody does it: Academic dishonesty among high school and college students'. *Contemporary Educational Psychology*, 27 (2), 209–28.

Johnson, D.W. and Johnson, R.T. (1994) *Learning Together and Alone: Cooperative, competitive, and individualistic learning.* 4th ed. Needham Heights, MA: Allyn and Bacon.

Kauffman, Y. and Young, M.F. (2015) 'Digital plagiarism: An experimental study of the effect of instructional goals and copy-and-paste affordance'. *Computers and Education*, 83, 44–56.

Keene, K. (2013) 'Blending and flipping distance education'. *Distance Learning*, 10 (4), 63–9.

Key, R. (2013) 'Boy saves sister from moose attack using "World of Warcraft" knowledge'. *Analog Addiction*, 31 January. Online. https://analogaddiction. org/2013/01/31/boy-saves-sister-from-moose-attack-using-world-of-warcraft-knowledge/ (accessed 15 September 2017).

Kimmerle, J., Moskaliuk, J., Oeberst, A. and Cress, U. (2015) 'Learning and collective knowledge construction with social media: A process-oriented perspective'. *Educational Psychologist*, 50 (2), 120–37.

Kolikant, Y.B.-D. (2010) 'Digital natives, better learners? Students' beliefs about how the internet influenced their ability to learn'. *Computers in Human Behavior*, 26 (6), 1384–91.

Kühn, S., Gleich, T., Lorenz, R.C., Lindenberger, U. and Gallinat, J. (2014) 'Playing Super Mario induces structural brain plasticity: Gray matter changes resulting from training with a commercial video game'. *Molecular Psychiatry*, 19 (2), 265–71.

Kuiper, E., Volman, M. and Terwel, J. (2005) 'The web as an information resource in K–12 education: Strategies for supporting students in searching and processing information'. *Review of Educational Research*, 75 (3), 285–328.

Lancaster, T. and Clarke, R. (2014) 'An observational analysis of the range and extent of contract cheating from online courses found on agency websites'. In *Proceedings of the 8th International Conference on Complex, Intelligent and Software Intensive Systems (CISIS 2014), 2–4 July 2014, Birmingham, United Kingdom.* Piscataway, NJ: Institute of Electrical and Electronics Engineers, 56–63.

Lave, J. and Wenger, E. (1991) *Situated Learning: Legitimate peripheral participation.* Cambridge: Cambridge University Press.

Learning Space Toolkit (n.d.) 'About'. Online. http://learningspacetoolkit.org/about/ (accessed 15 September 2017).

Leo, J., Lacasse, J.R. and Cimino, A.N. (2011) 'Why does academic medicine allow ghostwriting? A prescription for reform'. *Society*, 48 (5), 371–5.

Lessig, L. (2008) *Remix: Making art and commerce thrive in the hybrid economy.* New York: Penguin Press.

Lines, L. (2016a) 'Ghostwriters guaranteeing grades? The quality of online ghostwriting services available to tertiary students in Australia'. *Teaching in Higher Education*, 21 (8), 889–914.

Lines, L. (2016b) 'Substantive editing as a form of plagiarism among postgraduate students in Australia'. *Assessment and Evaluation in Higher Education,* 41 (3), 368–83.

Löfström, E. (2011) '"Does plagiarism mean anything? LOL": Students' conceptions of writing and cheating'. *Journal of Academic Ethics,* 9 (4), 257–75.

Ma, H., Lu, E.Y., Turner, S. and Wan, G. (2007) 'An empirical investigation of digital cheating and plagiarism among middle school students'. *American Secondary Education,* 35 (2), 69–82.

MacCallum-Stewart, E. (2011) 'Stealth learning in online games'. In de Freitas, S. and Maharg, P. (eds) *Digital Games and Learning.* London: Continuum, 107–28.

Macdonald, R. and Carroll, J. (2006) 'Plagiarism: A complex issue requiring a holistic institutional approach'. *Assessment and Evaluation in Higher Education,* 31 (2), 233–45.

Mahmood, Z. (2009) 'Contract cheating: A new phenomenon in cyber-plagiarism'. *Communications of the IBIMA,* 10, 93–7.

Mao, J. (2014) 'Social media for learning: A mixed methods study on high school students' technology affordances and perspectives'. *Computers in Human Behavior,* 33, 213–23.

Marques de Albuquerque, R. (2016) *Digital Game Education: Designing interventions to encourage players' informed reflections on their digital gaming practices.* PhD thesis, University of Nottingham.

Marsh, J. (2011) 'Young children's literacy practices in a virtual world: Establishing an online interaction order'. *Reading Research Quarterly,* 46 (2), 101–18.

Mazuch, R. (2013) 'Sense sensitive design and the learning environment'. Keynote presentation at the Learning Spaces Pedagogic Research Group Conference, Cardiff, 11 March 2013. Online. http://pedagogic.research.southwales.ac.uk/work/ (accessed 15 September 2017).

McCabe, D.L., Butterfield, K.D. and Treviño, L.K. (2012) *Cheating in College: Why students do it and what educators can do about it.* Baltimore: Johns Hopkins University Press.

McClintock, J. and McClintock, R. (1970) 'Architecture and Pedagogy'. In McClintock, J.A.R. (ed.) *Henry Barnard's School Architecture.* New York: Teachers College Press.

McGrail, E. and McGrail, J.P. (2015) 'Exploring web-based university policy statements on plagiarism by research-intensive higher education institutions'. *Journal of Academic Ethics,* 13 (2), 167–96.

Monahan, T. (2002) 'Flexible space and built pedagogy: Emerging IT embodiments'. *Inventio,* 4 (1), 1–19. Online. http://publicsurveillance.com/papers/built_pedagogy.pdf (accessed 15 September 2017).

Mueller, P.A. and Oppenheimer, D.M. (2014) 'The pen is mightier than the keyboard: Advantages of longhand over laptop note taking'. *Psychological Science,* 25 (6), 1159–68.

Naace (n.d. a) 'ICT Mark'. Online. www.naace.co.uk/school-improvement/ict-mark/ (accessed 15 September 2017).

Naace (n.d. b) 'Third Millennium Learning Award'. Online. www.naace.co.uk/thirdmillenniumlearningaward/ (accessed 15 September 2017).

Newton, P.M. and Lang, C. (2016) 'Custom essay writers, freelancers, and other paid third parties'. In Bretag, T. (ed.) *Handbook of Academic Integrity*. Singapore: Springer, 249–71.

Northcutt, C.G., Ho, A.D. and Chuang, I.L. (2016) 'Detecting and preventing "multiple-account" cheating in massive open online courses'. *Computers and Education*, 100, 71–80.

Park, C. (2003) 'In other (people's) words: Plagiarism by university students – literature and lessons'. *Assessment and Evaluation in Higher Education*, 28 (5), 471–88.

Poole, D. (2007) 'A study of beliefs and behaviors regarding digital technology'. *New Media and Society*, 9 (5), 771–93.

Potter, J. (2012) *Digital Media and Learner Identity: The new curatorship*. New York: Palgrave Macmillan.

Rigby, D., Burton, M., Balcombe, K., Bateman, I. and Mulatu, A. (2015) 'Contract cheating and the market in essays'. *Journal of Economic Behavior and Organization*, 111, 23–37.

Risquez, A., O'Dwyer, M. and Ledwith, A. (2013) '"Thou shalt not plagiarise": From self-reported views to recognition and avoidance of plagiarism'. *Assessment and Evaluation in Higher Education*, 38 (1), 34–43.

Ritter, D. and Eslea, M. (2005) 'Hot sauce, toy guns, and graffiti: A critical account of current laboratory aggression paradigms'. *Aggressive Behavior*, 31 (5), 407–19.

Rogerson, A. (2014) 'Detecting the work of essay mills and file swapping sites: Some clues they leave behind'. Paper presented at the 6th International Integrity and Plagiarism Conference, Gateshead, 16–18 June 2014.

Ruedy, N.E., Moore, C., Gino, F. and Schweitzer, M.E. (2013) 'The cheater's high: The unexpected affective benefits of unethical behavior'. *Journal of Personality and Social Psychology*, 105 (4), 531–48.

Sams, A. and Bergmann, J. (2013) 'Flip your students' learning'. *Educational Leadership*, 70 (6), 16–20.

Schön, D.A. (1995) *The Reflective Practitioner: How professionals think in action*. Aldershot: Arena.

Schroeder, A., Minocha, S. and Schneider, C. (2010) 'The strengths, weaknesses, opportunities and threats of using social software in higher and further education teaching and learning'. *Journal of Computer Assisted Learning*, 26 (3), 159–74.

Seely Brown, J. and Duguid, P. (2000) *The Social Life of Information*. Brighton, MA: Harvard Business School Press.

Selwyn, N. (2008) '"Not necessarily a bad thing …": A study of online plagiarism amongst undergraduate students'. *Assessment and Evaluation in Higher Education*, 33 (5), 465–79.

Shachaf, P. (2010) 'Social reference: Toward a unifying theory'. *Library and Information Science Research*, 32 (1), 66–76.

Simkins, D.W. and Steinkuehler, C. (2008) 'Critical ethical reasoning and role-play'. *Games and Culture*, 3 (3–4), 333–55.

Sisti, D.A. (2007) 'How do high school students justify internet plagiarism?'. *Ethics and Behavior*, 17 (3), 215–31.

Sivasubramaniam, S., Kostelidou, K. and Ramachandran, S. (2016) 'A close encounter with ghost-writers: An initial exploration study on background, strategies and attitudes of independent essay providers'. *International Journal for Educational Integrity*, 12 (1), 1–14.

Spence, I. and Feng, J. (2010) 'Video games and spatial cognition'. *Review of General Psychology*, 14 (2), 92–104.

Steinkuehler, C. (2015) 'Parenting and video games'. *Journal of Adolescent and Adult Literacy*, 59 (4), 357–61.

Steinkuehler, C. and Duncan, S. (2008) 'Scientific habits of mind in virtual worlds'. *Journal of Science Education and Technology*, 17 (6), 530–43.

Stewart, O.G. (2015) 'A critical review of the literature of social media's affordances in the classroom'. *E-Learning and Digital Media*, 12 (5–6), 481–501.

Stöckelová, T. and Virtová, T. (2015) 'A tool for learning or a tool for cheating? The many-sided effects of a participatory student website in mass higher education'. *British Journal of Educational Technology*, 46 (3), 597–607.

Stogner, J.M., Miller, B.L. and Marcum, C.D. (2013) 'Learning to e-cheat: A criminological test of internet facilitated academic cheating'. *Journal of Criminal Justice Education*, 24 (2), 175–99.

Sutton, A. and Taylor, D. (2011) 'Confusion about collusion: Working together and academic integrity'. *Assessment and Evaluation in Higher Education*, 36 (7), 831–41.

Sutton, A., Taylor, D. and Johnston, C. (2014) 'A model for exploring student understandings of plagiarism'. *Journal of Further and Higher Education*, 38 (1), 129–46.

Szabo, A. and Underwood, J. (2004) 'Cybercheats: Is information and communication technology fuelling academic dishonesty?'. *Active Learning in Higher Education*, 5 (2), 180–99.

Tanner, C.K. (2009) 'Effects of school design on student outcomes'. *Journal of Educational Administration*, 47 (3), 381–99.

Townley, C. and Parsell, M. (2004) 'Technology and academic virtue: Student plagiarism through the looking glass'. *Ethics and Information Technology*, 6 (4), 271–7.

Turnitin (2012) *The Plagiarism Spectrum: Instructor insights into the 10 types of plagiarism*. Online. www.ed.ac.uk/files/atoms/files/10-types-of-plagiarism.pdf (accessed 15 September 2017).

Tyack, D. and Cuban, L. (1995) *Tinkering Toward Utopia: A century of public school reform*. Cambridge, MA: Harvard University Press.

Ulrich, R.S. (1984) 'View through a window may influence recovery from surgery'. *Science*, 224 (4647), 420–1.

Unsworth, G., Devilly, G.J. and Ward, T. (2007) 'The effect of playing violent video games on adolescents: Should parents be quaking in their boots?'. *Psychology, Crime and Law*, 13 (4), 383–94.

Velliaris, D.M. (2017) *Handbook of Research on Academic Misconduct in Higher Education*. Hershey, PA: IGI Global.

Vitruvius (2006) *The Ten Books on Architecture*. Trans. Morgan, M.H. Originally 1914. Project Gutenberg. Online. www.gutenberg.org/files/20239/20239-h/29239-h.htm (accessed 15 September 2017).

Walker, M. and Townley, C. (2012) 'Contract cheating: A new challenge for academic honesty?'. *Journal of Academic Ethics*, 10 (1), 27–44.

Wallace, M.J. and Newton, P.M. (2014) 'Turnaround time and market capacity in contract cheating'. *Educational Studies*, 40 (2), 233–6.

Waycott, J., Gray, K., Clerehan, R., Hamilton, M., Richardson, J., Sheard, J. and Thompson, C. (2010) 'Implications for academic integrity of using web 2.0 for teaching, learning and assessment in higher education'. *International Journal for Educational Integrity*, 6 (2), 8–18.

Wenger, E., White, N. and Smith, J.D. (2009) *Digital Habitats: Stewarding technology for communities*. Portland, OR: CPsquare.

Whipple, W.R. (1987) 'Collaborative learning: Recognizing it when we see it'. *AAHE Bulletin*.

Whitton, N. and Maclure, M. (2017) 'Video game discourses and implications for game-based education'. *Discourse: Studies in the Cultural Politics of Education*, 38 (4), 561–72.

Williams, D., Martins, N., Consalvo, M. and Ivory, J.D. (2009) 'The virtual census: Representations of gender, race and age in video games'. *New Media and Society*, 11 (5), 815–34.

Yeo, S. (2007) 'First-year university science and engineering students' understanding of plagiarism'. *Higher Education Research and Development*, 26 (2), 199–216.

Zhang, J. (2009) 'Comments on Greenhow, Robelia, and Hughes: Toward a creative social web for learners and teachers'. *Educational Researcher*, 38 (4), 274–9.

Part Four

Helping learners get the most benefit from digital technology

4

Helping learners get the most benefit from digital technology

Rosemary Luckin and Mutlu Cukurova

In Part 1 of this book we discussed learning and presented seven principles for learning that can be applied to learning with technology. In this part, we look at how we can help learners get the most from the digital technologies available to them. In Chapter 4.1 David Baume and Eileen Scanlon present and discuss what we know about the digital capabilities that learners need in order to use contemporary technologies effectively. They present this work in terms of the principles of learning from Chapter 1. Keith Turvey and Norbert Pachler author Chapter 4.2 and critically explore what we know about the use of tablet devices in classrooms. They argue that we need to go beyond the face value of the research that often claims this technology can be effective, and also beyond the face value of the various controversies if we are to make better use of these technologies. In Chapter 4.3, Torben Steeg and David Barlex introduce the *maker movement* of people 'who like to make stuff ... often using high technology tools'. They discuss what the research says about the impact and potential of the maker movement in education. Finally, Ann Jones, Eileen Scanlon and Koula Charitonos consider the ways in which technology can support learning across contexts, and present three illustrative case studies in Chapter 4.4.

Chapter 4.1

A contemporary digital capabilities framework

David Baume and Eileen Scanlon

Introduction

In Chapter 1.1 we presented a discussion about what we know about learning from the reviews and meta-analyses of the research literature over a considerable number of years. Here we present an account of the contemporary digital capabilities that learners need to develop if they are to benefit from the potential of the digital technologies they use. Initially we explore the contemporary digital capabilities framework provided by JISC illustrated in Figure 4.1.1. The diagram suggests that digital capability requires:

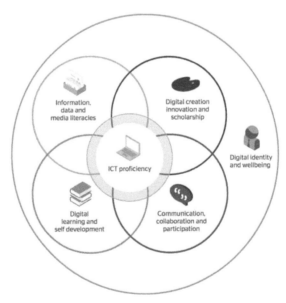

Figure 4.1.1: The skills needed to thrive in a digital environment. 'Building digital capability' *Source:* JISC (http://repository.jisc.ac.uk/6611/1/JFL0066F_DIGIGAP_MOD_IND_FRAME.PDF)

- Starting in the outer circle; whatever we are doing digitally, we must protect our digital identity and ensure our digital wellbeing. Of course we each have to decide what this means for us, what our standards and limits are. If our identity is never stolen or compromised, and if we don't let our use of digital technologies damage our physical, mental or social health or wellbeing, then we probably have this under control.
- Moving to the centre of the diagram; whatever technology we are using we need to be able to use it confidently, critically, skilfully and appropriately, which includes safely (safe to the technology and safe to us). We have to be able to turn it on and off, connect it and generally get it to do what we want it to do.
- The four intermediate circles suggest different kinds of uses of technology. Another approach to this model is to write our own intermediate circles, to describe the kinds of things and then the particular things that we want to use technology for, as suggested earlier, perhaps prompted by the titles of the four intermediate circles here, or something else. With the constant reminders to ensure our safety and wellbeing, and to use the technologies at least competently.

Developing our digital capabilities

A key question to be addressed is: how can we (continue to) develop the digital capabilities we decide or discover we need? In terms of the seven principles of learning that we introduced at the beginning of the book:

Learning principle 1

There may be three sources of structure or scaffolding for your learning about the digital:

- The structure of the task you are trying to undertake. This may involve a sequence of activities, or a number of things to be done more or less together, or perhaps some other structure.
- The structure of the programme, the app, the device. This may include the way it defines data and asks or tells you what to do; the form of data it outputs.
- Your own mental model of the task, of what is needed.

Things will go best in the short term if these three structures are similar, congruent and aligned.

Learning principle 2

You set your own goals. Of course you want to do it well – or, at any rate, well enough.

Learning principle 3

Prior knowledge can be a blessing and a curse. It can get us operational very quickly. But it's the tacit knowledge that can bite us, the things we didn't even know we knew but were, almost invisibly, part of our daily practice. Anyone who has moved between Mac and Windows, in either direction, will understand this. It's quicker to learn a new technology that we can assimilate into our current worldview, our current ways of thinking and working. But our next task may need us to use a new technology that forces us to think and act in a new way, to accommodate our world view to take on board something quite different. And that's where the important innovations may come from.

Learning principle 4

We have to learn actively. The technology almost demands active learning, and we should go along with this. The technologies have to be learned from the inside, by using them – not ignoring the instructions (more likely these days the context-specific help file), but by jumping in. Good technologies welcome and reward this approach. That is part of what makes them good.

Learning principle 5

You learn the technology by using the technology, and seeing how it goes. Time on task.

Learning principle 6

We can do it socially. Contrary to the cartoon image of the man (for some reason it is usually a man) alone at his keyboard, much of our computer time is spent online, and much online time is spent in communication with others. We suggested earlier that online communities are sources of information. They can also be sources of advice, of support, on safety and on proficiency and on our particular enthusiasms. And epic time-wasters. Be strong!

Learning principle 7

Mostly, the technology gives us feedback. It either does what we want it to or it doesn't, and sometimes it tells us why. We can ask friends, colleagues or the user group around the technology for help. 'How can I make it … ' is a common question in such forums. Often your question will already have been answered. Search the FAQs.

Conclusion

The contemporary digital capabilities that learners need to develop can be described in terms of the learning principles discussed in Chapter 1 and also in terms of the JISC framework presented in Figure 4.1.1:

1. We must protect our digital identity and ensure our digital wellbeing.
2. Whatever technology we are using, we need to be able to use it confidently, critically, skilfully and appropriately, which includes safely.
3. Different kinds of technology use can be described, including: information, data and media literacies; digital creation, innovation and scholarship; digital learning and self-development and communication, collaboration and participation.

No one promised that learning would be easy. But it will always be essential. It will take us to new places, to important and rewarding new achievements. It is absolutely worth the effort.

Tablet devices in education
Beyond face-value

Keith Turvey and Norbert Pachler

Introduction

If learners are to benefit educationally from the potential offered by tablet devices we must understand the nature of the legitimate concerns that are reported. In this chapter we therefore critically examine arguments and evidence relating to the use of tablet devices and smartphones in education. We do this by engaging with common concerns and issues: distraction from learning and potential negative impact on attainment, technology addiction and online safety. We present evidence that we believe suggests these genuine concerns associated with tablet devices and mobile digital technologies such as smartphones need to be engaged with beyond their face-value.

We take the view that tablet devices and smartphones bring new opportunities as well as raising imperatives for learners and teachers in formal educational contexts and beyond (Turvey and Pachler, 2016). The ubiquity and penetration of a global network of mobile technologies in so many aspects of our lives is intensifying. This prompts a call for action to all educators (parents, teachers and the wider community) to play an active role in supporting future generations to develop constructive and critical orientations towards mobile technologies, the media they bear, the functions they perform and the possibilities they bring forth in the present and future. What is not helpful, we suggest, are the reductionist 'black or white' dystopian versus utopian views that have tended to characterize debates about new and emerging technologies in the media over the decades.

Hype, crying wolf and genuine concerns

The guidance computer used in the Apollo moon landing on 20 July 1969 had a processor speed of 0.043 megahertz and a memory of 64 kilobytes (Saran, 2009). In theory, the gain in speed and storage capacity of an iPad Pro, at the time of writing, is in multiples of thousands and millions respectively. Such facts about digital technologies pique consumers' interest for the latest gadget as technology companies know only too well. Why would you not want to put such face-value computing power in the hands of learners? Of course, when it comes to computing capacity it is all relative. Data-hungry multimedia combined with the kinds of multitasking we require of digital devices has a tendency to put gains in computing power into perspective.

Digital technologies are often promoted superficially on their immediate face-value, as opposed to being thought through critically as to how they might merge with, extend or inhibit current pedagogical and cultural practices. Similarly, on the other side of the debate, the proscription of digital technologies, such as tablet devices, is often done through appeals to face-value concerns. Consider for a moment the grave concerns expressed by some about the future of language as texting became commonplace with the use of mobile phones. This was accompanied by fears that the younger generation in particular, would use *textspeak* inappropriately in essays and examinations, leading to a decline in the quality of spoken or written English. However, Crystal (2009) highlighted the mythology surrounding these concerns, arguing that 'texting has added a new dimension to language use' and that there is no evidence of a widespread detrimental impact on standard English.

We do not dismiss face-value concerns or claims about the potential impact of digital devices in formal education contexts. But these do need to be examined more deeply, drawing on research evidence to shed light on the place of mobile technologies such as tablet devices and smartphones. However, while it is an issue that rightly concerns parents and children as much as teachers, it is probably true to say that often parents, children and, to some extent, teachers have little say about important decisions regarding the rationale, purchase and setup of digital technologies in schools. Selwyn (2016) has questioned what appears to be a tradition of seeing educational technology as an inherently *good thing*, which has led to top-down government and school policy initiatives. Yet children, parents and teachers are key players in terms of the ways in which the devices will be used. User agency and context are also important factors when considering 'personal' devices as tablets that have implications beyond the formal education context. Available research and monitoring and evaluation evidence has often been ambivalent (Weston and Bain, 2010).

Many of the various stakeholders' concerns regarding the introduction of iPads or Android tablets in schools relate to areas in which there are already useful bodies of research knowledge. In any case, although we would argue that research can only help us to gain a deeper understanding of the issues, questions about what does or doesn't work when deploying educational technologies are problematic. Effective use of any educational technology is contingent upon understanding the multiple complexities of the context in which it is deployed and, most importantly, *how* it is used and for what purposes (Cox *et al.*, 2003). Tablet devices are no exception in this respect despite the hype often associated with them (Clark and Luckin, 2013).

Research can inform our understanding as educators so that we can make better intuitive decisions in response to the pedagogical complexities of specific educational contexts. But parents and children can also benefit from deeper consideration of the place they choose to grant mobile technologies in their lives, shedding light on the genuine face-value concerns they have about the increasingly anthropomorphic relationship we, as humans, develop with digital technologies. It is impossible to cover comprehensively the whole field relating to tablet and other mobile devices in the classroom but we offer an introduction to those issues we believe give the general public most cause for concern. These are: concerns about the potential to distract from learning and technology addiction, neurological concerns about the long-term effects of technologies on the brain and educational perspectives about online safety.

Beyond research face-values

At face-value, a meta-analysis carried out for the Education Endowment Fund, consisting of 14 different studies in the use of digital technologies, found that the introduction of digital technologies *on average* can offer 'moderate learning gains' of approximately four months' progress (Higgins *et al.*, 2012). Hattie (2009) using similar methods estimates similar potential effects for the introduction of digital technologies. However, beyond face-value, the actual effect sizes of the different studies in Higgins *et al.*'s 2012 analysis vary significantly, ranging from the negative effect size of -0.03 to a positive effect size of 1.05. In other words, the face-value is misleading and such meta-analyses merely tell us that technology can have both a positive or negative impact on attainment and learning. Another recent meta-review (Haßler *et al.*, 2016) that looked specifically at research on the use of tablet devices in schools found more positive results in terms of learning outcomes. Out of 23 studies, Haßler and colleagues found 16 reported positive learning outcomes, five reported no difference and two reported negative learning outcomes. However, they also make the important point that much of the research included in their review did not go beyond face-value, stating that 'a large proportion of identified research offers limited or no details of the activities that learners engaged in' (Haßler *et al.*, 2016: 151).

It is not unreasonable to put the variability in impact of these various studies down to *how* the technology is actually appropriated by teachers and children and for what purposes in what contexts. These are far more complex questions to answer. The use of econometrics in educational research often tells us very little in terms of direct cause and effect between pedagogical practices, digital technologies and learning gains or loses. Randomized Controlled Trials (RCTs) form the basis of most meta-reviews where the results from a number of RCTs are synthesized to gain a meta-view of a field of research often over a number of years. A significant issue is that meta reviews or analyses can end up amplifying the significance of poorly conducted RCTs. To try to guard against this, selection criteria are used to decide which RCTs will be included. However, as Wiliam (2014: 4) points out, when conducting Randomized Controlled Trials (RCTs) it 'turns out to be quite difficult to get people to implement the programs as designed', which raises further concerns about such face-value analyses of the impact of tablets and other mobile devices on learning. Unfortunately, much of the large scale quantitative research into the impact of digital technologies on learning continues to take a face-value approach, often comparing the banning of digital devices with the blunt and undefined instrument of not banning digital technologies (Beland and Murphy, 2015). What is particularly interesting in Beland and Murphy's study, beyond the correlation between a blanket ban on mobile phones and higher attainment, is that the impact varied according to student characteristics, having no positive or negative impact on higher attaining children. This suggests that student dispositions towards, as well as teachers' pedagogical decisions about, digital technologies are vitally important.

Concerns about distractions from learning

An important factor here in terms of pedagogical design and student dispositions is clearly the issue of distraction and what constitutes distraction from learning. When a family sits down at a table to eat and share conversation over food, the issue of distraction can be more straightforward. The purpose of the activity is to eat and share conversation as a group. Such family rituals might indeed involve sharing photographs through a mobile device but the use of a mobile phone or tablet device by a member of the group can be more easily perceived as a distraction from the shared purpose of the group. Distraction in a learning context involving the use of tablet devices or smartphones is much more complex to determine, as has been noted from various case studies of teachers in the field (Pimmer and Pachler, 2014; and Turvey, 2014). In particular, it is important to ask what it is that children are being distracted from. We believe it is more productive to focus on distraction from the conceptual knowledge and understanding that is being taught and therefore to draw on research from the field of instructional design and cognitive psychology.

In the 1980s and 1990s cognitive psychologist Alan Baddeley (1986), among others (Sweller, 1988) provided evidence to support their theories about the ways in which memory functions in relation to stimuli and distraction during the process of learning or solving problems. Working memory in these studies is defined theoretically as a 'store' where small amounts of information are retained for a short period of time, such as the duration of solving a problem. A familiar scenario is holding in one's mind the cost of several items being ordered in a café. Long term memory involves the retention of much larger amounts of information 'stored' for much longer periods of time and retrieved as and when required. Returning to our café scenario, this would be the procedural knowledge one retrieves to calculate the costs held in working memory. Because working memory appears to be limited, the relevance of material presented and the way in which material is presented to learners is assumed to be vital for effective learning to take place (Kirschner and Kester, 2016). The theory, usually termed *cognitive load theory,* can be summed up as follows: the more extraneous material learners are required to process and/or the more effort they have to go to in making the material relevant or accessible for processing, the more distracted from the learning and the more impeded learning is likely to become as working memory becomes overloaded.

At face-value this would appear to offer a strong argument for banning the use of mobile devices such as iPads in schools, due to the potential to overload students with sensory stimuli that may not be germane to their understanding. However, Baddeley's research into *how* stimuli are processed by working memory and become established as longer term memories (Baddeley in Tulving and Craik, 2000) highlights the importance of relevant semantic connections between different media and modalities (auditory, visual, textual) for understanding to develop and become established as long term memory, as 'deeper semantic processing leads to the best retention' (Baddeley, 2000: 82). In other words, the explicit and effective combination of relevant text, image and auditory stimuli can be highly conducive to learning and understanding. Tablet devices bring with them the opportunity to exploit media and modality in learning but, as Kirschner and Kester argue, it turns out that more evidence is needed to inform our decisions about what media and instructional designs 'should be used in what situations with what groups to achieve what goals under what circumstances' (2016: 538). Mayer (2008) unravels some of these fine-grained complexities and identifies principles for the design of multimedia instruction, based upon what is known about the limited capacity of working memory and also the way the brain appears to process visual and auditory information via separate channels.

However, most importantly here we believe, is Mayer's suggestion that learning with multimedia is also contingent upon learners' 'active processing – the idea that deep learning depends on the learner's cognitive processing during learning (e.g., selecting, organizing and integrating)' (2008: 761). This emphasizes the importance of metacognition or the importance of learners learning how to learn in a multimedia rich world. The more we understand about contingencies for, or barriers to learning and understanding with digital technologies, the more, we would argue, it becomes necessary to educate learners about how to optimize their opportunities to learn and to be critical about what they learn.

It is worth adding a note of caution here. There has been a tendency to popularize over-simplistic models and theories relating to learning and memory. In interpreting models from cognitive psychology, the complexities of the sensory register and the executive functions are sometimes underplayed. Executive functions such as learner motivation and emotions affect memory and retention, and are difficult to account for under laboratory conditions, far removed from the complexities and dense variability of the classroom. Over-simplistic interpretations of metaphorical models of memory have led some policymakers to over-emphasize a reliance on impoverished approaches to learning and teaching based upon rote learning and repetition of facts, with very little concern for deeper levels of understanding or issues about helping children to learn how to learn.

Despite these caveats, it is not unreasonable to assume, based on the evidence available, that the use of media-rich mobile technologies such as tablet devices, without careful attention to *how* they are used and without any attempt to teach children how to optimize their opportunities to learn with digital technologies and self-regulate their use, could impede or distract from learning as much as it could support it. Mills highlights the vital role of self-regulation in militating against 'negative consequences experienced from Internet use' (2016: 5). Media, it seems, as McLuhan forewarned as long ago as 1964, can be used to beguile, distract and exploit. The potential of digital technologies such as tablet devices to distract from or hamper learning is not an argument for the banning of mobile phones and tablet devices in schools unless, as a society, we are content to leave future generations' critical media literacy and metacognitive capacity to chance. If anything, it creates new imperatives to support learners in optimizing their capabilities to use such digital technologies more critically and effectively.

Indeed, in a recent meta-review on the potential effects of Internet use on adolescents' cognitive development, Mills suggests that cognitive changes that 'are likely taking place' might better be seen as an adaptive process that is necessary for 'emerging adults' ability to successfully navigate our highly-connected world' (2016: 10). This is more than merely a cognitive issue, it is also a socio-cultural one, as we consider later in this chapter.

Concerns about neurological impact

From a neuroscience perspective, the issue of learning in relation to mobile devices has led to some hypothetical and as yet only partly evidenced speculation relating to potential long-term effects on what is often termed the cognitive architecture of the brain. Some have popularized neuroscience perspectives (Greenfield, 2014), speculating as to whether, due to digital technologies, as a species our brains are becoming 'rewired'. The speculative evidence for 'rewiring' claims about the brain are often linked to Magnetic Resonance Imaging (MRI) studies that show grey matter differences in the brain as a correlation with occupational and environmental stimuli; for example, Maguire, Woollett and Spiers's (2006) comparative MRI study of London taxi and bus drivers. Others have approached this issue of distraction from the perspective of cognitive engagement (Howard-Jones *et al.*, 2015). Paul Howard-Jones and colleagues explored how the design of an app gamified learning – specifically, applying elements of game design to non-game contexts via varying the certainty of the rewards learners received, which is linked to the production and uptake of dopamine in the brain. Dopamine is a chemical that functions, among other things, as a neurotransmitter for the reward system in the brain. The theory being tested was the intensity of emotional response – as indicated by levels of dopamine – and its capacity or otherwise to support the encoding of memories, during a gamified process of learning. Howard-Jones *et al.*'s (2015) study provides evidence that engaging with multimedia through tablets or other digital technologies, in a gamified learning context, stimulates short-term responses in the brain. It suggests the extent of such changes (such as levels of dopamine) can to some degree be designed into activities with digital devices. However, it is important to emphasize that these are short-term changes, the like of which we also experience moment to moment in response to everyday stimuli and activities such as: consuming food and drink, meeting friends, sleeping, experiencing disappointment or pleasure and so on. In relation to whether our engagement with tablet devices and digital stimuli can be linked to any long-term changes in the cognitive or physiological architecture of the brain, there is currently no conclusive evidence to support any such assertions. Kim and Han offer some insight in their review of the neurobiological features of problematic Internet and video game use. They point to the fact that a range of conditions such as ADHD, major depression, and social phobia often 'coexist with problematic Internet and video game use ... [but] it is an open question whether such brain changes are the result of problematic Internet and video game use, pre-existing or coexisting psychiatric disorders, or other causes altogether' (2015: 75).

While a technology effect should not be ruled out, it is unlikely that a single technological cause could be isolated. It seems more likely that technology addiction is symptomatic of deeper and more complex neurological, biological, emotional and behavioural factors. This view of digital technologies as symptom rather than cause of addictive behaviour is further supported by population studies that have consistently found the issue of pathological Internet use to be prevalent in only a minority of the populations studied (Durkee *et al.*, 2012; Strittmatter *et al.*, 2016). News media reports tend to lay blame for addictive behaviours towards digital technologies squarely with the technologies themselves in a simplistic linear cause and effect explanation of the phenomenon. Reports often utilize the problematic *digital natives* meme to characterize children and young people as 'lost' to their digital technologies. But such simplified and superficial commentary also ignores the socio-cultural complexity and scope of this issue. Taking only a medical view of Internet or digital technology addiction inadvertently places the remedy beyond our own actions and beyond the socio-cultural structures we choose to co-construct as communities and societies that could also play a more constructive role. At worst a purely medical perspective renders us increasingly powerless to address the issue. As Turkle notes:

> To combat addiction, you have to discard the addicting substance. But we are not going to 'get rid' of the Internet. We will not go 'cold turkey' or forbid cell phones to our children ... We have to find a way to live with seductive technology and make it work to our purposes. (Turkle, 2011: 294)

Faced with such important concerns, there is an imperative, we would argue, for education to play a significant role in helping future generations orientate towards the purposeful, critical and creative use of digital technologies. On the one hand, the seductive qualities of digital technologies such as tablet devices create genuine tensions but, on the other, new opportunities for personalization, collaboration and authenticity (Burden and Kearney, 2016) offer significant potential for purposeful and creative use in education. For example, the playing of video games is often portrayed by the media in a negative light in relation to genuine issues of technology addiction but the evidence suggests this issue is far more complex with potential to develop children's computer literacy and logical problem solving skills (Greitemeyer and Mügge, 2014). See Chapter 3.1 for a more detailed discussion of the problems associated with computer games.

Online safety: Restriction versus trust

Smartphones and tablet devices bring multiple, personalized gateways to the Internet and the world beyond the classroom. The idea of 'control' in this scenario is far more complex than with other educational technologies such as Interactive Whiteboards (IWBs). Tablets and mobile phones challenge established forms of pedagogy because they put the window on the world in the hands of the child in such a way that requires a reconfiguration of pedagogy based on trust and participation for protection.

Since the inception of the Internet in schools, the approach has prioritized protection over participation, minimizing the risk of exposure to inappropriate content or harm through restriction (the filtering or banning of certain technologies, for example). Rather than prioritizing the education of children about the risks and opportunities of the Internet to help them to develop the skills and dispositions to protect themselves, greater emphasis has been placed on restricting access (Male and Burden, 2014). The very real risks, such as cyberbullying, commercial exploitation of young people, exposure to pornography and the potential for sexual grooming are well documented in the media. However, the Byron Review in 2008 highlighted the problem with prioritizing protection through restriction over protection through participation:

> Children and young people need to be empowered to keep themselves safe – this isn't just about a top down approach. Children will be children – pushing boundaries and taking risks. (Byron, 2008: 2)

Livingstone's European collaboration (Livingstone *et al.*, 2011) exploring the online lives of children and young people identified further evidence of the necessity for a more active and progressive stance towards online protection based on developing critical media literacy through participation. Content, or the worldwide web, like the infrastructure – the Internet – is not static and nor are the risks that children and young people face or are yet to face. Livingstone and colleagues highlighted the ongoing emergence of new risks that often parents and teachers are unaware of and, therefore, draw attention to the need to listen to children and young people in order to understand the emergent risks that they may often be first to encounter.

It is beyond human possibility to police the Internet or the worldwide web yet under the recent Investigatory Powers Act (United Kingdom Parliament, 2016) new measures in England have been brought in that pursue an agenda of blanket surveillance of children and young people's online activities. It is now statutory (DfE, 2015a) for schools to have filters and monitoring systems in place to restrict children's access to inappropriate material and keep log files in order to identify individual users' search histories. Brought in to address most recent concerns about the radicalization of children and young people, such measures, we would argue, could serve to merely heighten the probability of exposure to risk, driving some children and young people towards more covert practices with mobile technologies. It is unlikely that the introduction of tablets or any digital technology into a school context where digital surveillance is of the utmost priority can lead to the openness and trust between young people and their elders that is required to tackle the difficult and emergent issues of online safety. As the UN Special Rapporteur remarks, these measures merely limit 'right to freedom of expression' and put 'children in greater danger by inhibiting discussion about online risks' (UNHCR, 2014: 18).

Conclusion

The way that a technology is actually appropriated by teachers and learners and for what purposes in what contexts, plus student dispositions towards as well as teachers' pedagogical decisions about digital technologies are vitally important when it comes to the extent to which any technology does or does not support learning. Based on the evidence available, the use of media-rich technologies such as tablet devices, without appropriate attention to *how* they are used, could impede or distract from learning as much as they could support it.

The negative potential of technology to provoke addiction is not well evidenced and it is unlikely that a single technological cause could be isolated. It seems more likely that technology addiction is a symptom of deeper and more complex neurological, biological, emotional and behavioural factors. Education must play a significant role in helping future generations orientate towards the effective use of digital technologies.

The issue of online safety gets to the heart of the purposes of education and the place of mobile technologies within any vision for their use. What is the likely output of a risk-averse education system in which digital technologies serve an agenda of restriction and surveillance while paradoxically exposing the next generation to the commercially driven incentives of technology companies? It would appear now more than ever what is needed is an approach to digital technologies in education that goes beyond restriction and face-value approaches to online protection. Such approaches would put children and young people's rights at the centre of the use of digital technologies; that is, their right to open, accurate and critical debate of the difficult issues of our time that will no doubt shape their futures. This can only be built upon trust that gives children and young people active agency over digital technologies in order to develop the kinds of creative and critical media literacy needed. Anything less than this may merely 'exacerbate rather than diminish children's vulnerability to risks' (UNHCR, 2014: 12).

The maker movement and schools

Torben Steeg and David Barlex

Introduction: Who are makers and hackers?

Even if you haven't had any direct involvement with them, you've probably heard of folk who call themselves 'makers' or 'hackers', or of the 'Maker Movement' and its Maker Faires (http://makerfaire.com), or of FabLabs (www.fabfoundation.org/fab-labs), makerspaces or hackspaces (www.hackspace.org.uk), or of open source hardware projects such as the Arduino (www.arduino.cc) and the RepRap 3D printer (http://reprap.org). These are all aspects of maker activity.

It's worth noting that in everyday usage (especially by popular media) the term 'hacker' is generally used to describe those who illegally break into other people's computers. However, such people are known as 'crackers' by those technically minded experts in their world. In maker culture, 'hacker' is used much more widely and positively to describe folk who are clever programmers, adept at taking apart code and tweaking it for new purposes and, by extension, those who like to do the same with hardware.

'Maker' is a term used to describe people who like to make stuff, often, but not always, using high technology tools (microcontrollers, laser cutters, 3D printers, for example) and in some cases designing and making such tools themselves. It is a largely self-defining term (if you call yourself a maker, you probably are one) and takes in a broad swathe of interests that include crafting, heavy engineering, electronics, embedded control, programming, robotics and biotech among many other things. There is a strong bias among makers towards open-source tools, both hardware and software and a belief that the products you make (as well as those that you use) should be covered by 'open' licences, such as those from Creative Commons (https://creativecommons.org) and the Open Source Initiative (http://opensource.org), thus allowing them to be developed and modified (hacked) by others; this world view is summarized in the Maker's Bill of Rights (Figure 4.3.1) and the Open Source Hardware Association's 'Open Source Hardware May and Must' document (Figure 4.3.2).

THE MAKER'S BILL OF RIGHTS

■ Meaningful and specific parts lists shall be included.
■ Cases shall be easy to open. ■ Batteries shall be
replaceable. ■ Special tools are allowed only for darn
good reasons. ■ Profiting by selling expensive special
tools is wrong, and not making special tools available
is even worse. ■ Torx is OK; tamperproof is rarely OK.
■ Components, not entire subassemblies, shall be
replaceable. ■ Consumables, like fuses and filters, shall
be easy to access. ■ Circuit boards shall be commented.
■ Power from USB is good; power from proprietary
power adapters is bad. ■ Standard connectors shall
have pinouts defined. ■ If it snaps shut, it shall snap
open. ■ Screws better than glues. ■ Docs and drivers
shall have permalinks and shall reside for all perpetuity
at archive.org. ■ Ease of repair shall be a design ideal,
not an afterthought. ■ Metric or standard, not both.
■ Schematics shall be included.

Make:
technology on your time

Drafted by Mister Jalopy, with assistance from Phillip Torrone and Simon Hill

Figure 4.3.1: The Maker's Bill of Rights (http://makezine.com/2006/12/01/the-makers-bill-of-rights)

Open Source Hardware

MUST

Allow anyone to study, modify, distribute, make, and sell the hardware.

Provide publicly accessible design files and documentation (the source).

Clearly specify what portion of the design, if not all, is being released under the license.

Not imply that derivatives are manufactured, sold, warrantied, or otherwise sanctioned by the original designer.

Not use the trademarks of other companies without permission.

Not be released as non-commercial or no derivatives.

MAY

Require attribution be given.

Use the open source hardware logo to signify their hardware follows the open source hardware definition.

Require derived works to carry a different name or version number from the original design.

Be copied directly or have derivitives created from it.

Require a viral license.

Created by the Open Source Hardware Association
Learn more at oshwa.org

Figure 4.3.2: Open Source Hardware May and Must (www.oshwa.org/wp-content/uploads/2014/08/OSHW-May-and-Must.pdf)

The things that makers produce may appear quirky and are often produced for themselves or their immediate community (rather than being made with an immediate eye to mass production). Often they are a result of 'tinkering' or 'playing' with materials (Wilkinson and Petrich, 2014). However, there are also examples of things created by makers becoming the basis of a commercial company – many products on funding sites like Kickstarter (www.kickstarter.com) have their origins with makers.

Growth of the maker movement

The desire to make stuff is hardly new. DIY has been around a long time and became more of a leisure pursuit and less a necessity during the second half of the last century. What is new is the coming together of this DIY mindset with a collection of digital tools and resources that have enabled the maker movement to do more and to communicate better. These include the rapidly dropping costs of digital manufacturing tools, the availability of powerful free software, the rise of open hardware, social networking via the Internet and the growth of community spaces where makers can gather (Dougherty and Conrad, 2016).

Two significant things happened in 2005. One was the publication by Neil Gershenfeld of 'Fab' (Gershenfeld, 2005), a book that detailed the development of a making course at MIT open to all students, and the subsequent creation, as a spinoff, of what he called a FabLab (Fabrication Laboratory). FabLabs are workshops stocked with state-of-the-art but low-cost digital designing and making tools with a focus on community use. There are now more than 400 FabLabs worldwide, including more than 20 in the United Kingdom (exact numbers are difficult to track as new ones are frequently popping up, and in some cases closing down, so rapidly) (Walter-Herrmann and Büching, 2013).

Also new in 2005 was the launch of Maker Media (http://makermedia. com) and the publishing of *Make* magazine and its associated website (http:// makezine.com). The website has grown to include a shop of equipment and resources for makers (www.makershed.com) as well as a large and growing repository of step-by-step maker projects.

In 2006, Maker Media ran the first Bay Area Maker Faire, with the strap line: 'The greatest show (and tell) on earth'. In 2015, the tenth Bay Area Maker Faire hosted more than 1,200 exhibits and 145,000 attendees. In fact, by 2015 there were more than 150 Maker Faires around the world, including seven in the United Kingdom, with more than a million visitors (Maker Faire, 2016). Numbers certainly grew again in 2016.

However, while FabLabs and MakerMedia are significant influences they are also just facets of the wider maker community, which is incredibly diverse. Across the world makers get together to hack and make in a wide range of settings from informal gatherings in cafés, through a wide range of 'makerspaces' and 'hackspaces' to professionally run membership organizations such as TechShop (www.techshop.ws). In the United States,

100K Garages (www.100kgarages.com) is an organization that helps connect makers with each other and to those with fabrication facilities. Maker's Row (https://makersrow.com) has similar aims. In the United Kingdom, the UK Hackspace Foundation (www.hackspace.org.uk) lists 66 affiliated hackspaces. But this certainly isn't the total number of makerspaces.

Making (and designing) in school education

The most obvious subject with which to link the maker movement is design and technology (D&T). The UK government laid the foundations for D&T in England in 1988 with the publication of the National Curriculum Design and Technology Working Group Interim Report, generally known as the Parkes Report:

> This is literally a visionary activity, a mode of thought which is non-verbal and which has been a characteristic of design and technology throughout history. Such imaging finds its representation in drawings, diagrams, plans, models, prototypes and computer displays and simulations, before its eventual realisation in a product, which may be an artefact, system or environment. (DES, 1988)

Failure to meet the high aspirations of the Parkes Report, compounded by legislative changes with unintended consequences, have led to a significant reduction in the number of young people studying the subject to the age of 16 years over the past 25 years; from 95 per cent of the cohort in 1990 to 35 per cent of the cohort in 2015 (Choulerton, 2015; Barlex, in press).

During the last 15 years, there have been significant attempts to modernize the design and making that pupils carry out in their D&T lessons through continuing professional development (CPD) activities. These include a national CADCAM initiative and a national Electronics in School Strategy, with a focus on programmable control, which was eventually combined into a national Digital Design and Technology Programme (Barlex, 2011). As part of this CPD the ways in which design and technology is taught have been developed to include:

- designing without making
- making without designing
- designing and making
- considering the consequences of technology.

Orchestrated appropriately these provide variety, breadth, balance and depth to enable pupils to achieve technological capability and perspective while making the progress required to achieve a GCSE qualification in the subject. The new D&T GCSE (DfE, 2015b), introduced in September 2017, requires all candidates to work across a range of material areas and to engage with digital making and embedded control.

The maker education movement

Many UK school Design and Technology (D&T) departments were at least as well equipped as the minimum specification for a FabLab (at that time the first schools were installing 3D printers, a technology that didn't then figure in the list of prescribed FabLab equipment). This suggested that here was a great opportunity to open schools to their communities – as well as to open the D&T curriculum to new ways of working (Steeg, 2008). But discussions with schools at the time were not positive, partly because the idea of makerspaces was novel and few had heard of FabLabs and, probably more significantly, it was hard for schools to see past the barriers of things like insurance, health and safety, and security.

The Maker Movement is much stronger in the United States and those who have lost faith in schools to engage young people in technically focused, modern designing and making are looking to the Maker Movement to provide this. The Obama administration viewed the maker movement very favourably, referencing it in several key speeches and, in 2014, hosting the first, annual White House Maker Faire (www.whitehouse.gov/nation-of-makers). The result of this interest is that significant federal money, for example from the Defense Advanced Research Projects Agency (DARPA) (Dougherty, 2012), followed by substantial funding from industry, for example, Cognizant (Dorph and Cannady, 2014) was made available to set up the Maker Education Initiative ('MakerEd'; http://makered.org) with the aim of developing and supporting Makerspaces associated with schools. Because of the very diverse nature of the US education system this initiative is focused, at least to start with, on extracurricular activity.

Making, hacking and pedagogical thinking

MakerEd is based firmly on constructivist and constructionist (Papert, 1993; Kafai and Resnick, 1996) views of learning and sees engagement with making as a powerful lever to support learning. A growing number of US schools are embracing making as a core element of their curriculum. Prominent among these is High Tech High (www.hightechhigh.org), a network of 12 charter schools in San Diego. Even more radical is Brightworks (www.sfbrightworks.org), a private school where the whole curriculum is built around collaborative, mixed-age projects in which making is a core activity.

Maker education activity has been explored and explained in number of recent books (including Martinez and Stager, 2013; Honey and Kanter, 2013; Fleming, 2015; Carlson, 2016) that make the case for making as a core component of a rounded education and provide case studies from a range of schools as well as advice on how to get started. However, it is important to note that, because the idea of maker education is so new, solid quantitative research on its merits (or otherwise) is only just beginning to emerge (Peppler *et al.*, 2016a, 2016b), though there is a longer tradition of similar constructivist and constructionist approaches to draw on such as Project/Problem/Inquiry-Based Learning (Larmer *et al.*, 2015). What is clear is that as making as a community activity moves into classrooms and schools there is a need to think carefully about how to preserve its essential features as it inevitably bends to accommodate the structures of schooling.

Developing making and hacking as a core element of good education

Those advocating a 'maker approach' to education criticize practice in schools as being overly constrained by too much instruction, too much interruption and too much intervention, that is: the curriculum experience is teacher centred/controlled as opposed to pupil centred, with the pupil having agency concerning both what to do and how to do it (Martinez and Stager, 2013). Southall (2016) has argued that there is a gap between the professed aims of D&T education and the actual teaching of D&T, due to narrow conceptions of how learning should be planned for and assessed. She argues that changes need to be made to the way that D&T learning is planned for and her suggestions would move D&T pedagogic practice closer to the openness of a maker approach.

Gershenfeld's (2005) idea of 'just in time' learning prevails in the maker space in which there is no shame in asking for help from those who know more or are more skilled than you are, or in using pre-existing items (chunks of code, parts scavenged from broken/worn-out products). The thrust is doing what it takes to make something and that something is often, if not always, personal, an item of fun or simply 'cool' without the necessity of meeting a significant outside need or want. And, of course, makers are under no obligation to provide evidence of how they have done what they have done for assessment purposes (though very often the maker sharing imperative means that projects are well documented in a form that others can follow – which opens up assessment potential).

It seems clear that if in the informal space the emphasis is on doing by whatever means possible, then it will not be on learning a prescribed curriculum. Arguably a wide range of learning will be taking place in maker activities, but what this is may well emerge as the making activity progresses. Ito *et al.* (2010), exploring the closely allied, even overlapping, area of learning using 'new media', describe children's progressive engagement with a tinkering approach in three stages of *hanging out, messing around* and *geeking out.* These descriptions underline the difficulty of developing transfer from the informal maker space to the more formal classroom space.

Moving making and hacking into schools' curricula will inevitably challenge much prevailing practice since looking at maker activity through the eyes of traditional education, it appears irreverent, if not actually heretical, about the serious business of preparing young people for examinations where learning needs to be structured and organized by teachers so that their pupils can gain the qualifications required to progress through the education system into the world of work.

There is something inherently engaging in making as carried out in maker spaces and perhaps our focus in schools should be not so much on the content of *what* is being learned but *how* it is being learned and the influence this might have on the learners' ways of learning and ways of doing. If such ways of learning/doing are experienced often enough, then it can be argued that they will inform and influence the way such learners behave and think. It was this consideration that led the Royal Academy of Engineering to instigate research concerned with exploring 'engineering habits of mind' that led to the report 'Thinking like an engineer' (Lucas *et al.*, 2014). This identified six engineering habits of mind (EHoM) that, taken together, describe the ways engineers think and act (although this list may fail to capture either the obsessive attention to detail or the conservatism born of 'safety-first' thinking that characterizes much work in engineering):

- systems thinking
- adapting
- problem finding
- creative problem solving
- visualizing
- improving.

The report also suggested ways in which the education system might be redesigned to develop engineers more effectively, recommending that the engineering teaching and learning community seize the opportunity of the revised National Curriculum to bring about a mindset shift in schools and redesign engineering education, especially at primary level. This recommendation has been taken up by the Tinker Tailor Robot Pi project (Bianchi, 2014) which explores the notion of *tinkering*, with particular regard to primary schools (Bianchi, 2016). The project arrived at the following definition of tinkering:

> Tinkering is exploring through fiddling, toying, messing, pottering, dabbling and fooling about with a diverse range (of) things that happen to be available in a creative and productive pursuit to make, mend or improve. (Bianchi, 2016)

Although this is very much in tune with the maker way of working described above, some may find the explicit alignment of tinkering with engineering education questionable. Indeed, the Tinker Tailor Robot Pi project itself asks the following:

1. Is tinkering engineering?
2. Is tinkering a habit of mind in itself?
3. If tinkering provides a pedagogy, how do we develop children's ability to tinker?
4. How do we measure the impact of this technique within a school system that is so individualistic and product outcome driven?

It is the last question that is the most pertinent especially if we see the benefits of a tinkering pedagogy and want to move such pedagogy from the primary school to the secondary school. An interesting aspect of the Tinker Tailor Robot Pi project is the high involvement of professional engineers in collaboration with teachers in providing experiential professional development for teachers who become confident enough to allow their pupils to tinker.

Exploring maker education through partnership

In any partnership it is important that there are benefits to all the partners and that the commitment and activities required of partners are realistic and not over-burdensome. Hence while the knowledge and skill embedded in a maker community may well be extremely useful to a teacher and her pupils we must ask:

1. What are the mechanisms by which such knowledge can be made available to the teacher and pupils?
2. How can this knowledge and skill be incorporated into the school curriculum?

3. What benefits are there to the maker community in providing this knowledge and skill?

An example might prove instructive. Barclays Bank is funding the Eagle Labs scheme that includes incubators giving entrepreneurs and start-ups access to state-of-the-art workspaces. They also provide maker spaces operated by Makerclub (https://makerclub.org). At the time of writing there are four such maker spaces in England (Birmingham, Bournemouth, Brighton and Cambridge) equipped with 3D printing, laser cutters, workshop spaces with a range of traditional making tools, meeting rooms, presentation areas with AV equipment and high speed WIFI; while they are staffed by mentors with the expertise to support those attending the labs. The aim of the labs is to introduce members of the public, particularly young people, to new technologies and create communities of practice that learn through informal making. The Eagle Lab in Brighton, for example, runs a Mend it Mondays session every week at which attendees bring in broken artefacts and are helped to mend them by the Lab Technicians using the Lab's resources. Most recently they are developing the teaching of programming with special reference to robotics.

Conclusion

There is a case for maker education to be a core component of a rounded education, but solid quantitative evidence about its merits is only just beginning to emerge and the well-established traditions of constructivist and constructionist learning are required to bolster support. The informal practices of making emphasize doing by whatever means is possible, and they do not lend themselves easily to a prescribed curriculum. The transfer of an informal maker space to the more formal classroom space is not an easy task. It may be more productive to focus school activity on *how* learning by making happens. For example, the Royal Academy of Engineering has instigated research concerned with exploring six 'engineering habits of mind' (EHoM).

Partnerships may provide a useful way forward for making in education through initiatives such as the Barclays Eagle Labs scheme. It is not difficult to see how a design and technology teacher who lacked expertise in the use of 3D printing or laser cutting could visit the lab and acquire such expertise. There are staff at the lab who are tasked with providing such expertise. This could lead to equipment in the school being better used or the school purchasing such equipment for the first time. It would also be possible for the teacher to bring a small group of pupils to the lab to develop similar knowledge and skills and then organize design and technology lessons in which these pupils acted as 'in-class experts' to support the learning of other pupils.

Such labs have the potential to bridge the gap between the informal maker space and the more formal school space without compromising the integrity of either. The benefit for the schools in this arrangement is that the labs can provide dedicated, bespoke CPD for design and technology teachers who are faced with developing their curriculum in response to the modernization of the subject and the introduction of a radically different GCSE qualification from September 2017. The benefit for the lab is that the pupils will (it is hoped) begin to attend the lab independently as a leisure time activity and become part of the maker community of practice centred on the lab.

It is also possible to imagine a reversal of this situation in which schools' design and technology departments act as maker spaces for the community using the expertise of teachers and technicians plus the equipment in the department. However, given the emphasis on achieving good and improving examination results and the requirement to modernize the design and technology curriculum this is unlikely to be seen as feasible or desirable by most schools.

Chapter 4.4

Learning across locations and settings

Ann Jones, Eileen Scanlon and Koula Charitonos

Introduction

There has been increasing interest in recent years in how to support children in making connections between learning at school and out of school in all kinds of different settings. After all, our brains do not divide what we understand into what we learn in school and what we learn elsewhere. Technology has a role to play here. Researchers in technology-supported learning have investigated learning in different settings, such as schools and universities (formal settings), after school clubs and girl guides (non-formal settings), and in our own homes or simply out and about (informal settings) (see Eshach, 2007, for a discussion of the differences between formal, informal and non-formal settings). Researchers have also looked at how learning can be supported across different settings, for example between schools and after school clubs or between museums and schools.

There are many reasons for this growing interest in learning across contexts. For example, research has suggested that where learners are outside institutional settings and constraints they have the freedom to choose their own goals and agenda, which can have a positive effect on motivation. Meanwhile, mobile technologies have been shown to have potential to support learning activities that move between formal and informal settings. Research has also shown that learning across different settings can be very powerful, as we will illustrate.

Here we will consider what the research tells us about learning across locations and settings by focusing on three interrelated themes that emerge from the research just mentioned:

1. The mobile learner.
2. Context-based learning.
3. The informal learner.

And we will illustrate each theme with research examples drawn from three case studies: the nQuire after-school club; learning in and from museums, and the iSpot project. We begin by summarizing our themes.

The mobile learner

A great many of us use smartphones to find information quickly, wherever we are. Mobile devices such as smartphones give us the potential to use this information for learning, and to engage in context-based learning. Indeed, courses that were once mostly accessed via websites on laptops or computers are increasingly being provided in 'mobile-friendly' form. So what is meant by mobile learning? Different definitions have been offered with most encompassing the idea that mobile devices are often used, but also that the learner himself or herself is mobile. Brown and colleagues, for example, argue that:

> the distinguishing aspect of mobile learning is the assumption that learners are continually mobile. Rather than seeing learners as physically present in a certain place, such as a classroom or a museum, learners are active in different contexts and frequently change their learning contexts. (Brown *et al.*, 2010: 4)

Interestingly, research shows that learners will use whatever technological resources (e.g., laptop, mobile phone, tablet) they have available in order to work on the task in hand (Kukulska-Hulme *et al.*, 2009; Jones, 2015). So research into mobile learning encompasses both how learners use such technological resources and also how they learn in different locations, using fixed as well as mobile technologies.

Context-based learning

Much has also been written on the role of context in learning and its implications, and in this book Chapter 1.3 tackles the thorny issue of context (see also for example, Brown *et al.*, 2010). For instance, a known challenge in the classroom is for children to be able to apply what they have learnt to new and different settings (see Gilbert, 2006; Brown and Duguid, 1991; Anderson *et al.*, 1996 for discussions of knowledge transfer). More recently, the development of mobile technologies and an increasing focus on mobile learning has led to interest in how we can best learn *in* particular contexts and *from* particular contexts.

What do we mean by context? At The Open University, a series of annual reports has explored new forms of teaching, learning and assessment

(Sharples *et al.*, 2015). One topic discussed in the 2015 report is context-based learning, where context is described as follows.

> Context enables us to learn from experience. By interpreting new information in the context of where and when it occurs and relating it to what we already know, we come to understand its relevance and meaning. In a classroom or lecture theatre, the context is typically connected to a fixed space and limited time. Beyond the classroom, learning can come from an enriched context such as visiting a heritage site or museum, or being immersed in a good book. We have opportunities to create context, by interacting with our surroundings, holding conversations, making notes, and modifying nearby objects. We can also come to understand context by exploring the world around us, supported by guides and measuring instruments. (Sharples *et al.*, 2015: 6)

An example of context-based learning is provided by the MASELTOV project that developed a suite of apps for use on mobile phones to support informal contextual language learning for migrants in their new cities (Gaved *et al.*, 2014). Imagine that Teresa, with limited knowledge of English, has the MASELTOV language app (for learning English) on her smartphone and enters a grocery store or a supermarket. She is offered some vocabulary resources to help her find the items she wants to buy. She is also told that there are some lessons available that she could study later at home. When she goes to find a bus on the way home, she is offered support and vocabulary about travel. Another tool that she has available as part of her suite of apps is called a 'Text-lens'. With this she can take a photograph of a sign that is puzzling her, and get a translation. Hence she is able to learn both *in* the context (immediate help on grocery or travel vocabulary) and later, at home, *from* the context, when she works through the lesson. She can then reapply what she has learnt on her next shopping trip and reinforce it: she is learning informally in the course of her everyday life. Tools such as the MASELTOV apps are able to 'know' about the learner's context through using a combination of the smartphone's hardware (e.g. GPS receiver) and customized software (in this case a 'recommendation engine' that suggests choices based on a learner's previous activities). The MASELTOV apps are also examples of informal learning – which is our final theme.

The informal learner

For many years we have known that the extent of informal learning, when compared with the learning that takes place in classrooms or other educational institutions, is often ignored (Coffield, 2000). More recently, there has been considerable interest in informal learning, how it might connect to formal learning, and where informal learning takes place (such as on the Internet: Preece, 2016). As with mobile learning and contextual learning there are different definitions of both informal and non-formal learning (Dierking, 1991; Livingstone, 2001; Burbules, 2006). One view that we find helpful considers learning on a continuum ranging from formal to informal, with one important factor being the amount of control the learner has over their learning. Who decides what is going to be learned? Will the learning be assessed? Is a teacher involved? Is there a curriculum and, if so, who decides what is part of that curriculum? And when will the learning take place and for how long and who decides? Where many of these decisions are taken by the learner, we are likely to refer to the learning as *informal* learning. In less formal contexts, *learners* may decide *what* they learn and *how* they go about it. Learning may also occur *without* the learner's intention to learn (which is the kind of language learning supported in the MASELTOV project discussed earlier: Kukulska-Hulme *et al.*, 2015).

One of the typical outcomes of informal learning is that motivation can be high. Evidence suggests that informal learning contexts, in which the learner has decided to involve herself and which are usually based on her particular interests, can be more motivating (Eshach, 2007). This might also be because the learner has a personal stake in the learning and is more in control. As Song and Bonk (2016) note:

> Though there has not been a consensus for the definition, motivational aspects of self-directed learners were found in most of the informal learning definitions. Thus, informal learners are characterised as motivated to choose or self-direct their own learning. (Song and Bonk, 2016: 3)

As we have seen, informal learning, mobile learning and learning in, from and across contexts often overlap. For this reason, rather than considering any further these approaches in isolation from one another, we will adopt the perspective of three very different case studies, each an example of technology-supported research across contexts.

Case studies
Case study 1: The nQuire after-school club
Although after-school clubs vary considerably, they tend to be much less formal than school itself. In the nQuire after-school club (which is part

of a large project called 'Personal Inquiry' (PI)), pupils chose their own investigations, within constraints, although some school rules applied (e.g. how they addressed the teachers). For this reason we use the term *non-formal learning* to refer to learning happening as a result of participating in this club. The aim of the PI project was to support children to conduct *personally relevant* scientific inquiries where they gathered and assessed evidence, conducted experiments and engaged in informed debate in contexts ranging from formal to informal. The children used small netbooks, so that when they moved from the classroom to home for example, these mobile devices supported the inquiry they were making, wherever they were.

In this after-school club, researchers worked with teachers to support students in planning and conducting evidence-based inquiries at home on the theme of sustainability. The students decided what topic to investigate (hence the personal relevance) and worked independently in small groups of their choice. For example, once they had settled on exploring 'food rotting' they designed inquiries into the storage and decomposition of food, including investigations into packaging. They used the nQuire software (Mulholland *et al.*, 2012), to help them structure the different stages of an inquiry, including: deciding on a topic, generating a hypothesis, collecting and analysing data, and drawing valid conclusions. Support from the software included reminding pupils of the stage they were at in their inquiry, storing their data and providing different ways of presenting information graphically.

The researchers interviewed two groups of pupils who attended the club, their teachers and a number of parents, and kept records of the students' work. Data was collected on how motivated the students were, their attitudes and their skills. Overall, the students were clearly excited and motivated to learn about food sustainability, and all of them were positive about working in a non-formal context where they had more control and choice. For example, one said: 'I wanted to find out and learn new things and the fact that we could choose what sort of sustainability project we did was really good.'

Each group presented their work to the other groups and designed a poster that they used to discuss their inquiries. The focus of discussion was on reflecting on the inquiry, and how the inquiries could have been improved. Here there was evidence of students' understanding of planning a scientific inquiry. For example, the 'cheese' group realized that their decision to rot cheese in three different houses made their investigation unfair since temperature was not controlled, which could have affected their results. The data suggested that the club influenced pupils' attitudes towards food production and packaging. The students talked about being 'more sustainable', giving comments such as 'it is important to try to be sustainable and try ... not to be greedy', 'get free range eggs. Buy these bananas that aren't in packaging.'

The researchers also found that the web-based software supported the pupils' inquiries at home when there was no teacher support, and could support a limited range of different personal inquiries. As the software was implemented on mobile devices, students had it with them wherever they were. For this reason, it supported the inquiry process, and allowed for representations of the students' personalized inquiries to be developed. It was seen as bridging different contexts such as home and school – and in addition to keeping student data, it also supported data interpretation and representation.

The research discussed in this case study shows how students were able to conduct science investigations, learning about the scientific inquiry process, across contexts out of school, in a non-formal setting (the after-school club) and in informal settings (at home). They were supported in doing this by their use of mobile devices and specific software.

Case study 2: Learning in and from museums

This case study is again concerned with learning contexts that are usually less formal than the school classroom: museums, which are visited by individuals, families and schools. How can technology best be used to support learning in and from museums, and help children to make links between museum visits and their everyday lives – i.e. across contexts?

Sawyer (2014), in discussing the learning sciences, notes how attributes of successful learning include learning through conversation and collaboration – both types of learning that can be well supported by technology (as illustrated in our first case study above). In considering how to enable innovative forms of learning with museums, Sharples describes Sprake's (2012) work on 'learning through touring', where visitors create tours by moving through constructed spaces, *'creating experiences from their interactions with people, locations and objects'* (Sharples, 2015: 2).

Charitonos also uses the idea of tours in her study on children's use of microblogging in museums (Charitonos *et al.*, 2012). Her research investigated how history students aged 13–14 years, in a UK secondary school, used social and mobile technologies in school field trips. As part of this study the students used the social media platform Twitter as part of their visit to the Museum of London. The researcher was particularly interested in how the young people's interactions on Twitter (on smartphones lent to them) helped them to engage meaningfully with the museum content and to make sense of their experiences – in other words, whether Twitter was able to support the children's conversations around artefacts in the museum and to support meaningful interpretations of the museum objects. She was also interested in how group postings translated into learning trails (or 'tours') that might then be used as the basis of a meaningful dialogue both inside and outside the museum (i.e. across contexts).

The study included classroom work before and after the museum trip and aimed to integrate part of the History curriculum work with the museum visit. In particular, the work focused on how the children's understanding of the theme of civil rights ('Get up, stand up: fight for your rights!') could be supported and developed. As in our first case study, the children were asked to carry out inquiries, in this case historical inquiries, to investigate questions such as: Which methods do people use to remove inequalities in society? They would then select and interpret evidence (historical sources), in order to evaluate and critically reflect on their inquiries and reach reasoned conclusions. Finally they presented their interpretations to an audience of fellow pupils.

The students, working in groups of three or four, followed pre-defined trails in the museum, with instructions and activities being given to each group in a booklet. For example, in response to the task 'In the Suffragette case find an object with which Suffragettes chained themselves to parts of government buildings as a form of protest. What do you think of this method of protest?', the students took photographs and tweeted (posted a comment on Twitter). The data included these tweets, the photographs and interviews with the students.

The outcomes of this research were complex. For example, while many of the groups' Twitter postings did not lead to protracted online conversations, the students did value the online social space as a place to contribute, view and reflect on others' opinions. For example, as one of the students noted, ' ... some people don't have the confidence to put the hand up and talk about what they've seen. With the technology they could write it down ... and I saw a lot of people write down some really good ideas and maybe the use of technology could help them get their point across.'

Using Twitter also helped the participants to extend their museum experience. They frequently used the photographs that they took as the basis of brief discussions, through which they developed their understanding and interpretation of the objects that they saw (which is an example of learning through collaboration and conversation as discussed by Sawyer (2014)). Twitter also enabled the discussion to be preserved: 'Without technology you wouldn't have remembered it and looking back at them [tweets] when you can.'

The interviews also revealed that the children were very positive about their use of the mobile technologies in this visit: 'seeing everyone's reactions, like different things around the museum and what they thought about it on Twitter ... it was really interesting to think of what other people thought of the visit'. Children also highlighted how the technology allowed them to stay connected: 'you got to see other people's opinions ... you can see how they interpret it [an object] ... I like the fact you were staying in touch with everyone, even though they were not there.'

As in our first case study, the students use of a mobile technology (here Twitter on mobile telephones) supported their interest in and engagement with the learning activities. However, although no specific software needed to be developed, the learning activities depended on considerable planning before the visit. In addition, the visit itself was well supported by a teacher, assistant and the researcher. Nevertheless, the use of mobile technology here supported some conversations and collaboration about the objects of interest in the museum and the concepts being studied, and helped them make connections between contexts (here between the non-formal context of the museum and the formal context of school).

Case study 3: The iSpot project

While our first two case studies concerned learning contexts that are less formal than the school classroom, our third and final case study moves into a fully informal context (although the technology has also been used in formal settings). iSpot (www.ispotnature.org) is an online tool and community that aims to encourage a new generation of naturalists by helping students and people of all ages learn how to identify organisms from gardens, fields and forests. Although species identification is a skill that underlies all of biodiversity science, it is no longer part of the UK school curriculum. iSpot has been successfully used in the United Kingdom and far beyond, in informal and formal settings. For example, it has been incorporated into The Open University's OpenScience Laboratory (that allows anyone, anywhere, to access practical science education) and into various OU courses.

iSpot facilitates novices and experts to work together to identify living organisms and crowdsourcing identification. Anyone, anywhere, can upload an image for identification, while the community participates and helps with the identification. A contribution on the iSpot website is a shared social object (Knorr Cetina, 2001), while participation in the website is scaffolded by these contributions and identifications to allow participation in the community of practice. The information gathered by iSpot is deposited with biodiversity databases and networks, allowing them to use this data for conservation purposes.

At the time of writing iSpot has gained 53,000 registered users who have made more than 550,000 observations of many thousands of species, including two not recorded in the United Kingdom before. For example, in 2009, a six-year-old girl discovered a moth on her windowsill. The moth, native to Asia, had never before been spotted in the United Kingdom. After identification on iSpot the species was also confirmed by experts and the moth was taken into the Natural History Museum collection. Other notable examples have been described by Silvertown and colleagues: 'In South Africa, a doctor submitted a photograph of unknown seeds that were the cause of poisoning in several children presenting at a clinic and these were identified 35 seconds after posting on iSpot (iSpot, 2013). Hitherto unknown populations of South African endemic plant species are regularly discovered on iSpot' (Silvertown *et al.*, 2015: 142).

A number of studies have been conducted on the impact of participation with iSpot, and on which features can be identified as important in the design of community projects (e.g. iSpot Local and iSpot Mobile). For example, attention has been paid to how learners can be supported to be members of a natural history community, with participation structured around a shared social object, engaging in knowledge building as active contributors to knowledge. In particular, Scanlon and colleagues showed that iSpot offers 'new opportunities for learners to engage with science on the move' and provides 'an inquiry learning approach to identification of wildlife with support provided by a community developing round the resource' (Scanlon *et al.*, 2014: 58).

The overall experience of the iSpot project, with its analysis of the improvement in identification as users become more experienced, provides some evidence of knowledge development. However it was also possible that the users are simply becoming more proficient with the system – which means that there is room for further investigation of learning taking place with the system. This was considered further by Silvertown *et al.*:

> While we have anecdotal evidence from comments made by participants that they have learned, we do not have direct, quantitative evidence of learning in iSpot yet. However, we do know from a previous analysis of 400 participants' behaviour that they provided determinations for fewer than 40 per cent of

their very first observations, but that they themselves determined more than 60 per cent of their 50th observations (Scanlon *et al.*, 2014). This change in behaviour probably reflects learning, although other causes of the trend are possible. (Silvertown *et al.*, 2015: 142)

In other words, the research suggests that, as users of iSpot become more experienced with the tools, they are improving their identification knowledge. However, further study is needed (which might be facilitated by a quiz service now incorporated within iSpot) to assess whether learning is taking place.

Unlike our previous two case studies, iSpot does not involve teachers when it is being used in informal settings, although it does involve participation from experts. iSpot is also an example of an informal learning context-based (gardens, parks and forests) mobile tool that has been used across contexts, in various formal settings (such as schools and universities).

Conclusion

The three case studies discussed in this chapter involve students in a range of learning activities across contexts. As we have seen, students have investigated the scientific process of investigation, coming to understand the flaws in their investigation design (case study 1); they have collaboratively developed interpretations of museum objects, which they have used to further their understanding of civil rights in a historical context (case study 2); and they have collaborated with experts in order to develop their identification skills (case study 3).

While each of these case studies has illustrated ways in which learning can take place across contexts, they do not provide strong quantitative evidence of testable learning. Nevertheless, our first case study, nQuire, does show students learning across the contexts of home and school, by means of mobile technology, and suggests that control of learning (being able to decide on the topic of investigation) is important for motivation. Our second case study, which involved learning in museums, illustrates a successful use of social media in a museum context. Finally, while our first and second case studies both involve learning about the context in which the learning is taking place, and our third case study, iSpot, involves learning in the natural world, all of our case studies emphasize learning *in context* and *between contexts*. In fact, all three case studies (and other projects mentioned such as MASELTOV) show the importance of context for learning: the context *in which* one learns and *from which* one learns. Some technologies, especially mobile devices that learners can carry with them all the time such as smartphones, are increasingly able to use knowledge of a learner's context. This allows the technology to offer appropriate and different content or suggestions in each setting to different learners. Such 'intelligence' can be part of a mobile device's hardware or software.

Conclusion

Rosemary Luckin and Mutlu Cukurova

We started Part 4 with a brief discussion about contemporary digital capabilities and the need for learners to develop these if they are to be effective learners. For example the JISC contemporary digital capabilities framework suggested the need for us to: protect our digital identity and ensure our digital wellbeing; use whatever technology we have access to confidently, critically, skilfully and appropriately, which includes safely, and to acknowledge and value the different kinds of use that can be made of technology, including: information, data and media literacies; digital creation, innovation and scholarship; digital learning and self-development and communication, collaboration and participation.

The chapter by Keith Turvey and Norbert Pachler illustrated the need for us to probe the evidence concerning tablet devices and not take any of it merely at face value. Students' dispositions towards, as well as teachers' pedagogical decisions about digital technologies are vitally important. The dangers of over-simplistic interpretations of research about memory was used as an example that showed how these have led some policymakers to over-emphasize a reliance on impoverished approaches to learning and teaching based upon rote learning and repetition of facts.

We are urged to pay careful attention to *how* devices are used and to focus on teaching students how to optimize their opportunities to learn with digital technologies, and to self-regulate their use. Technology addiction as it suggested is symptomatic of deeper and more complex neurological, biological, emotional and behavioural factors. The issue of online safety was seen as central. We were encouraged to move on from the risk-averse education system in which digital technologies serve an agenda of restriction and surveillance to an approach that would put children and young people's rights at the centre of their use of digital technologies.

Chapter 4.3 provided an extensive description of maker education activity and encouraged the idea that making should be a core educational component in any system. Torben Steeg and David Barlex acknowledge that solid evidence about maker education is only just beginning to emerge. However, they point to constructivist and constructionist approaches as further evidence for why making could support learning effectively. The emphasis within making activity in schools should be on the process of making and how learning is happening rather than what should be included in the curriculum. Work by the Royal Academy of Engineering illustrates this point well with its exploration of 'engineering habits of mind' that describe the ways engineers think and act and include: systems thinking, adapting, problem finding, creative problem solving, visualizing and improving. Partnerships with non-educational partners are seen as a possible way forward for education with initiatives such as Barclays Bank's Eagle Labs being seen as a possible way to bridge the gap between the informal maker space and the more formal school space without compromising the integrity of either.

Chapter 4.4 sees Ann Jones, Eileen Scanlon and Koula Charitonos explore learning across different locations and settings. Three case studies are discussed, each of which illustrates ways in which learning can take place across locations. These case studies provide evidence that: control of learning (being able to decide on the topic of investigation) is important for motivation; and that both the context *in which* one learns and the context *from which* one learns are important. Technologies, such as mobile devices, are increasingly able to use knowledge of a learner's context to offer appropriate individualized content or suggestions.

What the research says about helping learners get the most benefit from digital technologies

- Digital capabilities are those that enable us to function (live, learn and work) in a digital society, that enable us to confidently, critically, skilfully and appropriately select and use digital technologies to achieve our goals.
- Digital capabilities constantly need to be updated, as new technologies emerge and old ones die, and also as our goals and our methods change.
- The responsibility for maintaining our digital capability lies with each of us. We need to work out what it is that we need to be able to do, and then find the technology, the training, the support, to help us to be able to do it.
- Teachers, parents and children should understand that tablet devices can have a positive, negative or indeed no effect on learning or attainment.
- The actual effect on learning and attainment cannot be linked wholly to the use of tablet devices and will be dependent on how they are used (as was also reported in Chapter 1.6), in what contexts and for what purposes.
- Increasing attainment is not the only purpose for incorporating tablet devices into education; they have an important place in children and young people's developing media literacy.
- The opportunity that tablets afford to combine visual with textual information or narrated audio with animation can contribute to learning and conceptual understanding.

- There is currently no evidence to suggest the use of tablet devices per se can cause addictive behaviours, but teachers and parents should play an active role in helping children to develop the self-control to moderate and critically mediate their use of tablet devices and mobile technologies.
- An overemphasis on a culture of surveillance may be counterproductive and expose children and young people to increased risk and vulnerability when adopting tablets or mobile technologies.
- There is no room for complacency in adopting mobile technologies such as tablet devices into formal education contexts; there should be regular opportunities for children, teachers and parents to discuss and critically review the ways the technology is being used and consider how they could use it more effectively.
- There is an emerging maker movement in the United Kingdom, United States and elsewhere that is receiving attention from government and industry as a means of engaging young people with technical skills and enterprise.
- Due to the novelty of maker education, solid quantitative research on its practice is only just beginning to emerge but educational researchers are investigating approaches to teaching and learning that draw on the nature of maker activities.
- The maker movement challenges conventional approaches to learning that are taking place in schools.
- Various stakeholders are now actively engaged in developing synergy between maker activity and mainstream learning in schools.
- Learning takes place in many contexts, from formal contexts such as schools or universities, to non-formal contexts like after-school clubs, to informal contexts such as at home.
- Learning in non-formal or informal contexts may have an impact on student motivation, because typically they choose what they want to learn.
- Various technologies (such as mobile devices and specific software including nQuire and iSpot) have been developed to facilitate learning in specific settings, and also to facilitate learning across settings. Such technologies also have the potential to respond adaptively to the context in which the learning is taking place, delivering appropriate content or providing appropriate tools.

- While the evidence that appropriate technologies can support learning in non-formal and informal settings is detailed and positive, the research has not yet provided strong quantitative evidence of testable learning.

Acknowledgements

Thanks to Professor Bob Farmer for conversations about the work of James Hattie, and to Professor Alan Tait and Dr Roger Mills for collaboration on an earlier synthesis of the research on learning.

References (Part 4)

Anderson, J.R., Reder, L.M. and Simon, H.A. (1996) 'Situated learning and education'. *Educational Researcher*, 25 (4), 5–11.

Baddeley, A. (1986) *Working Memory*. Oxford: Clarendon Press.

Baddeley, A. (2000) 'Short-term and working memory'. In Tulving, E. and Craik, F.I.M. (eds) *The Oxford Handbook of Memory*. New York: Oxford University Press, 77–92.

Barlex, D. (2011) 'Achieving creativity in the technology classroom: The English experience in secondary schools'. In Barak, M. and Hacker, M. (eds) *Fostering Human Development through Engineering and Technology Education*. Rotterdam: Sense Publishers, 103–29.

Barlex, D. (in press) 'D&T in England (history and rationale)'. In de Vries, M.J. (ed.) *First International Handbook of Technology Education*. The Netherlands: Springer.

Beland, L.-P. and Murphy, R. (2015) *Ill Communication: Technology, distraction and student performance* (CEP Discussion Paper 1350). London: Centre for Economic Performance.

Bianchi, L. (2014) *Tinker Tailor Robot Pi: Embracing engineering in the school curriculum*. Manchester: University of Manchester. Online. http://epsassets.manchester.ac.uk/medialand/fascinate/projects/tinker-tailor-robot-pi.pdf (accessed 10 March 2017).

Bianchi, L. (2016) *Tinker Tailor Robot Pi: Exploring a signature pedagogy for engineering in primary schools: Learning together with teachers and engineers*. Manchester: University of Manchester.

Brown, E., Brner, D., Sharples, M., Glahn, C., de Jong. T. and Specht, M. (2010) *Location-Based and Contextual Mobile Learning: A STELLAR small-scale study*. STELLAR European Network of Excellence in TEL (EU).

Brown, J.S. and Duguid, P. (1991) 'Organizational learning and communities-of-practice: Toward a unified view of working, learning, and innovation'. *Organization Science*, 2 (1), 40–57.

Burbules, N.C. (2006) 'Self-educating communities: Collaboration and learning through the internet'. In Bekerman, Z., Burbules, N.C. and Silberman Keller, D. (eds) *Learning in Places: The informal education reader*. New York: Peter Lang, 273–84.

Burden. K. and Kearney, M. (2016) 'Future scenarios for mobile science learning'. *Research in Science Education*, 46 (2), 287–308.

Byron, T. (2008) *Safer Children in a Digital World: The report of the Byron Review*. London: Department for Children, Schools and Families.

Carlson, M. (2016) *180 Days of Making*. CreateSpace Independent Publishing Platform.

Charitonos, K., Blake, C., Scanlon, E. and Jones, A. (2012) 'Museum learning via social and mobile technologies: (How) can online interactions enhance the visitor experience?' *British Journal of Educational Technology*, 43 (5), 802–19.

Choulerton, D. (2015) 'From here to where? The current state of design and technology: What we know, what the data is telling us and the threats, challenges and opportunities ahead'. Design and Technology Association (DATA) Summer School keynote speech, 9 July 2015. Online. www.slideshare. net/Ofstednews/design-and-technology-association-data-summer-school-keynote-2015 (accessed 10 March 2017).

Clark, W. and Luckin, R. (2013) *What the Research Says: iPads in the classroom*. London: London Knowledge Lab. Online. https://digitalteachingandlearning. files.wordpress.com/2013/03/ipads-in-the-classroom-report-lkl.pdf (accessed 10 March 2017).

Coffield, F. (ed.) (2000) *The Necessity of Informal Learning*. Bristol: Policy Press.

Cox, M., Webb, M., Abbott, C., Blakeley, B., Beauchamp, T. and Rhodes, V. (2003) *ICT and Pedagogy: A review of the research literature* (ICT in Schools Research and Evaluation 18). London: Department for Education and Skills. Online. https://wiki.inf.ed.ac.uk/twiki/pub/ECHOES/ICT/ict_pedagogy_ summary.pdf (accessed 10 March 2017).

Crystal, D. (2009) *Txtng: The gr8 db8*. Oxford: Oxford University Press.

DES (Department of Education and Science) and Welsh Office (1988) *National Curriculum Design and Technology Working Group Interim Report*. London: HMSO.

DfE (Department for Education) (2015a) *Design and Technology GCSE Subject Content*. London: Department for Education.

DfE (Department for Education) (2015b) 'New measures to keep children safe online at school and at home'. Press Release, 22 December. Online. www.gov. uk/government/news/new-measures-to-keep-children-safe-online-at-school-and-at-home (accessed 10 March 2017).

Dierking, L. (1991) 'Learning theory and learning styles: An overview'. *Journal of Museum Education*, 16 (1), 4–6.

Dorph, R. and Cannady, M.A. (2014) *Making the Future: Promising evidence of influence*. Berkeley: University of California. Online. www.cognizant. com/about-cognizant-resources/Cognizant-making-the-future.pdf (accessed 10 March 2017).

Dougherty, D. (2012) 'Makerspaces in education and DARPA'. *Make*, 4 April. Online. http://makezine.com/2012/04/04/makerspaces-in-education-and-darpa (accessed 10 March 2017).

Dougherty, D. and Conrad, A. (2016) *Free to Make: How the maker movement is changing our schools, our jobs, and our minds*. Berkeley, CA: North Atlantic Books.

Durkee, T., Kaess, M., Carli, V., Parzer, P., Wasserman, C., Floderus, B., Apter, A., Balazs, J., Barzilay, S., Bobes, J., Brunner, R., Corcoran, P., Cosman, D., Cotter, P., Despalins, R., Graber, N., Guillemin, F., Haring, C., Kahn, J.-P., Mandelli, L., Marusic, D., Mészáros, G., Musa, G.J., Postuvan, V., Resch, F., Saiz, P.A., Sisask, M., Varnik, A., Sarchiapone, M., Hoven, C.W. and Wasserman, D. (2012) 'Prevalence of pathological internet use among adolescents in Europe: Demographic and social factors'. *Addiction*, 107 (12), 2210–22.

Eshach, H. (2007) 'Bridging in-school and out-of-school learning: Formal, non-formal, and informal education'. *Journal of Science Education and Technology*, 16 (2), 171–90.

Fleming, L. (2015) *Worlds of Making: Best practices for establishing a Makerspace for your school*. Thousand Oaks, CA: Corwin.

Gaved, M., Luley, P., Efremidis, S., Georgiou, I., Kukulska-Hulme, A., Jones, A. and Scanlon, E. (2014) 'Challenges in context-aware mobile language learning: The MASELTOV approach'. Paper presented at the 13th World Conference on Mobile and Contextual Learning (mLearn 2014), Istanbul, Turkey, 3–5 November 2014.

Gershenfeld, N. (2005) *Fab: The coming revolution on your desktop – from personal computers to personal fabrication*. New York: Basic Books.

Gilbert, J.K. (2006) 'On the nature of "context" in chemical education'. *International Journal of Science Education*, 28 (9), 957–76.

Greenfield, S. (2014) *Mind Change: How digital technologies are leaving their mark on our brains*. London: Rider Books.

Greitemeyer, T. and Mügge, D.O. (2014) 'Video games do affect social outcomes: A meta-analytic review of the effects of violent and prosocial video game play'. *Personality and Social Psychology Bulletin*, 40 (5), 578–89.

Haßler, B., Major, L. and Hennessy, S. (2016) 'Tablet use in schools: A critical review of the evidence for learning outcomes'. *Journal of Computer Assisted Learning*, 32 (2), 139–56.

Hattie, J. (2009) *Visible Learning: A synthesis of over 800 meta-analyses relating to achievement*. London: Routledge.

Higgins, S., Xiao, Z. and Katsipataki, M. (2012) *The Impact of Digital Technology on Learning: A summary for the Education Endowment Foundation*. Durham: Durham University. Online. https://educationendowmentfoundation.org.uk/public/files/Publications/The_Impact_of_Digital_Technologies_on_Learning_(2012).pdf (accessed 15 September 2017).

Honey, M. and Kanter, D.E. (eds) (2013) *Design, Make, Play: Growing the next generation of STEM innovators*. New York: Routledge.

Howard-Jones, P., Holmes, W., Demetriou, S., Jones, C., Tanimoto, E., Morgan, O., Perkins, D. and Davies, N. (2015) 'Neuroeducational research in the design and use of a learning technology'. *Learning, Media and Technology*, 40 (2), 227–46.

Ito, M., Baumer, S., Bittanti, M., Boyd, D., Cody, R., Herr-Stephenson, B., Horst, H.A., Lange, P.G., Mahendran, D., Martínez, K.Z., Pascoe, C.J., Perkel, D., Robinson, L., Sims, C. and Tripp, L. (2010) *Hanging Out, Messing Around, and Geeking Out: Kids living and learning with new media*. Cambridge, MA: MIT Press.

Jones, A. (2015) 'Mobile informal language learning: Exploring Welsh learners' practices'. *eLearning Papers*, 45, Article 6, 4–14.

Kafai, Y. and Resnick, M. (eds) (1996) *Constructionism in Practice: Designing, thinking, and learning in a digital world*. London: Routledge.

Kim, S.M. and Han, D.H. (2015) 'Neurobiological aspects of problematic internet and video game use'. In Aboujaoude, E. and Starcevic, V. (eds) *Mental Health in the Digital Age: Grave dangers, great promise*. New York: Oxford University Press, 69–85.

Kirschner, P.A. and Kester, L. (2016) 'Towards a research agenda for educational technology research'. In Rushby, N. and Surry, D.W. (eds) *The Wiley Handbook of Learning Technology*. Chichester: John Wiley and Sons, 523–41.

Knorr Cetina, K. (2001) 'Objectual practice'. In Schatzki, T.R., Knorr Cetina, K. and von Savigny, E. (eds) *The Practice Turn in Contemporary Theory*. London: Routledge, 175–88.

Kukulska-Hulme, A., Gaved, M., Paletta, L., Scanlon, E., Jones, A. and Brasher, A. (2015) 'Mobile incidental learning to support the inclusion of recent immigrants'. *Ubiquitous Learning*, 7 (2), 9–21.

Kukulska-Hulme, A., Sharples, M., Milrad, M., Arnedillo-Sánchez, I. and Vavoula, G. (2009) 'Innovation in mobile learning: A European perspective'. *International Journal of Mobile and Blended Learning*, 1 (1), 13–35.

Larmer, J., Mergendoller, J. and Boss, S. (2015) *Setting the Standard for Project Based Learning: A proven approach to rigorous classroom instruction*. Alexandria, VA: Association for Supervision and Curriculum Development.

Livingstone, D.W. (2001) *Adults' Informal Learning: Definitions, findings, gaps and future research*. (Working Paper 21). Toronto: Centre for the Study of Education and Work.

Livingstone, S., Haddon, L., Görzig, A. and Ólafsson, K. (2011) *EU Kids Online: Final report*. London: LSE. Online. http://eprints.lse.ac.uk/39351 (accessed 10 March 2017).

Lucas, B., Hanson, J. and Claxton, G. (2014) *Thinking Like an Engineer: Implications for the education system*. London: Royal Academy of Engineering.

Maker Faire (2016) 'Fast facts'. Online. https://makerfaire.com/media-center/#fast-facts (accessed 15 September 2017).

Maguire, E., Woollett, K. and Spiers, H. (2006) 'London taxi drivers and bus drivers: A structural MRI and neuropsychological analysis.' *Hippocampus*. 16 (12), 1091–101.

Male, T. and Burden, K. (2014) 'Access denied? Twenty-first-century technology in schools'. *Technology, Pedagogy and Education*, 23 (4), 423–37.

Martinez, S.L. and Stager, G.S. (2013) *Invent To Learn: Making, tinkering, and engineering in the classroom*. Torrance, CA: Constructing Modern Knowledge Press.

Mayer, R.E. (2008) 'Applying the science of learning: Evidence-based principles for the design of multimedia instruction'. *American Psychologist*, 63 (8), 760–9.

Mills, K.L. (2016) 'Possible effects of internet use on cognitive development in adolescence'. *Media and Communication*, 4 (3), 4–12.

Mulholland, P., Anastopoulou, S., Collins, T., Feisst, M., Gaved, M., Kerawalla, L., Paxton, M., Scanlon, E., Sharples, M. and Wright, M. (2012) 'nQuire: Technological support for personal inquiry learning'. *IEEE Transactions on Learning Technologies*, 5 (2), 157–69.

Papert, S. (1993) *Mindstorms: Children, computers, and powerful ideas*. 2nd ed. New York: Basic Books.

Peppler, K., Halverson, E.R. and Kafai Y.B. (eds) (2016a) *Makeology: Makerspaces as Learning Environments (Vol. 1)*. New York: Routledge.

Peppler, K., Halverson, E.R. and Kafai Y.B. (eds) (2016b) *Makeology: Makers as Learners (Vol. 2)*. New York: Routledge.

Pimmer, C. and Pachler, N. (2014) 'Mobile learning in the workplace: Unlocking the value of mobile technology for work-based education'. In Ally, M. and Tsinakos, A. (eds) *Increasing Access through Mobile Learning*. Vancouver: Commonwealth of Learning and Athabasca University, 193–204.

Preece, J. (2016) 'Citizen science: New research challenges for human–computer interaction'. *International Journal of Human–Computer Interaction*, 32 (8), 585–612.

Saran, C. (2009) 'Apollo 11: The computers that put man on the moon'. *Computer Weekly*, 17 July. Online. www.computerweekly.com/feature/Apollo-11-The-computers-that-put-man-on-the-moon (accessed 10 March 2017).

Sawyer, R.K. (ed.) (2014) *The Cambridge Handbook of the Learning Sciences*. New York: Cambridge University Press.

Scanlon, E., Woods, W. and Clow, D. (2014) 'Informal participation in science in the UK: Identification, location and mobility with iSpot'. *Journal of Educational Technology and Society*, 17 (2), 58–71.

Selwyn, N. (2016) 'The dystopian futures'. In Rushby, N. and Surry, D.W. (eds) *The Wiley Handbook of Learning Technology*. Chichester: John Wiley and Sons, 542–56.

Sharples, M. (2015) 'Seeding, wonder rooms and curatorial inquiry: New forms of museum communication and learning'. In *DREAM Conference: "Museum Communication: Practices and Perspectives", Royal Danish Academy of Sciences and Letters, Copenhagen, 27–28 August 2015: Position Papers*. Odense: Danish Research Centre on Education and Advanced Media Materials, 26–30.

Sharples, M., Adams, A., Alozie, N., Ferguson, R., FitzGerald, E., Gaved, M., McAndrew, P., Means, B., Remold, J., Rienties, B., Roschelle, J., Vogt, K., Whitelock, D. and Yarnall, L. (2015) *Innovating Pedagogy 2015: Exploring new forms of teaching, learning and assessment, to guide educators and policy makers* (Open University Innovation Report 4). Milton Keynes: Open University.

Silvertown, J., Harvey, M., Greenwood, R., Dodd, M., Rosewell, J., Rebelo, T., Ansine, J. and McConway, K. (2015) 'Crowdsourcing the identification of organisms: A case-study of iSpot'. *ZooKeys*, 480, 125–46.

Song, D. and Bonk, C.J. (2016) 'Motivational factors in self-directed informal learning from online learning resources'. *Cogent Education*, 3 (1), Article 1205838, 1–11.

Southall, M. (2016) 'What does design and technology learning really look like?'. *Design and Technology Education*, 21 (3), 51–62.

Sprake, J. (2012) *Learning-through-Touring: Mobilising learners and touring technologies to creatively explore the built environment*. Rotterdam: Sense Publishers.

Steeg, T. (2008) 'Makers, Hackers and Fabbers: What is the future for D&T?'. In Norman, E.W.L. and Spendlove, D. (eds.*) The Design and Technology Association International Research Conference Loughborough University, 2-4 July*. Wellesbourne: The Design and Technology Association, 65–73.

Strittmatter, E., Parzer, P., Brunner, R., Fischer, G., Durkee, T., Carli, V., Hoven, C.W., Wasserman, C., Sarchiapone, M., Wasserman, D., Resch, F. and Kaess, M. (2016) 'A 2-year longitudinal study of prospective predictors of pathological internet use in adolescents'. *European Child and Adolescent Psychiatry*, 25 (7), 725–34.

Sweller, J. (1988) 'Cognitive load during problem solving: Effects on learning'. *Cognitive Science*, 12 (2), 257–85.

Turkle, S. (2011) *Alone Together: Why we expect more from technology and less from each other*. New York: Basic Books.

Turvey, K. (2014) 'iPads in education? A participatory design for professional learning with mobile technologies'. In Passey, D. and Tatnall, A. (eds) *Key Competencies in ICT and Informatics: Implications and issues for educational professionals and management: IFIP WG 3.4/3.7 International Conferences, KCICTP and ITEM 2014, Potsdam, Germany, July 1–4, 2014, Revised Selected Papers* (IFIP Advances in Information and Communication Technology 444). Heidelberg: Springer, 106–23.

Turvey, K. and Pachler, N. (2016) 'Problem spaces: A framework and questions for critical engagement with learning technologies in formal educational contexts'. In Rushby, N. and Surry, D.W. (eds) *The Wiley Handbook of Learning Technology*. Chichester: John Wiley and Sons, 113–30.

UNHCR (2014) *Report of the Special Rapporteur on the Promotion and Protection of the Right to Freedom of Opinion and Expression* (A/69/335). New York: United Nations General Assembly. Online. www.ohchr.org/EN/newyork/Pages/HRreportstothe69thsessionGA.aspx (accessed 10 March 2017).

United Kingdom Parliament (2016) Investigatory Powers Act, 2016. Online. https://services.parliament.uk/bills/2015-16/investigatorypowers.html (accessed 29 October 2017).

Walter-Herrmann, J. and Büching, C. (eds) (2013) *FabLab: Of machines, makers and inventors*. Bielefeld: Transcript Verlag.

Weston, M.E. and Bain, A. (2010) 'The end of techno-critique: The naked truth about 1:1 laptop initiatives and educational change'. *Journal of Technology, Learning, and Assessment*, 9 (6), 5–25. Online. http://ejournals.bc.edu/ojs/index.php/jtla/issue/view/150 (accessed 10 March 2017).

Wiliam, D. (2014) 'Randomized control trials in education research'. *Research in Education*, 6 (1), 3–4.

Wilkinson, K. and Petrich, M. (2014) *The Art of Tinkering: Meet 150+ makers working at the intersection of art, science and technology*. San Francisco: Weldon Owen.

Suggested reading 3

Dougherty, D. and Conrad, A. (2016) *Free to Make: How the maker movement is changing our schools, our jobs, and our minds.* Berkeley, CA: North Atlantic Books.

Gabrielson, C. (2013) *Tinkering: Kids learn by making stuff.* Sebastopol, CA: Maker Media.

Martinez, S.L. and Stager, G.S. (2013) *Invent To Learn: Making, tinkering, and engineering in the classroom.* Torrance, CA: Constructing Modern Knowledge Press.

Wilkinson, K. and Petrich, M. (2014) *The Art of Tinkering: Meet 150+ makers working at the intersection of art, science and technology.* San Francisco: Weldon Owen.

Suggested reading 4

1. If you were particularly interested in the iSpot project you might enjoy reading Jennifer Preece's article in the *Interactions* magazine about how citizen scientists (such as those participating in iSpot) can help address the challenge of species extinctions through recording biodiversity data. See: Preece, J. (2017) 'How two billion smartphone users can save species!'. *Interactions*, March–April, 26–33 (http://interactions.acm.org/archive/view/march-april-2017/how-two-billion-smartphone-users-can-save-species).

2. A video about the nQuire project, entitled 'Next generation problem solvers' can be found here on YouTube: www.youtube.com/watch?v=c-h92gXWb6A

3. Context based learning and incidental learning (the latter relevant to the MASELTOV project discussed in the chapter) feature in the 2015 *Innovating Pedagogy* report: Sharples, M., Adams, A., Alozie, N., Ferguson, R., FitzGerald, E., Gaved, M., McAndrew, P., Means, B., Remold, J., Rienties, B., Roschelle, J., Vogt, K., Whitelock, D. and Yarnall, L. (2015) *Innovating Pedagogy 2015: Exploring new forms of teaching, learning and assessment, to guide educators and policy makers* (Open University Innovation Report 4). Milton Keynes: Open University (http://proxima.iet.open.ac.uk/public/innovating_pedagogy_2015.pdf).

Part Five

Technology for adult
learners in and beyond
formal institutions

Introduction

Technology for adult learners in and beyond formal institutions

Stuart Edwards

Digital technology and the Internet offer an alluring prospect for education: not only 'anytime, anywhere' but 'anyone', indeed 'everyone', able to learn almost 'anything'. MOOCs, free online courses that provide learning at scale, have attracted significant attention for their potential to open up education, particularly higher education, to learners around the world. The two key questions running through this chapter are: (1) how far is educational technology fulfilling its potential to provide education for all; and (2) what issues need to be addressed and what developments made to go further in fulfilling that potential?

We begin in Chapter 5.1 with an exploration as to whether there is evidence of an impact on UK rates of adult participation in learning. This groundwork is followed by two further chapters. Chapter 5.2 is from Rebecca Ferguson, Christothea Herodotou, Tim Coughlan, Eileen Scanlon and Mike Sharples. It examines research carried out in the United Kingdom in order to identify priority areas for MOOC development. In Chapter 5.3 I look at other areas of learning, beyond MOOCs, and beyond HE, reviewing examples of educational technology with potential to extend access.

Technology, the Internet and adult participation in learning

Stuart Edwards

Introduction

In 2015, 22 per cent of adults aged 17 or over in the United Kingdom reported that they were currently participating in learning of one kind or another (National Institute for Adult and Continuing Education [NIACE], 2015). That would amount to more than 11 million adult learners, most of whom were not at school or university. In this chapter we explore the question: what do we know about how technology is helping the adult population to access learning? We look at national survey data from the United Kingdom and the United States to find out the extent to which adults are using their technology for learning and whether this is impacting on overall rates of participation in learning.

Access to learning through technology

First, it is worth looking at how many adults are using technology to access learning. There is a regular annual survey of Internet usage carried out by the Office for National Statistics in Great Britain (ONS, 2015). In that year, adults 16 and over in Great Britain reported the following 'learning activities carried out over the Internet for educational, professional or personal purposes' within the last three months:

- 11 per cent 'doing an online course'
- 19 per cent 'online learning material other than a complete online course'
- 10 per cent 'communicating with instructors or students'
- 6 per cent 'other'
- 57 per cent 'none of these'.

And responding to other questions about their Internet activity within the last three months:

- 37 per cent reported 'looking for information about education, training or courses'

- 56 per cent reported 'consulting wikis to obtain knowledge or information'.

As might be expected, the trends are positive over time. The number of adults who used the Internet to undertake some form of online course has increased steadily in recent years, from four per cent of adults in 2007 to 11 per cent in 2015. And there have been similar increases in the numbers saying that they are using the Internet for other forms of learning that do not amount to a complete online course.

This all seems encouraging for technology's potential to promote education for all. But two questions need to be probed:

- Are all groups in society gaining new opportunities to access learning online?
- Is the upward trend in learning online leading to an overall increase in learning participation?

In terms of access for all groups, the ONS surveys for Great Britain show that although Internet usage has increased steadily since 2006, in 2015 there were still 10 per cent of adults who reported never having used the Internet. Many of these were 65 years old and over, and the figure was still 12 per cent for 55–64s. Of those who are disabled, 27 per cent have never used the Internet. Unsurprisingly, lower rates of Internet usage translate through to lower figures for use of the Internet for learning activities. The proportion of those with disabilities doing an online course in 2015 was half that of those without a disability – 6 per cent against 12 per cent). The rate was also 6 per cent for 55–64s. So while the Internet may be helping to extend education opportunities to many of the adult population, there is still a significant number of people for whom the technology is another barrier rather than an enabler.

We have attempted to answer the second question by looking at how the ONS data for online learning compare with the results of the NIACE (2015) survey of adult participation in learning conducted in the same year, though it should be noted that the two surveys ask different questions of slightly different populations and therefore cannot be mapped directly onto each other. NIACE (now part of the Learning and Work Institute: an independent policy and research organization in the United Kingdom that combines the 'National Institute of Adult Continuing Education' (NIACE) and the 'Centre for Economic and Social Inclusion'), has been conducting this annual survey since 1996. It reports on the proportion of adults aged 17 and over taking part in learning, without distinguishing between online and offline, and provides a breakdown of who participates and who does not. While it is of course a moot point what exactly should be counted as learning for these purposes and what individuals responding to surveys interpret as being learning, the data reported across the two surveys are interestingly different.

Somewhat counter-intuitively, more adults now report doing some form of online learning in the ONS survey than say they are participating in learning (online and offline) in the NIACE survey. In the 2015 NIACE survey, just over a fifth of adults (22 per cent) reported that they were currently learning. In the ONS survey for the same year 43 per cent of adults reported some form of 'learning activities carried out over the Internet for educational, professional or personal purposes'. The ONS figure includes adults from a year younger at 16 and covers a three-month period rather than just current learning activity, but even if the comparison is made with the NIACE survey result for those who report taking part in some form of learning in the past three years, the ONS figure for online learning activities alone is still slightly higher.

It is also striking that, although use of the Internet by adults to access learning is undoubtedly increasing, the overall levels of adult participation in learning (online and/or offline) as reported in NIACE surveys has remained relatively unchanged over the past two decades. In the 1996 NIACE report, 40 per cent of respondents reported having taken part in some form of learning in the previous three years; in 2015 the equivalent figure was 41 per cent. This would tend to suggest:

- If the Internet is having a positive impact on the participation of adults in learning, this may largely be in terms of counteracting other factors that might otherwise have reduced participation, such as reductions in some areas of public funding and the impact of austerity, as opposed to facilitating a net increase (unless this has been masked by under-reporting as a result of Internet-based learning not yet always being counted as 'proper learning').
- The main beneficiaries may be those who are already likely to be adult learners, providing them with an additional, more flexible and perhaps cheaper means of access to learning, rather than significantly extending access to new groups of learners.

There is further evidence to support this latter point from similar research undertaken in the United States.

A comparison with the United States

In the United States, the Pew Research Center, which describes itself as a 'non-partisan fact tank', commissioned research in 2016 on Lifelong Learning and Technology. Based on differently worded questions from the UK NIACE survey, a much higher proportion – 74% – of Americans identified themselves as undertaking lifelong learning activities. But in terms of the use of technology to support learning, the evidence, as in the United Kingdom, tends to suggest the impact of technology on barriers to access has been limited so far. The report concludes:

> There are broad patterns associated with personal and professional learning related to socio-economic class, people's access to technology, the kinds of jobs they have, their learning outlooks, and their racial and ethnic backgrounds. *As a rule, those adults with more education, household incomes and Internet-connecting technologies are more likely to be participants in today's educational ecosystem and to use information technology to navigate the world* (our emphasis).

> These findings offer a cautionary note to digital technology enthusiasts who believe that the Internet and other tools will automatically democratize education and access to knowledge. The survey clearly shows that information technology plays a role for many as they learn things that are personally or professionally helpful. Still, those who already have high levels of education and easy access to technology are the most likely to take advantage of the Internet. For significant minorities of Americans with less education and lower incomes, the Internet is more on the periphery of their learning activities. Fewer of the people in those groups are professional or personal learners, and fewer of them use the Internet for these purposes. Overall, the Internet does not seem to exert as strong a pull toward adult learning among those who are poorer or less educated as it does for those in other groups.

There is though one interesting finding in the United Kingdom that seems to run slightly counter to this general conclusion. In general, the unemployed are less likely to participate in learning than the employed (for example, 35 per cent compared to 49 per cent, NIACE, 2015). However, this position was reversed when the 2013 ONS survey of Internet usage in Great Britain compared the figures for those 'doing an online course' between employed, unemployed and economically inactive. While participation among the economically inactive is clearly much lower at 4 per cent, the participation rate for the unemployed is higher than among employed – 13 per cent vs 11 per cent. This is still only a relatively small sub-set of the unemployed, but it is one area where the research shows a relatively disadvantaged group making greater use of the Internet to access learning.

Conclusion

The data appears to show clearly that the number of adults who used the Internet to undertake some form of online course has increased steadily in recent years, from 4 per cent of adults in 2007 to 11 per cent in 2015 (ONS 2015 survey data). And there have been similar increases in the numbers saying that they are using the Internet for other forms of learning that do not amount to a complete online course. However, as yet, there is no clear evidence that this growth in learning online is leading to an increase in overall rates of adult participation in learning. As reported in NIACE surveys, participation has changed little from 1996 to 2015.

Beyond the broad question of how the Internet and technology are impacting on adult participation in learning, there are more specific questions about the impact in particular spheres of adult learning, and the issues to be addressed and developments necessary if they are to go further in fulfilling the promise of education for all. It is likely that the Internet is most beneficial for learning among the more privileged socio-economic groups and those who are already taking part in some form of learning. This is a concern for those who see technology as a mechanism to engage new learners in educational pursuits.

MOOC development

Priority areas

Rebecca Ferguson, Christothea Herodotou, Tim Coughlan, Eileen Scanlon and Mike Sharples

Introduction

Free online courses that provide learning at scale have the potential to open up education around the world. MOOCs now engage millions of learners. For example, FutureLearn, the United Kingdom's largest MOOC provider, passed 6m registered learners in 2017, 75 per cent of these outside the United Kingdom. Coursera, the world's largest platform, claimed 24m learners worldwide in March 2017, of which more than half a million were UK learners.

In this section, we explore what the research tells us about how MOOCs need to be developed in order to help provide education for all. This research was carried out at UK universities partnered with the FutureLearn MOOC platform. When it was carried out, FutureLearn had 64 university partners, including 29 within the United Kingdom, all linked by the FutureLearn Academic Network (FLAN).

The majority of UK universities that have engaged significantly with MOOC research are FutureLearn partners. They have already published a substantial body of work in this area, which moves from initial exploration to focused investigations. The first postgraduate students in this area are now early-career researchers who add their experience to active research teams. Some strong research provides a platform for others to build on, while the overall spread of work adds breadth to the field. An overview of this body of work provides a national perspective on priorities for development.

UK universities store and share their peer-reviewed research in large repositories. In order to locate work on MOOCs, we searched the relevant repositories for publications that included 'MOOC' in their title or abstract. After setting aside work that did not focus on MOOCs or that was not accessible, this resulted in a list of 167 publications from 19 UK universities, covering MOOCs on more than 30 platforms.

We produced a short summary of all 167 publications, including recommendations made as a result of the research. We then gathered these together and grouped them in terms of their main priorities. This resulted in a set of eight priority areas for MOOC development.

1. Develop a strategic approach to learning at scale.
2. Develop appropriate pedagogy for learning at scale.
3. Identify and share effective learning designs.
4. Support discussion more effectively.
5. Clarify learner expectations.
6. Develop educator teams.
7. Widen access.
8. Develop new approaches to assessment and accreditation.

These areas are explored in the following sections. The full report on our survey and analysis is available at https://r3beccaf.files.wordpress. com/2017/03/moocs-2016.pdf

Develop a strategic approach to learning at scale

Universities' engagement in this area began in a spirit of exploration. Now they need to consider their motivations and develop a strategic approach that encompasses the position of MOOCs inside and outside the organization, now and in the future (White *et al.*, 2015b). MOOCs require substantial investment, so they must offer value to their providers as well as workable business models in order to be sustainable (Weller, 2014). Possibilities for raising revenue in an open environment include Freemium (basic services provided free of charge while more advanced features come at a price), sponsorship, grants, donations, merchandise, sale of supplementary material, selective advertising, data sharing and follow-on events (Liyanagunawardena *et al.*, 2015).

These courses can be used to enhance the skills and reputation of academics, academic departments and the organization as a whole (White *et al.*, 2015a, 2015b), but they also play other important roles. A strategic approach can support the development of lasting collaborations and the enablement of impact by linking MOOCs with other open education initiatives. Such links enable providers to draw on decades of experience of open learning and help widen the options for learners (McAndrew and Scanlon, 2013; Weller, 2014).

Universities can blend MOOC materials with other courses, so that campus students benefit from access to excellent video presentations and engagement in online discussion. Classes can use the 'flipped classroom' model whereby students access core teaching materials online, engage in online discussion and testing, and use campus time for academic discussion and problem solving. Courses that run at many institutions, such as study skills and introductory statistics, could be replaced by high quality MOOCs for students or for prospective students.

As lifelong learning becomes increasingly important, learning journeys including MOOCs could offer people different routes through education (Nkuyubwatsi, 2016). An individual might move from just-in-time learning such as watching a video about an immediate concern, to a series of MOOCs about related issues, into a full-time degree, a part-time postgraduate course and career-spanning workplace training. The distinction between students and alumni would be replaced by a group of lifelong learners who maintain active engagement with their university. MOOCs can form an essential part of blended learning that connects campus and online learners.

MOOCS already build capacity for collaborative networks. In the future, such learner communities could be used as effective think tanks. Members, whether in student or alumni mode, could enjoy discussing the big issues of the day with a large worldwide community. Such debates, combined with universities' expert knowledge, could produce reports and recommendations that go far beyond what has been possible for smaller, national groups (Ferguson *et al.*, 2015).

Develop appropriate pedagogy for learning at scale

These communities may be very diverse. Learner characteristics and engagement show MOOCs have the potential to connect both inter-generational and international networks (Wintrup *et al.*, 2015a). However, massive numbers on a course can provide a negative experience for participants, so it is crucial that MOOC developers are aware of what is educationally valuable about learning at scale and work with the massive rather than against it (Knox, 2014).

Some teaching and learning methods, such as lecturing, work at both large and small scales. Others benefit from the effects of large-scale participation. There is more than 70 years of evidence that exposition and instruction through educational radio and television can bring learning benefits to millions if they receive adequate local support (Imhoof, 1985).

Networked learning has also been shown to scale well. This is a process of collaborative meaning making through mutual support and interaction amongst learners (Goodyear *et al.*, 2004). Networked communities share expertise through organized clusters of contributions and responses. Methods of reputation management and reward, including 'liking' posts and badging people who have provided evidence of expertise, add community-defined value to the contributions (Clow and Makriyannis, 2011).

Networked learning, and its close relation, connectivist learning, formed the educational basis of the original MOOCs (Siemens, 2005). Connectivism is another approach that scales. It views learning as distributed within a technologically enhanced social network, associated with recognizing and interpreting patterns of interaction.

The FutureLearn platform has been developed around conversational learning, another approach that benefits from scale. The premise of this approach is that learning takes place when people engage in conversations. These may be internal conversations in which they reflect on understanding and consider issues, conversations with educators in which they receive and query information, or conversations with peers in which they discuss differences in opinion and try to reach agreement (Ferguson and Sharples, 2014).

For learners to benefit from the support of a wide range of peers, MOOCs must take into account the points at which they are likely to need support, find opportunities for asking questions, and build in motivation for offering help to others. This means platforms should not only provide opportunities for learners to communicate with each other, but should also include ways of judging which people are offering helpful and reliable advice. Social factors (rating and voting) to assess reliability, the user's profile and badges to demonstrate competence can all be used to support this approach (Liu *et al.*, 2012).

MOOCs can provide access to a huge set of resources and a global range of perspectives. Educator teams need to consider how the diversity, commitment and focused interests of MOOC learners can best be harnessed and used to promote the formation of networks and communities. Teams could also consider possibilities for the creation of more effective opportunities for self-directed and open-ended learning (Wintrup *et al.*, 2015a).

Identify and share effective learning designs

When sharing successful implementations of pedagogy with others, learning design is a useful tool. It uses descriptive frameworks for teaching and learning activities, helping educators to share and adopt teaching ideas (Dalziel *et al.*, 2016). Learning design enables educators to showcase successful learning activities and design innovations across faculties and institutions (Hatzipanagos, 2015). It not only covers the use of resources and the timings of activities, it also looks at how those resources are deployed to support learning.

The same resource may support many different methods of learning – see Table 1 for examples derived from studies of how people learn with technology (Manches *et al.*, 2010a; 2010b), as reported in Chapter 2.1. A video can form the stimulus for an inquiry, the basis for a conversation, instructions for an embodied fitness exercise, or part of a problem-solving exercise. Changes to the basic pedagogic elements of a course are associated with shifts in patterns of engagement (Ferguson *et al.*, 2015).

Table 5.2.1: Learning methods and technology-based examples

Learning method	Technology-based example
Assessing	engaging in online peer review
Browsing	using search engines to find educational materials
Case-based	investigating medical cases online
Collaborative	creating shared Google doc
Construction	engaging with Minecraft
Cross-context	learning between classroom and home with tablet
Conversational	engaging in online discussion
Delivered	watching an online video
Embodied	monitoring exercise with Fitbit activity tracker
Game-based	multiplayer educational game, e.g. Endless Ocean
Inquiry-driven	using digital probes to collect and analyse data
Networked	educational social networking
Performative	learner blogging
Problem-solving	working in online teams to solve environmental problems
Reflective	reviewing e-portfolio of learning activities
Simulation	learning science in a virtual world

Learner dropout is a concern with MOOCs, and much of this takes place in the first week (Nazir *et al.*, 2015; Ferguson and Clow, 2015; Jordan, 2014; Jordan, 2015). Changes to learning design can provide bridges between course weeks, stressing links between these weeks, pointing learners forward, supporting latecomers and engaging learners who are out of step with the cohort.

Support discussion more effectively

Most of the pedagogies that scale effectively (networked learning, conversational learning and connectivism) require discussion among learners. To engage in successful conversations, all parties need access to a shared representation of the subject matter as well as tools for commenting, responding and reflecting.

Highlighting content that contributes to learning by commenting on it is one way of encouraging discussion. Another is asking learners to link to videos and photographs and then commenting on these to initiate interactions. Groups can be used to organize learners in discussion areas, helping them identify and comment on content of interest. MOOC learners are often nomadic, forming sub-communities on different platforms, so hashtags can be used to bring those groups together (Bozkurt *et al.*, 2016).

Early socialization experiences have a long-term impact on newcomers' satisfaction, performance and intention to stay in a group (Nazir *et al.*, 2015). One way to address this is to pair new arrivals with more experienced MOOC learners, who can help them to understand the way the MOOC operates. As first-time posters who receive a response in an online community are more likely to post again, a learner's first post should be prioritized. Newcomers may not have much experience of online interaction but good practice can be encouraged through specific guidance and provision of good examples. This includes using inclusive language, demonstrating respect for alternative viewpoints and encouraging different forms of acceptable social interaction (Murray, 2014; Wintrup *et al.*, 2015b).

Clarify learner expectations

Within most MOOCs, a significant percentage of learners have never experienced online learning or learning at this level before. They may have registered to gain access to a single piece of content, or to a series of discussions, or to find out more about open learning. As with other forms of informal learning, learners set their own goals in MOOCs, and these do not necessarily align with the learning outcomes proposed by the educator. Learners take multiple paths, so traditional ways of measuring success are unlikely to prove sufficient. However, many will be aiming to complete the course successfully. 'Students seek not merely access, but access to success, which the institution should do everything to facilitate while maintaining standards' (Daniel, 2012).

Each MOOC therefore needs to make explicit the learning objectives, how to study in this context, how to use course resources, and how to participate in a learning conversation. Approximate guidance on how long more complex activities require, if deeper learning and integration is to take place, will help guide decisions about which activities to engage in and for how long (Wintrup *et al.*, 2015b). A balance needs to be struck between providing guidance on how to be an effective MOOC learner and getting started with the course content.

Learners also look for information about what is expected of them, whether their learning is expected to develop incrementally or the MOOC is structured in discrete blocks of learning. Making this information easily visible, but not dominant, facilitates the learning experience and helps to manage learners' expectations. Learners can be strategic and make informed choices about how to spend time if it is clear to them how social learning and interactivity contribute to engaged learning, and which learning activities are most important if a learner does not have time to complete them all (Wintrup *et al.*, 2015a).

Develop educator teams

Pedagogy, learning design, promoting discussion and clarifying expectations are all roles for educator teams. Many people, often from different departments, are involved in the production and presentation of most MOOCs. Close collaboration is required between academic teams, producers and academic librarians on issues such as copyright and licensing of resources for MOOCs (Gore, 2014), support for MOOC design, access to resources and support for digital literacies for educators and learners on MOOCs. Learners may encounter mentors, facilitators or guides – these staff may or may not have been involved in course design and production (Ferguson and Whitelock, 2014).

Educators are often willing to put in extra hours on new MOOCs. However, as these MOOCs become business as usual, it is important to reconsider the allocation of educator time (Teplechuk, 2013) and how educators are supported. Forums, discussion areas and chances to meet up both online and offline offer opportunities to extend and share practice, to share possibilities for creating or accessing resources that are not available when working at a smaller scale, and to build on success.

Widen access

One area where new approaches must be built is accessibility. Current MOOC learners are primarily individuals with prior experience of higher education (Cannell and Macintyre, 2014). While MOOCs have widened their access to education, there is little evidence that MOOCs are widening participation for those distanced from education. This may be because people with a higher education have better access to MOOCs, are better prepared for the self-learning required in these courses, or are less worried about recognition than learners without qualifications who have to prove their skills to employers (Liyanagunawardena, 2015).

MOOCs need to reach different sections of the population if the objective of widening access to study is to be achieved. At a basic level, those communicating key messages about MOOCs need to consider how to attract a more diverse cohort. Educators need to ensure that no elements of learning design unnecessarily exclude people on the grounds of disability, age or location, and should engage actively with the challenges that exclude learners due to disability and disadvantage (Ferguson and Sharples, 2014).

Resources need to be available in many languages, perhaps drawing on the power of the crowd to carry out crowd-sourced translations. At the same time, learners whose physical restrictions have limited their access to face-to-face learning will be expecting accessible online options (Rodrigo and Iniesto, 2015). Challenges such as providing mathematical notation for those with restricted vision will have to be overcome. These cannot be seen simply as technological challenges; they also require changes in environment and attitude.

Develop new approaches to assessment and accreditation

Changes are also needed to the assessment and accreditation of learning. MOOCs need to make use of the full range of computer-based assessment options, including selected response (such as multiple-choice questions); constructed response (in which learners construct the response); short-answer questions and essays; and the use of e-portfolios, blogs and wikis, and peer assessment (Jordan, 2013).

Peer assessment can be implemented in different ways. In one case, progression in peer assessment capability and responsibility might be deliberately structured, using a learning design that includes phases of activity, peer assessment, reviewing and reflecting upon the assessor's assessment, learning to be a better assessor, further activity and further assessment. In another case, each student, over time, would have opportunities to develop a portfolio of peer assessment work. In a third case, various kinds of recognition such as ratings or badges could be built into technical platforms in order to manage the peer assessment workflow (O'Toole, 2013).

Badging provides a soft route from assessment to accreditation (Law and Law, 2014). Badges in MOOCs offer opportunities to reflect on intended learning outcomes. If badges are used, their value needs to be clearly explained and the badge schema should be given a prominent place so that it is accessible to learners at all times and encourages badge collection. Badge award messages should be pushed out as soon as badges have been awarded, in order to establish a clear link between the award and the associated task (Hauck and MacKinnon, 2016).

Full qualifications are also an option. MOOCs provide international education, so the credits they offer should be recognized worldwide and form part of a credit transfer system (Witthaus *et al.*, 2016). Quality assurance agencies will require evidence that qualifications are consistent, that they are assessed rigorously, and that the potential for cheating and misconduct is low. A workable qualification system will require improved authentication technology that establishes firm links between the registered learner, the learning activity and the qualification. Stakeholders, particularly learners, should be aware of the options for validation and accreditation, and these options should take into account why recognition is sought.

Conclusion

MOOCs have shown that they can engage millions of learners, but more work is needed. If MOOCs are to be sustainable, the universities that offer them must have a clear strategy in place that balances expenditure on MOOCs with value to the institution. If MOOCs are to provide opportunities to widen participation, then more attention must be paid to accessibility and to removing some of the barriers that are currently in place. If MOOCs are to live up to their promise of providing lifelong learning at a massive scale, they will require experienced educator teams who can make use of appropriate pedagogies, develop learning designs that lead to student success, clarify learner expectations, respond to them and engage them in knowledge-building conversations. In time, MOOCs may become one component in a global education system that blends campus and online learning, combining free and paid-for courses, leisure learning and professional development.

Widening adult learning participation

Stuart Edwards

Introduction

In this chapter we explore the role of technology to extend opportunities for adult participation in learning. We consider what the research says about the impact of technology on extending opportunities for technical, vocational and basic skills learning and we explore the potential of 'brain training'.

Technical and vocational learning

The majority of adult learning is vocational in one form or another. Vocational learning encompasses apprenticeships, other work-based training (some of which leads to formal qualifications, some not), and courses and qualifications delivered by FE colleges and private providers. It is also of course an important element of some HE. Here we focus largely on what could be described as technical and vocational learning. Most of this is funded by employers and is job specific, or focused on health and safety or first aid (Gloster *et al.*, 2016). There is also significant state funding through the Education and Skills Funding Agency (Snelson and Deyes, 2016).

For employers' use of technology-enabled learning, there is now a substantial body of evidence that has been collected by an organization called Towards Maturity (https://towardsmaturity.org/) through an annual benchmarking survey run since 2003. Over the past 11 years, more than 4,400 companies and 18,000 learners have taken part in its longitudinal studies. The data for its 2015 benchmark report (Towards Maturity, 2015) was drawn from: (a) a detailed online Benchmark review process with more than 600 learning and development (L&D) professionals from 55 countries, 61 per cent of whom were UK based; and (b) a sample of 1,600 learners undertaking a learning landscape survey, of whom 88 per cent were from the United Kingdom.

The Benchmark findings need to be caveated by the fact that they are based on what a self-selecting group of participants self-report, but they include some interesting pointers:

- on average, 19 per cent of training budget is spent on e-learning and learning technologies
- 26 per cent of formal training is e-enabled or blended, 19 per cent is online only and 55 per cent is face to face
- 36 per cent are using technology-enabled learning for non-compliance-related training
- 66 per cent are using technology-enabled learning for compliance-related training
- 77 per cent predict an increase for blended learning, 69 per cent for online only but just 6 per cent for face to face only (74 per cent predict a decrease).

Another angle is provided by the research of an organization called Learning Light (www.learninglight.com) that has developed an economic forecasting model based on training expenditure for each industry sector and has published a series of reports on the value and growth prospects of UK and other international e-learning markets. The fourth report in the series (Learning Light, 2014) applies the model to e-learning markets in the United Kingdom, European Union and China, and also reflects the results of more than 90 semi-structured qualitative interviews with UK-based HR and L&D executives involved in the training and development sector.

Learning Light's findings are broadly consistent with those of Towards Maturity. For example, their estimate was that 17 per cent of training budgets were devoted to e-learning in 2012/13, with a total UK e-learning market value of £528m to £565m, up from £313m in 2009. They are clear that this growth in e-learning has been largely through displacing more traditional training programmes in a training market that has only been growing very slowly. As with other statistics, there is no indication here that the growth of e-learning is leading to a significant growth of learners and learning activity. Buyers' and commissioners' top concerns are to get 'more for less' from their budget and the quality of learning materials, and the majority of what they spend – some 60 per cent – is on compliance training.

However, this may not be the full picture. Towards Maturity research (Towards Maturity, 2015) also looks at the attitudes and behaviour of learners in the workplace. Their findings broadly confirm the so-called '70:20:10 model' (Lombardo and Eichinger, 1996) that suggests formal courses are only a small part of how people learn in a work context, and that learning and development strategies need to give more attention to creating conditions for effective informal learning that takes place directly in the flow of work. They also draw on the concept of the 'self-directed learner' who their research shows is pro-active in learning from others, harnesses technology to learn through web search and mobile devices, and demands flexibility in terms of learning at their own pace. Although the nature of what is happening in this informal sphere may be harder to pin down, the impact of technology here could be more significant for extending learning opportunities than through formal learning in the workplace.

Turning to the predominantly publicly funded FE and skills sector, the importance of education technology is widely recognized but there is limited research evidence.

The 2013 Commission for Adult Vocational Teaching and Learning (CAVTL) sought to establish the principles, characteristics and distinctive features of excellent adult vocational teaching and learning, and the factors to enable these (CAVTL, 2013). This was done through a largely qualitative approach including visits to observe practice, seminars and calls for evidence. Although technology was not its main focus, the commission took specific evidence (Laurillard, 2013) and visited examples of innovative practice. Key technology related conclusions included:

- The importance of access to up-to-date technology – not necessarily educational technology – in vocational teaching and learning 'because keeping on top of technological advances is an essential part of the occupational expertise required in any workplace' – this links to CAVTL's key principle of 'line of sight' to work.
- The ability of technology to enable the distinctive features of excellent adult vocational teaching and learning, but its use being no guarantee of excellence.
- The need – in order to realize the benefits – for continuing professional development and for 'a model that enables teachers to know how to select, design, develop, share and review different types of digital teaching and learning activities'.
- The [particularly striking] potential of digital simulations to complement real work experience and to offer a pedagogically valuable way for vocational learners to practise and be assessed safely.

Previously, the Association of Colleges (AoC, 2012) undertook a survey of its members (which include both FE and sixth form colleges). The survey results, based on 101 responses, showed continuing investment in a wide range of technologies, though there is no estimate for the overall proportion of budget spent. The survey also sought to assess the confidence of college staff in the ability of technology to achieve certain outcomes and the barriers to effective implementation. The results in terms of confidence are summarized in the table below. Generally, the levels of confidence are quite high, including for widening participation, but the survey also revealed concerns about the ability to manage the deployment of technology effectively. The need for more staff training and specific funding, and the lack of integration within strategic planning and business processes are all cited as barriers.

Table 5.3.1: Confidence levels regarding Learning Technologies delivery of outcomes

How confident are you that Learning Technologies can deliver the following outcomes?			
	Very confident	Confident	Not very confident	Not at all confident
Improved flexibility to deliver a wider range of learning opportunities	52.4%	42.7%	4.9%	0.0%
Increased student engagement	47.6%	49.5%	2.9%	0.0%
Widening participation through learning materials that can be used for distance learning and are accessible	44.1%	49.0%	6.9%	0.0%
Improved retention	22.3%	62.1%	15.5%	0.0%
Improved student achievement	26.2%	67.0%	6.8%	0.0%
Improved communication with learners with disabilities, language and other difficulties to achieve learning outcomes	42.7%	45.6%	10.7%	1.0%
Enhance delivery of literacy, numeracy and informal adult learning	34.7%	47.5%	15.8%	2.0%

Source: AoC, 2012

The Further Education Learning Technology Action Group (FELTAG), a group commissioned in 2013 by the then minister of state for skills and enterprise at BIS, Matthew Hancock, undertook two further workforce attitudes and experience surveys to inform its recommendations aimed at ensuring the effective use of learning technology in the sector (FELTAG, 2014). The first reviewed teaching practitioners' current perspectives. The principal findings demonstrated that 'while there is a trend towards more teachers innovating with digital technology, this is *on their individual initiative* and support comes only from *peers* within their organization'. So while there was evidence of growing confidence and capability, what appeared to be missing was the means to share these ideas and developments across the sector. The second survey, like the AoC one, was conducted with managers, and highlighted some similar issues, but also brought out more clearly external factors that work against the use of learning technology, including funding and audit regimes, Ofsted inspection, policies focused on 'security' and 'e safety' – all of which tended to stifle innovation and experimentation. FELTAG concluded that 'the FE sector is keen to innovate, and is already doing so, but on a small scale and in a fragmented manner, without strategic support'. Their wide-ranging recommendations attempted to address the issues identified, including the capability and capacity of FE and skills providers, investment, regulation and funding.

Research has also been undertaken more recently on the expectations and experiences of technology by students. JISC, the body that provides digital services to the higher education, further education and skills sectors, completed a Digital Student research project in 2016. This included research focused on FE and skills students as well as HE students. The FE project report (Sharpe and Browne, 2015) was based on a literature review of reports from FE and skills, 12 focus groups with 220 learners across six FE colleges and speaking to more than 300 staff at events. The main findings include that:

- Little research has been undertaken with learners. Although there are many examples of creative uses of technology in case studies in the sector, these are not based on a body of research evidence and in this respect FE and skills is different from HE where there has been an 'exponential increase' in studies of how students experience technology.
- From what research does exist, it is clear that learners in FE 'experience the digital environment in a myriad of different ways'. The authors view this as unsurprising given the diversity of learners, but note that it is not always reflected in sector and institutional documents that tend to represent all learners as confident, motivated and positive about

the use of IT in education. The report highlights three broad groups of learners: those with basic skills and access issues; a majority, who may have the basics but still have issues of use and recognize they have more to learn; and another minority who are skilled and enthusiastic technology users, but whose experiences are dominated by the extent to which they are able to transfer their personal and social uses of technology to a learning context.

- Learners in FE, in general, have high expectations of technology use, in particular that it will enhance their learning in practical ways. This is similar to HE students' expectations, but the authors emphasize that more engagement with learners is often required as FE cohorts are likely to include more learners who are less experienced with technology. Like HE students, FE learners also expect robust, fast and reliable services and up to date equipment, but with FE there can be another distinct dimension in terms of expecting industry standard hardware and software to prepare them for work. This mirrors points in the CAVTL report about equipment and 'line of sight'.

Overall, the main conclusion drawn is that more needs to be done to capture the learner perspective both through engagement and more formal research. This is seen as particularly important for FE both because of the diversity of learners and the dangers of making assumptions, and the lack of research in comparison with HE.

Basic skills

The United Kingdom has a long standing and persistent problem with low levels of literacy and numeracy among its adult population and compares poorly with other OECD countries. Significant public funding has been invested over the past two decades to try to address this problem, which remains a major barrier to many other forms education for millions of adults.

In 2011, the then Department for Business, Innovation and Skills (BIS) published a *Review of Research and Evaluation of Improving Adult Literacy and Numeracy* (Vorhaus, *et al.*, 2011). This included a review of the evidence on the use of technology. While acknowledging a wider evidence base on learning technology in general terms, a key conclusion was that the evidence base on the effectiveness of the use of learning technology in adult literacy and numeracy (ALN) provision remained thin. There were few rigorous evaluations of the impact of using learning technology to support the delivery of literacy and numeracy, whether in FE, workplaces or other learner contexts. Based on this limited evidence (often individual sources rather than a body of work), the authors felt that following conclusions could be drawn:

- Learning technology may improve learner progress and achievement, but the evidence is at best mixed.
- Learning technology can make learning more flexible in how, when and where learning takes place. Such flexibility is particularly valued in the delivery of workplace provision and also underlies the success (in terms of enrolments at least) of learndirect [an ALN provider that, using a supported online delivery model, had more than 2.75 million people complete its courses between 2000 and 2010].
- A small body of evidence suggests that learning technology helps to attract, engage and motivate learners. Learners (and also employers) are more likely to perceive basic skills training to be relevant where it is marketed under the guise of ICT training. Other evidence suggests that mobile technologies, including applications for iPhones, online interactive games and social media are motivating many learners.
- Learners value the flexibility that the use of ICT offers, along with the opportunity for instant feedback and the ability to engage in non-conventional exercises such as quizzes, games and pictorial approaches to learning.
- The value of technology for ALN is conditional on the learners' existing ICT skills. Learners with poorer ICT skills are more likely to drop out if their acquisition of these skills is unsupported.
- Although learning technology is potentially attractive to 'hard-to-reach' learners and to those who have not benefited from conventional educational models, it may represent a barrier to learning for older learners and those on low incomes without access to technology and the Internet at home.'

It was also noted that findings suggest ICT skills and basic (literacy and numeracy skills) may benefit from simultaneous development. But the overriding conclusion was the need for more research:

> In the light of the rate of development of ICT, including mobile technologies, and the potential to support learning and learning progress, it is recommended that robust trials are conducted to clarify which are the effective practices in using technology for different groups of learners, and for different types of learning outcome. (Vorhaus *et al.*, 2011)

So where do things stand now? The United Kingdom still has a very significant problem with adult basic skills in literacy and, in particular, numeracy. In 2016, the OECD published a review of policy insights based on the results of an international survey of adult skills undertaken in England in 2012 (Kuczera, Field and Windisch, 2016). The main headlines were:

- an estimated nine million working-age adults in England (more than a quarter of adults aged 16–65) have low literacy or numeracy skills or both
- England's overall performance is around average for literacy, but well below average for numeracy relative to other OECD countries in the survey
- a further concern is that, unlike in most other countries, young adults (16–24-year-olds) perform no better than older adults approaching retirement age (55–65-year-olds) – 16–18-year-olds actually perform worse.

The costs, both for individuals and the country as a whole, are very high. For example, it has been estimated (Pro Bono Economics, 2014) that the overall cost to the UK economy of outcomes associated with low levels of numeracy is around £20.2 billion per year, or about 1.3 per cent of GDP. While the priority, as recognized by the OECD review, must be early intervention to ensure all young people have stronger basic skills, the challenge remains what more can be done for the generation of young adults who have now joined the labour market with inadequate basic skills, many of whom still have more than 50 years of working life ahead of them.

This same generation is of course by far the most digitally literate and connected; and they have been failed for one reason or another during at least 11 years of school education, with billions spent on conventional classroom teaching with qualified teachers. If ever, in terms of enabling education for all, there were a challenge for which edtech ought now to be part of the answer, then surely this should be it.

There are certainly people and organizations trying to take up this challenge. Looking specifically at numeracy:

- National Numeracy is an independent charity established in 2012 to help raise low levels of numeracy among both adults and children and to promote the importance of everyday maths skills. A major part of its effort has been to commission a suite of National Numeracy tools including an online National Numeracy Challenge, for which over 100,000 adults have registered, and Mobile Maths, a new smartphone app game aimed at 16–25-year-olds. The Challenge involves some introductory attitudinal questions, a set of diagnostic tests that assess the user's current level, up to Level 2, and then links to a set of resources on other sites such as Khan Academy that can be used to learn specific areas before retaking the Challenge check-up. There has not as yet been any systematic independent evaluation, but National Numeracy state that of those retaking the challenge, 75 per cent show more positive attitudes and 80 per cent have improved their level of attainment. They have also found that positive responses to some of the attitudinal questions are highly predictive of likelihood to improve, and that working with a partner where the Challenge is 'quasi-compulsory' also improves engagement and final outcomes.

- Citizen Maths is a free online Level 2 maths course for self-motivated adults, which has been developed by a partnership of Calderdale College, OCR (an awarding body) and the UCL Institute of Education with advice from the Google course builder team and funding from the Ufi Charitable Trust (which is also supporting the Mobile Maths smartphone app). The course, designed according to principles supported by research, consists of five units structured around 'powerful ideas in action' – Proportion, Uncertainty, Representation, Pattern and Measurement – with a mix of video, apps and quizzes setting each in the context of everyday life at work or home. The final units went live in 2016, and more than 13,000 people had registered for the course by June 2017. There has been positive feedback from individual users, and some initial evaluation, but as yet no direct evaluation of Citizen Maths's educational effectiveness (Ufi Charitable Trust, 2016).

These are all developments with interesting potential, but in terms of the evidence base little has changed since the BIS review findings in 2011. The need still remains for robust trials and a more concerted development and evaluation programme through which projects and tools can be tested. This would of course need significant funding, but only a minute fraction of what it is costing to have 25 per cent of the adult population without basic skills or indeed what was spent on the provision that failed them at school.

Brain training

Somewhere on the borderline between basic skills, informal adult learning and gaming, another interesting area is the use of technology for 'brain training'. Globally, including in the United Kingdom, millions of adults regularly play 'brain training' games through websites, apps and gaming consoles. These generally follow a similar format: collections of mini-games designed to test various mental skills; encouragement to undertake selections of these games as part of a regular training regime; and statistics and graphs to show the user how their capabilities are improving over time and how they compare with others. Varying claims have been made for the efficacy of these games, such as improvements in memory, attentiveness, speed and all-round intelligence, and the ability to stave off various forms of decline in cognitive functions in an aging population. So what does the evidence show?

The first point to make – putting aside for a moment questions of impact and efficacy – is that these forms of technology-based brain training games have been very successful at engaging would-be adult learners, as well as commercially. For example, *Dr Kawashima's Brain Training: How old is your brain?* sold more than three million copies in the United Kingdom between June 2006 and July 2009, making it then the most popular video game ever in the country. Other players have emerged in the market since with websites and apps including names such as *Lumosity*, *Elevate*, *Peak*, *Fit Brains* and *BrainHQ*. Lumosity, which is a US operation run by Lumos Labs Inc. based in California, is probably the most well-established, and by 2015 reported having more than 70 million users worldwide.

The claims made for these brain training games vary considerably. Nintendo has always been careful not to make direct claims that their games have been scientifically validated, positioning them rather as a fun and challenging entertainment product, like crosswords and sudoko, though still seeking some credence by association and being 'inspired by' the work of Dr Kawashima, a Japanese neuroscientist. Lumosity, however, have gone much further and it has landed them in legal trouble. The Federal Trade Commission (FTC), which protects US consumer interests, brought charges alleging that they deceived consumers with unfounded claims that Lumosity games can help users perform better at work and in school, and reduce or delay cognitive impairment associated with age and other serious health conditions. Without fully accepting these charges, in January 2016 Lumos Labs agreed to pay $2 million in redress.

So what does the research tell us? It is an interestingly mixed picture. There are examples of trials and experiments that have shown no significant impact. Typically, people improve their performance in a particular test or game when they practise it regularly, but this does not then transfer to a more generalized improvement in cognitive functioning that can be measured in other ways. However, there are also examples where what appears to be rigorous and independent research has demonstrated significant and promising impacts. Much of course depends on the specificity of the 'brain training' intervention and the impact it is seeking to achieve.

A large and influential experiment to test the impact of braining training games on IQ was undertaken in 2009, under the title of Brain Test Britain. This was promoted by the BBC popular science programme, *Bang Goes the Theory*, and designed by researchers at King's College London and Cambridge University. More than 11,000 volunteers completed the initial six-week brain training period. At the start of the experiment all participants took a set of benchmarking tests to assess specific brain skills. They were then randomly assigned to one of three groups: two groups undertook different types of brain training games, either focused on reasoning (planning, problem-solving and analysis) or non-reasoning (short-term memory, attention to detail, maths and interpreting visual information); the third group undertook a general knowledge quiz using the Internet to find the answers. At the end of the six weeks they were tested again on the benchmarking tests. The results were published in the journal *Nature* (Owen *et al.*, 2010), as well as being presented on television.

The headline finding was that the study uncovered no evidence that playing brain training games can meaningfully boost 'brain power' in the general population. The people who played the brain training games got better at those specific games, but there was no evidence that this transferred to the brain skills measured by the benchmarking tests.

However, that was not the whole story. When specific age groups were looked at separately, there was some measurable impact for older people in the benchmarking tests after six months of brain training games (Corbett *et al.*, 2015). Those over 50 improved in verbal learning and reasoning skills. Those over 60 also became better at daily life tasks like handling finances or remembering to take medication. These effects were seen with both reasoning and non-reasoning brain training games.

Further trials and studies have been undertaken since and there is a growing number of examples of promising results with respect to older adults. A small scale randomized controlled trial study in Japan reported findings in 2012 showing that playing the Brain Age (Nintendo) game for four weeks could lead to improved cognitive functions in some areas (executive functions and processing speed) in the elderly (Nouchi *et al.*, 2012). In the United Kingdom, a large scale randomized controlled trial involving almost 7,000 adults aged over 50 was undertaken by researchers at the Institute of Psychiatry, Psychology and Neuroscience (IoPPN) at King's College, London, with funding from the Alzheimer's Society. Their results provided further evidence that an online brain training package can not only improve memory and reasoning skills – but also how well older people carry out everyday tasks (Corbett *et al.*, 2015). Other very promising results were reported by US researchers at the Alzheimer's Association International Conference in Toronto in July 2016 (Edwards *et al.*, 2016). The Active Study (Advanced Cognitive Training for Independent and Vital Elderly) tracked 2,832 healthy elderly people with an average age of 74 at the beginning through a ten-year randomized controlled trial. Their most dramatic finding was that a particular form of speed of processing computer exercises, undertaken for a total of 11 to 14 hours, has the potential to cut by as much as 48 per cent the risk of developing dementia ten years later.

Another interesting angle is whether games explicitly designed and promoted as 'brain training' are necessarily more likely to be effective at enhancing cognitive functions than those designed purely for entertainment. A US research study (Shute *et al.*, 2015) undertaken at the Florida State University College of Education tested 77 undergraduate students who were randomly assigned to play either Portal 2 ('a first-person puzzle-platform video game') or Lumosity for eight hours. All participants were pre/post tested on problem solving, spatial skills and persistence. Interestingly, the Portal 2 players scored higher than Lumosity in all three areas and showed significant gains on spatial tests. The Lumosity players showed no gains on any measure.

So, what overall does the research tell us about the contribution that brain training games could make to adult learning? It is not easy to summarize and this is a highly-contested area. For example, in 2014 a group of nearly 70 leading brain scientists co-ordinated by the Stanford Center on Longevity issued an open letter headed 'A Consensus on the Brain Training Industry from the Scientific Community', that was critical of the industry and concluded: 'We object to the claim that brain games offer consumers a scientifically grounded avenue to reduce or reverse cognitive decline when there is no compelling scientific evidence to date that they do.' Two months later, a larger group of more than 120 neuroscientists issued a rebuttal, 'Scientists to Stanford: Research shows brain exercises can work' (Stanford Center on Longevity, 2014), which while agreeing some companies overstated their claims, pointed to a large body of evidence that brain training programmes could offer a scientifically based way to reduce cognitive decline. Attempting to pick a way through this minefield, the following points appear relatively clear:

- Brain training type games have the ability to engage large numbers of adults – including perhaps some not well-represented in more conventional adult learning – in regular activity through which they are seeking to maintain or improve cognitive skills in a way that is fun and entertaining.
- Claims made for the types of impact achievable through playing some of these games have been exaggerated for commercial gain and sometimes gone well beyond what could be supported by the existing evidence base derived from rigorous independent research.
- There is nevertheless some very promising, rigorous independent research that has demonstrated specific cognitive benefits for specific groups of people from specific types of brain training in specific circumstances – though games designed as brain training are not necessarily the only ones that can be effective, and indeed there are many other forms of activity that can have cognitive benefits.
- An approach with large numbers of players generating large volumes of data that can be relatively easily analysed lends itself to large-scale research and rigorous trials, and these types of games are at an interesting intersection between education and medical research. Over time it ought to be possible to undertake far more research that can be used to develop a more secure evidence base, refine games design and narrow down what is most effective (and to be fair to companies like Lumosity they do invite researchers to work with them and use their data in this way).
- While there are always likely to be limitations to the types of skills and learning that could be tackled through such games, there could well be more scope for them to be developed and used alongside other forms of teaching and learning, particularly for basic skills like maths and English.

Conclusion

As we live longer, and expect to work longer, lifelong learning becomes more important for all adults. Reviewing the current evidence, it seems fairly clear that technology has significant, arguably game-changing, potential to extend education for the adult population, and if key needs are to be addressed, such as the deficit in basic skills, it is difficult to imagine solutions at the required scale that do not exploit that potential. However, while the potential may exist, there is limited evidence as yet that it is being fulfilled or that technology is having a transformative impact on adult access to education.

It is significant that 11 per cent of the adult population now say that they are using the Internet to do an online course and 40 per cent in total say they are undertaking some form of learning activity online (as reported in Chapter 5.1). However, there is little or no robust research evidence to indicate that the overall volume of adult learning has increased as a result, that access is being significantly extended to new groups of learners, or that particular learning outcomes are being improved. There are of course all kinds of promising case studies, development projects and surveys of subjective opinion, as well as significant trends in how industry is investing its training budgets and a growing e-learning industry serving a vocational market: but that does not yet amount to a rigorous evidence base.

This should perhaps not come as a surprise and is not itself a reason to question the potential. The gaps in what the research says probably tell us more about the research than the use of technology for adult learning. However, this is another issue for the deployment of technology, which requires new business models and patterns of investment that are difficult to justify without firmer evidence. That said, it is also another area where technology could help move things forward through its ability to capture large volumes of data that can then underpin more rigorous research.

Perhaps then a different question is needed: not what does the research say, but what should the research be asking. Experts in the field of education technology have increasingly turned their attention to trying to understand and address the gap between potential and actual impact to date.

The Technology Enhanced Learning (TEL) Research Programme's 2013 report, *Beyond Prototypes*, sought to establish 'what can be done to move from academic research and innovative prototypes to effective and sustainable products and practices'. A multi-disciplinary team analysed the field, made detailed studies of particular examples of TEL innovation and undertook in-depth interviews with key figures from research and industry. The report recognizes that: 'arenas for informal learning, non-formal learning, lifelong and professional learning are very much part to the TEL research agenda' which should extend beyond formal education. A key conclusion is the need to 'look beyond product development and pay close attention to the whole process of implementation'. Evidence is crucial but this needs to go beyond proving the technology under laboratory conditions. 'Methods of evaluation are required that can be applied to processes of innovation and to institutional change, as well as those that can be applied to shifts in technology usage.' Furthermore, the researchers describe 'education as a super stable system' in which technological innovation can only be introduced successfully based on a sophisticated understanding of how to affect change in such a system.

The Ufi Charitable Trust's report, *Scaling Up* (Shepherd *et al.*, 2012), investigated opportunities for and barriers to the application of digital learning, focusing specifically on adult learning to inform future use of the trust's funds to support research and development in the sector. Their findings – based on desk research, an online questionnaire and in-depth interviews with researchers, business people, learning professionals and civil servants – identified opportunities and barriers under four headings:

- 'capability building and advocacy' – gaps in skills and understanding among practitioners and decision-makers are identified as a major obstacle to a step change in vocational learning in the United Kingdom
- 'new models for the organization of learning' – the argument that there is now 'the opportunity to transform the learning process, rather than just automate it', through developments such as peer supported and assessed learning, flipped classrooms and separating learning from assessment
- 'interaction and immersion' – 'making better use of the power of computers to deliver intelligent and adaptive learning simulations, games and virtual worlds'
- 'learning infrastructure' – making use of the availability of cloud services, and highly powered mobile devices and e-book readers.

Perhaps lessons can learned too from the current debate about brain training, being fought out primarily in the domain of medical rather than educational research. For all the concerns about quackery and miss-selling, millions of adults are engaged and generating data, and there is an emerging body of evidence proving one way or another whether particular interventions can do what they claim. It is also increasingly recognized that asking the question 'does brain training technology work' is not a sensible question, and that it can only be established whether a particular example of the technology applied in a particular context with a defined group of individuals has a particular impact. It is equally not sensible to ask the general question 'does education technology work?'.

Looking to the future, there are promising developments aimed at creating a more robust evidence base for the further education and adult skills sector as a whole. The 2013 Commission on Vocational Teaching and Learning was a landmark and there are now programmes of research being initiated by bodies such as the Centre for Vocational Education Research, the Behavioural Research Centre for Adult Skills and Knowledge, the Education Endowment Foundation, and the Centre for Post-14 Education and Work. Specifically with regard to the application of education technology in the sector, the 2014 FELTAG report's recommendations put down some important markers and bodies like JISC, the Education and Training Foundation, and the UfI Trust are enabling follow up work.

Given the recurring concerns in research findings about professional development for practitioners, a particularly interesting example is the free *Blended Learning Essentials* MOOC supported by the UfI Trust, which was launched on FutureLearn in October 2015 for teachers and trainers in vocational education. At the half-way point in the first course runs there were already 25,000 sign-ups and 76 per cent of course participants in the first 'Getting Started' course said at the end that they now feel confident about using blended learning, compared with only 14 per cent prior to the course. Following this initial success, the range of courses has been expanded, with the original 'Getting Started' and 'Embedding Practices' courses being rerun, and two new courses added for 2017/18 on 'Developing Digital Skills' and 'Supporting Apprenticeships'.

The wider challenge for research on education technology will be to ensure that it connects with the broader framework of research on FE and skills, with developments across industry, as represented by Towards Maturity and Learning Light, and with the latest insights from other fields such as neuroscience and behavioural economics. Creating, disseminating and applying this more comprehensive evidence base, moving beyond sporadic initiatives, will be one of the key factors to realize the potential of education technology for lifelong learning.

Conclusion

Rosemary Luckin and Wayne Holmes

The research evidence and data reported across the three chapters in this part provide interesting reading about adult learning and the potential of technology to engage and enhance the experience. More adults in Great Britain report using the Internet to take part in some form of learning and yet the number of adults who report participating in any sort of learning, including but not limited to that involving the Internet, has remained remarkably stable for the past 20 years. One might conclude that technology, such as the Internet, is not bringing new learners into the fold. It would seem that we are not succeeding in widening participation beyond those who were already engaged in learning, even with the advent and growing popularity of innovations such as MOOCs and so-called 'brain training' games that have the capacity to top the game sale charts.

The chapter about MOOCs provides an interesting read and is based on a body of 167 publications. The priorities extracted from this research literature for those involved in developing and using MOOCs include the need to widen access and to develop new approaches to assessment and accreditation. These two priorities are likely to be interlinked, because many adults in need of learning opportunities have been failed by an education system that is steeped in traditional methods of assessment and accreditation.

The authors of Chapter 5.2 note that MOOC learners are primarily individuals with prior experience of higher education and there is little evidence that MOOCs are widening participation for those distanced from education. Therefore, while MOOCs have shown that they can engage millions of learners, this does not necessarily equate to widening participation. Clearly, more attention must be paid to accessibility and to removing some of the barriers that are currently in place.

The importance of both adult education and widening participation is cast in yet sharper relief when considered in light of the fact that across the globe, populations are living longer and the workplace is evolving swiftly as a result of increasing automation. It is clear that lifelong learning will be essential for all adults. It is also clear that while technology has significant potential to extend education for the adult population (indeed as Stuart Edwards points out in Chapter 5.3 it is hard to imagine any solution to the lifelong learning needs of a nation that does not exploit the potential of technology) there is limited evidence that technology is having a significant impact on adult access to education. In particular, the evidence suggests that those distanced from learning are not being engaged in education through technology.

The research provides promising case studies, including development projects and surveys of subjective opinion, as well as studies of new approaches such as digital games that appear to be useful for some older learners. There is also evidence of significant investment by industry in training with technology and a growing e-learning industry, and yet there is no rigorous evidence base to call upon. In fact, Stuart Edwards suggests that rather than asking what the research says, we should ask: *what should the research be asking?* The Ufi report (Shepherd *et al.*, 2012) provides some useful pointers in this respect: we need to tackle the gaps in skills and understanding among practitioners and decision-makers, we need new models for the organization of adult learning to make better use of computers for intelligent and adaptive learning simulations, games and virtual worlds, and we need to make better use of the available cloud services, and highly powered mobile devices and e-book readers. These issues require significant research to ensure a sound evidence-based foundation for future progress.

What the research says about technology for adult learners in and beyond formal institutions

- Technology-enabled learning has grown over the past decade: increasing numbers of adults are using the Internet for some form of online learning.
- Surveys suggest that UK employers are spending close to a fifth of their training budgets on e-learning and learning technologies, and this will continue to rise.
- Growth in the use of technology for learning does not appear to have widened participation. There is no clear evidence that the growth in the use of technology and online learning is having a significant impact in the United Kingdom on either the overall rate of adult participation in learning or the make-up of those participating.
- The evidence that does exist suggests that the main impact has been to provide an additional access route for those already likely to be engaged in learning.
- MOOC learners, for example, are primarily individuals with prior experience of higher education, and there is little evidence that MOOCs are widening participation for those distanced from education.
- Employers' growing investment in e-learning has been largely at the expense of traditional training programmes. Their major concern has been to get 'more for less' and 60 per cent of what is spent is on 'compliance training'.
- For adult basic skills – maths and English – despite the huge level of need and some promising developments, there is not yet evidence of impact at scale.

- Research has identified a range of issues to be addressed and developments made if technology is to better fulfil its potential to enable education for all.
- MOOCs now engage millions of learners. Research on MOOCs identifies eight priority areas for development relating to strategy, pedagogy, learning design, discussion, learner expectations, access, assessment and accreditation.
- MOOC sustainability depends on the universities offering them having a clear strategy that balances expenditure with value to the institution.
- To live up to their promise of providing lifelong learning at a massive scale, MOOCs will require experienced educator teams who can make use of appropriate pedagogies for learning at scale, develop learning designs that lead to student success, clarify learner expectations, respond to them and engage them in knowledge-building conversations.
- Across technical and vocational education, and basic skills, a lack of research is itself an issue; not having the evidence base to know what works and whether it can be implemented at scale. Gaps in the skills and understanding of practitioners and decision-makers also pose a key challenge.
- So-called 'brain training' games, though at the fringes of what might conventionally be regarded as education, may offer some interesting lessons in terms of their capacity to reach a different kind of mass audience and provide large volumes of data that could enable more rigorous research, whether that proves or disproves their claims of efficacy.
- As lifelong learning becomes more important, MOOCs and other digital technology are creating the potential for different routes through education over an individual lifetime, and more fluidity between HE, technical and vocational and other broader forms of adult learning.
- At this stage, the main factors to be addressed if technology is to fulfil its promise of adult education for all are not technological limitations, but rather:

  o the culture and context of learning and learners
  o the need for new business models and organizational structures

> o the need for a clearer framework to evaluate what works and to inform practitioners and
>
> o through a combination of all of these, a concerted challenge to the built-in inertia of seemingly stable education systems.

References (Part 5)

AoC (Association of Colleges) (2012) *AoC Learning Technology Survey Report.* London: Association of Colleges. Online. www.aoc.co.uk/sites/default/files/AoC_Learning_Technologies_Report_2012.pdf (accessed 15 September 2017).

Bozkurt, A., Honeychurch, S., Caines, A., Bali, M., Koutropoulos, A. and Cormier, D. (2016) 'Community tracking in a cMOOC and nomadic learner behavior identification on a connectivist rhizomatic learning network'. *Turkish Online Journal of Distance Education*, 17 (4), Article 1, 4–30.

Cannell, P. and Macintyre, R. (2014) 'Towards open educational practice'. In *Conference Proceedings: The Open and Flexible Higher Education Conference, hosted by AGH University of Science and Technology in Krakow, 23–24 October 2014: 'New Technologies and the Future of Teaching and Learning'.* Maastricht: European Association of Distance Teaching Universities, 109–19.

CAVTL (Commission on Adult Vocational Teaching and Learning) (2013) *It's about Work ... Excellent adult vocational teaching and learning.* London: Learning and Skills Improvement Service. Online. www.excellencegateway.org.uk/content/eg5937 (accessed 15 September 2017).

Clow, D. and Makriyannis, E. (2011) 'iSpot analysed: Participatory learning and reputation'. In *LAK'11: Proceedings of the 1st International Conference on Learning Analytics and Knowledge, February 27–March 1, 2011, Banff, Alberta, Canada.* New York: Association for Computing Machinery, 34–43.

Cognitive Training Data (2014) 'Scientists to Stanford: Research shows brain exercises can work'. Online. www.cognitivetrainingdata.org/%20the-controversy-does-brain-training-work/response-letter/ (accessed 6 November 2017).

Corbett, A., Owen, A., Hampshire, A., Grahn, J., Stenton, R., Dajani, S., Burns, A., Howard, R., Williams, N., Williams, G. and Ballard, C. (2015) 'The effect of an online cognitive training package in healthy older adults: An online randomized controlled trial'. *JAMDA*, 16 (11), 990–7.

Dalziel, J., Conole, G., Wills, S., Walker, S., Bennett, S., Dobozy, E., Cameron, L., Badilescu-Buga, E. and Bower, M. (2016) 'The Larnaca Declaration on Learning Design'. *Journal of Interactive Media in Education*, 1, Article 7, 1–24.

Daniel, J. (2012) 'Making sense of MOOCs: Musings in a maze of myth, paradox and possibility'. *Journal of Interactive Media in Education*, 3, Article 18, 1–20.

Edwards, J.D., Xu, H., Clark, D.O., Ross, L.A. and Unverzagt, F.W. (2016) *The ACTIVE Study: What we have learned and what is next?* Online. www.apa.org/news/press/releases/2016/08/active-study.pdf (accessed 15 September 2017).

FELTAG (Further Education Learning Technology Action Group) (2014) *Paths Forward to a Digital Future for Further Education and Skills: Recommendations for the Minister of State for Skills and Enterprise, Matthew Hancock MP*. London: FELTAG. Online. http://feltag.org.uk/wp-content/uploads/2012/01/FELTAG-REPORT-FINAL.pdf (accessed 15 September 2017).

Ferguson, R. and Clow, D. (2015) 'Consistent commitment: Patterns of engagement across time in massive open online courses (MOOCs)'. *Journal of Learning Analytics*, 2 (3), 55–80.

Ferguson, R., Clow, D., Beale, R., Cooper, A.J., Morris, N., Bayne, S. and Woodgate, A. (2015) 'Moving through MOOCs: Pedagogy, learning design and patterns of engagement'. In Conole, G., Klobučar, T., Rensing, C., Konert, J. and Lavoué, É. (eds) *Design for Teaching and Learning in a Networked World: 10th European Conference on Technology Enhanced Learning, EC-TEL 2015, Toledo, Spain, September 15–18, 2015, Proceedings* (Lecture Notes in Computer Science 9307). Cham: Springer, 70–84.

Ferguson, R. and Sharples, M. (2014) 'Innovative pedagogy at massive scale: Teaching and learning in MOOCs'. In Rensing, C., de Freitas, S., Ley, T. and Muñoz-Merino, P.J. (eds) *Open Learning and Teaching in Educational Communities: 9th European Conference on Technology Enhanced Learning, EC-TEL 2014, Graz, Austria, September 16–19, 2014, Proceedings* (Lecture Notes in Computer Science 8719). Cham: Springer, 98–111.

Ferguson, R., Sharples, M. and Beale, R. (2015) 'MOOCs 2030: A future for massive open learning'. In Bonk, C.J., Lee, M.M., Reeves, T.C. and Reynolds, T.H. (eds) *MOOCs and Open Education Around the World*. New York: Routledge, 315–26.

Ferguson, R. and Whitelock, D. (2014) 'Taking on different roles: How educators position themselves in MOOCs'. In Rensing, C., de Freitas, S., Ley, T. and Muñoz-Merino, P.J. (eds) *Open Learning and Teaching in Educational Communities: 9th European Conference on Technology Enhanced Learning, EC-TEL 2014, Graz, Austria, September 16–19, 2014, Proceedings* (Lecture Notes in Computer Science 8719). Cham: Springer, 562–3.

Gloster, R., Marvell, R., Buzzeo, J., Hadjivassiliou, K., Williams, J. and Huxley, C. (2016) *Mapping Investment in Adult Skills: Which individuals, in what learning and with what returns?* (BIS Research Paper 292). London: Department for Business, Innovation and Skills.

Goodyear, P., Banks, S., Hodgson, V. and McConnell, D. (eds) (2004) *Advances in Research on Networked Learning*. Boston: Kluwer Academic Publishers.

Gore, H. (2014) 'Massive open online courses (MOOCs) and their impact on academic library services: Exploring the issues and challenges'. *New Review of Academic Librarianship*, 20 (1), 4–28.

Hatzipanagos, S. (2015) 'What do MOOCs contribute to the debate on learning design of online courses?'. *eLearning Papers*, 42, 1–10.

Hauck, M. and MacKinnon, T. (2016) 'A new approach to assessing online intercultural exchange: Soft certification of participant engagement'. In O'Dowd, R. and Lewis, T. (eds) *Online Intercultural Exchange: Policy, pedagogy, practice*. New York: Routledge, 209–34.

Horrigan, J.B. (2016) *Lifelong Learning and Technology*. Washington, DC: Pew Research Center. Online. http://assets.pewresearch.org/wp-content/uploads/sites/14/2016/03/PI_2016.03.22_Educational-Ecosystems_FINAL.pdf (accessed 15 September 2017).

Imhoof, M. (1985) 'Interactive radio in the classroom: Ten years of proven success'. *Development Communication Report*, 48, 4–5.

James, D. and Unwin, L. (2016) *Fostering High Quality Vocational Further Education in Wales*. Cardiff: Public Policy Institute for Wales. Online. http://ppiw.org.uk/files/2016/01/PPIW-Report-Fostering-High-Quality-Further-Education-in-Wales.pdf (accessed 15 September 2017).

Jennings, C., Overton, L. and Dixon, G. (2016) *70+20+10=100: The evidence behind the numbers* (In-Focus Report). London: Towards Maturity. Online. https://towardsmaturity.org/2016/02/02/in-focus-702010100-evidence-behind-numbers/ (accessed 15 September 2017).

Jordan, K. (2014) 'Initial trends in enrolment and completion of massive open online courses'. *International Review of Research in Open and Distance Learning*, 15 (1), 133–60.

Jordan, K. (2015) 'Massive open online course completion rates revisited: Assessment, length and attrition'. *International Review of Research in Open and Distributed Learning*, 16 (3), 341–58.

Jordan, S. (2013) 'E-assessment: Past, present and future'. *New Directions*, 9 (1), 87–106.

Knox, J. (2014) 'Digital culture clash: "Massive" education in the E-learning and Digital Cultures MOOC'. *Distance Education*, 35 (2), 164–77.

Kuczera, M., Field. S., and Windisch, H. (2016) *Building Skills for All: A Review of England*. OECD.

Laurillard, D. (2013) *Technology as a Driver and Enabler of Adult Vocational Teaching and Learning*. London: Institute of Education. Online. www.excellencegateway.org.uk/content/eg5858 (accessed 15 September 2017).

Law, A. and Law, P. (2014) 'Digital badging at the Open University: Recognition for informal learning'. In *Conference Proceedings: The Open and Flexible Higher Education Conference, hosted by AGH University of Science and Technology in Krakow, 23–24 October 2014: 'New Technologies and the Future of Teaching and Learning'*. Maastricht: European Association of Distance Teaching Universities, 189–206.

Learning Light (2014) 'A review of the e-learning markets of the UK, EU and China 2014'. Online. www.e-learningcentre.co.uk/resources/market-reports/ (accessed 15 September 2017).

Liu, H., Macintyre, R. and Ferguson, R. (2012) 'Exploring qualitative analytics for e-mentoring relationships building in an online social learning environment'. In *LAK'12: Proceedings of the 2nd International Conference on Learning Analytics and Knowledge, April 29–May 2, 2012, Vancouver, British Columbia, Canada*. New York: Association for Computing Machinery, 179–83.

Liyanagunawardena, T.R. (2015) 'Massive open online courses'. *Humanities*, 4, 35–41.

Liyanagunawardena, T.R., Lundqvist, K. and Williams, S.A. (2015) 'Massive open online courses and sustainability'. Paper presented at the 6th International Open Education Conference (OER15), 'Mainstreaming Open Education', Cardiff, 14–15 April 2015.

Lombardo, M. and Eichinger, R. (1996) *The Career Architect Development Planner*. Minneapolis: Lominger.

Manches, A., Phillips, B., Crook, C., Chowcat, I. and Sharples, M. (2010a) *Shaping Contexts To Realise the Potential of Technologies To Support Learning*. Nottingham: Capital.

Manches, A., Phillips, B., Crook, C., Sharples, M., Patterson, W., Stokes, E., Balmer, K. and Chowcat, I. (2010b) *Technology and Education: Putting it in context*. Nottingham: CAPITAL Research Project (Curriculum and Pedagogy in Technology Assisted Learning).

McAndrew, P. and Scanlon, E. (2013) 'Open learning at a distance: Lessons for struggling MOOCs'. *Science*, 342 (6165), 1450–1.

Melby-Lervåg, M. and Hulme, C. (2013) 'Is working memory training effective? A meta-analytic review'. *Developmental Psychology*, 49 (2), 270–91.

Murray, J.-A. (2014) 'Participants' perceptions of a MOOC'. *Insights*, 27 (2), 154–9.

Nazir, U., Davis, H. and Harris, L. (2015) 'First day stands out as most popular among MOOC leavers'. *International Journal of e-Education, e-Business, e-Management and e-Learning*, 5 (3), 173–9.

NIACE (National Institute of Adult Continuing Education) (2015) *2015 NIACE Adult Participation in Learning Survey: Headline findings*. Leicester: NIACE. Online. www.learningandwork.org.uk/wp-content/uploads/2017/01/2015-Adult-Participation-in-Learning-Headline-Findings.pdf (accessed 15 September 2017).

Nkuyubwatsi, B. (2016) 'Positioning extension massive open online courses (xMOOCs) within the open access and the lifelong learning agendas in a developing setting'. *Journal of Learning for Development*, 3 (1), 14–36.

Nouchi, R., Taki, Y., Takeuchi, H., Hashizume, H., Akitsuki, Y., Shigemune, Y., Sekiguchi, A., Kotozaki, Y., Tsukiura, T., Yomogida, Y. and Kawashima, R. (2012) 'Brain training game improves executive functions and processing speed in the elderly: A randomized controlled trial'. *PLoS ONE*, 7 (1), Article e29676, 1–9.

ONS (Office for National Statistics) (2015) *Internet Access – Households and Individuals: 2015* (Statistical Bulletin). Newport: Office for National Statistics. Online. www.ons.gov.uk/peoplepopulationandcommunity/householdcharacteristics/homeinternetandsocialmediausage/datasets/internetaccesshouseholdsandindividualsreferencetables [(accessed 15 September 2017).

O'Toole, R. (2013) *Pedagogical Strategies and Technologies for Peer Assessment in Massively Open Online Courses (MOOCs)* (Discussion Paper). Coventry: University of Warwick.

Owen, A.M., Hampshire, A., Grahn, J.A., Stenton, R., Dajani, S., Burns, A.S., Howard, R.J. and Ballard, C.G. (2010) 'Putting brain training to the test'. *Nature*, 465 (7299), 775–8.

Pro Bono Economics (2014) *Pro Bono Economics Report for National Numeracy: Cost of outcomes associated with low levels of adult numeracy in the UK*. London: Pro Bono Economics. Online. www.nationalnumeracy.org.uk/sites/default/files/pbe_national_numeracy_costs_report_11mar.pdf (accessed 15 September 2017).

Rodrigo, C. and Iniesto, F. (2015) 'Holistic vision for creating accessible services based on MOOCs'. Paper presented at the Open Education Global Conference 2015, 'Innovation and Entrepreneurship', Banff, Alberta, Canada, 22–24 April, 2015.

Sharpe, R. and Browne, L. (2015) *Digital Student: Further education: FE learners' expectations and experiences of technology – synthesis report*. Bristol: JISC. Online. https://ugc.futurelearn.com/uploads/files/b4/9d/b49d8701-61e0-4264-9ef5-8298a5802ec9/JR0043_FE_DIGITALSTUDENT_REPORT_A.pdf (accessed 15 September 2017).

Shepherd, C., Moore, D., Schmoller, S. and Perry, A. (2012) *Scaling Up: Achieving a breakthrough in adult learning with technology*. London: Ufi Charitable Trust. Online. www.ufi.co.uk/sites/ufi.co.uk/files/Scaling%20up_21_5_V3.pdf (accessed 15 September 2017).

Shute, V.J., Ventura, M. and Ke, F. (2015) 'The power of play: The effects of Portal 2 and Lumosity on cognitive and noncognitive skills'. *Computers and Education*, 80, 58–67.

Siemens, G. (2005) 'Connectivism: A learning theory for the digital age'. *International Journal of Instructional Technology and Distance Learning*, 2 (1), 3–10.

Snelson, S. and Deyes, K. (2016) *Understanding the Further Education Market in England* (BIS Research Paper 296). London: Department for Business, Innovation and Skills.

Stanford Center on Longevity (2014) 'A consensus on the brain training industry from the scientific community'. Online. http://longevity3.stanford.edu/blog/2014/10/15/the-consensus-on-the-brain-training-industry-from-the-scientific-community-2/ (accessed 15 September 2017).

TEL (Technology Enhanced Learning Research Programme) (2013) *Beyond Prototypes: Enabling innovation in technology-enhanced learning*. London: Institute of Education. Online. http://oro.open.ac.uk/41119/1/BeyondPrototypes.pdf (accessed 15 September 2017).

Teplechuk, E. (2013) 'Emergent models of Massive Open Online Courses: An exploration of sustainable practices for MOOC institutions in the context of the launch of MOOCs at the University of Edinburgh'. Unpublished MBA dissertation, University of Edinburgh.

Towards Maturity (2015) *Embracing Change: Improving performance of business, individuals and the L&D team* (2015–16 Industry Benchmark Report). London: Towards Maturity. Online. https://towardsmaturity.org/2015/11/05/embracing-change-improving-performance-benchmark/ (accessed 15 September 2017).

Ufi Charitable Trust (2016) 'Blended Learning Essentials'. Online. www.ufi.co.uk/projects/blended-learning-essentials (accessed 15 September 2017).

Vorhaus, J., Litster, J., Frearson, M. and Johnson, S. (2011) *Review of Research and Evaluation on Improving Adult Literacy and Numeracy Skills* (BIS Research Paper 61). London: Department for Business, Innovation and Skills.

Weller, M. (2014) *The Battle for Open: How openness won and why it doesn't feel like victory*. London: Ubiquity Press.

White, S., Davis, H., Dickens, K., León, M. and Sánchez-Vera, M. (2015a) 'MOOCs: What motivates the producers and participants?'. In Zvacek, S., Restivo, M.T., Uhomoibhi, J. and Helfert, M. (eds) *Computer Supported Education: 6th International Conference, CSEDU 2014, Barcelona, Spain, April 1–3, 2014, Revised Selected Papers* (Communications in Computer and Information Science 510). Cham: Springer, 99–114.

White, S., León, M. and White, S. (2015b) 'MOOCs inside universities: An analysis of MOOC discourse as represented in HE magazines'. Paper presented at the 7th International Conference on Computer Supported Education (CSEDU 2015), Lisbon, Portugal, 23–25 May 2015.

Wintrup, J., Wakefield, K. and Davis, H. (2015a) *Engaged Learning in MOOCs: A study using the UK Engagement Survey*. York: Higher Education Academy.

Wintrup, J., Wakefield, K., Morris, D. and Davis, H. (2015b) *Liberating Learning: Experiences of MOOCs*. York: Higher Education Academy.

Witthaus, G., Inamorato dos Santos, A., Childs, M., Tannhäuser, A.-C., Conole, G., Nkuyubwatsi, B. and Punie, Y. (2016) *Validation of Non-Formal MOOC-Based Learning: An analysis of assessment and recognition practices in Europe (OpenCred)* (JRC Science for Policy Report). Luxembourg: Publications Office of the European Union.

Part Six

How technology can
support teaching

Introduction

What the research says about how technology can support teaching

Rosemary Luckin and Wayne Holmes

Much emphasis is placed on how technology can help learners with constant calls for the community to demonstrate that technology works and that it can improve learning outcomes. For example, when Nicky Morgan (2016), the then UK education secretary, opened the 2016 BETT show she stated that: 'Where technology is evidence based and outcome driven – where it really works – we will back it all the way'.

Artificial Intelligence (AI) is the subject of much media coverage and the implications of AI technologies for education are of increasing concern. Chapter 6.1 provides an excellent description of the way that AI technology can be used to produce software that can track and support student learning. These systems can also provide teachers with increased information about their students' progress that can be integrated into their future teaching practice.

Benedict du Boulay, Alexandra Poulovassilis, Wayne Holmes and Manolis Mavrikis use Chapter 6.2 to investigate how technology could be used to reduce the achievement gaps that even in developed countries like the United Kingdom dog the equalities agenda and prevent many people from achieving their potential.

In this chapter, the authors note the enormous challenge faced by teachers and university lecturers with students whose abilities are wide ranging and who require the kind of one-to-one attention that is impossible to provide in any normal classroom setting. They argue that we have the technologies to assist educators and as evidence they report case studies about artificial intelligence technologies that can provide personalized support for students, better information for teachers to increase their awareness of their learners' needs and more time for teachers to provide the individualized support that is their speciality.

Chapter 6.3 sees Kaśka Porayska-Pomsta, Christina Preston, Charlotte Laerke Weitze and Sarah Younie explore the assumptions that are made about teachers' knowledge and understanding of educational practice. They suggest that the often aspirational rhetoric in many reports stands in stark contrast to the reality of many educators' capabilities and training. The research evidence they report about teaching expertise illustrates that the abilities required of teachers are complex, shaped by multiple types of interactions and contexts operating at multiple levels of knowledge and skills.

Their chapter has a particular focus on the metacognitive skills required from teachers and they present three examples of how educational practitioners' continuous development of metacognitive skills may be supported through the design and application of different technologies across a variety of educational contexts. All three examples concern themselves with developing educational practitioners' critical reflection skills in order to support their adaptive decision making and pedagogical innovating capabilities.

Learning analytics, artificial intelligence and the process of assessment

Rosemary Luckin and Kristen Weatherby

Introduction

In this chapter we explore some of the ways in which technology can support and perhaps revolutionize the assessment process. Assessment of students' learning is a core element of teaching. Typically, assessment has focused on levels of attainment, measurement against set standards and comparisons across schools and countries at national and international levels. However, there is concern that such emphases lead to a focus on formal examinations, target-setting, teaching to the test and concerns about school performance and league tables that discourage teachers and schools from pursuing alternative assessment approaches that 'might unlock the potential of their pupils' (DfE, 2010: 16).

It is interesting to ponder why there is a global prevalence of formal exams and tests when we know that knowledge and understanding cannot be rigorously evaluated in this way. In addition, there are increasing reports of stress associated with exams and anxiety for both students and teachers. As reported in Luckin (2017), 'The prevailing exam paradigm is unpleasant, can turn students away from education, and requires that students and teachers take time away from learning.' There have been attempts over the years to find alternatives, but none have borne fruit at scale. In this chapter, we explore the possibility afforded by learning analytics and artificial intelligence to reduce the stress for teachers who must prepare their students for a range of tests and exams and then be judged by their students' subsequent performance.

The prevailing assessment paradigm

A 2009 report on national testing across Europe (EACEA, 2009) found that pupil assessment is complex and comprises a variety of assessment instruments and methods, both formative and summative, and that the assessment process is integral to the overall structure of educational systems. The report identifies three key purposes for assessment in formal education:

- **Summative** (assessment *of* learning) – summarizing the achievement of individual pupils at the end of a school year or key stage.
- **Evaluative** (assessment *of* education quality) – used as an indicator of individual school/teacher performance in terms of education quality and the effective application of policies and practice.
- **Formative** (assessment *for* learning) – focusing on the day-to-day learning needs of individual pupils and adapting teaching accordingly.

While highlighting the role of national and summative assessment in relation to teacher quality and school improvement, the report emphasizes that the core form of assessment and the most effective form of assessment for learning is *continuous assessment* – the ongoing monitoring and tracking of students' learning progress.

However, continuous assessment could be very labour intensive if all the detailed information about an individual learner's activities and progress must be hand recorded and analysed. Yet this is an area where technology can really help. It can be used to track the minutiae of student learning processes and performance as it happens over time, to analyse this information and to store it. In particular, big data, artificial intelligence (AI) and learning analytics have an important role to play.

Big data, learning analytics and assessment

For years, businesses have been using ever more detailed data to learn more about their customers so they might tailor their products and services to fit customer needs. From supermarket loyalty cards that provide information about their customers' preferences to the familiar recommendations from online retailers like Amazon and the personalized adverts that appear when one searches for information on the world wide web, we are increasingly subjected to personalized marketing.

The methods that companies and others use to obtain and analyse data are commonly referred to as data analytics and data mining. Data analytics is the practice of analysing data to drive decision-making in business, whereas data mining is slightly more technical and involves extracting business value from large datasets (Ferguson, 2012). With the advent of the Internet came the arrival of web analytics, in which data on website usage is examined in order to improve the online experience for users (Elias, 2011). Vast quantities of consumer data are collected from users' Internet browsing patterns and online purchase history and inform numerous business decisions.

When used in education, these data collection and analysis practices are called learning analytics (LA) and educational data mining (Baker and Siemens, 2014). These fields have developed separately but there are many similarities and differences between the two (Siemens and Baker, 2012). Both involve the analysis of large-scale datasets in education with the goal of recognizing patterns in the data in order to make predictions about the future (Elias, 2011). Both learning analytics and educational data mining are 'being used to answer increasingly complex questions about what a student knows and that a student is engaged' (Bienkowski *et al.*, 2012: 25) in order to provide improvements to teaching and learning (Siemens and Baker, 2012).

Educational data mining is automated, and focuses on developing new tools to identify patterns in the data (Bienkowski *et al.*, 2012, Siemens and Baker, 2012). It relies on the software to provide support for learners (Baker and Siemens, 2014) and concentrates less on pedagogy than learning analytics (Clow, 2013). Learning analytics (LA) have a foundation in constructivism and situated learning. LA can use automated analysis or human intervention to analyse the collected data and make decisions about the support that educators can provide to improve learning (Baker and Siemens, 2014). LA therefore require skills on the part of those reviewing the data, both in terms of understanding what the data mean and then in deciding the best course of action based on the analyses (Siemens and Baker, 2012). LA can differ from other educational research because it can take advantage of existing datasets and put them in a format (often through data visualizations) that makes them more accessible to end users (Ferguson, 2012).

In 2011, at the first Conference on Learning Analytics and Knowledge, the Society for Learning Analytics Research (SoLAR) defined learning analytics as 'the measurement, collection, analysis and reporting of data about learners and their contexts for the purposes of understanding and optimizing learning and the environments in which it occurs' (Ferguson, 2012). The basic aim of the field is to improve the teaching and learning experience for both educators and students (Martinez-Maldonado *et al.*, 2015).

Use of learning analytics in education

Since the recognition of 'big data' as a new concept, there have been many claims that it will revolutionize education (see, for example, Tulasi, 2013), mostly from the computer science and educational technology literature and the media, rather than educational research literature.

Although the learning sciences have been slower to adopt the use of analytics than have other fields of research such as the applied sciences (Baker and Siemens, 2014), its use in education has grown in recent years. This is mainly due to the rapid growth in the quantity of data being collected from students in schools and higher education. More education systems and universities are tracking student achievement data online and often these databases connect to other student social records to provide a more complete picture of learners and their contexts. Increasing numbers of schools and universities now use some type of online learning platform for homework, assessments and communication with parents or other stakeholders (Ferguson, 2012; Tempelaar *et al.*, 2015).

Teachers are using technology applications that can track student movement through their work or record their progress on various learning tasks. In addition, the data itself is easier to use because some standardized data formats now exist, as well as better analytical tools to manage and explore large datasets (Baker and Siemens, 2014, Karkalas *et al.*, 2016).

Although the use of data in education has been limited in comparison with many other fields, educational technologists are starting to see the potential benefits and myriad conceivable uses for the massive quantities of data that continue to be collected. Researchers agree that opportunities for LA are great in terms of presenting visual representations of data to help users interpret it, developing profiles of learners based on similar characteristics and performance and giving teachers the opportunity to continually develop and improve their practice based on evidence (Bienkowski *et al.*, 2012). In addition to shaping practice, LA also has the possibility to alter the common understanding of how students learn, thereby changing existing theories in education (Baker and Siemens, 2014). The use of LA can provide models of knowledge use, behaviour and experience and the identification of trends and changes over time (Bienkowski *et al.*, 2012). And additionally, LA allows educators and institutions to reflect on learners' progress at the individual learner level (by monitoring and analysing student progress) and at the institutional level (by revealing patterns of progress across areas of the institution) (Greller and Drachsler, 2012).

LA initially found its way into education at the university level and has since begun to trickle down into primary and secondary education. The timeliness of feedback on teaching that LA can provide initially appealed to many in higher education. For example, ordinarily professors relied on student surveys, administered at the end of a course, to gather data about their teaching over the term that had just ended. Once those data had been analysed, educators could begin to think about changes they would make to future courses (Elias, 2011). With LA, teachers and educators can use data they already have to make changes in their teaching immediately. It has to be said, however, that such practices are not as yet widespread.

Another use of LA in higher education involves predictive modelling to determine whether students will finish a course based on their personal characteristics and actions. A model is developed using information known about students before the beginning of the course, such as their background characteristics, educational history and rate of absenteeism in courses to date. Further data are collected during the course through the use of the online learning platform, which details how students have used the platform, how they have performed in any assessments and their actual attendance to date. Finally, whether each student has actually completed the course is added to the model, which can then be used to predict future students' likelihood of completing this course (Clow, 2013).

Already learning analytics has evolved into several different sub-types, a selection of which are listed below:

- Mobile learning analytics: involves collection and analysis of data from students' mobile devices to understand how more flexible interactions with learning materials can impact the learning process (Aljohani and Davis, 2012).
- Ubiquitous learning analytics: adds contextual information about learners to the data collected through mobile learning analytics and provides information on the relationships between learners and their contexts (Aljohani and Davis, 2012).
- Learner-centred analytics: is reminiscent of educational data mining in that it collects and analyses the traces learners leave behind through their so-called digital footprint to provide a better learning experience. However, the focus here is on helping learners use these data to improve their own learning process (Baker *et al.*, 2012: 20).
- Visual learning analytics: provides visualizations of the learning traces left behind by learners, revealing patterns (in usage, for example) that might guide teachers in providing additional support to learners (Baker *et al.*, 2012; Karkalas *et al.*, 2016; Mavrikis *et al.*, 2016).

The challenges involved in using learning analytics

The speed of technical progress means that the fields of LA and EDM are growing so quickly that the development of policies and practices to help the field develop effectively are often lagging behind. In addition, the rapid spread of LA is often not grounded in research (Siemens, 2012). This situation is largely due to the fact that many of the datasets being used in today's software applications are closed, school datasets that researchers are not allowed to access in order to validate their software (Greller and Drachsler, 2012, Siemens, 2012). There is not yet a well-established connection between corporate entities and the research community, and there is a gap between research and practice in the field as well. In an ideal world there would be a cycle of information sharing between companies, researchers and practitioners so that analytics could inform research and practice and vice versa (Siemens, 2012). Many academics argue that in order for LA to be successful in education, not only do LA researchers need to work hand in hand with the field of EDM (Siemens and Baker, 2012), but LA also needs to collaborate with other stakeholders from many different fields. Education researchers and practitioners, learning scientists, psychologists, human-computer interaction experts and software engineers need to be involved in the design process alongside LA and EDM researchers and developers (Martinez-Maldonado *et al.*, 2015).

Other technical challenges exist in the field as well. To date there is not a common format for much of these data, resulting in data from one system being unusable in another (Bienkowski *et al.*, 2012, Greller and Drachsler, 2012). Often data systems might not include certain data points that are needed in order to create a learner model or profile. This could result in an inaccurate picture of learners if certain key variables are not being considered in the development of the learner model (Bienkowski *et al.*, 2012). The quality of the data visualizations is also vital in providing accurate representations of the data analyses. In fact many believe that LA software needs to do more than just provide data visualizations. Products need to be based in pedagogy and provide next steps or recommendations to educators and learners based on the data (Elias, 2011; Ferguson, 2012; Cukurova *et al.*, 2016).

Some researchers believe that it is easier to address the technical challenges with AI than those challenges that involve people, their competencies and their culture. Teachers, who are frequently the end users for this technology, often do not have the skills necessary to interpret the data they see and determine the appropriate support for their students. The teaching profession does not have a history of data-driven decision-making in many countries (Bienkowski *et al*, 2012, Greller and Drachsler, 2012). One study found that the learning management system used by a university was mainly used for content delivery rather than data analysis and that the faculty were resistant to using the technology; only 30 per cent made use of it over the course of the year (Macfadyen and Dawson, 2012).

Furthermore, the purpose of using LA has to be made clear (Martinez-Maldonado *et al.*, 2015). It could be dangerous to use these data for high-stakes evaluations of teachers, due to the errors that might occur in inputting data, the limitations of the software or incorrect interpretations of the data and subsequent behaviour changes made by teachers (Bienkowski *et al.*, 2012, Greller and Drachsler, 2012). There is also a risk that school leaders or administrators might interpret and use data to put measures in place that do not involve the teacher at all (Clow, 2013). More support for the use of learning analytics is needed at an institution and practitioner level in order to avoid some of these issues.

Possibly the most challenging issues for LA researchers and developers are those relating to ethics. Some of the data issues preventing better connections between research and corporate entities are ethical ones. Policies have yet to be created that provide guidance as to the ownership, privacy and usage of these data (Bienkowski *et al.*, 2012, Ferguson, 2012, Greller and Drachsler, 2012). Privacy and ethics issues are especially important to consider given the fact that the datasets being used in LA contain much personal information about individual students, many of whom are minors (Bienkowski *et al.*, 2012). Other ethical challenges are related to the use of information that LA is able to provide that might not have been previously known by learners, teachers, parents or institutions. One such example is the model created to predict course completion, discussed previously. If this model predicts that certain students will not finish a course for which they have registered at university, should the university allow them to take the course at all (Clow, 2013)?

Looking forward with artificial intelligence

The continual growth of LA and EDM indicate that the possibilities for personalization of learning and improving teaching are greater than the inherent risks. Greller and Dreschler (2012) believe that LA can only be successful if the following are considered:

1. Limitations of the individual user (competencies, acceptance).
2. External constraints (data conventions, norms).
3. Instruments (technology, algorithms, theories).
4. Data (open or protected).
5. Objectives (reflections, prediction).
6. Stakeholders (institutions, teachers, learners, parents).

In addition, we need to develop analytics that take into account the context of use. And we need to ensure that learning scientists, and in particular educationalists, are able to influence what gets measured, how it is analysed, and who the analysis is for. We need research that addresses the aforementioned issues and builds a knowledge base that details what actually makes a particular learning analytics tool suitable for a particular learner or situation (Scheffel *et al.*, 2015).

Artificial intelligence, learning analytics and the future of assessment

Artificial intelligence (AI) is a popular topic for scientists and the media. AI can be and is being used to increase the effectiveness and efficiency of learning analytics. However, not all data and learning analytics use AI methods and approaches and there are other key ways in which AI might be used to improve assessment for learners and teachers.

What is artificial intelligence and why is it relevant to assessment?

Applications of AI are used in many areas such as medical diagnosis, language translation, face recognition, autonomous vehicle design and robotics. To understand the implications of AI for assessment we first need to understand what AI is and does, so let's take the definition of AI used in the *Oxford Dictionary of English* (Oxford Dictionaries Online, 2017; Russell *et al.*, 2010), which defines AI as: 'computer systems that have been designed to interact with the world through capabilities (for example, visual perception and speech recognition) and intelligent behaviours (for example, assessing the available information and then taking the most sensible action to achieve a stated goal) that we would think of as essentially human'.

This definition is where the complexity of AI starts to unfold, because the definition itself relies upon an understanding of the word *intelligence*, an expression that is also the subject of multiple definitions. For example, is intelligence the ability to acquire and apply knowledge and skills, or is it wisdom, or is intelligence the ability to handle criticism without denial, blame, excuses or anxiety? AI is concerned with increasing our understanding about how the mind works by investigating the problem of designing machines that have intelligent abilities.

In addition to the many definitions of intelligence, we also need to contend the fact that AI involves the integration of many different subject areas, such as psychology, philosophy and computer science into the 'discipline' of AI. This makes AI a complex field to understand. In addition, humans have a tendency to dismiss the intelligence of something or someone once it becomes commonplace and part of everyday life. AI can seem like magic until we understand how it works and its use has become so general that we often don't even think of it as being AI. If I ask a lecture hall full of people who are not AI experts to imagine an AI, it is likely that they will imagine some sort of technology: a robot, an intelligent personal assistant or perhaps one of the smart game playing technologies, such as those that perform better than grand masters when playing chess. However, if we focus on what it means to behave intelligently, then the most important aspect of AI is to identify the problem to which intelligence is to be applied and to design *a clear understanding and representation of that problem*. Without this problem specification process, there is no chance of developing a good solution to which AI technology can be applied. The AI designer must have a good understanding of the problem an AI is supposed to solve, as well as the type of AI technique that might be appropriate. The features of the problem must be specified along with the features of the environment in which the AI must operate. The AI's intelligence or knowledge will enable it to contribute to the problem solution within the constraints of the problem environment. Once we recognize the importance of the AI design stage we can start to unpack the relevance of AI to teaching and learning and the vital role that educators need to play if AI is to meet its potential in the benefits it provides to education.

How can artificial intelligence and LA support the assessment process?

We noted earlier that there is a growing belief that LA software should do more than merely provide data visualizations. The software should embody a pedagogy and provide next steps or recommendations based on the data. This is where AI and the learning sciences come into the picture. The data that is collected and analysed by the LA software could be subjected to artificially intelligent algorithms that are based on both a pedagogical theory of choice and specific evidence about how learning takes place. For example, there is a wealth of evidence that metacognitive skills are important for successful learning. There is also evidence that specific metacognitive skills, such as help-seeking, can be taught through the intelligent provision of feedback to learners as they learn (Luckin and du Boulay, 2016). It would therefore be possible for information about the effectiveness or not of a learner's use of help and assistance could be tracked using LA software and then modelled through AI techniques. The resultant model would enable the software to provide appropriate feedback to learners to build their help-seeking skills. It would also permit visualizations of the AI to be provided to inform learners and teachers about each student's metacognitive progress as well as their progress at the subject level of their study.

We can expand this example a little further to one of the key problems for educators today: the changing nature of the workplace that means that we cannot be sure exactly what skills will be most important for our students as they progress into employment. The only thing we can be sure about is that the future workplace will be uncertain and unpredictable, so that our students will need to be able to cope with this uncertainty, to be resilient lifelong learners. As educators, we must therefore ensure that our students are able to be effective learners for themselves and with and for others and society too. The key skill people will need for their future work lives will be self-efficacy. In other words, every individual needs to have an evidence-based and accurate belief in their ability to succeed in specific situations and to accomplish tasks both alone and with others. A person's sense of self-efficacy plays a key role in how people tackle tasks and challenges, and how they set their goals, both as individuals and as collaborators. It is something that can be taught and mentored and it requires an extremely good knowledge of what one does and does not know, what one is and is not so good at, where one needs help and how to get this help. This self-knowledge is not just about subject specific knowledge and understanding, but also about one's wellbeing, emotional strength and intelligence.

This self-knowledge and efficacy is also particularly important, because these are skills that AI cannot replicate. No AI developed to date understands itself; no AI has the human capability for metacognitive awareness and self-knowledge. We must therefore ensure that we develop our human knowledge and skills to take advantage of what is uniquely human and use AI wisely to do what it does best: the routine cognitive and mechanical skills that we have spent decades instilling in learners and testing in order to award qualifications. The implications of this for school systems, the curriculum and teaching are profound and educators must engage in discussing what needs to change as a matter of urgency. This is not a job for the technologists, but if we do not motivate educators to engage in discussions about what AI could and should be used for in education the large technology companies may usurp the educators and occupy the AI vacuum that a lack of engagement will produce.

Can we leverage artificial intelligence and re-imagine the teaching?

What we hope is clear from the discussion about the future of the workforce is that we need to review what and how we teach and ensure that AI is designed and used as a tool to make our students (and ourselves) smarter, not as a technology that takes over human roles and 'dumbs us down'. To achieve this outcome, we need to concentrate on developing teaching that develops the uniquely human abilities of our students as well as instilling within them the requisite subject knowledge in a flexible, interdisciplinary and accessible manner. The parallel in teaching is that we need AI assistants to relieve teachers from the routine automatable parts of their job and enable them to focus on the human communication, the sensitive scaffolding and the provision of support for the wellbeing of students so that they can build the self-knowledge and self-efficacy that will ensure that they are able to advance in their chosen workplace.

Three examples of the ways in which teaching could be re-imagined are presented below. Each is driven by a significant educational challenge.

Assessing what can't be automated, not what we can easily automate

The current outdated testing and examining system assesses the routine cognitive subject knowledge that can easily be automated. As we noted at the start of this chapter, these assessment systems are also ineffective, time consuming and the cause of great anxiety for learners, parents and teachers. However, there is now an alternative due to the potential information we can gain from combining big data and AI and applying it to the problem of assessing learning. There is a rather beautiful irony in the fact that while unable to understand itself or develop any self-knowledge, AI can help us to understand ourselves as learners, teachers and workers and to develop our self-knowledge. Let me explain what I mean by this:

- The careful collection, collation and analysis of the data that can be harvested through people's use of technology gives us a rich source of evidence about how learners are progressing, cognitively, meta-cognitively and emotionally.
- Continuing work in psychology, neuroscience and education has increased our understanding of how humans learn. This increased knowledge can be used to specify signifiers or behaviours that evidence learner progress.

- Our increased knowledge about human learning can also be used to design AI algorithms and models that can analyse data about learners, recognize signifiers of learning and build dynamic models of each individual students' progress holistically so that we can chart their development of self-knowledge and self-efficacy as well as their increased knowledge and understanding of key subject knowledge.
- The final step in the process is to design ways in which we can visualize the data that has been analysed to define each learner's progress cognitively, metacognitively and emotionally. These visualizations can be used by learners, educators, parents and managers to understand the detailed needs of each learner and to develop within each learner the skills and abilities that will enable them to be effective learners throughout their lives.

An AI assessment system that was composed of these AI tools and that illustrated to every learner the analysis of their progress in an accessible format would support learning and teaching through continually assessing learning of both subject specific knowledge and the skills and capabilities that the AI augmented workforce will require, such as negotiation, communication and collaborative problem solving. This AI assessment system would be more accurate and cheaper than the human intensive examination systems currently in place (Luckin, 2017) and it would free up time for teaching and learning that is currently taken up when we stop teaching in order for people to sit tests and exams. Assessment would happen continuously while people learn. This assessment change requires political will as well as investment in technology development and engagement with teachers, students and parents so that they fully understand the AI assessment proposition (for a more detailed account of this argument for AI assessment see Luckin, 2017).

Conclusions

LA and AI can help us to improve the accuracy of our assessment systems and help us ensure that learners understand much more about their own skills, abilities and learning needs. However, in order to benefit from the potential of these technologies we need to address some key issues:

- Socially, we need to engage teachers, learners, parents and other education stakeholders to work with scientists and policymakers to develop the ethical framework within which AI assessment can thrive and bring benefit.
- Technically, we need to build international collaborations between academic and commercial enterprise to develop the scaled-up AI

assessment systems that can deliver a new generation of exam-free assessment.

- Politically, we need leaders to recognize the possibilities that AI can bring to drive forward much needed educational transformation within tightening budgetary constraints. Initiatives on these three fronts will require financial support from governments and private enterprise working together.
- Practically, we need to provide action points for discussion and focus on the problem specification and solution design elements of AI where educators' input is vital.

Artificial intelligence and big data technologies to close the achievement gap

Benedict du Boulay, Alexandra Poulovassilis, Wayne Holmes and Manolis Mavrikis

Introduction

> Currently, we are failing to meet the needs of all learners. The gap between those who achieve the most and those who achieve the least is a challenge that teachers, school leaders, administrators, and government officials face every day, in every country. Globally, students from poorer backgrounds perform worse than students from richer backgrounds (Carnoy and Rothstein, 2013). The results of this achievement gap impacts upon a country's economy as well as the social well-being of their population (Hanushek and Woessmann, 2010). The reasons behind the achievement gaps in different countries vary, but the fact remains that not all learners are achieving their potential at school. (Luckin et al., 2016: 42)

We observe achievement gaps even in rich western countries, such as the United Kingdom, which in principle have the resources as well as the social and technical infrastructure to provide a better deal for all learners. The reasons for such gaps are complex and include the social and material poverty of some learners with their resulting other deficits, as well as failure by government to allocate sufficient resources to remedy the situation. On the supply side of the equation, a single teacher or university lecturer, even helped by a classroom assistant or tutorial assistant, cannot give each learner the kind of one-to-one attention that would really help to boost both their motivation and their attainment in ways that might mitigate the achievement gap.

In this chapter, we argue that we now have the technologies to assist both educators and learners, most commonly in science, technology, engineering and mathematics subjects (STEM), at least some of the time. We present case studies from the fields of artificial intelligence in education (AIED) and big data. We look at how they can be used to provide personalized support for students and demonstrate that they are not designed to replace the teacher. In addition, we also describe tools for teachers to increase their awareness and, ultimately, free up time for them to provide nuanced, individualized support even in large cohorts.

Artificial intelligence and big data in education

The name 'artificial intelligence' (AI) can be a little scary, especially at present where the notion of (an) AI taking over the world to the detriment of society is a popular contemporary nightmare.

Artificial intelligence in education is not about educational robots taking away jobs from teachers and brainwashing children. It is much more prosaic and consists of programs running on tablets and laptops that help teach learners on a one-to-one basis in a way that adapts the tasks, assistance and the feedback to the capabilities and progress of the individual learner.

Artificial intelligence in education is a computer-based technology that tries to provide insightful, adaptive and personalized teaching, at the level of competence of an expert human tutor, for individuals and groups. In particular, such computer-based systems attempt to choose appropriate tasks for the learner to work on and then react dynamically to how they go about dealing with these tasks. These reactions can take the form of specific hints on individual steps taken and on requests for help, as well as providing general assistance (or 'scaffolding'). Note that the reactions of the system are not only provided once the learner has submitted an answer but can also be provided in response to individual steps towards that answer. Such systems are also known as 'intelligent tutoring systems' (ITS). Other systems are more open-ended and sometimes less individually adaptive but provide opportunities for a learner to explore a domain; they are referred to as exploratory or open-ended learning environments (ELE). We will refer to all of these here as 'AIED systems'.

The term 'big data' is also a little scary, especially where corporations and governments hoover up huge amounts of personal data, where there seems to be endless breeches of privacy and data hacking, and the boundary between secure and insecure data is very porous. In an educational context, big data can be beneficial in that it can collect information about how a cohort of learners is interacting with a learning environment and making progress with their learning. This information can be used by teachers and instructional designers to improve the environment and the support it offers to students. So big data enables learning environments to be adapted by showing where they work well and where they do not.

This chapter is organized as follows. In the next section, we describe in more detail what an AIED system is and provide some examples. We then describe some exploratory learning environments. We then move to big data, both to describe it and give examples. In the final part of the chapter we examine the evidence for the educational value of AIED systems and big data.

The key parts of AIED systems

The capability to individualize its teaching and assist even with partial answers depends on an AIED system having the following four components:

1. The **domain knowledge model** is the component that provides the capability of the system to complete the tasks that it sets the students and to judge which steps contribute towards a solution, or which parts of an answer are correct. In other words, the system needs to understand the material that it is teaching, unlike a book or a website that can merely present that material. Because STEM subjects lend themselves much more readily to having their domains represented in ways that can be automatically reasoned about, most AIED systems have been built to teach these areas.

2. The **student model** is the component that provides a representation of the learner in terms of their developing knowledge and skills. This is needed so that tasks of an appropriate complexity and difficulty can be set. As the learner works through various tasks, the system builds up a 'student model' of what the learner can reliably get right, what they seem to partially understand, and what they seem to be as yet very poor at. This model can never be exact, but is a best guess and can be used, for example, to select the next task for the learner or to give a little bit of challenge in areas not yet mastered, and also practise in areas that seem well understood.

3. The **model of pedagogy** is the component that represents the teaching capability of the system. This is used to make decisions about how best to present new material, how best to deal with requests for help, how best to deal with incorrect steps and answers and so on. This might also include an understanding of how to motivate the learners if they become demotivated and tactics to deal with students who try to 'game the system' (Baker *et al.*, 2008) by demanding so much help that the system might otherwise give them all the answers.

4. The **interface** is the component that provides the channel through which the learner and the system communicate. This channel might be through spoken dialogue, or text and diagrams provided either by the learner or the system (see Figure 6.2.2). Such an interface may also include an animated pedagogical agent taking the role of a tutor or of a fellow student.

We present below some examples of AIED systems illustrating their domain model, student model, pedagogical model and interface. We chose a variety of systems and their potential to support students in different contexts.

Examples of AIED systems

Procedural skills – the Cognitive Algebra Tutor

Our first example is an older and 'traditional' intelligent tutoring system. It teaches algebraic skills such as equation solving. In the Pittsburgh Algebra Tutor, and other similar systems derived from it, the overall form of interaction is that the system chooses an individualized sequence of algebraic problems for the learner to solve and then monitors each step that the learner takes in solving each problem. The system has gone through several iterations. The interface shown in Figure 6.2.1, taken from a much-cited early paper (Koedinger *et al.*, 1997), offers a problem specific worksheet for the learner to fill out their partial answers to each sub-step of the problem. Later versions, such as the one used in a large evaluation described later, provide a more modern look and feel with access to a number of other tools to help the learner and find information (Koedinger and Aleven, 2016).

The system uses its domain model and student model to sequence the problems for each learner on an individual basis, depending on their rate of progress in mastering the various algebraic subskills needed for each problem (see bottom right of the interface). They are also used to reason about partial answers in various representations, such as a graph, spreadsheet and equation solver, to decide when a partial answer is a step in the right direction to solving the overall problem and when it is not. The pedagogical model makes the system react quickly to any mistake made by the learner so as to reduce the chance that they stray too far from the solution and get muddled. It also dynamically assesses what is the best next problem for the learner to work on so as to ensure that new skills are encountered and old skills practised.

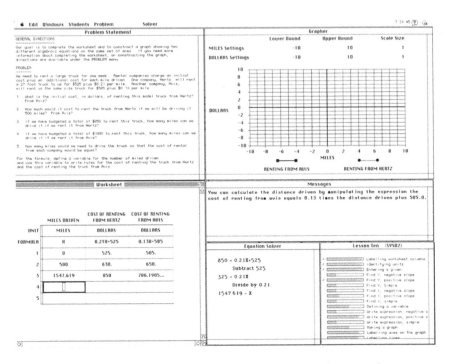

Figure 6.2.1: Interface for the Pittsburgh Algebra Tutor (Koedinger *et al.*, 1997)

Exploratory learning environments for conceptual understanding – BETTY's Brain

Our second example is Betty's Brain, a system designed to teach scientific *conceptual* understanding of river ecosystems (Leelawong and Biswas, 2008). In particular it aims to help learners appreciate the complexity of the causal and other relationships between different processes occurring in such ecosystems; for example, that fish produce waste and that this waste is food for bacteria (see Figure 6.2.2). There is also skill building in the learner's interactions with Betty's Brain, such as following causal chains of reasoning and developing generic study skills, but the main focus is still on conceptual understanding.

The heart of the system is the Concept Map Editor pane in the top right of the interface. This is where the learner builds up a conceptual map of the river ecosystem, using nodes and links via the Editor on the top left of the screen. The conceptual map can also be understood by the system and this enables it to answer questions based on it.

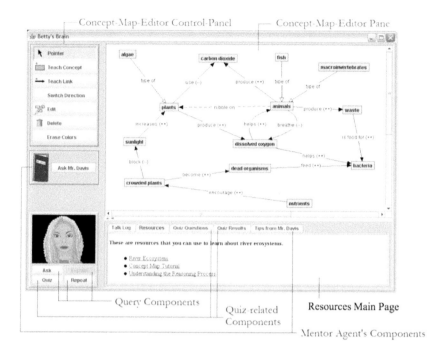

Figure 6.2.2: Betty's Brain interface (Reprinted with permission of Springer from Leelawong and Biswas, 2008: 181)

The narrative behind the interaction is that the human learner is attempting to teach fellow student, Betty, seen on the bottom left of the screen in Figure 6.2.2. The conceptual map is a record of what the learner has so far taught Betty – hence 'Betty's Brain'. The learner can test the adequacy of what Betty has learnt by asking her to take a quiz administered by Mr Davis, the teacher. Mr Davis assesses Betty's answers to the quiz questions and provides feedback to the learner, who then has the chance to edit the conceptual map in an attempt to help Betty get a better quiz score. Mr Davis assesses Betty's answers to the quiz by reasoning from the conceptual map created by the human learner. This slightly indirect way of learning has a particular advantage for the human learner in terms of somewhat forestalling any negative reactions from the student to mistakes in the quiz, as they are Betty's mistakes.

The learner can test the adequacy of the conceptual map directly by asking Betty such questions as 'If macro-invertebrates increase what happens to bacteria?' Betty can answer such a question and explain that answer by following the causal reasoning indicated in the conceptual map using qualitative reasoning techniques.

The system also provides learning materials that the learner is encouraged to use – see the lower part of the screen in Figure 6.2.2. In addition to feedback about the domain of river ecosystems, Mr Davis also makes suggestions at the metacognitive level, for example about making better use of the reading materials, in an effort to help the learner develop good study skills.

In terms of the four components mentioned in the previous section, we note that the domain knowledge of the system is its ability to reason using the conceptual maps produced by the learner. Its student model is made up of a record of the various actions taken by the learner and the partial but growing understanding of the domain as exemplified in the conceptual map. In pedagogical terms the system is driven by the actions of the learner, although the overall educational goal of having Betty pass all the quizzes is clearly provided by the system. The system does have a model of pedagogy that drives how and when it makes comments at the metacognitive level, for example when Betty reacts to being asked to take a second quiz even though there has been no change to the conceptual map. Finally, the interface is key to the interaction as the conceptual map built by the learner is both an expression of their evolving understanding and can be reasoned about by the system (even if the map is wrong or partial).

eXpresser and the MiGen system

Another example of an exploratory environment is a mathematical microworld called eXpresser that aims to support 11–14-year-olds' learning of algebraic generalization, as part of a system called MiGen (Noss *et al.*, 2012). (eXpresser is one of a set of tools making up the MiGen system, which was developed through funding from the ESRC/EPSRC Technology Enhanced Learning programme, award no. RES-139-25-0381.) Using eXpresser, students are asked to construct two-dimensional tiled models and associated algebraic rules. The algebraic rules relate to the number of tiles of each colour required to paint each pattern and their model overall (see Figure 6.2.3).

Figure 6.2.4 illustrates a feedback message given by the eXpresser to a student who has constructed a correct pattern and a correct colouring rule for it, nudging the student towards 'unlocking' a number (i.e. turning it into a variable) so as to now generalize their pattern and rule. Figure 6.2.5 shows a message of encouragement but also a stronger prompt to guide the student towards generalizing their construction.

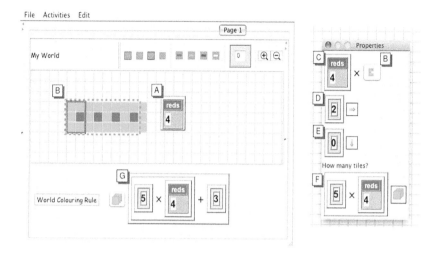

Figure 6.2.3: The eXpresser microworld. Letters highlight the main features: (A) An 'unlocked' number (i.e. variable) is given the name 'reds' and signifies the number of red (dark grey) tiles in the pattern. (B) Building block to be repeated to make a pattern. (C) Number of repetitions (in this case, the value of the variable 'reds'). (D; E) Number of grid squares to translate B to the right and down after each repetition. (F) Units of colour required to paint the pattern. (G) General expression that gives the total number of units of colour required to paint the whole pattern.

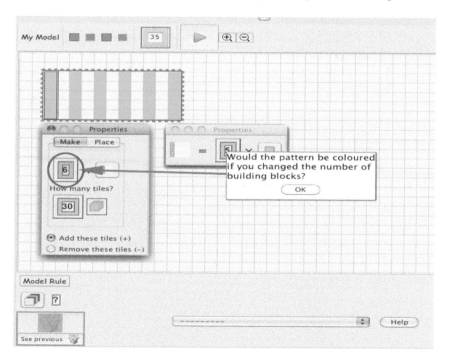

Figure 6.2.4: A 'nudge' from the eXpresser

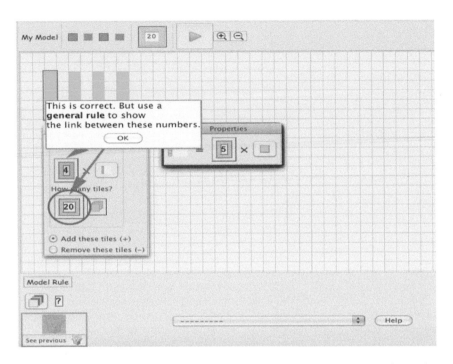

Figure 6.2.5: A message of encouragement and a stronger 'prompt' from the eXpresser

In terms of the four components of AIED systems mentioned earlier, the domain knowledge of the system is its internal model of mathematical concepts relating to algebraic generalization. The student model records the learner's gradual mastery of these concepts as they work through successively harder tasks, as well as a history of the learner's constructions and interactions with the system. In pedagogical terms, each task comprises a set of learning goals that the learner needs to achieve as they work on the task using eXpresser. The system provides adaptive support based on how the student is approaching the task and how they are interacting with the system. Again, the eXpresser interface is key to the student-system interactions and the student's growing conceptual knowledge, as their construction of models and rules can be reasoned about by the system in order to provide appropriate support, and it also demonstrates the student's evolving understanding of the domain.

Combining ITS and ELE – the case of iTalk2Learn

Intelligent tutoring systems like Cognitive Algebra Tutor and exploratory environments like eXpresser do not have to exist in isolation. The iTalk2learn project developed an adaptive digital learning platform for primary school mathematics that allows interaction via direct manipulation and speech to provide intelligent interventions and individualized task sequences. (The iTalk2Learn system was developed through co-funding from the EU FP7 programme, ref. no. ICT-318051.) Importantly, for the discussion here, iTalk2Learn combines structured and exploratory activities to improve learners' procedural as well as conceptual knowledge (Rummel *et al.*, 2016). It does so by offering activities from a commercial intelligent tutoring system (Math-Whizz, www.whizz.com) to support procedural knowledge, and from a microworld called Fractions Lab to improve students' conceptual knowledge of fractions (Hansen *et al.*, 2016). In Fractions Lab, students are asked to construct one or more fractions and, using the affordances of the system, to compare, add or subtract fractions. In Figure 6.2.6, for example, the student has been asked to create a fraction, and then to create four equivalent fractions with increasingly larger denominators. So far the student has created their first fraction, but has not yet created any equivalent ones. The glowing lightbulb at the top of the screen indicates that there is help currently available from the system (Grawemeyer *et al.*, 2015b). Clicking on the lightbulb results in the feedback message shown in Figure 6.2.7, which is aiming to nudge the student towards the next step. Figure 6.2.8 shows that the student has indeed made their first equivalent function. After a period of inactivity, Figure 6.2.9 shows a message of encouragement and also an unsolicited prompt (Grawemeyer *et al.*, 2015b) to guide the student towards the next step.

As students are undertaking tasks, they are encouraged to talk aloud. A speech recognition system extracts keywords that are combined with prosodic features also extracted from the speech signal and used as input to methods for the classification of students' sentiment and cognitive load. The outcomes of this emotion and affect recognition serve as input for providing intelligent support to the student and automatic selection of interventions. This relies on large amounts of data and student modelling, as described in the next section on big data.

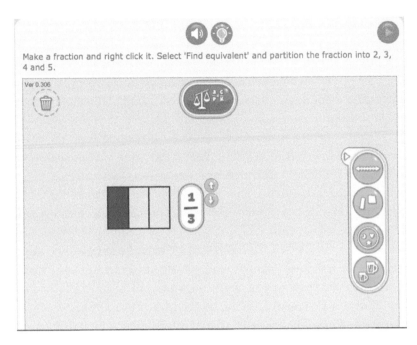

Figure 6.2.6: Fractions Lab microworld, showing the availability of low-interruption feedback

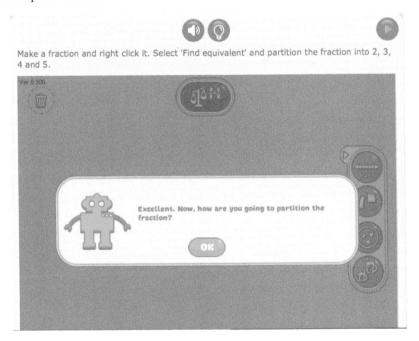

Figure 6.2.7: Fractions Lab microworld, showing the elective display of low-interruption feedback

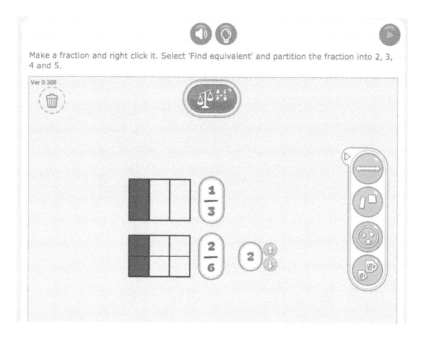

Figure 6.2.8: Fractions Lab microworld, showing that the student has progressed to the next step

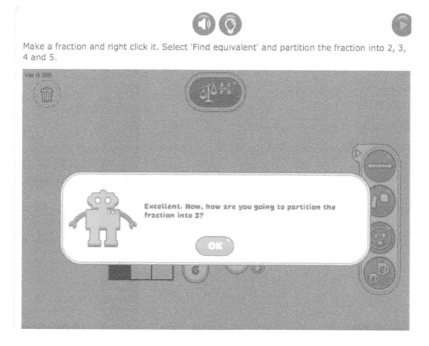

Figure 6.2.9: Fractions Lab microworld, showing a message of encouragement and also a stronger prompt to guide the student towards accomplishing the subsequent step

In terms of the four components of AIED systems, these are similar in functionality to those of eXpresser, except that in Fractions Lab the student model also includes information about the student's evolving affective state as the student works on a task using the microworld.

Two ways in which AIED systems might be used

There are two main ways that AIED systems can be used effectively in schools. First, such systems can be deployed as classroom assistants in the following sense. While whole group teaching or small group teaching by a human teacher continues to be the norm, it is commonplace for an individual or a small group to be handed over to a human classroom assistant. This might be to provide individual help for pupils who are not doing so well, or it might be to assist pupils who have already mastered the material ahead of the rest of the class and who need a bit more of a challenge. The idea here is that in addition to the human classroom assistant, an AIED system could be used by an individual pupil or a group of pupils who need extra practice or who need exposure to more challenging material. The ability of such systems to monitor the individual problem-solving steps of the pupil and to provide help, hints and scaffolding specifically appropriate to the individual could be a valuable extra tool in the classroom.

There are also potential benefits for a group of pupils working with such a system to discuss and argue about different possible answers to problem-solving steps, as well as the meaning and intent of feedback on their errors received from the system. For the more able pupils running ahead of the rest of the class, such systems can provide more challenging problems, possibly with less help and scaffolding, thus maintaining their motivation.

The second way that AIED systems can be used is as assistants in after-school classes, revision classes or for homework. In these situations, the classroom teacher is typically less available, but the pupil will still need the kind of detailed assistance that such systems are able to provide. Just as we have mentioned that groups of pupils can discuss an ongoing interaction with an AIED system to help create better understanding, so a child and a parent at home can have a similarly fruitful discussion together in the context of using an AIED system.

Note that our use cases have the AIED system working in tandem with the classroom teacher and not as a replacement. Those visions of future education involving simply computer-based instruction without the social and pedagogic support of human teachers are barren indeed. It is instructive to note the high drop-out rates when college-level courses are delivered solely via Massive Open Online Courses (MOOCs) direct to the individual learner, with little in the way of face-to-face interaction with either the teacher or with fellow students (Liyanagunawardena *et al.*, 2013).

Big data in education

Emergent web, mobile, and pervasive digital technologies are generating data at unprecedented scales and speeds in virtually all areas of human activity. Across industry, commerce and the public sector this 'big data' is being digitally collected and computationally analysed in order to gain better understanding of providers' services and products, consumers' needs and preferences, and, more fundamentally, to expand human knowledge across the sciences, social sciences and humanities.

Originally, big data was taken to mean data sets that are beyond the management and analysis capabilities of traditional software tools. The generation of such data sets led to the development of new data storage and data processing paradigms, such as NoSQL data stores (Cattell, 2010), massively data-parallel distributed processing frameworks (Dean and Ghemawat, 2008; EMC, 2015) and cloud computing platforms (Armbrust *et al.*, 2010).

Big data is distinguished from other data by exhibiting the so-called 'V' attributes. These include:

- *volume* – the size of the datasets;
- *velocity* – the rapid rate at which the data may generated;
- *variety* – different types of data being generated from multiple sources, needing to be cross-referenced and combined in order to be fully exploited;
- *veracity* – the incompleteness of the data being collected, and the imprecision of inferences being made from it; and
- *volatility* – data being collected or inferred may become less relevant over time.

More recently there is recognition that these 'V' attributes are not the whole story and that what is most important is the ability to extract *value* from such data while also complying with given time, human and technical resource constraints.

Learning analytics and educational data mining

Big data in the education sector is the focus of two complementary academic fields: **learning analytics** and **educational data mining**.

The field of **learning analytics (LA)** is concerned with *gathering, analysing and visualizing* data about learners and learning processes, so as to increase stakeholders' understanding of these and hence *to improve learning and the environments in which it occurs* (Siemens, 2012; Drachsler and Greller, 2012; Ferguson, 2012). This data may be collected from many different sources:

- virtual learning environments (VLEs) that track and support students' activities, interactions, reflections and progress through learning tasks;
- students' assessment activities – both formative and summative;
- students' personal records and records of prior achievement;
- learner profiling and learner modelling software;
- software supporting social networking, peer support and collaboration;
- audio and video recordings;
- gesture and physiological sensor recordings (e.g., heart rate, galvanic skin response, blood pressure, EEG readings); and
- mobile learning apps, gathering large-scale user-centred and context-aware data.

This exceptionally broad range of data sources is allowing increasingly *individualized*, *detailed* and *longitudinal* data to be collected and analysed, bringing with it the potential to derive new insights and to provide more effective support to learners and tutors.

The fields of **educational data mining** (EDM) and LA have already been described in Chapter 6.1. Here we note in particular that LA and EDM can be regarded as parts of a larger interdisciplinary continuum of research and practice involving disciplines such as computer science, education and psychology, as well as teachers, learners, learning designers, policymakers and other stakeholders in learning processes from across the public and private sectors. The computing techniques developed and applied in the LA and EDM fields include: data modelling; data cleansing, transformation and integration; knowledge representation and reasoning; data mining, analytics and visualization; learner modelling; recommender systems; predictive modelling; social network analysis; and discourse analysis. We refer readers to Poulovassilis (2016) for a more detailed discussion of these different techniques, their applications and references to the relevant technical literature.

The sources and design process of big data in education

Collection and analysis of learning-related data has been used in Technology Enhanced Learning research and practice for many years. Big data, however, start playing a particular role when considering data from systems such as the AIED ones presented in the previous section. We can see from the description of these systems that the data they generate include:

- Event-based data: log data of students' interactions with the system; students' responses, ranging from simple answers to a question to more complex reflections, e.g., through text (in MiGen) or speech (in iTalk2Learn); occurrences of key indicators as students interact with the system; generation and provision of feedback by the system.
- Students' constructions: the diagrams in Betty's Brain, or the models and mathematical expressions being constructed by students in eXpresser, including a full history of how each was constructed.
- Task information: task descriptions, task learning goals, common solution approaches to each task.
- Learner models: information about students' level of attainment of concepts and skills, recent history of interactions with the system, progress with tasks set, achievement of learning goals, affective states.

We can see that this data exhibits all of the 'V' attributes we discussed earlier. As well as its evident volume and velocity, under the 'variety' attribute we have unstructured data (e.g. the students' reflections), semi-structured data (e.g. the log data, task information and students' constructions) and structured data (e.g. the learner models and indicator data). Under 'veracity' there is the inherent imprecision of the inferences being made by the system's intelligent components, e.g. in the detection of task-dependent indicators (Gutierrez-Santos *et al.*, 2012) or students' affective states (Grawemeyer *et al.*, 2015b). Under 'volatility', a student's history of interactions, inferred indicators and affective states may become less relevant with time.

The rich range of data that can be collected by an AIED system provides not only the possibility to generate personalized feedback for the learner, but also the opportunity to design visualization and notification tools for the teacher. The provision of such tools can help the teacher to formulate her own interventions to support both individual students and the class as a whole.

To be fully effective in the classroom, such tools need to be designed by multi-disciplinary teams involving teachers, pedagogical experts and computer scientists. In our own work in this area, we have used an iterative participatory methodology, comprising successive phases of prototyping, requirements elicitation, incremental development and evaluation (Gutierrez-Santos *et al.*, 2012; Mavrikis *et al.*, 2016; Gutierrez-Santos *et al.*, 2017). The next section illustrates this through examples.

Examples of applications of big data in education
Student modelling from big data – the case of affective learning
Perhaps the most common use of data from digital learning environments is to inform the system's internal conception of the learner and its learner modelling, as already mentioned in the previous section. One of the most innovative applications of such data is for the detection of a student's *affective state*. Such information can be used to enhance learning by means of nudges that move students out of negative states such as boredom or frustration that inhibit learning into positive states such as engagement or enjoyment. Affective states can be detected through computational analysis of data extracted from speech, facial expressions, eye tracking, body language, physiological signals or combinations of these (D'Mello and Kory, 2015). In the iTalk2Learn system, for example, a student's affective state is determined through detection of keywords and prosodic features in their speech as they talk aloud when interacting with the system (Grawemeyer *et al.*, 2015a). Such detailed student modelling can enable affect-aware support for the student, which has been shown to contribute to reducing boredom and off-task behaviour, with promising effects on learning (Grawemeyer *et al.*, 2017).

In addition, rich data from such systems can be used by designers and researchers to investigate the system's performance and efficacy and to identify areas requiring further development. For example, the system-student interaction data arising from iTalk2Learn have been recently remodelled using graph-based methods so as to more easily investigate the effectiveness of the intelligent support being provided by the system. Figure 6.2.10 illustrates one possible visualization of how a student's affective state changes during a learning task.

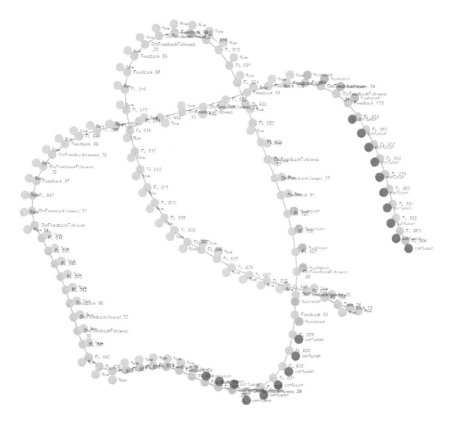

Figure 6.2.10: Graph-based modelling and visualization of students' interactions; the figure illustrates how one student's affective state changes between states of Engagement (green), Frustration (amber) and Confusion (red). Successive events are shown in blue and are connected by red edges

Teacher tools for exploratory learning environments

We described earlier the eXpresser mathematical microworld, which is one of the tools making up the MiGen system. Figures 6.2.11 and 6.2.12 illustrate two of that system's teacher assistance tools, each of which draws on the data generated by students' use of eXpresser: the classroom dynamics (CD) tool and the goal achievements (GA) tool. In the CD tool, each student present in the classroom is represented by a circle containing their initials. At the outset of the lesson, the teacher can drag-and-drop these circles so that their positions on the screen reflect the students' spatial positioning in the classroom. The colour of a student's circle reflects their current activity status, as inferred by the system. Green indicates a student working productively on the task set. Amber indicates a student who has not interacted with eXpresser for some time (by default, five minutes). Red indicates a student who has requested help from the system in a situation where the intelligent support cannot help any further: in such cases, the eXpresser displays the message 'The teacher will come to help you now' to the student, and the student's circle becomes coloured red to attract the attention of the teacher.

Most of the time the teacher will have the CD tool selected for display on her handheld computer. When students show as amber, she can approach them and encourage them to resume working on the task set. If students who are not showing as red call out for help she can encourage them to first seek help from the system, knowing that if the intelligent support cannot help, the student's circle will automatically appear as red in the CD tool. If a student does appear as red, the teacher can click on the student's circle on her way over to the student so as to see their current model and rule, which helps her to prepare her feedback for the student.

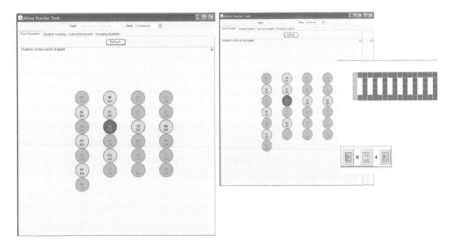

Figure 6.2.11: MiGen's classroom dynamics tool. On the left, a classroom with the students sitting at benches in rows. On the right, the teacher has clicked on the 'red' student to see their construction and rule on the way over to help them

From time to time, the teacher will also consult the GA tool, which again visualizes part of the big data being generated by the system (in this case, indicators inferring the current status of the student's achievement of the expected learning goals of the task). The GA tool presents a tabular display of students and task goals. Each row of the table shows the progress of one student (identified by their initials) in completing the task goals. A white cell indicates a goal that has not yet been achieved by the student. A green cell indicates that the goal is currently being achieved by the student's construction. An amber cell indicates that the goal was achieved at some point, but is not currently being achieved by the student's construction. Knowing which students have accomplished all the task goals allows the teacher to set them additional activities, for example comparing their construction approach with that of a peer (see below). If the GA tool shows that many students are not achieving a particular task goal, the teacher can interrupt the lesson to help all the students at the same time.

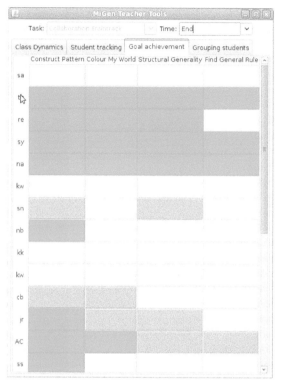

Figure 6.2.12: MiGen's goal achievements tool. We see that some students have achieved all or most task goals, some students have not made any progress yet, and some students are moving back and forth

Another of MiGen's teacher tools – the grouping tool (GT) (Gutierrez-Santos *et al.*, 2017) – supports the teacher in managing group discussion activities after students have finished their individual construction activities, by automating the pairing of students based on their constructions. Identifying appropriate pairs would be very time-consuming for the teacher to do manually during a lesson: it would require the teacher to investigate every student's construction, identify pairs of constructions that are sufficiently dissimilar to lead to fruitful student discussions and reflections, and then put the students into pairs, also taking into account interpersonal factors. The GT generates an initial set of pairings, aiming to minimize the overall similarity across all pairings. The proposed pairings are presented visually to the teacher, who can then confirm or change each pairing – see Figure 6.2.13 (we note that in the case of an odd number of students, one of the 'pairings' generated will be a triplet!). In the GT, students are represented by their initials within a circle. The degree of similarity between pairs of constructions is represented by a small green rectangle for low similarity; medium-sized yellow rectangle for moderate similarity; or large red rectangle for high similarity. The teacher can select students' circles and drag them into different groups in order to change the pairings suggested by the system so as to take into account factors that are beyond the system's knowledge, such as students' interpersonal relationships.

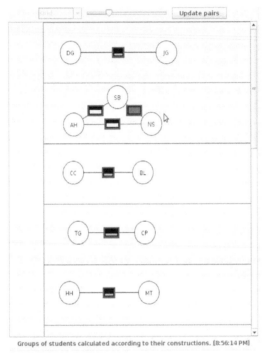

Groups of students calculated according to their constructions. [8:56:14 PM]

Figure 6.2.13: MiGen's grouping tool

The immediacy of the big data presented through MiGen's teacher tools can help teachers formulate their interventions during the current lesson, set additional homework, plan the next lesson, as well as adjust the design of future tasks to be set for a given class of students. The availability of such tools allows teachers to use ELEs in the classroom in new ways because they provide a greater sense of awareness than is possible with general-purpose student monitoring tools. Moreover, such tools can support teachers in providing evidence of students' learning, even in a context that is less subject to formal assessment, and to engage in their own enquiry into more conceptual student learning.

Tools for planning and reflecting on learning
So far we have seen examples of educational software in which data volume and velocity arise from the fact that the majority of the data are being

generated by the system as users interact with it. There are other categories of system (most notably, social networking and collaboration software) in which high data volume and velocity arise from the numbers of users and where the majority of the data are user-generated. Research in the L4All and MyPlan projects provides an example of this latter category of system. (L4All – Lifelong Learning in London for All; MyPlan – Personal Planning for Learning throughout life. Funded by JISC Distributed e-learning Pilot Call, 2005–8.) The prototype L4All system developed by these projects aimed to support adult learners in exploring learning opportunities and in planning and reflecting on their learning. The system allows users to create and maintain a chronological record of their learning, work and personal episodes – their timelines. Users' timelines are encoded as RDF triples, compliant with an RDFS ontology. (See www.w3.org/standards/semanticweb/ for information about RDF and RDFS.) There are some 20 types of episode, each belonging to one of four categories: educational, occupational, personal and other. Figure 6.2.14 illustrates a fragment of the overall L4All ontology.

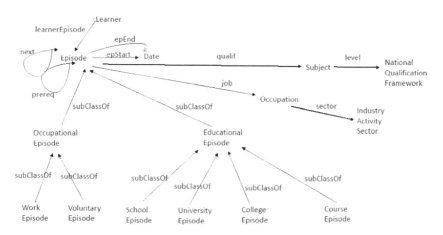

Figure 6.2.14: Fragment of the L4All ontology. Each instance of the episode class is: linked to other episode instances by edges labelled 'next' or 'prereq' (indicating whether the earlier episode simply preceded, or was necessary in order to be able to proceed to, the later episode; linked either to an occupation or to an educational qualification (subject) by means of an edge labelled 'job' or 'qualif'. Each occupation is linked to an instance of the Industry Activity Sector class by an edge labelled 'sector'. Each qualification is linked to an instance of the National Qualification Framework (NQF) class by an edge labelled 'level'. The Occupation, Subject, Industry Activity Sector and NQF hierarchies are drawn from standard UK occupational and educational taxonomies (see Labour Force Survey User Guide, Vol 5, www.ons.gov.uk/ons/guide-method/method-quality/speci_c/labour-market/labour-market-statistics/index.html)

Users can choose to make their timelines 'public' and thus accessible by other users. This sharing of timelines exposes future learning and work possibilities that may otherwise not have been considered, positioning successful learners as role models to inspire confidence and a sense of opportunity. The system's interface provides screens for the user to enter their personal details, to create and maintain their timeline (see Figure 6.2.15), and to search over the timelines of other users based on a variety of search criteria.

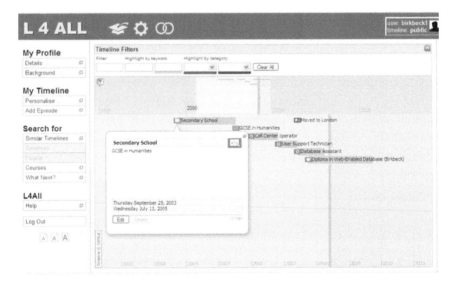

Figure 6.2.15: The main screen of the L4All system. At its centre is a visual representation of the user's timeline, and the system functionalities are organized around this. Each episode of learning or work is displayed in chronological order, depicted by an icon specific to its type and a horizontal block representing its duration. Details of an episode can be viewed by clicking on the block representing it, which pops-up more detailed information about the episode (dates, description), as well as access to edit and deletion functions

Van Labeke *et al.* (2009, 2011) describe two of the search facilities provided by the system, one to search for 'people like me' and another to find recommendations of 'what to do next'. The latter is illustrated in Figure 6.2.16 where we see one of the recommended timelines being displayed beneath the user's own, for easy visual comparison.

Figure 6.2.16: The 'What Next' user interface. Episodes in the recommended (lower) timeline that match episodes in the user's own (upper) timeline are shown in blue; episodes that start after all blue episodes are shown in orange – these are deemed by the system to be relevant for this user as they occur after the matching episodes, and thus represent possible choices that the user may be inspired to explore further for their future learning and career development; episodes that occur earlier than all blue episodes, or have no matches within the user's own timeline, are shown in grey

The technical basis for both the 'people like me' and the 'what to do next' facilities is the users' annotation of their episodes with concepts drawn from the L4All ontology. The availability of this metadata allows similarity algorithms to be used to compare the user's own timeline with all other timelines (Van Labeke *et al.*, 2009; 2011; Poulovassilis *et al.*, 2012).

In terms of the four components of AIED systems, the domain knowledge of the system is represented in the L4All ontology. Its 'student model' is the timeline that is created and annotated by the user. The pedagogical model is encapsulated in the 'people like me' and 'what to do next' functionalities offered to users, to help them explore possible future learning and career options and to plan and reflect on their lifelong learning. Again, the system's interface is key to the user's growing knowledge and confidence as they interact with their peers' timelines.

Evidence of effectiveness

Over the last 35 years or so a great variety of AIED systems have been developed and evaluated in the laboratory and in schools, colleges and universities. Such evaluations have compared AIED systems against more traditional teaching methods, such as whole class teaching by an individual human teacher, one-to-one tutoring by a human teacher, or the use of a textbook on its own, or some blend of these and other teaching methods. The evaluations have usually looked at either comparative learning gains or the study time needed to reach some mastery criterion. To date there have been few comparative evaluations of big data-enabled interventions (although see Ferguson *et al.*, 2016, for a recent review of the use of learning analytics in education), so our scope in this chapter is AIED systems in general.

There has now been a sufficient body of work published to allow a number of meta-reviews to be created. These are reviews that look at a large number of individual evaluations and try to draw general conclusions, typically by computing an average of the comparative learning gains. This chapter focuses on the meta-review evaluations of AIED systems, comparing them either against one-to-one human tutoring or against whole class teaching by a single instructor. These include using an AIED system blended into whole class teaching as compared to simply whole class teaching by an individual teacher.

Table 6.2.1 shows the results from six meta-reviews as well as a large study that evaluated a single AIED system, the Cognitive Algebra Tutor described earlier, in a large number of schools in the United States. Some meta-reviews involved more than one kind of comparison. In the table positive effect sizes and percentile rank changes indicate that the AIED system produced better learning outcomes than the human method it was compared with. Negative effect sizes and percentile rank changes indicate the opposite.

Table 6.2.1: Six meta-reviews and a large scale study (adapted from du Boulay, 2016)

	1 Meta-review	2 Comparison	3 No. of Comparisons	4 Mean Effect Size	5 Standard Error	6 Approx. percentile rank change
1	VanLehn (2011)	AIED system *vs* one-to-one human tutoring	10	-0.21	0.19	-8
2	Ma, Adesope, Nesbit, and Liu (2014)	AIED system *vs* one-to-one human tutoring	5	-0.11	0.10	-4
3		AIED system *vs* 'large group human instruction'	66	0.44	0.05	17
4	Nesbit, Adesope, Liu, and Ma (2014) *examining systems to teach computer science*	AIED system *vs* 'teacher led group instruction'	11	0.67	0.09	25

	1 Meta-review	2 Comparison	3 No. of Comparisons	4 Mean Effect Size	5 Standard Error	6 Approx. percentile rank change
5	Kulik and Fletcher (2016)	AIED system *vs* 'conventional classes'	63	0.65	0.07	24
6	Steenbergen-Hu and Cooper (2014) *examining college level use*	AIED system *vs* one-to-one human tutoring	3	-0.25	0.24	-10
7		AIED system *vs* 'traditional classroom instruction'	16	0.37	0.07	15
8	Steenbergen-Hu and Cooper (2013) *examining school level use*	AIED or Computer-aided Instruction (CAI) system *vs* 'traditional classroom instruction'	26	0.09	0.01	3
	Overall weighted mean	AIED system *vs* one-to-one human tutoring	18	-0.19		-7
	Overall weighted mean	AIED system *vs* conventional classes	182	0.47		18
9	Pane, Griffin, McCaffrey, and Karam (2014) *Examining the Algebra Tutor*	Blended learning including a AIED system *vs* traditional classroom instruction	147 schools	-0.1	0.10	-4
				0.21	0.10	8
				0.01	0.11	0
				0.19	0.14	7

Column 2 in the table shows the kind of comparison being made and column 3 the number of such comparisons collected in that meta-review. Column 4 shows the mean effect size across the comparisons (bigger indicates a larger effect). Column 5 shows the standard error of the mean effect size (smaller indicates reduced disparity between the individual studies examined).

The effect size measures how far the mean of the experimental group is from the mean of the control group measured in terms of the standard deviation of the control group scores, with effects above 0.4 'worth having' (Hattie, 2009). Note that although most of the effect sizes in Table 6.2.1 are positive, some are negative. A negative effect size indicates that the AIED systems produced worse learning outcomes than human tutoring (see rows 1, 2, 6 and 9).

Column 6 shows the equivalent increase/decrease in percentile rank as a result of using the AIED system in the comparison. For example, a change in percentile rank of ten would mean that on average students using the AIED system would have increased their ranking by ten percentage points compared to the control group.

The final study, Row 9 in Table 6.2.1, was different from the others. This was an evaluation of a single system, The Cognitive Tutor for Algebra (this is a successor to the Pittsburgh Algebra Tutor, see earlier) across a large number of matched pairs of schools in the United States (Pane *et al.*, 2014). The comparisons were between schools that included the AIED system 'blended' into their algebra teaching *versus* schools that carried on teaching in a traditional manner. There were four comparisons. The study was conducted over two years in both middle schools and high schools. The most positive result (an effect size of 0.21) was in the second year of the study in the high schools. The other results were more mixed, but still broadly positive with respect to the utility of the AIED system used in a blended fashion.

The overall picture from the meta-reviews is positive with respect to the use of AIED systems compared to whole class teaching. The weighted mean (weighted by number of comparisons) of the effect size from the meta-reviews is 0.47. When AIED systems have been compared to one-to-one human teaching they do not do so well, with a weighted mean of -0.19. This is hardly surprising at this stage of the development of such systems.

The authors of these meta-reviews made the following comments. For example, VanLehn found that AIED systems were, within the limitations of his review, 'just as effective as adult, one-to-one tutoring for increasing learning gains in STEM topics' (VanLehn, 2011: 214). While Nesbit and colleagues found 'a significant advantage of ITS over teacher-led classroom instruction and non-ITS computer-based instruction' (Nesbit *et al.*, 2014: 99). Likewise, Kulik and Fletcher concluded that:

> This meta-analysis shows that ITSs can be very effective instructional tools ... Developers of ITSs long ago set out to

improve on the success of CAI tutoring and to match the success of human tutoring. Our results suggest that ITS developers have already met both of these goals. (Kulik and Fletcher, 2016: 67)

Steenbergen-Hu and Cooper found that:

ITS have demonstrated their ability to outperform many [human led] instructional methods or learning activities in facilitating college level students' learning of a wide range of subjects, although they are not as effective as human tutors. ITS appear to have a more pronounced effect on college-level learners than on K-12 students. (Steenbergen-Hu and Cooper, 2013: 344)

Two points are of special note. First, there is some double counting in that there is overlap in the papers that the meta-reviews examined. Second, most of the comparisons concerned STEM subjects, as it is these kinds of domain that are best suited to the development of AIED systems (see the earlier section on artificial intelligence in education).

Conclusions

This chapter has described, on the one hand, the nature of AIED systems in terms of their four major components and provided examples of such systems and, on the other hand, examples of some of the opportunities that big data brings to children's and adults' learning.

We have argued that AIED systems have been sufficiently evaluated through a number of meta-reviews to demonstrate their effectiveness as part of blended learning in STEM subjects. These meta-reviews have shown that AIED systems do rather better than conventional classroom teaching, though a bit worse than one-to-one human tutoring. We have also made the case that the provision of personalized and adaptive feedback to students can enhance students' engagement, motivation and self-confidence, leading to improved learning outcomes.

No argument in favour of replacing teachers by AIED systems has been offered or is implied by these results. Human teachers are still the essential factor in any classroom to take control of the overall learning trajectory of the students, to motivate the unmotivated and the demotivated and to answer queries from students, particularly those who do not exactly know what it is that they do not understand. Indeed it is acknowledged that some students may not have the study skills and reasoning powers to take advantage of such systems (Biswas *et al.*, 2016) and so need support beyond what the system itself can provide.

However, we do argue that provision of individual automated feedback to students for common occurrences can free up time for the teacher to formulate more complex or nuanced support for students, particularly in larger classes. In addition, the rich data generated by such systems are being used to design visualization and notification tools for the teacher. Such tools can increase the teacher's awareness of the classroom state and of individual students' progress on the task set, and hence help the teacher in supporting both individual students and the class as a whole.

Despite these opportunities, there are still many challenges to fully exploiting the potential of AIED and big data in education. For example, this chapter has not addressed the issue of the cost-effectiveness of such systems. They are time-consuming to create and, for them to be effective, multi-disciplinary teams of pedagogical experts, learning designers and computer scientists must work together to understand what information is useful to whom and in what learning contexts, and to design computational techniques for detecting or inferring such information and generating appropriate feedback for users. Also, many AIED systems cover only a small part of the curriculum. However, both these factors are changing for the better as authoring tools emerge that allow more cost-effective design of intelligent systems without the need for specialist computing expertise. Moreover, as AIED systems are increasingly used, the data they collect can be analysed so as to design improvements to them.

There are also wider socio-technical challenges. As we have already argued, the design of AIED systems and of methods for collecting, managing, integrating, analysing and visualizing their big data needs to be both practically feasible and pedagogically meaningful. Moreover, it requires teachers, learners and other stakeholders to be sufficiently empowered, involved and trained to make effective use of these systems and the information that can be obtained from them. Lastly, agreements need to be framed between different educational stakeholders so as to allow sharing of learning-related data for the benefit of learners. This exposes numerous ethical questions, such as: what data about an individual should require their explicit consent in order to be collected, combined, used and shared? Likewise, what knowledge should be allowed to be inferred from the data, and what uses of such knowledge should be permitted? What levels of information and explanation are needed so that individuals can make fully informed decisions? What are appropriate anonymization, privacy, authorization and preservation policies for both data and inferred knowledge in different contexts of usage? From the opposite perspective, what inequalities may be faced by students (for example from less advantaged backgrounds) whose learning-related data is *not* being collected and used to offer them enhanced educational opportunities? Some of these ethical issues are explored by Manca and colleagues (2016), focusing specifically on the information being gathered by large-scale web-based learning platforms and social media applications.

In our own research projects, we aim to address these challenges through close collaboration between researchers, developers, students, teachers and other stakeholders. We draw on multi-disciplinary expertise from across computer science, the learning sciences and education. In the absence, as yet, of sufficiently broad and robust ethical frameworks we address ethical challenges on a project-by-project basis, fully engaging with our institutions' processes for ethical review of research, and also aiming to inform and shape these anticipating an era where artificial intelligence and big data are pervasive.

Technology to provide educational practitioners with the expertise they need

Kaśka Porayska-Pomsta, Christina Preston, Charlotte Laerke Weitze and Sarah Younie

Introduction

In this chapter we explore how technology can help teachers gain the skills and expertise they need to be effective. It is often assumed that the primary role of an educational practitioner is to create effective and motivating learning opportunities for learners. Following some initial training, educational practitioners are expected to be ready to take on the challenge of supporting learning in diverse contexts and specific subjects of their specializations. As such they are expected to be experts in their trade, to know how to design for learning and how to create motivating environments that will bring optimal outcomes for learners (Duffy, 2005; Lin *et al.*, 2005; Porayska-Pomsta, 2016). However, research related to educational practice and to the nature of teaching expertise suggests that such assumptions and the aspirational rhetoric that accompanies them stand in stark contrast with the reality of many educators' ability and readiness to consistently provide such stimulating environments. Pre-service teacher training alone seldom develops educational practitioners into adaptive decision-makers who are able to cope with the dynamic and only partly predictable learning contexts (Duffy, 2005; Buchmann, 1990; Windschitl, 2002, Lin *et al.*, 2005).

Research concerned with defining teaching expertise reveals that it is a complex construct that is shaped by the multifarious, transactional and context-dependent nature of learning and teaching and that it operates at multiple levels of knowledge and skills. For example, Shulman (1990) defines teaching expertise in terms of four broad types of knowledge:

1. repertoire of content knowledge
2. pedagogical content knowledge

3. curricular knowledge, including a good grounding in the philosophy of the subject
4. knowledge of how to negotiate between those aspects of the learning situations that are related to the learner and those that are related to the content taught.

Narciss (2004) refers to such expertise as educational practitioners' ability to recognize and match their feedback to the specific cognitive mindsets experienced by learners moment-by-moment and to their ability to adapt their support routines to the specific content being taught, and to the individual knowledge and motivations of the learners.

Verschaffel *et al.* (2009) and Godau *et al.* (2014) distinguish between routine expertise and *adaptive expertise*, drawing on Hatano and Inagaki's (1984) description of adaptive expertise in terms of a teacher's flexibility to use multiple strategies and their ability to choose between such strategies adaptively. Both *flexibility* and *adaptivity* are considered essential to teachers' ability to support learners' individualized learning processes and to their ability to cope with 'the cyclical and recursive dynamic of [such processes, along with] the implications of this dynamic on motivational, cognitive and emotional [states of learners]' (Christophel *et al.*, 2014: 2). Dale (1998) suggests that to become a professional teacher, the educator must be able to reflect on and to develop their practice systematically in collaboration with colleagues and with reference to professional theory. Dale calls this collaborative development a teacher's *third competence level* (Comp3), with the first competence level being the execution of teaching (Comp1), and the second level – the planning and discussions with peers about everyday challenges (Comp2). The third (Comp 3) level represents a space for teachers to interrogate their learning designs and for critical reflection thereupon, as well as for the professional development and research. Although the process of engaging in such critical reflections typically extends beyond teachers' daily obligations, it is of fundamental importance to the development of best teaching practices.

The predominant picture that emerges from the various accounts of what constitutes teaching expertise is that teaching is a 'dilemma ridden endeavour' (Duffy, 2005; Buchmann, 1990; Windschitl, 2002), whereby teachers have to make decisions about how to handle several and frequently competing aspects of learning situations, and where they must adapt to such situations *on-the-fly*. Christophel *et al.* (2014) use the term *adaptive expertise* to refer to the combination of those two competencies, whereas Duffy (2005) refers to *adaptive decision making* and he, like several other researchers, links the development of such competencies to the need for an investment in supporting teachers in learning how to engage in a continuous and targeted introspection, reflection *in* and *on* action (Schön, 1987), and adaptive metacognition (Lin *et al.*, 2005).

Research evidence suggests that adaptive metacognition is key to supporting both the understanding and the establishment of best and innovative teaching practices and to offering an effective basis for educators' life-long professional development (Lin and Schwartz, 2005; Hewitt *et al.*, 2003; Lin *et al.*, 2005; Laurillard, 2012; Cohen and Manion, 1980; Conlon and Pain, 1996). However, one of the primary challenges in supporting teachers' metacognitive development relates to helping them recognize that apparently routine situations often have a number of hidden features. Frequently, teachers' practices are entrenched in their perceptual abilities and habits through which they make sense of complex teaching situations and which rarely if at all involve conscious reflection or judicious application of principles of good practice (see also Hewitt *et al.*, 2003 for a discussion of 'gestalt'). Nevertheless, Korthagen and Kessels (1999). Hewitt *et al.* (2003) and Lin *et al.* (2005) show that teachers' habitual practices and interpretations of teaching situations may be changed when externalized in the form of conscious mental representations and when critically reflected upon. Lin *et al.* (2005) and Hewitt *et al.* (2003) provide some compelling evidence of the relationship between teachers' purposeful rooting for and observing the hidden features in the teaching situations they encounter and their adaptive metacognition (see also Lin and Schwartz, 2003; Dweck, 1999). Lin *et al.* (2005) provide evidence that teachers' searching for detailed information in the situations studied increases the specificity of their analysis of those situations, as well as revealing hidden aspects of those situations. Hewitt *et al.* (2003) highlight that the timing of the reflections is of crucial importance, with reflections immediately following the events of interest facilitating greater, more situated and precise recall. Finally, Lin *et al.* also emphasize the key role of digital technology in capturing and accessing both the critical episodes and in scaffolding teachers' perceptions thereof in learning situations, especially in helping them to home in on the absence of important information.

This chapter presents three examples of how educational practitioners' continuous development of metacognitive skills may be supported through design and application of different forms of technologies in a variety of educational contexts. The first example describes a small-scale design-based research process of engaging professional teachers in Denmark in a scaffolded reflection on and design of best pedagogical support practices in the context of a technology-enhanced learning environment called Global Classroom. The example also discusses the need for the development of sustainable means for interrogating pedagogical support practices by investigating how the establishment of a community of practice in the specific institution might allow teachers to engage in a continuous and on-demand access to collaborative critical reflection, which is of crucial importance to enabling pedagogical innovation. The second example illustrates the use of in-class video technology in combination with real-time coaching feedback delivered through an in-ear device to front-line teachers. Combining such technologies with human coaching in real time teaching situations aims to improve teachers' self-awareness while delivering learning support, and to allow them to interrogate and improve their practices. The third example demonstrates how engaging university tutors in the process of designing an intelligent tutoring system through knowledge elicitation may serve to enhance their awareness of students' specific behaviours at a fine-grained level of detail and their understanding of the relationship between such awareness and tutors' feedback choices during learning interactions. Although very different in terms of the technologies described and their epistemological origins, all three examples are concerned with enhancing educational practitioners' critical reflection skills as a way of enabling them to become adaptive decision makers and pedagogical innovators. The questions of shareability of the practices related to teachers' metacognitive competencies and pedagogical innovations, as well as the question of how and when best to facilitate educational practitioners' reflective processes, are of central concern in all three examples.

Example 1: Developing innovative pedagogical space and practice

Global Classroom (GC) is a learning environment implemented in a two-year full-time upper secondary general education programme for adult students, where students can choose between in-class participation or learning through video conferencing (Figure 6.3.1). GC has been introduced in the adult education centre (VUC) in Storstrøm, Denmark, to deliver learning support in a variety of different subjects. However, to date, there have been no guidelines available for employing best practice for supporting learning in this new context. Initially, when faced with this new learning environment, teachers reported that they:

1. lacked the competence to teach within it and that their previous learning designs could not be used,

2. lacked the time to develop learning designs that would suit the new technological learning environment, and
3. had a need for extended support in pedagogical innovation from the educational organization.

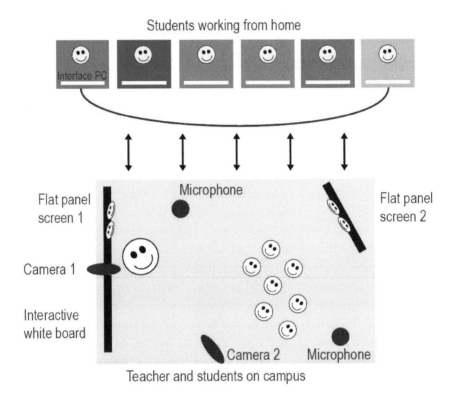

Figure 6.3.1: The Global Classroom – a hybrid synchronous video-mediated learning environment (Weitze, 2016)

In response to the teachers' reports, six workshops were organized with the purpose of exploring and establishing new practices of relevance to the VUC's GC and to allow teachers to engage in co-design of new practices of relevance to this new environment (Figure 6.3.2). Three different teacher teams participated in the workshops over the six meetings. The overarching aims of the six workshops were to:

1. Develop approaches which were both grounded in theory and that were feasible and effective at a practical level.

2. Construct an agile working practice that enabled the teachers to change teaching strategies in relation to the dynamically emerging demands in specific learning situations and to any strategic changes of the organization.
3. Provide a structured, reflective means for teachers to experiment with different designs and to enable rapid adoption by VUC as an institution of the solutions proposed.

Learning goals were established to provide the basis for the professional development and for the creation of learning designs during the workshops. After the course, the team members will be able to do the following:

1. Describe own learning design and identify and formulate possible problem areas in the current educational context.
2. Select and plan the use of and create a process of collective reflection about relevant literature in relation to the team's experience of current issues.
3. Develop and carry out a process leading to individual goals for innovation, both in the short and long term.
4. Master innovative tools that can be used in the innovation process in a pedagogical team.
5. Be innovative concerning their own teaching, involving technology as well as new/innovative learning designs.
6. Organize and lead an innovative team process.
7. Choose a strategy and method for knowledge development, knowledge sharing and anchoring in the team.

The workshops were intended to allow the participating teachers to:

- Carry out appropriate planning, execution and theorising with respect to their own teaching in IT-based and video-mediated teaching programmes.
- Make informed and relevant choices in the use of educational technology for their learning designs in a professional academic context.
- To investigate the means for knowledge sharing, communication and decision flow between the administration and the teachers.

Figure 6.3.2: A teacher team working together partly on-line during workshops made it easier to meet

An IT-pedagogical think tank for teacher teams (henceforth referred to as ITP4T) was developed as a consequence of the workshops. The ITP4T was a framework for facilitating reflection and learning design creation by teams of teachers at VUC. Teachers met every week for two hours over a six-week period to address specific pedagogical challenges of their own choosing. During this process they followed a specific procedure (described in detail later), requiring them to set the goals and milestones for their own continuous competence development and to collaborate with one another with respect to those goals.

To identify the goals and milestones, during the initial two meetings teachers clarified the problem areas through discussion and brainstorming. They recorded their problem areas both individually and as teams in a written form. They created a 'problem-bank' of all the challenges that they wanted to address and ultimately solve as well as a 'wish-list' of the specific competences they wanted to develop. They wrote this up in an online interactive project development tool called Trello (www.trello.com). This made it accessible for all team members and made it possible for teachers to jointly set priorities and to return and to alter them if needed. In this way the specific problem and competence development areas were turned into short and long term goals. This is illustrated as the black goal-dots on the coloured lines in Figure 6.3.3 (see end of chapter). As time passed, new goals were set and the teacher's level of competence increased. For example, teachers' areas of interest included:

1. problematic themes from the technology enhanced learning environment (TELE),
2. ways in which to create innovative learning designs for the learning environment,
3. questions around innovative use of educational technology, and
4. issues and questions related to teachers having to study professional theoretical literature, new research, Edu-blogs, videos, etc.

Teachers discussed how to evaluate whether the issues and challenges identified were solved or the goals reached. By being very clear on their goals for competence development, learning and innovation, they became aware of how and when they gained new competences. Furthermore, they reported that the competences gained were relevant and inspiring for their daily teaching practices.

The ITP4T think-tank process for reaching the goals was structured around a cycle involving five stages of design and reflection, including:

(a) input/presentation
(b) reflection/innovation/discussion
(c) evaluation
(d) anchoring/documentation/dissemination
(e) 'I dare you'.

Teachers worked in teams through this process during weekly two-hour meetings, at each meeting covering all five stages. Teachers reported that working within this structure provided the support they needed to achieve pedagogically innovative results. We now explain each of the stages in turn.

Input/presentation

Input/presentation (this is indicated in Figure 6.3.4 by the node A) of the chosen problem area/theme was conducted by the team leader of the day. The team members took turns at being team leaders. The problem area/theme chosen was always one that related to a real *burning problem* or to an idea for a solution to a burning problem, and it was inspired by the teachers' competence development goals (See Figure 6.3.3 at end of chapter). Every week all team members prepared for an hour for the theme of the week, which was laid out by the team leader. By preparing and investigating the subject in advance, the team leader would become the expert in relation to the specific problem and the possible solution to it.

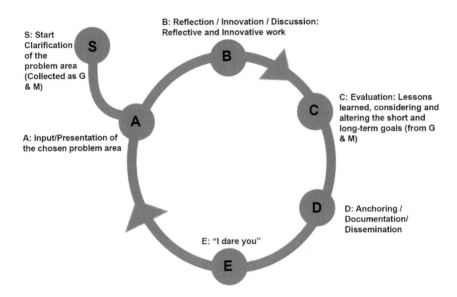

Figure 6.3.4: Weekly points consulted when working in the IT-pedagogical think tank for teacher teams (ITP4T) (Weitze, 2014)

Reflection/innovation/discussion

Reflection/innovation/discussion (node B) relates to the ideation and development part of the think-tank. Grounded in theory and inspired by the team leaders' presentations, the teachers engaged in brainstorming and informed discussions about the theme chosen for the week. The team leader of the day had planned activities for how the team could work and discuss a given theme. For example, this could take the form of discussions about the burning problem, drawings of new learning design concepts, or experimentation with technological devices. During the sessions teachers came up with suggestions for new learning designs and were able to explore the pedagogical challenges that were familiar to them, and invent new ways of addressing those challenges. They engaged in reflective and innovative work (Dale, 1998; Darsø, 2011) in a way that corresponds directly to Dales' (*ibid*) third level of teacher competence (Comp3). This level involves teachers abandoning their daily practical routines and instead creating a professional space for pedagogical reflection. This space is a place for dialogues, indepth critical reflections, development and research. The participating teachers also kept track of *what they knew* and *what they did not yet know,* and they used structured methods to conceptualize and discuss the problem areas. They also aimed to create a friendly and open space for this conceptualization, reflection and innovation to take place. Teachers emphasized the importance of one person taking responsibility for keeping discussions at the Comp3 level of Dale's competence description in order to enable collaborative reflection; in this way they avoided a pitfall common to group work of focusing on high-level discussions about common projects or venting frustrations rather than creating new solutions and solving their own complex and burning problems (Tingleff Nielsen, 2013). Teachers emphasized the advantages of consciously developing positive team relationships within which asking provocative questions that went beyond the team members' established experiences and teaching norms was acceptable. For example, some team members believed that they had tried everything in the approach to solve a problem, but still failed to reach satisfactory results. By allowing themselves to ask challenging questions, the teacher teams were able to move beyond the frustrating experiences to finding and rehearsing new solutions to their burning pedagogical problems.

Evaluation

Evaluation is node C. Following the development part of the workshop, teachers discussed new learning designs or new concepts identified in relation to the challenges explored by them within the context of the GC learning environment. They both evaluated the various competence goals they had set themselves for the current day or the long term, and they discussed additional future aims and goals for competence development. These new goals were then added to the list of goals defined previously. The teachers found this evaluation process important and helpful because it forced them to formulate their new concepts in a language common to all participants. This in turn allowed them to critique and to receive the critique from other team members. The evaluation process also supported the team in prioritizing and formulating their future goals for competence development.

Anchoring/Documentation/Dissemination

Anchoring/Documentation/Dissemination is node D. For the benefit of memorization and common explicit conceptualization of the innovations and solutions, knowledge sharing took place in a structured way within an online platform that was available to all teachers and to the organization. When the teachers collaborated in the ITP4T to create new learning designs, one of the digital tools they experimented with was *Learning Designer* (Laurillard, 2012). The teachers often used this tool in the documentation phase in the ITP4T. The tool makes it possible to create 'pedagogical patterns' for learning designs that can later be shared and discussed with other teachers. Teachers could choose between a range of features, for example, various pedagogical approaches or activity types: (read–watch–listen, collaborate, discuss, investigate, practise and produce). This gave everyone an opportunity to participate in the creation and use of the new knowledge. This tool enabled collaboration during the creation of new learning designs, because teachers could easily compare and discuss approaches to good learning designs even though they taught different subjects.

Several of the teachers identified a need for *anchoring and dissemination* of the new knowledge at the school. They proposed to establish regular open workshops, during which all teachers would have the opportunity to meet and learn from each other. A continuous practice like this, with various participating teacher teams, could establish common ground and create a foundation for a community of practice in this area. Since well-designed communities of practice are forums that support the 'living nature of knowledge', the types of new practices explored within the ITP4T could serve to support sharing of new knowledge (Wenger, 1998). One suggestion about how to disseminate the new knowledge was that since each team leader had researched specific problems and solutions when working in the ITP4T they had hereby become experts in the subjects for which they had been 'primary investigators'. Therefore, they could take a new role as disseminating experts within their specific area of interest in the educational organization. Another example of dissemination, suggested by one member of the ITP4T was: '[...] making small videos with each individual teacher's new innovations and ideas. Then it would also be available for everyone to be inspired by, independently of time and place.' These are only two of several suggestions made by teachers about the possible ways in which to anchor, document, disseminate and share the new knowledge created by the teachers in the organization beyond the ITP4T.

'I dare you'

'I dare you' (node E) consisted of teachers having to create a *product* and to *reify* their thinking for the next team meeting to enable them to engage in a grounded and concrete discussion. This activity was initiated by the team leader of the following week. It was important that some of the tasks consisted of conducting experiments in the class since the main aim for this think tank was to create motivating learning designs for the students. The tasks also consisted of finding and reading new materials related to a specific problem area, or finding and experimenting with new educational technology. Teachers noted that this product creation or reification was crucial to their being able to move forward in their competence development (Wenger, 1998). They also emphasized that 'I dare you' made a big difference to them. As one teacher stated: 'this is a big difference from traditional team meetings – in *I dare you* we change roles, becoming students and innovators, and by studying or experimenting between the team meetings we meet each other on informed ground at the next meeting, and this gives us an opportunity to move beyond the experiences we have from our daily working life – this really provides tools to move in new directions'. Having experienced the value of such in-between-meeting activities to their creative competence development, teachers made a commitment to each other to dedicate as much time to such activities as possible. Following the completion of the 'I dare you stage', the ITP4T cycle involving the five stages of design and reflection would start all over again the following week using a different challenge, thus enabling continuous competence development for and by the teachers (Figure 6.3.4).

While the ITP4T proved a good frame within which to enable teachers to engage in developing and evaluating new learning designs and in trialling the possible ways in which knowledge sharing and co-creation could be facilitated at the VUC, these innovations would not have gained much traction within their real practices without buy-in from someone with executive powers within the organization. This is why the workshops also involved the manager (the head of the department) who participated for ten minutes in every workshop. He reported that it was valuable for him to get insight into how and what the teachers discussed and innovated on. By participating in ITP4T sessions the manager was inspired to find new ways to share knowledge in the organization, and also learned about the teachers' new skills. The teachers reported that the manager's participation made them feel that he was interested in their new designs and that this was motivating for them.

To conclude this example, the teachers participating in the ITP4T found that the relatively tight structure of the five stages worked well insofar as it enabled them to develop many new ideas. They all used their new learning designs with the students, and some of the designs were used by several of the teachers. One teacher working in ITP4T said that: 'pedagogically, it's very much about how to think new thoughts and how to think outside the box, and this is perhaps what we have come a long way doing. This also means that in the future we will be able to explore different places than we normally would.'

The teachers agreed that it would be valuable to go through four or five ITP4T workshops twice a year, depending on the number of team members. This would make the foundation for continuous competence development and would meet the teachers' continuous need for pedagogical innovation. As a consequence, the organization has decided to educate a member of the pedagogical IT staff to co-ordinate the initial phases for new ITP4T teams as they learn to work in the model.

This example illustrates how innovation, knowledge-development and knowledge-sharing processes may be supported when teachers create learning designs in a concrete model such as ITP4T and how this process might contribute to the organizational learning process. When using this framework, the teachers became innovative learning designers developing new knowledge about learning designs, new use of technology and new ways of sharing knowledge in their educational institution. All teachers engaged in developing new pedagogical strategies, exploring and applying new technology and new learning designs in their existing practices. All teachers contributed to reflections on how to design a strategy and method for knowledge development, knowledge sharing and anchoring at the organization. They co-designed and tested the development of a practice for a new organizational learning design. Using this new practice enabled the teachers to transform non-knowledge or problems into ideas and pedagogical innovation and then back into new anchored knowledge. They acted as team managers for each other and were able to design and create pedagogical processes with collective reflection using relevant tools and methods to facilitate the common ideation phases for the team, leading to individual as well as team-based goals for innovation (Brown, 2009; Dale, 1998; Darsø, 2011). Their technological literacy (Hasse and Storgaard Brok, 2015), i.e. their ability to choose, use and evaluate specific technologies in the context of particular pedagogical approaches in given learning designs, was developed though experiments, theory and practice-based discussions with peers. The teachers became able to identify and formulate possible problem areas in their educational contexts, always with the central aim of creating motivating learning designs for the students. The teachers and the principal found it motivating and effective to work in the ITP4T; it provided them with a new framework and the support needed to take responsibility for their own learning processes. The ITP4T experience showed that teachers and organizations must develop an understanding of the need to allocate resources for ideating and developing new learning designs involving the use of technology.

The relation between innovation and learning could be observed in the following processes. When the teachers found a satisfactory solution (a new innovation) for one of their stated problems or goals, at a later stage they could examine how they had arrived there, tracing the learning trajectory to their solution (Dewey, 1933; Weitze, 2015). By reflecting on their decisions during the collaborative design, the innovation turned into knowledge again, making the new learning design, the new learning process or the new way of sharing knowledge in the organization possible to repeat. This new knowledge could then be communicated to other teachers in the organization making the whole organization benefit from these innovative processes.

The contribution of the ITP4T model is its ability to provide a theory-based learning design that supports a continuous practice and a structure focused on pedagogical innovation and reflection, with a foundation in teachers' and organizations' relevant professional challenges. This enables change and structured anchoring of the new concepts and may result in a visionary contribution to the educational institution.

The use of this new practice inside the VUC school empowered the teachers and created a new organizational learning design that could support innovation, help interrogate complex questions, create new organizational knowledge and anchor new knowledge and practices. These findings address the need for new knowledge in this area (Hasse and Storgaard, 2015; Laurillard, 2012; Law *et al.*, 2005; Somekh, 2007). The team practice gave teachers an identity not only as teachers but also as self-regulated learners, and the teachers had a more positive perspective of their own abilities to create change after participating in the workshops. In addition, the teachers valued the professional support they gave and received when developing new learning designs and when innovating together in teams. Though the example presented in this section represents a small-scale design-based research experiment, the pace at which the teachers progressed through the issues and came up with pedagogical innovations indicated the great potential for use of the model in other new educational environments involving technology. The principles of the ITP4T have been developed into a course for master students at Aalborg University, where students are taught how to create pedagogical practices for teacher teams in their respective organizations. The intention is that this course will serve to impact prospective teachers and support them in becoming creators of pedagogical innovative teacher teams in their educational institutions.

Currently, six projects are taking place at various educational institutions in Denmark, using the ITP4T. These institutions include primary schools, vocational schools, Bachelor Universities, technical colleges and high schools/upper secondary schools. The humble hope is that the ITP4T model will inspire future teacher teams to innovate and learn together.

Example 2: Using a video-based platform for coaching

The second example relates to real-time coaching of teaching during classroom practice using web-based audio and video tools carried out as part of the MirandaNet Fellowship research (MirandaNet Fellowship (Mirandanet.ac.uk) at the Institute of Education Futures, De Montfort University) undertaken on behalf of MirandaNet Associate, IRIS Connect (www.irisconnect.co.uk/), using their collaborative professional development system. This study is based on the findings from the first quantitative stage with 100 teachers (Preston, 2015). This research shows that real-time coaching can generate a range of benefits and improvements. The example explores some of these benefits using short case studies of individual participants. Also explored is the wider context that needs to be established in order for these benefits to be realized with schools, teachers and coaches working in partnership to develop and improve best practice in a live school and classroom situation.

The involvement of the teachers as co-researchers meant that they have all been invited to comment on the data as a means of increasing knowledge sharing and ensuring participant validation.

The IRIS Connect video and audio capture technology has two components: the first is the LiveView camera system, which is used to observe and capture classroom activity. It includes an in-ear receiver so that the teacher may hear feedback and suggestions from the coach in real-time. The LIveView camera is able to pan to the teacher because the teacher wears a special 'necklace' with a dongle that the camera can track. The coach is typically not in the classroom but observes the classroom activity through the video and audio feed (the coach may even be in a remote location beyond the school). The second component is the Discovery Kit, which is used to review and annotate the video data and recorded feedback. A significant aspect of the IRIS Connect system design is that all data is kept securely under the control of the teacher, not the school managers, senior teachers or the coach. The teacher controls the video data and coaching feedback and decides what data will be examined, shared and discussed, and this is a crucial aspect of the effectiveness of this real-time in-ear video coaching.

Research design

The findings of the research reported here are based on interviews with six teachers, two female, four male; in this chapter we refer to the interviewees simply as Female A and Female B, and Male A to Male D. The six teachers had been using the IRIS Connect web-based video system for at least four months and worked in schools where the use of in-ear coaching had been established for at least a year. The profiles of the teachers ranged from those who were just beginning in teaching to senior leaders who were well established in their profession and either learning to be coaches or already an experienced in-ear coach. The interviews aimed to explore the effectiveness of in-ear coaching and the professional working conditions that promote its effectiveness.

All the teacher interviewees were, in general, enthusiastic and positive about the value of in-ear coaching but also articulate about the potential pitfalls and risks. A key point that emerged is that the effectiveness of this method could not be divorced from the design, ethos and values of the school's CPD programme. What also emerges from the profiles of the interviewees is that there is a crossover between being a coach and being a coachee. The coaches do not set themselves up as the ultimate arbiter of good practice. Coaching is a joint enterprise that demonstrates the tacit agreement that, no matter how experienced, everybody gains from the coaching experience.

In the interviews, particular attention was given to those critical incidents that led the teachers to realize the value of the experience for their professional learning, anecdotes that might indicate a new direction, new idea or pinpoint learning. Critical incidents can illustrate how the experience might feel to teachers at different points in their professional lives and are used here to indicate how complex and varied human reactions can be to this innovative method of professional learning.

CASE STUDIES

Interviewee (FA) was an early career teacher who felt herself fortunate to have had access to a wide and varied range of CPD, which was especially formative during her NQT year. The CPD process first required working with the coach to identify aspects of her teaching that she wanted to improve. Following each period of observation she selected the video clips or 'reflections' she wanted to discuss with the coach.

Critical incident:

> 'One of my targets was the need to eliminate low-level disruption
> and to ensure that the pupils followed my instructions. At the
> time, I thought that the two targets that I had to tackle were very
> distinct. However, as the coaching session developed it became
> clear that the problem was not necessarily that my instructions
> were not clear enough. In fact the children were struggling to
> understand me. I was speaking too quickly and in a [strong
> regional] accent that few of the children had ever heard before.
> I immediately changed the way I spoke to the children ensuring
> that I spoke very slowly and enunciated clearly.'

Interviewee (FB) had in-ear coaching as an early career teacher when she was
an English Subject Leader at an inner-city school with a high proportion of
disadvantaged pupils, a multi-ethnic mix and a higher than average number
of pupils categorized as special educational needs (SEN) or entitled to free
school meals (FSM). She found in-ear coaching valuable at the start of her
career. As a result she is now learning to be a coach in her school where she
is a senior leader.

Critical incident:

> 'I was struggling because my Think, Pair and Share routine was
> not being effective. The children were not working well together
> and there was low-level disruption. The in-ear coach suggested I
> asked the pairs to go knee-to-knee and eye-to-eye. The quality of
> the paired work rose exponentially. It was such a useful tip.'

Interviewee (MA) was a male internal supply teacher who had been going
through 'a bad patch' in his career, beginning to wonder if teaching was
the right job for him. The school was in special measures and has a high
proportion of disadvantaged children with nearly 50 per cent of pupils from
disadvantaged backgrounds.

As a young teacher with little confidence, he dreaded being observed.
He remembers vividly his first observation using web-based video. He said,
'I felt pretty resigned by that time – whatever happens, happens.' However,
the in-ear coach was encouraging because although he felt he was a terrible
teacher the review of his reflections encouraged him to realize that he was
'actually quite good at teaching'. That was a turning point.

Critical incident:

> 'I was in a bad place. The in-ear coaching saved my teaching career, but even further, had a big impact on my life. I am now so much more confident.'

Interviewee (MD) is an experienced coach of several years standing, who reflected:

> 'The most powerful example I have done five times now: If the behaviour needs modifying, I've directed the teacher to have a child come to the coaching room and observe the lesson with the task of identifying the most effective and the most destructive learning behaviours of their peers. At times the child, facilitated by me, has coached the teacher ... it's fascinating. When they go back to class, their behaviour is modified ... In-ear coaching helps a teacher to focus not so much on planning and performance but more nuanced reflection on how the class can be engaged. A lesson plan is important but with in-ear coaching the teacher's attention shifts to the effectiveness of the implementation. It stops being about delivering a lesson and becomes about teaching learners.'

The teachers interviewed found the coaching process to be supportive, creative and, crucially, resulted in some significant insights into their practice leading to change and improvement. The teachers also enjoyed contributing to a face-to-face and online community of teachers who share ideas and support each other. One school leader commented:

> 'The long-term impact of web-based video I am seeing is that behaviour, thinking and language changes sustainably because of some well-timed comments from someone else in an in-ear coaching relationship.'

One coachee tried to explain why the immediacy of in-ear coaching mattered:

> ' ... the immediacy of the feedback – the relationship between how long after the session the feedback is given and its impact. If that is the case, extrapolating backwards, if you receive feedback at the exact moment you are doing something, then if that works this will be the most effective way to modify your behaviour, compared with the feedback that would happen in a post-coaching dialogue.'

Case study discussion

Several key points emerged from this study. Overall, all the teachers interviewed found the coaching process to be supportive, creative and, crucially, resulted in some significant insights into their practice leading to change and improvement. Much of the recognition of the practices that required attention also seemed to arise from the teacher's own review of their video observations and where these touch on personally sensitive issues changes in practice can meet with less resistance.

- A teacher moderating strong regional accent and the speed of delivery because she realized that the pupils could not understand her.
- A teacher recognizing that an aggressive and negative tone was hindering behaviour and learning.
- A teacher realizing that her use of assessment techniques was limited.

A further interesting aspect is how pupils can become involved in the coaching process. Inviting pupils to review video observations, be more reflective about their behaviour in class, or inviting them to comment on what coaching advice they might offer to a teacher also led participants to comment on how they had learnt to respect their pupils' own views about what is effective in the classroom.

The teachers had also enjoyed contributing to a face-to-face and online community of teachers who share ideas and support each other. One school leader commented:

> 'The value of the video platform is teachers can edit, share and comment to a range of people and then meet as a group to discuss a probe point – we look for one probe point within a reflection. The long-term impact of web-based video I am seeing is that behaviour, thinking and language changes sustainably because of some well-timed comments from someone else in an in-ear coaching relationship. The kids get used to it. But a sensible school will not use the system with pupils for whom it will not work: for example, autistic students who do not want to be filmed.'

In-ear coaching cannot be used effectively to develop teaching techniques unless the teachers work out techniques for observing their behaviour in their own time. The willingness of teachers to learn and improve is crucial to success. Trust is a key ingredient. The teacher must be in full control over all recorded video which is stored automatically into the teacher's individual user account on the web platform, protected by a personal password, and only they can decide if, when and with whom they might share their videos. This avoids any suggestion of surveillance and puts the teacher in control of their own improvement process.

One coach who had tried to sign up all the staff in his first programme had experienced hostility from those who were nervous about being observed and were afraid of the surveillance implications. He had had more success when he invited a small group of teachers to lead a change in the school CPD culture by signing up voluntarily. They then became advocates for change in CPD processes. As a general model this approach may be the best way to introduce in-ear coaching into school for the first time.

A general view was that a school that engages with web-based video in CPD should adopt a sample code of practice with their staff and also be prepared to change this code as experience and circumstances changed. A jointly developed code of practice should include clear principles about the ownership and control of data, that surveillance of teacher behaviour is not the purpose, that individuals safeguard their own and others' data, that new uses of the tools should be agreed collectively, and that clear principles of transparency are adopted when the tools are in use in the classroom (i.e. that pupils are aware that in-ear coaching is being carried out).

Views about feedback were varied but what was valued was that each individual teacher can specify a different style of feedback related to the context and to their preferences and perceived expertise:

> *'It's an individual thing about how you like the in-ear feedback in real-time – you can give a signal when you want to hear feedback, e.g. when you feel you have no idea what to do next, ask the coach to help out. Everyone has different approach and style – it might be difficult for some people to change their teaching style on receiving the feedback but that was not an issue for me with in-ear coaching.'*

One coachee tried to explain why the immediacy of in-ear coaching mattered:

> *'I have come across research that talks about the immediacy of the feedback – the relationship between how long after the session the feedback is given and its impact. If that is the case, extrapolating backwards, if you receive feedback at the exact moment you are doing something, then if that works this will be the most effective way to modify your behaviour, compared with the feedback that would happen in a post-coaching dialogue. The model we are*

> *looking at is this: the coached or observed lesson. Without video*
> *we draw on the different individual memories – both the observer*
> *and the teacher: with video it's a shared memory.'*

One coach and coachee partnership in this study invited pupils to be
behaviour coaches and, where trust is good and ethical considerations have
been met, for even pupils to offer comments:

> *'Children are highly sophisticated individuals; they appreciate the*
> *fact that I am trying to improve. I ask them what has gone well*
> *what hasn't and they are positive about it and give their input.'*

Example 3: Developing tutors' metacognitive skills through the process of designing intelligent tutoring systems: LeActiveMath project

Our last example derives from the work undertaken as part of the
LeActiveMath research project (henceforth LeAM), which was funded by the
European Commission under the Framework 6 Programme. (LeActiveMath
was funded by the European Commission Framework 6 Programme, grant
number: FP6-IST-2003-507826.) LeAM is a system in which learners at
different stages in their education can engage with mathematical problems
through natural language dialogue. LeAM consists of components, which
are typical within any standard intelligent tutoring system (du Boulay, *in
press*). These components include

1. a learner model, needed to track learners' behaviours as they interact
   with the system to allow the system to infer whether and what the
   learner knows and is learning
2. a tutorial component needed to represent different aspects of the subject
   domain and the pedagogical approach to supporting learning within the
   domain tutored
3. an exercise repository and a domain reasoner, which enable the system
   to reason about the key elements of the domain and their various
   attributes, e.g. difficulty level of a particular type of exercise or different
   solutions that are available to a given problem.

In addition to these key elements, LeAM also has:

4. natural language dialogue capabilities, which enable the system to
   select and deliver pedagogical feedback to the learner through natural
   language. LeAM's design is based on the premise that the context of a
   situation along with the interactions between learners and tutors are

integral to both regulating learners' emotions and to recognizing and acting on them in pedagogically viable ways.

To inform LeAM's learner and the natural language dialogue models, studies were conducted using a Wizard of Oz (WOZ) design methodology and a bespoke chat interface through which students and tutors interacted. WOZ is a methodology that emerged with the advent of computer technology and intelligent tutoring systems (Porayska-Pomsta *et al.*, 2013). WOZ utilizes computers' real-time data logging capabilities to capture moment-by-moment actions committed by users during their interactions with computers. The method is so called because its implementation typically involves a lightweight interface that can be manipulated by a human operator (the wizard) as if it were driven by artificially intelligent algorithms without the user knowing that they are in fact interacting with a human. The idea behind the approach is that WOZ interfaces can be mocked up to resemble those of the desired fully functional tutoring systems, without involving the full cost of such an implementation. In the present example the student-teacher communication channel was restricted to a typed interface with no visual or audio inputs to resemble the interface of the final LeAM learning environment that needed to be designed (see chat and history interface on the left-hand side of Figure 6.3.5). As such WOZ methods provide ecologically valid, contextually relevant means through which to evaluate some of the design and functionality ideas *a priori*. Importantly they also allow the designers of such technologies to elicit detailed knowledge from users (in this case learners) and experts (in our example – university maths tutors) needed to inform the design of technologies in terms of their functionality and prospective usability.

Five experienced tutors participated in the LeAM WOZ studies where they had to tutor individual learners in real time, delivering natural language feedback. They were told that the final goal of the study was to inform the specific components of the LeAM tutoring system, especially the user model and the dialogue model, which provided them with an overall frame within which to examine their own and their students' decisions and actions. The tutors were asked to talk aloud about their feedback decisions as they engaged in tutoring and to further qualify those decisions by selecting situational factors, e.g. student confidence or difficulty of material, that they considered important in those decisions. The tutors were asked to make their factor selections through a purpose-built tool every time they provided feedback. To aid them in this task some factors were predefined (based on previous research – see Porayska-Pomsta and Mellish, 2013), but these were not mandatory as the tutors could add their own factors to the existing set. The tutors could access and represent the situational factors through drop-down lists (see right hand side of Figure. 6.3.5), with each containing fuzzy-linguistic values such as *very high*, *high*, *medium*, etc., each value reflecting a relative degree to which they believed a factor expressed the current state of the world. For example, the factor *student confidence* could have five possible values from *very high* to *very low*, with the tutor being able to add further values if necessary. This factor-value selection was used directly to implement the Bayesian network (both its structure and the prior probabilities therein), which was responsible in the LeAM system for performing the fine-grained situational diagnoses in line with those performed by the human tutors (Porayska-Pomsta *et al.*, 2008).

Students' screens were captured during each session for the purpose of replay and tutors' post-task walkthroughs, following each completed interaction. In post-task walkthroughs, the recording of the student screen, the tutors' verbal protocol, and the selected situational factors-values for the given interaction were synchronized to facilitate replay. Walkthroughs allowed the tutors and the researchers to view specific interactions again, to discuss them in detail, to explain their *in-the-moment* choices of factors, and to change their assessment of the situations. Any changes made during walkthroughs were recorded in addition to the original factors' selections.

The data elicited provided rich information about the relationship between tutors' feedback and the specific contexts that they take into account when diagnosing learners' cognitive and affective states. It also provided a concrete basis for the implementation of the user and dialogue models in the system and the corresponding knowledge representations. However, the studies also provided important insights into the potential impact that the *knowledge elicitation* process had on the participating tutors. Specifically, the demand on teachers to report on the situational factors of importance to their feedback decisions brought to their attention that such factors may indeed play a role and forced them to think explicitly about them while making those decisions. Verbal protocols facilitated verbalization of those decisions *while* they were made and later provided an important tool for facilitating situated recall. Although initially all tutors had a clear understanding of, and an ability to identify the factors such as the difficulty of the material or correctness of students' answers, they were much less fluent in diagnosing and explaining students' affective states.

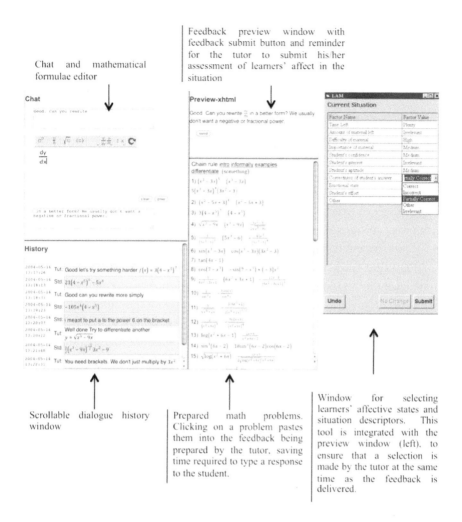

Figure 6.3.5: Wizard of OZ dialogue and data collection interface used in Porayska-Pomsta *et al.* (2008)

However, after an initial familiarization period involving up to two sessions, their willingness to engage in situational analysis and the fluency of their reports increased, while the tentativeness in identifying student behaviours at a fine level of detail seems to have decreased. This was evidenced in the increased speed at which they offered feedback to students, the level of elaboration in and the targeted quality of their verbal protocols and post-hoc interviews. For example, during the initial interactions, all of the tutors had their attention fixed on the correctness of students' answers, with the selection of the next problems or sub-problems to give as feedback to the students having been their chief concern. Initially, the tutors found it difficult (and at least three out of five of them even unnecessary) to pay attention to the language used by the individual students and to having to pay such persistently detailed attention to the different factors that were seemingly unrelated to the task of supporting learners in solving differential equations. Yet, on average, by the third interaction, all tutors except one began to verbalize explicitly their observations with respect to multiple situational dimensions such as content matter, students' possible cognitive states (e.g. confusion), emotional predispositions and states (e.g. confidence) (one found it difficult to accept that her reporting on what, how and why she was doing in this context was not intended to evaluate her as a tutor, but to learn more about the tutoring process more generally). The tutors were also able to identify reasons in the actual dialogue interactions for particular students' diagnoses, e.g. they reflected on some students using question marks at the end of statements as a potential sign of lack of confidence. Importantly, although the tutors were not burdened with having to understand the intricacies of the formal implementation intended within the LeAM system, i.e. the Bayesian knowledge representation and reasoning that was eventually employed to capture the dynamics of the situational diagnoses, having to represent their selections of situational factors in terms of the degree to which they believed those factor-values to be manifest in learners' behaviours highlighted to them the nuances in individual situations' and learners' idiosyncratic needs in the face of seemingly the same learning challenges and/or student misconceptions. This was reflected in the tutors' feedback to the learners, which over time became more positive, more elaborate, and more targeted to the actual factor diagnoses made than was the case initially. This was especially visible with respect to partially correct situations, in which some tutors (three out of five) made increasingly consistent effort first to provide praise for the correct part of the answer, e.g. *'This is so nearly right. Maybe you can spot the mistake before I send the right answer ... '* or encouragement, e.g. *'You are doing well up to now ... '* (for details of the analysis see Porayska-Pomsta *et al.*, 2008).

The use of verbal protocols during the interactions, followed by semi-structured interviews, and then post-task walkthroughs provided tutors with an opportunity to first formulate and record their diagnoses of the student in context, then reflect on and finally re-examine them. The post-hoc walkthroughs allowed the tutors to assess the consistency of their interpretations and further, to analyse those situations where they did not agree with themselves, leading, according to some tutors, to deep reflection and grounding of their understanding of (a) what matters to them the most in tutoring situations; and (b) the kinds of tutoring they would like to deliver *ideally*. At the end of the study some tutors expressed a need for a tutoring system for tutors, through which they could rehearse, experiment with and perfect their understanding of the different nuances of educational interactions, showing a real appreciation of the value of having to explicitly go through the effort of externalising, explaining and critiquing their practices.

Conclusion

In this chapter we presented three examples of the use of technology for supporting educational practitioners in developing their adaptive metacognitive skills and pedagogical expertise. The technologies discussed through the three examples differ in terms of their respective functionalities as well as their application and fit to the different contexts of use.

The first example discussed the utility and the application of the video conferencing tools in combination with a well-defined framework for collaborative reflection and problem solving by teachers working in further education. This example illustrated both the feasibility and the value of using a well-defined framework (ITP4T) as a means for scaffolding self- and collaborative reflection by teachers. Providing teachers with such a framework helped them articulate and share with other practitioners the pedagogical challenges that they faced daily. Such strictly scaffolded process over several design and reflection cycles led to teachers developing a common language and familiarity with a routine of co-creation and collaboration with others. Both the language and the routine provided the necessary tools for expression, in-depth reflection and introspection. While the process allowed the teachers to explore and experiment with the different solutions, it also highlighted the importance of explicit articulation and sharing of the challenges in a collaborative context where solutions could be co-designed by other practitioners. The ability of educational practitioners to share their professional challenges and solutions has been highlighted by Lin *et al.* (2005) as being critical to engendering pedagogical innovation. Comparison of perspectives through a carefully scaffolded process and the social aspect of such comparisons seems key to helping practitioners to shift their gestalts, to observe and then in turn be able to generate novel solutions to the specific challenges, leading them to more in-depth questioning, while also increasing their willingness to innovate, experiment and reinvent what they do. Furthermore, having other practitioners to position themselves against one's perspective may also help evaluate the potential effects of acting in particular ways. Identification of missing information and whether/why it is needed to clarify challenge situations may help educators in diagnosing them in tangible terms. Such identification can be accomplished through sharing perspectives with other practitioners and, equally, it can serve as a basis for sharing different points of view. Either way, it can help practitioners make informed decisions with respect to diverse possible actions that address the particular challenges, while also allowing them to contemplate the possible consequences of those actions.

In the second example, we presented case studies of teachers being coached by a human expert while teaching through an in-ear device. This coaching was intended to draw the individual teachers' attention to the potential areas for improvement in their practice. The *in situ* element of the coaching offered a unique opportunity for:

1. delivering immediate and contextualized feedback that the coached teachers could instantly put into practice,
2. the promotion of reflective practice and ultimately sharing of practice across and between schools, and
3. an opportunity for pupils to become more reflective about their own learning and behaviour.

As has been already discussed in the introduction the timing of the reflections has been highlighted by Hewitt *et al.* (2003) as key to facilitating the development of adaptive decision-making and metacognitive competencies by teachers. However, although Hewitt *et al.* emphasized the importance of immediate post-hoc introspection, this second example provides a powerful case for the value and feasibility of real-time self-monitoring and professional self-regulation. Nevertheless, the caveat is that the participating teachers need to know from the outset that the system will not be used as a means of surveillance or assessment of capability and that the whole process is based around teacher control and empowerment. Since the professional development landscape is becoming increasingly more fragmented and localized (Pachler *et al.*, 2010), this technology provides a platform that teachers themselves are using to share their practice internationally in order to improve their practice.

The third example illustrated how knowledge elicitation methods derived from and used in artificial intelligence research can also serve to support educational practitioners in articulating, reflecting on and improving their practices. The LeAM technology demanded knowledge about moment-by-moment decisions made by university maths tutors in a tutorial interaction with students. Of particular interest here was the relationship between tutors' observations of specific situations, including their interpretations of students' motivational and emotional states and their feedback decisions. In line with the first two examples, the process of tutors' reflection and self-reporting was aided through a strictly controlled means involving a bespoke interface designed especially for this purpose. Similar to the other examples, tutors' access to the recorded interactions and the fine-grained detail of self-reflection along with the permanent trace of those self-reflections that was afforded by the technology used proved invaluable to teachers increasing their self-understanding and self-monitoring during tutorial interactions.

All of the examples show that an investment in teachers' metacognitive competencies leads to their ability and willingness to inspect and improve their professional practices. All examples make a strong case for a need to develop formal frameworks, reflective routines and communities of practice within which educators can engage in reflection and where their thinking can be accomplished. Such framework should scaffold the practitioners in identifying first *what* it is that they think about the specific challenge situations before helping them to determine *how* they think. All examples and case studies presented illustrate some ways in which this could be achieved and this is further supported by examples from other studies such as by Hewitt *et al.* (2003) and Lin *et al.* (2005).

Use of multimedia and multimodal access to the learning situations (e.g. as in LeAM's synchronized WOZ interface) are important for anchoring practitioners' reflections, but they have to be coupled with active and targeted questioning as shown through the ITP4T framework introduced in this chapter's first example, with comparison with the perspectives as well as appropriately timed opportunities for reflection and experimentation (second and third example), in order to be effective.

All of the examples along with the literature reviewed suggest that with appropriate set-ups and willing practitioners their adaptive metacognition and professional decision making competencies can be developed into innovative practices in real educational contexts. Studies by Hewitt *et al.* and Lin *et al.* seem to corroborate these conclusions showing that teachers' established and long-unquestioned points of view can be changed through careful scaffolding, that pedagogic creativity can be fostered by exposing educators to different perspectives and that the two can serve to elicit in-depth, explicit descriptions of what the practitioners consider best practice in specific contexts. Although the sustainability, efficacy and scalability of such practices is still an open question, research points to the need and value of rethinking what we consider to constitute educational practitioners' expertise and the investment that we make in supporting the development of educators' adaptive decision making and metacognitive competencies.

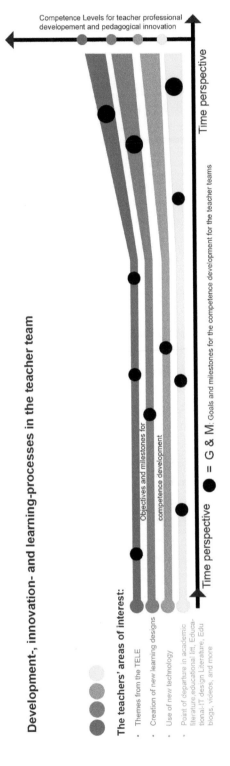

Figure 6.3.3: Goals, milestones and competence levels in four types of processes in professional development and innovation for teacher teams (Weitze, 2014)

Conclusion

Rosemary Luckin and Wayne Holmes

This final part of the book is arguably the most important, because it highlights the key role that educators play in helping learners to become successful at learning as well as knowledgeable about core curriculum subjects and essential skills. The key skill people will need for their future uncertain work lives will be self-efficacy. This requires self-knowledge, not just about subject specific knowledge and understanding, but also about one's wellbeing, emotional strength and intelligence. We therefore need to concentrate on developing teaching that develops the uniquely human abilities of our students as well as instilling within them the requisite subject knowledge in a flexible, interdisciplinary and accessible manner. This means that we must also focus on developing the skills of educators so that they can in turn develop the appropriate knowledge and skills in their students.

Chapters 6.1 and 6.2 illustrate how learning analytics and artificial intelligence can provide vital tools to help teachers develop both their own knowledge and skills and those of their students. An AI assessment system that illustrates to every learner (and their teachers) the analysis of their progress in an accessible format would support learning and teaching through continually assessing learning of both subject specific knowledge and the skills and capabilities that the AI augmented workforce will require. It would also free up all important teacher time by eliminating the need for exams and tests and detailed record keeping. AI can also help us tackle the problem that students from poorer backgrounds perform worse than students from richer backgrounds. AIED technology has been shown to be more effective than group tuition but not (yet) quite as effective as individual tuition. It is most effective when it is working in tandem with the classroom teacher.

The focus of Chapter 6.3 on teaching expertise highlighted its complex nature. Teachers often have to make difficult decisions *on the fly*, which requires adaptive metacognition. Evidence illustrates that practitioners' adaptive metacognition and professional decision-making competencies can be developed. Surely we must therefore invest in the formal frameworks, reflective routines and communities of practice that have been shown to scaffold practitioners to develop these competencies.

What the research says about how technology can support teaching

- Assessment of students' learning is a core element of teaching. However, the global prevalence of stop and test methods is unpleasant, inefficient, stressful and reduces the time available for teaching.
- The most effective form of assessment for learning is continuous assessment – the ongoing monitoring and tracking of students' learning progress.
- Technology can be used to track the minutia of student learning processes and performance as it happens over time, to analyse this information and to store it, and in so doing it can support continuous formative assessment of learning.
- The research fields of learning analytics (LA) and educational data mining (EDM) have developed separately but both involve the analysis of large-scale datasets in education with the goal of recognizing patterns in the data in order to answer complex questions about student learning and to suggest improvements to teaching.
- LA requires skills on the part of those reviewing the data, both in terms of understanding what the data means and then deciding the best course of action based on the analyses.
- Researchers agree that opportunities for LA are great in terms of presenting visual representations of data to help users interpret it, developing profiles of learners based on similar characteristics and performance, and giving teachers the opportunity to continually develop and improve their practice based on evidence.
- The timeliness of feedback on teaching that LA can provide enables teachers and educators to use data they already have to make changes in their teaching immediately.

- LA in higher education has been used for predictive modelling to determine whether students will finish a course based on their personal characteristics and actions.
- There are challenges involved in the fields of LA and EDM: the speed of technical progress is so quick that the development of policies and practices often lag behind, the rapid spread of LA is often not grounded in research, there is not a common format for much of the data, resulting in data from one system being unusable in another, and teachers often don't have the skills necessary to interpret the data they see and determine the appropriate support for their students.
- Possibly the most challenging issues for LA researchers and developers are those relating to ethics. Policies have yet to be created that provide guidance as to the ownership, privacy and usage of these data.
- AI can be and is being used to increase the effectiveness and efficiency of LA. There is a growing belief that LA software should embody a pedagogy and provide next steps or recommendations based on the data. The data that is collected and analysed by the LA software could be subjected to pedagogically grounded artificially intelligent algorithms that provide the intelligent provision of feedback to learners as they learn.
- LA and AI can help us to improve the accuracy of our assessment systems in a cost effective way that will help learners to understand much more about their own skills, abilities and learning needs. However, in order to benefit from the potential of these technologies we need to address some key issues. We need to:

  - Engage educational stakeholders in the development of an ethical framework within which AI assessment can thrive and bring benefit.
  - Build international collaborations between academic and commercial enterprise to develop the scaled up AI assessment systems.
  - Persuade political leaders to recognize the possibilities that AI can bring to drive forward much needed educational transformation within tightening budgetary constraints.

- Globally, students from poorer backgrounds perform worse than students from richer backgrounds. Artificial intelligence in education (AIED) and big data in education are technologies that can help with this problem.
- AIED might be used both in classrooms (to support teachers much as human classroom assistants support teachers) and at home (enabling students to build on what they have learned in the classroom while being given personalized support).
- The AIED known as intelligent tutoring systems (ITS) have been shown in many classroom studies to be more effective than group tuition but not (yet) quite as effective as individual tuition.
- AIED is most effective when it is working in tandem with the classroom teacher.
- Digital educational systems, such as VLEs, ITS and ELEs, are generating data at unprecedented scale and speed. Computational techniques can extract value from such data.
- The two complementary fields of learning analytics and educational data mining are devising multiple computational techniques to gather, analyse and visualize data about learners and processes of learning.
- Visualization and other tools can help teachers integrate AIED systems in the classroom, increase their awareness and, ultimately, free up time to provide nuanced support to students beyond what is possible through the system.
- There remains a range of challenges – pedagogical, technical, socio-technical and ethical – that need to be addressed by multidisciplinary teams.
- Teaching expertise is a complex construct that is shaped by many interactions and contexts operating at multiple levels of knowledge and skills. Teachers have to make decisions about how to handle several frequently competing aspects of learning situations, and adapt to such situations *on the fly*.
- Research evidence suggests that we need to rethink what we consider to constitute educational practitioners' expertise and the investment that we make in supporting the development of educators' adaptive decision making and metacognitive competencies. Adaptive metacognition is key to supporting both the understanding and the establishment and development of best and innovative teaching practices.

- One of the primary challenges in supporting teachers' metacognitive development relates to helping them recognize that apparently routine situations often have a number of hidden features. Nevertheless, teachers' habitual practices may be changed when externalized in the form of conscious mental representations and when critically reflected upon.
- The research evidence reviewed in this section indicates that practitioners' adaptive metacognition and professional decision making competencies can be developed into innovative practices in real educational contexts. However, the sustainability, efficacy and scalability of such practices are still open questions.
- The development of practitioners' adaptive metacognition and professional decision making competencies requires formal frameworks, reflective routines and communities of practice to scaffold practitioners in identifying first *what* it is that they think about the specific challenge situations before helping them to determine *how* they think.
- An IT-pedagogical think tank for teacher teams (ITP4T): a theory-based framework for facilitating reflection and learning design creation by teams of teachers was shown to engage teachers in developing new pedagogical strategies, exploring and applying new technology and new learning designs in their existing practices. They were seen to act as team managers for each other and were able to design and create pedagogical processes with collective reflection using relevant tools and methods leading to individual as well as team-based goals for innovation. The teachers became able to identify and formulate possible problem areas in their educational contexts, always with the central aim of creating motivating learning designs for the students.
- A real-time coaching system using web-based audio and video tools (IRIS Connect, found at www.irisconnect.co.uk) illustrated that real-time coaching can generate a range of benefits and improvements for teachers. The research evidence illustrates that teachers found the coaching process resulted in some significant insights into their practice leading to change and improvement. Pupils also become involved in the coaching process and were seen to become more reflective about their behaviour in class. The willingness of teachers to learn and improve is crucial to success and trust is a key ingredient

to avoid any suggestion of surveillance: a jointly developed code of practice including clear principles about the ownership and control of data is helpful in this respect.

- Knowledge elicitation methods derived from and used in artificial intelligence research can serve to support educational practitioners in articulating, reflecting on and improving their practices. Technology can provide access for teachers to recorded interactions and fine-grained detailed trace of their self-reflection that was shown to be invaluable in increasing their self-understanding and self-monitoring during tutorial interaction.

Acknowledgements

Chapter 6.2 is based on earlier papers by du Boulay (2016) and Poulovassilis (2016). We would like to thank Margarita Steinberg for her comments on parts of this chapter. We also thank the MiGen, L4All, iTalk2learn and GRASIDELE team members for our very fruitful collaborations, invaluable help and insights.

References (Part 6)

Aljohani, N.R. and Davis, H.C. (2012) 'Significance of learning analytics in enhancing the mobile and pervasive learning environments'. In Al-Begain, K. (ed.) *Proceedings of the 6th International Conference on Next Generation Mobile Applications, Services, and Technologies (NGMAST 2012), 12–14 September 2012, Télécom ParisTech, Paris, France.* Piscataway, NJ: Institute of Electrical and Electronics Engineers, 70–4.

Armbrust, M., Fox, A., Griffith, R., Joseph, A.D., Katz, R., Konwinski, A., Lee, G., Patterson, D., Rabkin, A., Stoica, I. and Zaharia, M. (2010) 'A view of cloud computing'. *Communications of the ACM*, 53 (4), 50–8.

Baker, R.S., Duval, E., Stamper, J., Wiley, D. and Buckingham Shum, S. (2012) 'Panel: Educational data mining meets learning analytics'. In *LAK'12: Proceedings of the 2nd International Conference on Learning Analytics and Knowledge, April 29–May 2, 2012, Vancouver, British Columbia, Canada.* New York: Association for Computing Machinery.

Baker, R. and Siemens, G. (2014) 'Educational data mining and learning analytics'. In Sawyer, R.K. (ed.) *The Cambridge Handbook of the Learning Sciences.* 2nd ed. New York: Cambridge University Press, 253–74.

Baker, R., Walonoski, J., Heffernan, N., Roll, I., Corbett, A. and Koedinger, K. (2008) 'Why students engage in "gaming the system" behavior in interactive learning environments'. *Journal of Interactive Learning Research*, 19 (2), 185–224.

Bienkowski, M., Feng, M. and Means, B. (2012) *Enhancing Teaching and Learning through Educational Data Mining and Learning Analytics: An issue brief*. Washington, DC: US Department of Education.

Biswas, G., Segedy, J.R. and Bunchongchit, K. (2016) 'From design to implementation to practice in a learning by teaching system: Betty's Brain'. *International Journal of Artificial Intelligence in Education*, 26 (1), 350–64.

Brennan, K. and Resnick, M. (2012) 'New frameworks for studying and assessing the development of computational thinking'. Paper presented at the Annual Meeting of the American Educational Research Association, Vancouver, British Columbia, Canada, 13–17 April 2012.

Brown, T. (2009) *Change by Design: How design thinking transforms organizations and inspires innovation*. New York: HarperCollins.

Buchmann, M. (1990) 'Beyond the lonely, choosing will: Professional development in teacher thinking'. *Teachers College Record*, 91 (4), 481–508.

Carnoy, M. and Rothstein, R. (2013) *What Do International Tests Really Show about US Student Performance?* Washington, DC: Economic Policy Institute.

Cattell, R. (2010) 'Scalable SQL and NoSQL data stores'. *ACM SIGMOD Record*, 39 (4), 12–27.

Christophel, E., Gaschler, R. and Schnotz, W. (2014) 'Teachers' expertise in feedback application adapted to the phases of the learning process'. *Frontiers in Psychology*, 5, Article 858, 1–4.

Clow, D. (2013) 'An overview of learning analytics'. *Teaching in Higher Education*, 18 (6), 683–95.

Cohen, L. and Manion, L. (1980) *Research Methods in Education*. London: Croom Helm.

Collins, A. and Halverson, R. (2010) 'The second educational revolution: Rethinking education in the age of technology'. *Journal of Computer Assisted Learning*, 26 (1), 18–27.

Conlon, T. and Pain, H. (1996) 'Persistent collaboration: A methodology for applied AIED'. *Journal of Artificial Intelligence in Education*, 7 (3–4), 219–52.

Cukurova, M., Avramides, K., Spikol, D., Luckin, R. and Mavrikis, M. (2016) 'An analysis framework for collaborative problem solving in practice-based learning activities: A mixed-method approach'. In *LAK'16: Proceedings of the 6th International Conference on Learning Analytics and Knowledge, April 25–29, 2016, University of Edinburgh, Edinburgh, United Kingdom*. New York: Association for Computing Machinery, 84–8.

Dale, E.L. (1998) *Pædagogik og Professionalitet*. Århus: Forlaget Klim.

Darsø, L. (2011) *Innovationspædagogik: Kunsten at fremelske innovationskompetence*. Frederiksberg: Samfundslitteratur.

Dean, J. and Ghemawat, S. (2008) 'MapReduce: Simplified data processing on large clusters'. *Communications of the ACM*, 51 (1), 107–13.

Dewey, J. (1933) *How We Think: A restatement of the relation of reflective thinking to the educational process*. Lexington, MA: Heath.

DfE (2010) *The Importance of Teaching. The schools white paper, 2010*. London: HMSO.

D'Mello, S.K. and Kory, J. (2015) 'A review and meta-analysis of multimodal affect detection systems'. *ACM Computing Surveys*, 47 (3), Article 43, 1–36.

Drachsler, H. and Greller, W. (2012) 'The pulse of learning analytics understandings and expectations from the stakeholders'. In *LAK'12: Proceedings of the 2nd International Conference on Learning Analytics and Knowledge, April 29–May 2, 2012, Vancouver, British Columbia, Canada.* New York: Association for Computing Machinery, 120–9.

du Boulay, B. (2016) 'Artificial intelligence as an effective classroom assistant'. *IEEE Intelligent Systems*, 31 (6), 76–81.

Duffy, G.G. (2005) 'Developing metacognitive teachers: Visioning and the expert's changing role in teacher education and professional development'. In Israel, S.E., Block, C.C., Bauserman, K.L. and Kinnucan-Welsch, K. (eds) *Metacognition in Literacy Learning: Theory, assessment, instruction, and professional development.* Mahwah, NJ: Lawrence Erlbaum Associates, 299–314.

Dweck, C.S. (1999) *Self-Theories: Their role in motivation, personality, and development.* Philadelphia: Psychology Press.

EACEA (2009) *National Testing of Pupils in Europe: Objectives, organisation and use of results.* Brussels: Eurydice.

Elias, T. (2011) 'Learning analytics: Definitions, processes and potentials'. Online. http://learninganalytics.net/LearningAnalyticsDefinitionsProcessesPotential.pdf (accessed 6 November 2017).

EMC Education Services (2015) *Data Science and Big Data Analytics: Discovering, analyzing, visualizing and presenting data.* Indianapolis: John Wiley and Sons.

Ferguson, R. (2012) 'Learning analytics: Drivers, developments and challenges'. *International Journal of Technology Enhanced Learning*, 4 (5–6), 304–17.

Ferguson, R., Brasher, A., Clow, D., Cooper, A., Hillaire, G., Mittelmeier, J., Rienties, B., Ullmann, T. and Vuorikari, R. (2016) *Research Evidence on the Use of Learning Analytics: Implications for education policy* (JRC Science for Policy Report). Luxembourg: Publications Office of the European Union. Online. http://oro.open.ac.uk/48173 (accessed 29 April 2017).

Godau, C., Haider, H., Hansen, S., Schubert, T., Frensch, P.A. and Gaschler, R. (2014) 'Spontaneously spotting and applying shortcuts in arithmetic: A primary school perspective on expertise'. *Frontiers in Psychology*, 5, Article 556, 1–11.

Grawemeyer, B., Gutierrez-Santos, S., Holmes, W., Mavrikis, M., Rummel, N., Mazziotti, C. and Janning, R. (2015a) 'Talk, tutor, explore, learn: Intelligent tutoring and exploration for robust learning'. In Conati, C., Heffernan, N., Mitrovic, A. and Verdejo, M.F. (eds) *Artificial Intelligence in Education: 17th International Conference, AIED 2015, Madrid, Spain, June 22–26, 2015, Proceedings* (Lecture Notes in Artificial Intelligence 9112). Cham: Springer, 917–18.

Grawemeyer, B., Holmes, W., Gutiérrez-Santos, S., Hansen, A., Loibl, K. and Mavrikis, M. (2015b) 'Light-bulb moment? Towards adaptive presentation of feedback based on students' affective state'. In *IUI'15: Proceedings of the 20th International Conference on Intelligent User Interfaces, March 29–April 1, 2015, Atlanta, Georgia, USA.* New York: Association for Computing Machinery, 400–4.

Grawemeyer, B., Mavrikis, M., Holmes, W., Gutiérrez-Santos, S., Wiedmann, M. and Rummel, N. (2017) 'Affective learning: Improving engagement and enhancing learning with affect-aware feedback'. *User Modeling and User-Adapted Interaction*, 27 (1) 1–40.

Greller, W. and Drachsler, H. (2012) 'Translating learning into numbers: A generic framework for learning analytics'. *Journal of Educational Technology and Society*, 15 (3), 42–57.

Gutierrez-Santos, S., Geraniou, E., Pearce-Lazard, D. and Poulovassilis, A. (2012) 'Design of teacher assistance tools in an exploratory learning environment for algebraic generalization'. *IEEE Transactions on Learning Technologies*, 5 (4), 366–76.

Gutierrez-Santos, S., Mavrikis, M., Geraniou, E. and Poulovassilis, A. (2017) 'Similarity-based grouping to support teachers on collaborative activities in an exploratory mathematical microworld'. *IEEE Transactions on Emerging Topics in Computing*, 5 (1), 56–68.

Hansen, A., Mavrikis, M. and Geraniou, E. (2016) 'Supporting teachers' technological pedagogical content knowledge of fractions through co-designing a virtual manipulative'. *Journal of Mathematics Teacher Education*, 19 (2–3), 205–26.

Hanushek, E.A. and Woessmann, L. (2010) *The High Cost of Low Educational Performance: The long-run economic impact of improving PISA outcomes*. Paris: OECD Publishing.

Hasse, C. and Storgaard Brok, L. (2015) *TEKU-modellen: Teknologiforståelse i professionerne*. København: U Press.

Hatano, G. and Inagaki, K. (1984) 'Two courses of expertise'. *Research and Clinical Center for Child Development Annual Report*, 6, 27–36. Online. http://hdl.handle.net/2115/25206 (accessed 15 September 2017).

Hattie, J. (2009) *Visible Learning: A synthesis of over 800 meta-analyses relating to achievement*. London: Routledge.

Hewitt, J., Pedretti, E., Bencze, L., Vaillancourt, B.D. and Yoon, S. (2003) 'New applications for multimedia cases: Promoting reflective practice in preservice teacher education'. *Journal of Technology and Teacher Education*, 11 (4), 483–500.

Karkalas, S., Mavrikis, M. and Labs, O. (2016) 'Towards analytics for educational interactive e-books: The case of the reflective designer analytics platform (RDAP)'. In *LAK'16: Proceedings of the 6th International Conference on Learning Analytics and Knowledge, April 25–29, 2016, University of Edinburgh, Edinburgh, United Kingdom*. New York: Association for Computing Machinery, 143–7.

Koedinger, K.R. and Aleven, V. (2016) 'An interview reflection on "Intelligent tutoring goes to school in the big city"'. *International Journal of Artificial Intelligence in Education*, 26 (1), 13–24.

Koedinger, K.R., Anderson, J.R., Hadley, W.H. and Mark, M.A. (1997) 'Intelligent tutoring goes to school in the big city'. *International Journal of Artificial Intelligence in Education*, 8 (1), 30–43.

Koedinger, K.R., Baker, R.S., Cunningham, K., Skogsholm, A., Leber, B. and Stamper, J. (2010) 'A data repository for the EDM community: The PSLC DataShop'. In Romero, C., Ventura, S., Pechenizkiy, M. and Baker, R.S. (eds) *Handbook of Educational Data Mining*. Boca Raton, FL: CRC Press, 43–56.

Korthagen, F.A.J. and Kessels, J.P.A.M. (1999) 'Linking theory and practice: Changing the pedagogy of teacher education'. *Educational Researcher,* 28 (4), 4–17.

Kulik, J.A. and Fletcher, J.D. (2016) 'Effectiveness of intelligent tutoring systems: A meta-analytic review'. *Review of Educational Research,* 86 (1), 42–78.

Laurillard, D. (2012) *Teaching as a Design Science: Building pedagogical patterns for learning and technology.* New York: Routledge.

Law, N., Kankaanranta, M. and Chow, A. (2005) 'Technology-supported educational innovations in Finland and Hong Kong: A tale of two systems'. *Human Technology: An Interdisciplinary Journal on Humans in ICT Environments,* 1 (2), 176–201.

Leelawong, K. and Biswas, G. (2008) 'Designing learning by teaching agents: The Betty's Brain system'. *International Journal of Artificial Intelligence in Education,* 18 (3), 181–208.

Lin, X. and Schwartz, D.L. (2003) 'Reflection at the crossroads of cultures'. *Mind, Culture, and Activity,* 10 (1), 9–25.

Lin, X., Schwartz, D.L. and Hatano, G. (2005) 'Toward teachers' adaptive metacognition'. *Educational Psychologist,* 40 (4), 245–55.

Liyanagunawardena, T.R., Adams, A.A. and Williams, S.A. (2013) 'MOOCs: A systematic study of the published literature, 2008–2012'. *International Review of Research in Open and Distance Learning,* 14 (3), 202–27.

Luckin, R. (2017) 'Towards artificial intelligence-based assessment systems'. *Nature Human Behaviour,* 1, Article 28, 1–3.

Luckin, R. and du Boulay, B. (2016) 'Reflections on the Ecolab and the Zone of Proximal Development'. *International Journal of Artificial Intelligence in Education,* 26 (1), 416–30.

Luckin, R., Holmes, W., Griffiths, M. and Forcier, L.B. (2016) *Intelligence Unleashed: An argument for AI in education.* London: Pearson.

Ma, W., Adesope, O.O., Nesbit, J.C. and Liu, Q. (2014) 'Intelligent tutoring systems and learning outcomes: A meta-analysis'. *Journal of Educational Psychology,* 106 (4), 901–18.

Macfadyen, L.P. and Dawson, S. (2012). 'Numbers are not enough: Why e-learning analytics failed to inform an institutional strategic plan'. *Educational Technology & Society,* 15 (3), 149–63.

Manca, S., Caviglione, L. and Raffaghelli, J.E. (2016) 'Big data for social media learning analytics: Potentials and challenges'. *Journal of e-Learning and Knowledge Society,* 12 (2), 27–39.

Martinez-Maldonado, R., Pardo, A., Mirriahi, N., Yacef, K., Kay, J. and Clayphan, A. (2015) 'The LATUX workflow: Designing and deploying awareness tools in technology-enabled learning settings'. In *LAK'15: Proceedings of the 5th International Conference on Learning Analytics and Knowledge, March 16–20, 2015, Poughkeepsie, New York, USA.* New York: Association for Computing Machinery, 1–10.

Mavrikis, M., Gutierrez-Santos, S. and Poulovassilis, A. (2016) 'Design and evaluation of teacher assistance tools for exploratory learning environments'. In *LAK'16: Proceedings of the 6th International Conference on Learning Analytics and Knowledge, April 25–29, 2016, University of Edinburgh, Edinburgh, United Kingdom.* New York: Association for Computing Machinery, 168–72.

Morgan, N. (2016) 'The benefits of technology in education'. *Speech at BETT 2016*. Online. www.gov.uk/government/speeches/nicky-morgan-bett-show-2016 (accessed 6 November 2017).

Narciss, S. (2004) 'The impact of informative tutoring feedback and self-efficacy on motivation and achievement in concept learning'. *Experimental Psychology*, 51 (3), 214–28.

Nesbit, J.C., Adesope, O.O., Liu, Q. and Ma, W. (2014) 'How effective are intelligent tutoring systems in computer science education?'. Paper presented at the IEEE 14th International Conference on Advanced Learning Technologies (ICALT), Athens, Greece, 7–10 July 2014.

Noss, R., Poulovassilis, A., Geraniou, E., Gutierrez-Santos, S., Hoyles, C., Kahn, K., Magoulas, G.D. and Mavrikis, M. (2012) 'The design of a system to support exploratory learning of algebraic generalisation'. *Computers and Education*, 59 (1), 63–81.

Oxford Dictionaries Online (2017) *ODE: The Oxford Dictionary of English*. Online. www.oxforddictionaries.com/ (accessed 6 November 2017).

Pachler, N, Preston, C., Cuthell, J., Allen, A. and Pinheiro-Torres, C. (2010) *ICT CPD Landscape: Final report*. Coventry: Becta. Online. http://mirandanet. ac.uk/wp-content/uploads/2016/04/ICT_CPD_Landscape_report.docx (accessed 15 September 2017).

Pane, J.F., Griffin, B.A., McCaffrey, D.F. and Karam, R. (2014) 'Effectiveness of Cognitive Tutor Algebra I at scale'. *Educational Evaluation and Policy Analysis*, 36 (2), 127–44.

Porayska-Pomsta, K. (2016) 'AI as a methodology for supporting educational praxis and teacher metacognition'. *International Journal of Artificial Intelligence in Education*, 26 (2), 679–700.

Porayska-Pomsta, K., Mavrikis, M., D'Mello, S., Conati, C.and Baker, R.S. (2013) 'Knowledge elicitation methods for affect modelling in education'. *International Journal of Artificial Intelligence in Education*, 22 (3), 107–40.

Porayska-Pomsta, K., Mavrikis, M. and Pain, H. (2008) 'Diagnosing and acting on student affect: The tutor's perspective'. *User Modeling and User-Adapted Interaction*, 18 (1–2), 125–73.

Porayska-Pomsta, K. and Mellish C. (2013) 'Modelling human tutors' feedback to inform natural language interfaces for learning'. *International Journal of Human–Computer Studies*, 71 (6), 703–24.

Poulovassilis, A. (2016) *Big Data and Education* (Technical Report BBKCS-16-01). London: Birkbeck. Online. www.dcs.bbk.ac.uk/oldsite/research/ techreps/2016/bbkcs-16-01.pdf (accessed 15 September 2017).

Poulovassilis, A., Selmer, P. and Wood, P.T. (2012) 'Flexible querying of lifelong learner metadata'. *IEEE Transactions on Learning Technologies*, 5 (2), 117–29.

Preston, C. (2015) *Innovation in Teaching and Learning: Using web enabled video technology to build professional capital through reflective practice, coaching and collaboration*. London: MirandaNet. Online. http://mirandanet.ac.uk/ about-associates/associates-research/iris-connect-research-into-web-based-video-in-professional-development/ (accessed 15 September 2017).

Rummel, N., Mavrikis, M., Wiedmann, M., Loibl, K., Mazziotti, C., Holmes, W. and Hansen, A. (2016) 'Combining exploratory learning with structured practice to foster conceptual and procedural fractions knowledge'. In Looi, C.-K., Polman, J., Cress, U. and Reimann, P. (eds) *Transforming Learning, Empowering Learners: Proceedings of the 12th International Conference of the Learning Sciences (ICLS 2016), Singapore, 20–24 June (Vol. 1).* Singapore: International Society of the Learning Sciences, 58–65.

Russell, S.J., Norvig, P. and Davis, E. (2010) *Artificial Intelligence: A modern approach.* Upper Saddle River: Prentice Hall.

Scheffel, M., Drachsler, H. and Specht, M. (2015) 'Developing an evaluation framework of quality indicators for learning analytics'. In *LAK'15: Proceedings of the 5th International Conference on Learning Analytics and Knowledge, March 16–20, 2015, Poughkeepsie, New York, USA.* New York: Association for Computing Machinery, 16–20.

Schön, D. (1987) 'Educating the reflective practitioner'. Paper presented at the Annual Meeting of the American Educational Research Association, Washington, DC, 20–24 April 1987.

Shulman, L. (1990) 'The transformation of knowledge: A model of pedagogical reasoning and action'. Paper presented at the Annual Meeting of the American Educational Research Association, Boston, MA, 16–20 April 1990.

Siemens, G. (2012) 'Learning analytics: Envisioning a research discipline and a domain of practice'. In *LAK'12: Proceedings of the 2nd International Conference on Learning Analytics and Knowledge, April 29–May 2, 2012, Vancouver, British Columbia, Canada.* New York: Association for Computing Machinery, 4–8.

Siemens, G. and Baker, R.S. (2012) 'Learning analytics and educational data mining: Towards communication and collaboration'. In *LAK'12: Proceedings of the 2nd International Conference on Learning Analytics and Knowledge, April 29–May 2, 2012, Vancouver, British Columbia, Canada.* New York: Association for Computing Machinery, 252–4.

Somekh, B. (2007) *Pedagogy and Learning with ICT: Researching the art of innovation.* London: Routledge.

Steenbergen-Hu, S. and Cooper, H. (2013) 'A meta-analysis of the effectiveness of intelligent tutoring systems on K-12 students' mathematical learning'. *Journal of Educational Psychology*, 105 (4), 970–87.

Steenbergen-Hu, S. and Cooper, H. (2014) 'A meta-analysis of the effectiveness of intelligent tutoring systems on college students' academic learning'. *Journal of Educational Psychology*, 106 (2), 331–47.

Tempelaar, D.T., Rienties, B. and Giesbers, B. (2015) 'In search for the most informative data for feedback generation: Learning analytics in a data-rich context'. *Computers in Human Behavior*, 47, 157–67.

Tingleff Nielsen, L. (2013) *Teamsamarbejdets dynamiske stabilitet: En kulturhistorisk analyse af læreres læring i team.* København: Forlaget UCC.

Tulasi, B. (2013) 'Significance of big data and analytics in higher education'. *International Journal of Computer Applications*, 68 (14), 21–3.

Van Labeke, N., Magoulas, G.D. and Poulovassilis, A. (2009) 'Searching for "people like me" in a lifelong learning system'. In Cress, U., Dimitrova, V. and Specht, M. (eds) *Learning in the Synergy of Multiple Disciplines: 4th European Conference on Technology Enhanced Learning, EC-TEL 2009, Nice, France, September 29–October 2, 2009, Proceedings* (Lecture Notes in Computer Science 5794). Berlin: Springer, 106–11.

Van Labeke, N., Magoulas, G.D. and Poulovassilis, A. (2011) *Personalised Search over Lifelong Learners' Timelines Using String Similarity Measures* (Technical Report BBKCS-11-01). London: Birkbeck. Online. www.dcs.bbk.ac.uk/research/techreps/2011/bbkcs-11-01.pdf (accessed 29 April 2017).

VanLehn, K. (2011) 'The relative effectiveness of human tutoring, intelligent tutoring systems, and other tutoring systems'. *Educational Psychologist*, 46 (4), 197–221.

Verschaffel, L., Luwel, K.,Torbeyns, J. and Van Dooren, W. (2009) 'Conceptualizing, investigating, and enhancing adaptive expertise in elementary mathematics education'. *European Journal of Psychology of Education*, 24 (3), 335–59.

Weitze, C.L. (2014) 'Continuous competence development model for teacher teams: The IT-Pedagogical Think Tank for teacher teams (ITP4T) in Global Classroom'. Proceedings of the 13th European Conference on e-Learning ECEL-2014. Copenhagen: Academic Conferences and Publishing International, 578–88.

Weitze, C.L. (2015) 'Pedagogical innovation in teacher teams: An organisational learning design model for continuous competence development'. In Jefferies, A. and Cubric, M. (eds). Proceedings of 14th European Conference on e-Learning ECEL-2015. Reading: Academic Conferences and Publishing International, 629–38.

Weitze, C.L. (2016) *Innovative Pedagogical Processes Involved Educational Technology: Creating motivating learning through game design and teacher competence development in a hybrid synchronous video-mediated learning environment.* Aalborg Universitetsforlag. Ph.d.-serien for Det Humanistiske Fakultet, Aalborg Universitet.

Wenger, E. (1998) *Communities of Practice: Learning, meaning, and identity.* Cambridge: Cambridge University Press.

Windschitl, M. (2002) 'Framing constructivism in practice as the negotiation of dilemmas: An analysis of the conceptual, pedagogical, cultural, and political challenges facing teachers'. *Review of Educational Research*, 72 (2), 131–75.

Index

Index

Index

Ma, H. 115
McCabe, D.L. 112
McGrail, E. and J.P. 116
McLuhan, Marshall 159
magnetic resonance imaging (MRI) 160
Maguire, E. 160
maker activity xx, xxv–xxvi, 62, 149, 163–75 and education 171–4, 187–8, 190 growth of 168–9
Maker Bill of Rights 165–6
Maker Media 168
makerspace xx
malnourishment 13
Manahan-Vaughan, D. 70
Manca, S. 285
MApp application 77–8
Marques de Albuquerque, R. 109
MASELTOV project 76–7, 79, 178–9, 185
mashups 121
massive open online courses (MOOCs) xx, xxvi, 110, 112, 199, 205–13, 229–30, 232–3, 268–9 benefits from 207
mathematical ability 15–16
'May and Must' document 165, 167
Mayer, R.E. 159
Mazuch, Richard 129–30
Media Bias (website) xxxiii
memory xix, 69–71, 158–9
meta-analysis xvii, 2, 157, 280–3
metacognition and metacognitive skills xxi, xxvii, 159, 242, 251–2, 288–9, 313, 315, 318–19
microworlds xx
MiGen system 262, 273–6
Mills, K.L. 159–60
Milton Keynes 78
MirandaNet xxiv, 49, 300
misogyny 104
mobile learning xx different definitions of 177
Mobile Maths game 221–2
mobile technology and devices xxix, 76, 81, 89, 102, 154–64, 176–7, 186, 188, 190, 228, 231, 247 children's use of 86–7
Monahan, Torin 125–6
Morgan, Nicky 241
Moseley, D. xxxiii
motivation for learning 4, 179
'mountain climbing' metaphor 4
Mueller, P.A. 115
multimedia 69–72, 75, 159–60, 313
Murphy, R. xxix, 157
museums 177, 181–5
MyPlan project 277

Narciss, S. 287
National Aeronautics and Space Administration (NASA) 49

National Geographic Scociety 65
National Institute for Adult and Continuing Education (NIACE) 200–4
National Numeracy (charity) 221–2
Nesbit, J.C. 282–3
networking and networked learning 36, 42, 207–8
neurological impact of using digital technology 160–1
neuroscience 70, 75, 160
news reporting of research xxviii–xxxiv *shape* of stories xxxi–xxxii
Newton, P.M. 119
Nightingale Associates 129
Nintendo 223
Norfolk, Andrew xxx
Noss, Richard 34
'notes to editors' xxxi
nQuire after-school club 177, 179–81, 185, 190
nQuire-it (platform) 66
numeracy 219, 221

Obama, Barack 170
Office for National Statistics (ONS) 200–4
older people's learning 224–5
online communities 152
online source material and teaching aids xxv
Open Source Initiative xxi
Open University 177–8, 183
'open' licences for products 165
Oppenheimer, D.M. 115
Organization for Economic Co-operation and Development (OECD) xxix, 88, 221

pairing of students 275–6
Papert, S. 46–8
Parkes Report (1988) 169
participation in learning, extent of 202, 211–12, 230–2
participative acts of learning 36, 42
Pascarella, E.T. 2
passive learning 70
'patchwriting' 112
pedagogical models xviii, 251, 258–9, 262
pedagogy 210 *built* 126 innovation and creativity in 131, 289, 313, 319
pedagogy–video (PV) inter-section 75
peer assessment 212
peer interaction 5, 133, 208
performative acts of learning 36, 41
personalized feedback 271, 283–4
personalized learning 134
personalized marketing 244
Pew Research Center 203
Philips, Vicki 124
Piaget, Jean 5, 46–8
Pittsburgh Algebra Tutor 259–60, 282